D0509852

INSIGHT GUIDES
LAOS & CAMBODIA

APA PUBLICATIONS

Part of the Langenscheidt Publishing Group

INSIGHT GUIDES

LAOS & CAMBODIA

Editorial

Project Editor
Alexia Georgiou
Series Manager
Rachel Lawrence
Designer
Ian Spick
Map Production
**Original cartography Cosmographics,
updated by Apa Cartography
Department**
Production
**Tynan Dean, Linton Donaldson and
Rebeka Ellam**

Distribution

UK
Dorling Kindersley Ltd
A Penguin Group company
80 Strand, London, WC2R 0RL
customerservice@dk.com

United States
Ingram Publisher Services
1 Ingram Boulevard, PO Box 3006,
La Vergne, TN 37086-1986
customer.service@ingrampublisher
services.com

Australia
Universal Publishers
PO Box 307
St Leonards NSW 1590
sales@universalpublishers.com.au

New Zealand
Brown Knows Publications
11 Artesia Close, Shamrock Park
Auckland, New Zealand 2016
sales@brownknows.co.nz

Worldwide
**Apa Publications GmbH & Co.
Verlag KG (Singapore branch)**
7030 Ang Mo Kio Avenue 5
08-65 Northstar @ AMK
Singapore 569880
apasin@singnet.com.sg

Printing

CTPS-China
© 2012 Apa Publications (UK) Ltd
All Rights Reserved
First Edition 2000
Third Edition 2012

CONTACTING THE EDITORS

We would appreciate it if readers
would alert us to errors or out-
dated information by writing to:
**Insight Guides, PO Box 7910,
London SE1 1WE, England.**
insight@apaguide.co.uk

ABOUT THIS BOOK

The first Insight Guide pioneered the use of creative full-colour photography in travel guides in 1970. Since then, we have expanded our range to cater for our readers' need not only for reliable information about their chosen des-tination but also for a real under-standing of the culture and workings of that destination. Now, when the internet can supply inexhaustible (but not always reliable) facts, our books marry text and pictures to provide those much more elusive qualities: knowledge and discern-ment. To achieve this, we rely heav-ily on the authority of locally based writers and photographers.

Insight Guide: Laos & Cambodia is structured to convey an under-standing of the two countries and their people as well as to guide readers through their varied attractions:

♦ The **Best of Laos and Cambodia** section at the front of the guide helps you to prioritise what you want to do.
♦ The **Features** sections, indicated by a pink bar at the top of each page, cover the natural and cultural history of the two countries as well as providing illuminating essays on their respective economies, socie-ties, food, arts and architecture.
♦ The main **Places** sections, indi-cated by a blue bar, are a complete guide to all the sights and areas worth visiting. Places of special interest are coordinated by number with the maps.
♦ The **Travel Tips** listings sections, with a yellow bar, provide compre-hensive details on transport, hotels, activities, an A–Z section of essen-tial practical information, and handy language sections with basic Lao and Khmer words and expressions.

Mekong River and Angkor Architecture, this time around Andrew updated the Laos and Cambodia Features sections in their entirety, the majority of the Laos Places section and Laos Travel Tips, and also expanded on the Editor's Choice and on Cambodia Modern History. Helping with the work was fellow CPA manager **David Henley**, who put together the original Travel Tips for the book's first edition.

Adam Bray, an American freelance writer who has lived in the laid-back Vietnamese beach town of Mui Ne since 2003, updated the Cambodian Places section and Cambodia Travel Tips. For the previous edition, he provided the chapters on Cambodian food, Siem Reap and Battambang, and the photo essay on Festivals as well as the list of Top Attractions.

Simon Stewart, a freelance writer based in Bangkok who has lived and worked in southeast Asia for 10 years, updated the Northeast and Northwest Laos chapters and provided a new feature on cycling in Laos.

This new incarnation of *Insight Guide Laos & Cambodia* builds on the content of earlier editions largely written by **Peter Holmshaw**, **Brett Dakin** and **Simon Robson**, as well as Andrew Forbes and David Henley.

Bringing both countries to life was the principal photographer, **Peter Stuckings**. The Australian, who has photographed several Insight Guides, calls Ho Chi Minh City his home, even though he spends most of his time exploring the Indochina region with his trusty camera and motorbike.

The contributors

This fully revised and updated edition was managed by **Alexia Georgiou** at Insight Guides' London office, and edited by **Paula Soper**. The updating work undertaken by **Andrew Forbes**, **David Henley**, **Adam Bray** and **Simon Stewart**.

Andrew Forbes has been based in Chiang Mai for more than twenty years, where he runs the CPA Media agency. He has been involved in Southeast Asian studies for a quarter of a century, has travelled extensively throughout the region and has been published in *The Asian Wall Street Journal*, *Far Eastern Economic Review*, *Jane's Defence Weekly* and *The Guardian*. Having contributed many of the features chapters for the first edition of the book back in 2000 and, in the 2010 edition, provided the text for the photo essays on Lao Minorities, the Plain of Jars, the

Map Legend

▬ ∙ ▬	International Boundary
▬ ▬ ▬	Province Boundary
▬ ∙ ▬	National Park/Reserve
▬ ▬ ▬	Ferry Route
⊖	Border Crossing
✈ ✈	Airport: International/Regional
⊞	Bus Station
✉	Post Office
❶	Tourist Information
♟	Buddhist Temple
ψ	Hindu Temple
✝ ✝ ✟	Church/Ruins
✝	Monastery
✡	Synagogue
☾	Mosque
∴	Archaeological Site
∩	Cave
𝟙	Statue/Monument
★	Place of Interest
⚑	Beach
🗼	Lighthouse
☼	Viewpoint

The main places of interest in the Places section are coordinated by number with a full-colour map (eg ❶), and a symbol at the top of every right-hand page tells you where to find the map.

Contents

Maps

Inside front cover: Laos.
Inside back cover: Cambodia.

Travel Tips

THE BEST OF LAOS & CAMBODIA: TOP ATTRACTIONS

A selection of the top sights of the two countries, from the haunting Plain of Jars to romantic Luang Prabang, vibrant Phnom Penh and the unmatched splendour of Angkor.

△ **Luang Prabang.** This beautiful royal capital is the religious centre of Laos. The old stupas and temples give the city a unique ambience, populated in part by hundreds of saffron-robed monks. See page 121.

△ **Angkor.** Indochina's top attraction dates from almost 900 years ago, the golden years of the Khmer civilisation. The sprawling site is a unique repository of incredible craftsmanship on a staggering scale. The towers at Angkor Wat, the most famous site of all, appear otherworldly at sunset as they are flanked by hordes of flying foxes. See page 277

▽ **Vientiane.** A smaller and more unassuming capital city would be hard to imagine. French-flavoured Vientiane extends languidly along the Mekong – walk along the river banks at sunset and enjoy a Beer Lao. See page 99.

△ **Tonlé Sap.** Cambodia's extraordinary river system reverses its flow during the rainy season, making the Tonlé Sap lake – the region's largest – a perfect breeding ground for fish and rare birdlife. See page 274.

◁ **Phnom Penh.** Cambodia's animated capital is a city that has rediscovered itself. Wonderful restaurants, lots to see and a pleasant riverside setting. See page 255.

△ **French colonial architecture.** The French left more than baguettes and coffee. Numerous elegant villas, shops and administrative buildings remain throughout Indochina, and are well represented in cities like Vientiane, Luang Prabang, Savannakhet and Phnom Penh. See page 108.

△ **The Plain of Jars.** These mysterious giant stone vats are a highlight of any trip to Laos. Their origins are obscure, though one legend suggests they were built by giants to store rice wine. See pages 132 and 138.

△ **Si Phan Don.** These numerous Mekong islands in southern Laos make a wonderful antidote to the stresses of modern life. See page 171.

△ **Cambodian islands.** For snorkelling, diving, camping and lounging on tropical beaches, there's no better place than the islands off Sihanoukville. See page 309.

▷ **The Mekong River.** This mighty waterway is a thread that weaves its way through China, Burma, Thailand, Laos, Cambodia and Vietnam. It is one of the planet's top areas of biodiversity and the 11th-longest river in the world. See page 160.

The Best of Laos & Cambodia: Editor's Choice

Unique cultural attractions, glittering temples and ancient sites, colourful markets, wildlife-rich forests, mountains and the Mekong River... here at a glance are our recommendations on what to prioritise to make the most of your trip.

Only in Laos and Cambodia

Khmer Classical Dance
This highly stylised art flourished in the royal court and continues to be performed regularly. See pages 231, 236, 354.

Shadow Puppets
Often mixed with live performance and accompanied by an orchestra. See page 232.

Secret Caves
Remote caves around Vieng Xai in northeastern Laos provided shelter for communist guerrillas. See page 136.

Pristine Forests
Laos offers some of the best-preserved jungles in Asia. See page 38.

The Tai Lu minority of northern Laos
Weave some of the finest textiles available in Southeast Asia and have their own distinctive temple architecture. See page 146.

Above: traditional dance school, Phnom Penh.
Left: Jayavarman VII figure at Angkor.

Temples and Religious Complexes

Angkor Wat
Built in the early 12th century, this amazing temple-city in the jungle has long been a symbol of Cambodia. See page 280.

Banteay Srei
The "Citadel of Women", an exquisite, pink sandstone temple dating from the 10th century. See page 288.

Preah Vihear
Enjoy grand vistas across from Thailand at this wonderful temple. See page 300.

Wat Phu, Champasak
The only noteworthy Angkorean temple in Laos is a highlight of any visit. See page 168.

Wat Xieng Thong
Luang Prabang's most impressive and historically significant temple sits at the confluence of the Khan and Mekong rivers. See page 124.

That Luang
Built in 1566, Vientiane's iconic stupa is a monument to both Lao independence and national Buddhism. See page 106.

NATIONAL PARKS AND OUTDOOR ACTIVITIES

Koh Kong Conservation Corridor
At the southwest coastal corner of Cambodia, this matrix of protected forests, national forests, wildlife sanctuary and offshore islands is only now being properly explored. See page 311.

Ream National Park
One of Cambodia's most accessible National Parks sits just east of Sihanoukville and offers hiking, boating and wildlife. See page 307.

Vang Vieng
Indochina's adventure capital offers a full round of activities, including spelunking, rock climbing, trekking, mountain biking, abseiling, kayaking, rafting and tubing. See page 117.

The Mekong River
Enjoy a boat ride to watch Irrawaddy dolphins in Cambodia, or a leisurely meal at a riverside café in Luang Prabang to take in the ambiance of the river. See pages 121, 153, 160, 171, 295.

Bolaven Plateau
Dramatic waterfalls cut through lush scenery and rich coffee plantations in southern Laos. See page 173.

Phu Khao Khuai National Park Easily accessed from Vientiane, this protected forest shelters endangered wildlife and offers chances to visit plunging waterfalls and treks to minority villages. See page 114.

ABOVE: Khon Phapheng falls. **BELOW:** Wat Phu.

CULTURAL EXPERIENCES

Phare Ponleu Selpak
Acrobats blend French and Khmer artistry to tell contemporary Cambodian stories accompanied by a traditional orchestra. See page 274.

Monks in Alms
Every morning monks gather rice for their daily meal. Luang Prabang is the most popular place to observe the *sai baat* procession. See page 126.

Hill Tribe Villages
Northern Laos harbours a treasure trove of minority culture. See pages 76, 129, 141.

Bamboo Train
Battambang's unique railway utilises a great deal of creative ingenuity. See page 275.

Royal Ballet
Witness this refined art form in Phnom Penh. See pages 231, 236, 354.

BEST MARKETS AND SHOPPING

Central Market, Phnom Penh
You can find almost anything in the country's largest market. See pages 259, 357.

National Silk Centre, Siem Reap
Observe the entire silk-manufacturing process, from worm to weaving, then purchase some of the finest silk in Indochina. See page 358.

Talaat Sao, Vientiane
Modern supermarket and department stores meet traditional outdoor markets at the largest shopping venue in Laos. See pages 106, 331.

Old Market (Psar Chas) and Pithnou Street,

Siem Reap
Find local handicrafts and everyday items in the traditional market, or head up the adjoining Pithnou Street for higher-quality items sold in trendy boutiques. See pages 273, 357.

Handicraft Night Market, Luang Prabang
Countless clothes, shoes, jewellery, minority handicrafts and souvenirs. See page 125.

ABOVE: Khmer dance.
RIGHT: market stall.

ABOVE: water-throwing as part of New Year festivities, Luang Prabang.

FESTIVALS AND EVENTS

Boun Pi Mai Lao, Luang Prabang
A gentler version of the water-throwing New Year festival in Chiang Mai, held in April. See pages 127, 299, 330.

Bon Om Tuk, Phnom Penh
Unique October/November celebration of the reversal of the Tonle Sap River. See page 298.

Boun Awk Phansa, Vientiane
Boat racing on the Mekong and traditional Lao games at the end of Buddhist Lent. See pages 298, 330.

Boun Pha That Luang, Vientiane
In October/November, this is a three-day Buddhist festival at the Lao national symbol, with candle-lit procession. See page 330.

ROYAL PALACES

Royal Palace, Phnom Penh
Classic architecture in beautiful grounds in the heart of the Cambodian capital. See page 255.

Royal Palace Museum, Luang Prabang
The former palace of the kings of Luang Prabang now restored and housing royal regalia, art and paintings. See page 122.

Palace Hotel, Champasak
The elaborate residence built for Chao Boun Oum that has now been converted into an iconic hotel. See page 165.

King's Terraces, Angkor Thom
The Elephant Terrace and the Terrace of the Leper King used by the kings of Angkor in its prime to watch military reviews and other entertainments. See page 280.

FOOD AND CUISINE

Amok
Cambodia's signature dish is a delicate fish curry steamed in a banana leaf with lemon grass, galangal, turmeric, fish paste and coconut milk. See page 240.

Khao Jii with fresh coffee
This may be common enough in France, but not elsewhere in Southeast Asia. Lao or Cambodian baguettes make a really welcome breakfast served with scrambled eggs or pâté. See page 85.

Mango, Mangosteen and Rambutan
The range and quality of truly delicious exotic fruit in both Laos and Cambodia has to be seen and tasted to be believed. See pages 86, 241.

Pho noodle soup
A gift to both Laos and Cambodia from neighbouring Vietnam, but popular enough to count as indigenous. A broth of rice noodles topped with beef, fresh herbs, bean sprouts and a squeeze of lime makes a popular breakfast dish or anytime snack. See page 242.

ABOVE: Cambodian *amok*. **BELOW:** jade Buddha statue at Haw Pha Kaew temple, Vientiane.

MUSEUMS AND GALLERIES

National Museum, Phnom Penh
Purpose-built in Khmer style and opened in 1917, this houses one of the finest collections of Khmer artistic and cultural artefacts anywhere in the world – as well as an invisible but noisy community of bats. See page 258.

Haw Pha Kaew
The former royal temple of the Lao monarchy in Vientiane, now used as a museum and including many old Buddha images. See page 104.

S21 Tuol Sleng

Genocide Museum, Phnom Penh
With its instruments of torture and its poignant photographs of the victims, the former prison where, during the Pol Pot years, thousands were interrogated and murdered makes for a harrowing visit. See page 262.

21 Khmer heritage houses, Battambang
Outside the city, two of these old wooden stilt-houses are open to visitors, of which Khor Song is the more popular. See page 275.

MONEY-SAVING TIPS

Cambodia
When visiting Angkor – unless you are only planning on a day trip – buy a seven- or three-day pass, a substantial saving on a single-day pass.
For smaller purchases like street snacks or cold drinks, pay in the local currency, not the universally preferred US$ dollar. You will only get change from a dollar in riel or kip, and outside

Cambodia and Laos, the local currency is worthless.
Cutting back on beer, which carries a substantial government tax, will save a surprising amount of money.

Laos
Try a local baguette with pâté or cheese for breakfast, accompanied by a strong Lao coffee. The quality is excellent, and a street café is much

cheaper than a hotel restaurant.
Like Cambodia, Laos is a poor country, but souvenir vendors will certainly have factored bargaining into their first asking price: bargain for at least 20 percent off these items.
If you're entering Laos from Thailand, stock up on toiletries beforehand as these may cost double the Thai price in Laos.

LAOS AND CAMBODIA

Ignored for decades, these two countries are emerging as amongst the most exciting travel destinations in Southeast Asia.

Together, Laos and Cambodia form the little-known hinterland of Indochina. In the colonial period they were considered backwaters by the French, who concentrated on exploiting the resources of Vietnam – the third and dominant country in French Indochina. During the turbulent years that followed independence, the United States waged a viciously destructive "Secret War" against the North Vietnamese Army and its Lao allies, the Pathet Lao, while Cambodia, having been illegally carpet-bombed by the US Air Force, was then "liberated" by the genocidal Khmer Rouge. Both countries experienced impoverishment and isolation from the outside world.

Nowadays both have put this brutal period behind them, although it has been a long and tortuous process for Cambodia. Opening their doors to the international community and to overseas visitors, the governments in Vientiane and Phnom Penh perceive tourism as a way to increase national development and assure a more prosperous future.

There are good reasons for linking Laos and Cambodia in a single guidebook. Both countries have a long tradition of Indic culture, as well as being closely related through Theravada Buddhism (northern parts of Laos are rather different in this respect, however) and long years of interaction with neighbouring Thailand and Vietnam. Each is startlingly beautiful and relatively undeveloped, populated by generous and friendly people, and home to some unforgettable sights. Their dependence on the mighty Mekong River and a shared colonial past further bind them, with both having benefited from the French culinary tradition – as Cambodia's King Sihanouk once put it: "I am an anti-colonialist, but if one must be colonised it is better to be colonised by gourmets." Today both countries are members of ASEAN, are developing and are increasingly prosperous. There has never been a better time to visit them.

PRECEDING PAGES: Ta Prohm, Anghor. **LEFT:** That Makmo Stupa, Luang Prabang.
ABOVE, FROM LEFT: baguettes in Vientiane; fisherman casting his nets.

SPIRITUAL PEOPLES

Both Laos and Cambodia have a strong spiritual base. Buddhism is the major religion, but a significant number of people adhere to other faiths.

The dominant religion in both Laos and Cambodia is Buddhism – its followers account for around 65 percent of the population of Laos and 90 percent of the population of Cambodia, although other religions – Islam, Christianity and spirit cults – also flourish. As in Thailand, Burma and Sri Lanka, the Buddhists are followers of the Theravada system, or "Way of the Elders". In contrast, the Buddhism practised in neighbouring Vietnam (and among the Vietnamese population of Laos), as in China, Korea and Japan, is of the Mahayana school.

Buddhism in Laos and Cambodia

Buddhism is thought to have been introduced to Luang Prabang in the late 13th or early 14th century. The first ruler of the Lao Kingdom of Lan Xang, Fa Ngum, declared Buddhism the state religion, but it took centuries for the faith to spread throughout the lowland Lao inhabitants of the region – indeed, to this day pre-Buddhist spirit cults remain widespread.

While the Communist government in Laos made some effort to circumscribe or eliminate Buddhism in the first years after its seizure of power in 1975, such attempts met with the overt hostility of the population and were soon abandoned. Today the lowland Lao – that is, mainly, the people of the Mekong and other major river valleys – are overwhelmingly Buddhist and generally quite devout. The women are, perhaps, more pious than the men, but it

is commonplace throughout the country to see lines of both men and women offering alms to the saffron-clad monks early each morning.

Buddhism had an earlier impact in Cambodia, gradually spreading throughout the country from the 10th century onwards and receiving a significant boost during the reign of the Buddhist monarch Jayavarman VII (1181–1219). In time it replaced Hinduism as the state religion – although some residual respect for Vishnu and Shiva may still be encountered. Like other religions, it suffered terribly under the Khmer Rouge (see page 209), but in Cambodia today it has made a major comeback.

LEFT: stupa at Udong, near Phnom Penh. **RIGHT:** monks visit the Pak Ou caves near Luang Prabang.

Theravada and Mahayana Buddhism

The religious face of both Laos and Cambodia most immediately apparent to the visitor is Theravada Buddhist. Saffron- and orange-robed monks, white-robed nuns, richly ornamented temples with characteristic *chao-fa* "sky hook" eaves reaching to the heavens, alms bowls, *chedis* and *naga* serpents all epitomise the essence of Theravada Buddhism – closely paralleling the Theravada establishments in Thailand, Burma (Myanmar) and Sri Lanka.

Yet not far from the surface, in the dragon-ornamented temples of Vientiane's Chinatown,

arhat, ready to attain Nirvana ("self-extinction"). In essence this means an end to corporeal existence and the endless cycle of rebirth. Not many people seriously aspire to become an *arhat* or achieve extinction in this life – that is usually seen as many lifetimes away. Instead, most Theravada Buddhists aim to achieve a better rebirth, which can be realised by accruing good *karma* and minimising bad *karma*: in short, by being and doing good.

The Mahayanist ideal, on the other hand, is that of the *bodhisattva* – one who has perfected the virtues of generosity, morality, patience, vigour, concentration and wisdom, but elects vol-

or behind a shopfront in Phnom Penh or Battambang, a parallel Buddhist tradition, the Mahayana, also exists. This is best seen in the Chinese and Vietnamese temples, where the Mahayana Buddhist traditions of Central Asia merge and mingle with Chinese Confucianism, Daoism and the archaic spirit worship that is indigenous to the civilisations of mainland Southeast Asia (see page 19).

The main difference between Mahayana and Theravada lies in subtle issues of emphasis and interpretation. Theravadins stress the importance of personal salvation – that is, the temporary renunciation of personal salvation in order to help humanity achieve enlightenment. A Theravadin strives to become a worthy one, an

untarily to stay in this world and help others, rather than entering directly into Nirvana.

The Mahayana school of Buddhism considers that Gautama, "the Enlightened One", is just one of many manifestations of the Buddha. They believe that there are countless Buddhas and *bodhisattvas*. Together with an equally large number of Daoist divinities, these have combined to form a pantheon of deities and demi-gods whose aid and advice can be sought on any issue through invocations and offerings.

Despite Buddhism's division into two main sects, its central tenets are common to both – specifically, the principles contained in the Four Noble Truths and the Eightfold Path, the laws of *karma* and the goal of Nirvana.

Theravada is also known as the "Way of the Elders" variant of Buddhism, so called because of its great antiquity – it has existed for around 2,400 years, or as long as Buddhism itself. The Mahayana, by contrast, is regarded as a relative newcomer, having developed in South India a mere 1,900 years ago.

Spirit cults

Although frowned upon by both the Theravada Buddhist establishment and the Communist government, spirit cults have many adherents throughout Laos and remain the dominant non-Buddhist belief system in the country.

Phnom Penh's Catholic cathedral was totally demolished by the Khmer Rouge in 1975. For the radicals, Catholicism represented both the former French colonial power and the despised Vietnamese.

undergoing the ceremony; the *khwan* are implored to return to the body, and when they do equanimity is restored. Belief in spirits is very prevalent among the upland peoples of Laos, notably the Black Tai, while animism and shamanism play central roles in

Essentially, most Lao believe in the existence of spirits or *phii*. These are often associated with trees, rocks, waterfalls, and other natural elements or phenomena.

Spirits should be treated with proper caution and respect. Sometimes they need appeasing. Of special importance are the 32 *khwan* or guardian spirits necessary for good health and mental equilibrium. A common Lao spirit practice is the *basi* ceremony, which ensures that the 32 *khwan* are all present in a person's body. Respected elders tie loose loops of string around the wrists of those

ABOVE, FROM LEFT: Xieng Khuan Buddha Park, near Vientiane; Phnom Penh street scene.

RULES FOR A GOOD REBIRTH

Simple ways of achieving a good rebirth are: not taking life, refraining from alcohol, gambling and sexual promiscuity, keeping calm, not getting angry and honouring elderly people. Merit can be gained by giving donations to temples and monks, perhaps by regilding a *stupa* or donating a handful of rice to an itinerant monk. Above all, honour and respect should be paid to the *triratana*, or "Three Jewels": the Buddha, *sangha* (order of monks) and *dhamma* (sacred teachings). Most men will join the *sangha* and become monks at least once in their lives. Women may also be ordained as nuns, but this decision is often delayed until child-raising is complete.

the rites and religious beliefs of the Hmong, Akha and Mien minorities.

The spirit world is also very real to the people of Cambodia. Spirit houses are frequently found in Khmer homes, and tutelary spirits of good, bad and indifferent character are widely believed in and revered right across the country. Animism in Cambodia is generally limited to upland minority peoples – Khmer Loeu – such as the Kuy, Mnong, Brao and Jarai of northeastern Mondolkiri and Rattanakiri, and the Pear and Saoch of the southwestern Cardamom and Elephant Mountains.

Ancestor worship, known in Vietnamese

Christianity

Christianity, introduced to Indochina by the French, never made much headway among the Buddhist Lao or Khmers. In Laos, Vietnamese converts to Christianity migrated to the large cities, and because of this, Christianity in Laos is more closely associated with Vietnamese expats than with Europeans or indigenous Lao. The former French Roman Catholic Cathedral still stands in Vientiane, but these days it is attended by relatively few worshippers.

In Cambodia, too, Christianity is more associated with Viet Kieu – expat Vietnamese – than with Europeans or Khmers. This is probably

as *hieu*, or the ritual expression of filial piety, is also very important and widely practised in the Vietnamese immigrant community, alongside other belief systems. Yet even this truly heterogeneous mixture of beliefs is not enough to satisfy the spiritual needs of the eclectic Vietnamese. It may be that the Triple Religion of Buddhism, Daoism and Confucianism is just too Chinese for Viet tastes. After all, Vietnam's long relationship with the Middle Kingdom has been essentially a love–hate relationship, with greater emphasis on the latter emotion. The Vietnamese, Sinicised though their civilisation maybe, are still a Southeast Asian people, so locality spirits, too, must be appeased.

why the Khmer Rouge, who sought to exterminate the Vietnamese, went to the trouble of completely destroying Phnom Penh Cathedral so that not one brick remained. Today Christian missionaries are once more openly preaching the Gospel, although indigenous Christians – including Vietnamese residents of Cambodia – do not constitute more than 1 to 2 percent of the population.

Vietnamese and Chinese religions

Although the Vietnamese are associated with Catholicism, the majority of the ethnic Vietnamese in Laos are in fact Mahayana Buddhists. There are two practising *chua* or Vietnamese temples in Vientiane. The larger of these, Chua Ban Long, is located in a small Vietnamese enclave to the west of Khun Boulom Road and is well worth a visit.

With about 1 million people, the ethnic Vietnamese constitute the largest ethnic minority in Cambodia, and, as in Laos, most are Buddhists, of the Mahayana school. The distinction between Theravada and Mahayana Buddhism reinforces already deep cultural and social differences between the Khmer and Viet peoples.

Furthering the divide, the Vietnamese minority – made up of a wide cross section of Viet society – includes representatives of all

Laozi and Jesus among its saints – has in some cases bridged the wide Viet–Khmer divide to win Khmer converts.

The Chinese population of Laos comprises mostly urban-dwellers, whose temples are readily visible in the towns. They practise a mixture of Confucianism, Daoism, Mahayana Buddhism and ancestor worship.

Islam

There are almost no ethnic Lao Muslims, but the country does have a small Muslim minority made up of South Asian migrants of Punjabi and Tamil origin. More recently Cham Muslim

Vietnamese religious persuasions: as well as Buddhists, Confucians and Christians there are followers of such exclusively Vietnamese faiths as Cao Dai and Hoa Hao Buddhism (a kind of Buddhist cult, Hoa Hao is puritanical, opposed to established Buddhist clerical influence, and very patriotic to the Vietnamese state). The Holy See of the Cao Dai is in the Vietnamese province of Tay Ninh, close to the Cambodian frontier, and this extraordinary syncretic religion – which counts Victor Hugo,

ABOVE, FROM LEFT: ruins of a 19th-century French Catholic church at Bokor National Park, Cambodia; Cambodian Muslims, ethnic Chams, at the window of a mosque; inside Vientiane's Jamia Mosque.

THE TRIPLE RELIGION

For ethnic Chinese and Vietnamese believers, the "Great Vehicle" of Mahayana Buddhism is closely associated with *Khong Giao*, or Confucianism, an ethical system which originated in China and was based on the teachings of the great moral philosopher Confucius (551–479 BC).

Similarly linked is Daoism, or Lao Giao, founded in China during the 6th century BC by Laozi as a system of speculative philosophy centring on the concept of man's oneness with the universe. As the basic tenets of the three teachings are not in conflict they have practically fused, and are known as *Tam Giao*, or the Triple Religion.

refugees from Cambodia, victims of the Khmer Rouge reign of terror, have settled in Laos, while small numbers of Muslim Yunnanese or Chin Haw may be found in the north of the country. There are two mosques in Vientiane; one – the Jama' Masjid – is very central, close to Fountain Circle.

Perhaps surprisingly, Islam is Cambodia's second religion. Nearly all Cambodia's Muslims are ethnic Chams – at around 500,000 people they are the country's largest minority after the Vietnamese. Originally refugees from 18th-century Vietnam, the Chams practise a rather lax form of Sunni Islam: fasting one day a week

during the month of Ramadan, abstaining from pork but often drinking alcohol.

Since the time of the Khmer Rouge, when Islam suffered particularly severely, aid in the form of money, assistance in building new mosques, and the provision of books and educational help from Malaysia and the Middle East is gradually resulting in the establishment of a more orthodox Sunni Muslim tradition.

Buddhism and the Khmer Rouge

Traditionally Cambodia was considered the most Buddhist country in Southeast Asia. To be a Khmer meant being a Buddhist. The three jewels – the Buddha, *sangha*, *dhamma*

– were everywhere honoured, if not always followed, and the national religion was omnipresent. From the smallest upcountry village to the heart of Phnom Penh the country was studded with Theravada Buddhist temples and stupas. Everywhere, too, were spirit houses – those less orthodox but enduringly popular ancillary manifestations of Southeast Asian Buddhism.

Before the Khmer Rouge seized power in 1975, Cambodia had almost 3,000 registered temples, and most Khmer men became monks for at least some part of their lives. For example, in the mid-1930s the young Pol Pot spent several months as a novice at Wat Botum Vaddei, a monastery near the Royal Palace in Phnom Penh. Buddhism provided a spiritual explanation for existence, a moral code for living and a retreat from mundane concerns when this proved necessary or desirable. Disgraced politicians, or those who had fallen from power, often took refuge in the saffron robe.

All this changed with astonishing swiftness after the Khmer Rouge seized power. In the new society that Democratic Kampuchea (DK) was building there was no room for any spiritual or moral authority other than that of the Party. Angkar – the Organisation – would brook no rival in its bid to establish total control over the hearts and minds of the Cambodian people, and this alone would have been enough to seal the fate of Buddhism in Democratic Kampuchea.

Yet apart from the issue of control, there were ideological reasons for the Khmer Rouge leadership's determination to stamp out Buddhism. The driving force behind the ideology of the DK leadership – ideologues like Pol Pot and Ieng Sary – was nothing less than the complete transformation of Cambodian society. This goal was to be achieved by blending elements of China's Cultural Revolution with North Korea's *Juche*, or "self-reliance", but taking both processes further, and from an exclusively Khmer base.

Pol Pot and his comrades scorned ideas of a simple "great leap forward" and transitional stages to building socialism. Democratic Kampuchea would achieve Communism in a single bound, and that bound would be a "super great leap forward", trebling agricultural production at a stroke.

How could monks possibly fit into such a society? Monks were wandering mendicants, begging for their food and thus permitting others to improve their *karma* through the act of giving. They were prohibited by *dhamma* from working in the fields in case they harmed any living creature – even an insect – which might be crushed underfoot.

Worse still, from a Khmer Rouge viewpoint, monks preached the transience of mundane objectives (such as tripling the harvest, for example), and held the achievement of Nirvana, or self-extinction, as the ultimate purpose of existence. Clearly these

Nor did the spirits fare better – we have accounts of Khmer Rouge militiamen spraying spirit houses with machine-gun fire to prove to the superstitious peasantry that a new force was in charge, and one that would brook no interference, even from the spirit world.

Monks in the Killing Fields

From 1975 – even earlier in those areas that had been under Khmer Rouge control during the civil war – Buddhism was proscribed: it was not merely discouraged, or simply prohibited, but physically expunged. Temples were closed (and sometimes torn down), while resident monks

views, aims and objectives were at a variance with those of DK political leaders like Pol Pot and military commanders like Ta Mok. To the Khmer Rouge, therefore, monks were nothing more than worthless parasites who – rather like townspeople, only more so – lived free of cost, depending on the labour of the peasantry, contributing nothing to society other than a negative, non-productive superstition. Quite simply, they had to go. And go they did.

ABOVE, FROM LEFT: monks collect alms during the daily procession, or *sai baat*, at Don Khong, Siphandon, boy monks apply themselves to the study of scripture.

POL POT AND THE PARASITES

Pol Pot wished to build a controlled, collectivised society based primarily on agriculture, in which everyone worked. As monks were forbidden to work in the fields, they were parasites. "The monks are bloodsuckers, they oppress the people, they are imperialists," it was claimed. "Begging for charity... maintains the workers in a down-trodden condition." The people were forbidden to support the *sangha*: "It is forbidden to give anything to those shaven-arses, it would be pure waste"; and, more chillingly: "If any worker secretly takes rice to the monks, we shall set him to planting cabbages. If the cabbages are not fully grown in three days, he will dig his own grave."

were ordered to take off their robes, don black peasant garb and go to work in the fields. Those who refused were unceremoniously killed.

Khmer Rouge propaganda and slogans from this period provide a telling record of DK attitudes towards Buddhism and the Buddhist establishment. Pol Pot wished to establish a militarised, fiercely nationalistic state, which would be capable of taking back the Mekong Delta from Vietnam and the Khmer-speaking border regions of Surin and Buriram from the Thais. Buddhism abhorred violence, therefore, according to the Khmer Rouge: "The Buddhist religion is the cause of our country's weakness."

During a little more than three years of DK rule, between April 1975 and December 1978 – the terrible time called the "zero years" – the Khmer Rouge set out to disestablish Buddhism completely. Worship, prayer, meditation and religious festivals were forbidden. All Buddha figures, scriptures and other holy objects and relics were desecrated by fire or water, or simply smashed to pieces.

Pali, the theological language of Theravada Buddhism, was banned. Most temples were turned into storehouses or factories; some were destroyed, others were converted into prisons and execution centres. Only symbols of past Khmer greatness, such as Angkor Wat, were actively preserved, although many temple buildings in Phnom Penh and the other main cities survived the DK period in varying states of disrepair.

At the same time the brotherhood of monks was forcibly disbanded and almost completely destroyed. The most prominent, most senior and most popular monks, including the abbots of many temples, were simply taken outside and killed – on occasion the DK cadres responsible for such executions would display the saffron robes of the murdered monk on nearby trees for the people to see. Monks who agreed to abandon their robes were forced, against all their principles, to marry. Angkar needed a growing population to fight the more numerous Vietnamese, so celibacy ran counter to the interests of the revolution.

Slaughter of the Buddhists

Before the Khmer Rouge seizure of power, Cambodia supported an estimated 60,000 Buddhist monks. After 44 months of DK rule, in January 1979, fewer than 1,000 remained alive to return to their former monasteries. The rest had died – many murdered outright by the Khmer Rouge, but still more as a result of brutality, starvation and disease.

Only at Wat Ko, the birthplace of Nuon Chea, Pol Pot's shadowy right-hand man and DK's "Brother No. 2", was a monastery permitted to remain open. Here four monks – almost certainly the only practising monks left in the whole of Democratic Kampuchea – received alms from Nuon Chea's mother on an almost daily basis. She disapproved of DK anticlericalism, and clearly wasn't taking any notice of her doting son.

With the destruction of the DK regime and the expulsion of the Khmer Rouge from Phnom Penh in 1978, a concerted and increasingly successful attempt was made by the new Cambodian authorities to restore the national culture. At the forefront of this movement has been the return of organised religion. Monasteries have gradually reopened, prohibitions on making offerings and holding festivals have been lifted, and Cambodian Buddhism has made a rapid and lasting recovery from the Khmer Rouge onslaught.s

LEFT: prayer offerings at Phnom Bakheng temple, Siem Reap. **RIGHT:** the stupa at Udong, near Phnom Penh.

LAOS

Laos is a fascinating and rewarding country to visit. Definitively off the beaten track, it has retained its culture and charm, traditional village life, wild forests and beautiful countryside.

One of Southeast Asia's least-known countries, Laos is an ancient land with a surprisingly sophisticated culture; at the same time, it is easy-going and a great deal of fun to visit. From the 14th century to the 16th century, when the Kingdom of Lan Xang or "One Million Elephants" was at its peak, this was one of the most important states in Southeast Asia, and many of the country's religious and cultural traditions date from this period. Subsequently Lan Xang went into decline, and the Lao people found themselves dominated by their more powerful neighbours, Thailand and Vietnam.

Throughout the centuries it remained distinctively Lao, however – a society dominated by lowland, wet-rice growing Buddhists closely related to the neighbouring Thai. Yet in the mountains almost 50 percent of the population is still made up of widely varying minority groups, each with its own distinctive and colourful traditions, clothing and world-view.

A visit to Laos is, in many ways, a trip back into the past. Cultural links with neighbouring Thailand are immediately apparent in the saffron robes of the Buddhist monks, the similarities in temple architecture and the speech of the people – yet Laos is more like the Thailand of 30 years ago. Although it has opened up to tourism in the past decade, there is still little of the rampant commercialism and vibrant entertainment industry which characterise its neighbour. The waters of the Mekong River which forms the boundary between the two countries may flow past both Lao and Thai banks at the same rate, but the flow of life in the two countries proceeds at two entirely different speeds.

There is another side to Laos, too, which distinguishes the country from Thailand and further enriches an already sophisticated culture. At least in terms of architecture and cuisine, Laos has benefited from its long association with its other neighbours and from French influences. Lao food is delicious, but one is also able to eat in Chinese and Vietnamese restaurants, as well as enjoy excellent coffee, fresh baguettes, croissants and French haute cuisine.

PRECEDING PAGES: view from Mount Phu Si, Luang Prabang; the ruins at Wat Phu; the daily market at Luang Prabang. **LEFT:** *wat* detail, Luang Prabang. **ABOVE, FROM LEFT:** rice is the main crop; the most important temple in Laos, Pha That Luang.

THE LAY OF THE LAND

Laos is a mountainous country, cut through and
bounded to the west by the Mekong River.
Some 40 percent remains forested, a sanctuary
for many rare and endangered species.

Set firmly within tropical Southeast Asia
between latitudes 14°N and 23°N, the Lao
People's Democratic Republic, as it has
been known officially since 1975, covers just
over 236,800 sq km (91,400 sq miles). It shares
borders with China and Burma (Myanmar) in
the north and northwest, Thailand in the west,
Cambodia in the south and Vietnam in the east.
The familiarity of the alliterative cliché "landlocked Laos" perhaps disguises the significance
of the republic's geographical insularity. It is
the only country in Southeast Asia, an area traditionally heavily involved in maritime trade,
which doesn't have a coastline. What Laos does
have in abundance are mountains and rivers.
Over 90 percent of the country lies more than
180 metres (585ft) above sea level, and around
70 percent comprises mountains and plateaux.

There are no extensive areas of flatland anywhere in the country – the largest being around
the capital, Vientiane, and the southern city of
Savannakhet, although the northern region
is more consistently mountainous than the
south, and is characterised by rugged ranges cut
through by narrow river valleys. Most of these
rivers eventually flow into the Mekong (Mae
Nam Khong in Lao), which forms Laos's border
with Burma before sweeping east towards Luang
Prabang and then swinging south to Vientiane
to form much of the country's border with
Thailand before entering Cambodia. Rivers in
the far east drain through Vietnam into the Gulf
of Tonkin and the South China Sea.

LEFT: gathering rice on the Bolaven Plateau, a
highland region known for its relatively cool climate.
RIGHT: ferrying traffic across the Mekong to Don
Khong.

Mountains and plateaux

The country's highest mountains are found in
Xieng Khuang province in the central northeast. The landscape is typified by jagged limestone peaks, often severely eroded to form
serrated ridges and ranges. Many of the mountains exceed 2,000 metres (6,500ft) in height,
the highest being Phu Bia, which reaches 2,820
metres (9,165ft). Behind that peak is the extensive Xieng Khuang Plateau, the largest such feature in the country, which is principally rolling
grasslands rather than a flat plain. Prehistoric
stone jar-shaped vessels dot some of the plateau,
lending it its popular name, the Plain of Jars
(see page 132). Most of southern Laos is at a
lower elevation than the north, except for the

Annamite Cordillera, the principal mountain range, which runs northwest to southeast for some 1,100km (690 miles) – half the length of the country – comprising much of its border with Vietnam and forming the watershed between the Mekong and the South China Sea.

Geologically the range is a complex mix of rock formations. Ancient lava flows have formed several notable plateaux within central and southern Laos: the Khammuan Plateau, in the cordillera's central stretch, is an area of karst peaks, steep valleys and grottoes. Further south the beautiful Bolaven Plateau extends for 10,000 sq km (3,860 sq miles).

The mighty Mekong

The mountainous terrain of Laos makes much of the country relatively inaccessible and unsuitable for high-yield or commercial agriculture. It is no surprise, then, that the main population centres are found in the Mekong Valley, particularly in the southern flood plains. The two biggest cities – the capital, Vientiane, and Savannakhet, which are also the administrative centres of Laos's most populous provinces – are on the Mekong.

The transport infrastructure in Laos has improved, and the river remains a practical means of moving goods and people effectively and efficiently. The central stretch of the Mekong, from Luang Prabang to slightly north of the Khemmarat rapids in Savannakhet province, remains navigable all year round, but, despite the fact that the river swells to widths of almost 15km (9 miles) in the south (around the Si Phan Don area), the upper stretches beyond Luang Prabang can be treacherous and shallow in the dry months, impassable to most vessels. There are plans to blast these areas to afford the river year-round navigability and increase its potential as an international trade route, but there is opposition to such schemes, both in Laos and in neighbouring countries, especially Thailand and Cambodia.

Blasting is only one of a number of Mekong projects that have been discussed, most revolving around damming the river to provide irrigation and hydroelectric power. Upstream, China has already built four dams and a fifth is scheduled for completion in 2015. A major dam on the Nam Ngum River was constructed in 1975, flooding an area of 250 sq km (96 sq miles)

CONSERVATION IN LAOS

Timber is an important source of revenue, although at great cost to the environment. Areas which 30 years ago were covered in forest, for example the Bolaven Plateau in the far south, today have but a few trees left after irresponsible logging. Efforts have been made to curb the deforestation, including setting up 17 National Biodiversity Conservation Areas (NBCAS), covering just over 10 percent of the land area, but logging continues. Even within the NBCAS concessions are granted, and elsewhere the military runs its own concerns, in breach of all agreements and laws. The revenues are too high for laws to have much effect.

Despite such justifiable worries about logging in various parts of the country, Laos still has one of the most unspoilt environments in Southeast Asia and retains much of its wildlife. However, with few controls on hunting, trapping and exporting endangered species, and little public awareness of the value of maintaining biodiversity and the problems involved in species extinction, conservation measures seem unlikely. Laos has been slow to ratify the Convention on International Trade in Endangered Species (CITES), although how much difference this would make is questionable. Much of the Lao population beyond the few large cities still relies on "bush meat" to supplement its diet, and this is particularly true of the upland people such as the Hmong, who have hunted small game and birds for centuries, and see little reason to stop now.

and forming the Ang Nam Ngum Reservoir, 90km (55 miles) north of Vientiane. A hydro-electric power station here generates much of the capital city's power, and the excess is sold to Thailand. The Lao authorities commissioned the Name Theun II dam on the Nam Theun River in the Nakai district of Khammuan province in 2010; the completed dam is 50 metres (165ft) high and, at a cost of flooding 450 sq km (175 sq miles), provides 1,070MW of power for development and export.

At present, at least 11 possible future sites have been identified as other locations for new dams projected to be built by 2020 and to raise

to pay off foreign debt, while local people are rarely, if ever, properly compensated.

Climate and farming

The tropical climate of Laos revolves around the annual monsoon cycle, which produces three distinct seasons. The southwest monsoon arrives between May and July and continues until November, bringing most of the year's rainfall. From November to March the country is almost completely dry and relatively cool, catching breezes from the tail end of the northeast monsoon; from March to May temperatures edge higher, and with little rain the countryside

the country's power-generating capacity by at least 5,000MW. This would make hydroelectric power – already a key element in the Lao economy – a truly major contributor to the annual GDP, though understandably environmentalists worry about both the long-term effects of damming and the logging concessions that are invariably part of such ventures. While supporters argue that dams provide a stable and sustainable source of foreign exchange for a poor country such as Laos, opponents claim that much of the projected income will be needed

ABOVE, FROM LEFT: the limestone landscapes of Laos are riddled with caves; lodges at Si Phan Don; dusk falls on the Mekong River.

It is difficult to overestimate the importance of the Mekong to the Lao people and their country. In addition to depositing fertile alluvial silt, the river is a major artery of trade and travel and source of fish.

becomes ever drier and dustier. Through the year as a whole, the low-lying Mekong Valley is warmer and more humid than the more mountainous areas. The provinces of Vientiane and Savannakhet get more rainfall than the north-central provinces of Xieng Khuang and Luang Prabang but substantially less than the southern areas of the Annamite Cordillera.

The great majority of the Lao people still live and work in rural areas; for example, Vientiane – by some margin the largest city – has a population of less than 250,000 (although the metropolitan area is around three times that). Traditionally the lowland river valleys are inhabited by those who are ethnically Lao – about 50 percent of the population – and they are involved in subsistence wet-rice cultivation, which still accounts for most of the use of valley land. Upland areas are inhabited by other ethnic groups, who cultivate dry rice as well as practising slash-and-burn agriculture, and hunting and gathering. Agriculture, albeit at

subsistence level, occupies most of the population, although less than 10 percent of the land is suitable for cultivation. Apart from rice, crops include tobacco, wheat, corn, soybeans, fruits, nuts and vegetables in the lowlands, and tobacco, tea, coffee, maize and, still of significant economic importance, opium in the hills.

Flora and fauna

Laos has emerged as an ecotourism destination in recent years, with visitors attracted by some of the most pristine natural environments in Southeast Asia – and the wildlife that these environments sustain. Some 40 percent of the country remains forested (down from around 70 percent in the 1960s), with the largest

> In the 1990s scientists discovered a previously unknown mammal in the Annamite Cordillera, the spindlehorn or Vu Quang's ox, called nyang in Lao and also known as the saola.

surviving tracts of woodland in Indochina. Around 21 percent of the land is protected, although illegal hunting and poaching is a problem. The forests largely consist of tall thin dipterocarps, often reaching 30 metres (100ft), and valuable hardwood trees including teak and rosewood. Along river valleys bamboos are particularly prolific. A few regions have slightly different forest cover, including evergreen and tropical pine. On the plateaux of the Annamite Cordillera, forests give way to savannah.

These forests and grasslands support a diverse array of wildlife, some of which have been hunted to extinction in neighbouring countries. Among mammal species are the Asiatic black bear, the Malayan sun bear, the Asiatic jackal, red panda, concolor gibbon and giant barking deer. There are still a few hundred wild elephants, and over 1,000 more are used for logging and transport. A small number of rhinoceros *sondaicus* survive on the Bolaven Plateau, and elsewhere in the south there have been sightings of kouprey, a rare species of wild cattle. Other mammals that may be seen with luck and patience include the gibbon (of which there are five species in Laos), the douc langur, banteng, Fea's muntjac, Indian muntjac, marbled cat, leopard cat – perhaps even an extremely rare Indochinese tiger. The freshwater Irrawaddy dolphin can sometimes be seen in the Mekong around the Si Phan Don area in southern Laos.

Non-mammalian species include snakes, of which six are venomous (two types of cobra, three species of viper, and the banded krait), while the large Tokay gecko is a highly audible presence in villages throughout the country. There are many colourful birds, indigenous and migratory. Birdwatchers are rewarded with a huge variety, from the sub-Himalayan species found in the northern forests to spectacular birds such as the giant ibis and sarus cranes in the Mekong Valley – itself an important migration route.

LEFT: Lao woman from the Lantan tribe harvesting corn near Luang Namtha, in Northern Laos.
RIGHT: Khon Phapheng falls in southern Laos.

DECISIVE DATES

3000 BC–AD 1000
Laos is settled by Austro-Tai-speaking peoples.

The Kingdom of One Million Elephants

1353
Fa Ngum founds the Kingdom of Lan Xang. He makes Theravada Buddhism the state religion.

1421–1520
Lan Xang suffers 100 years of petty wars and rivalries.

1520
King Phothisarat comes to the throne and reunifies the kingdom. Forty years later his son Setthathirat moves the capital from Luang Prabang to Vientiane.

1637–94
King Sulinya Vongse presides over the Golden Age of Lan Xang from his capital at Vientiane.

1700
After the death of Sulinya Vongse, Lan Xang begins to break up.

Fragmentation and Decline

1775–1800
The Siamese absorb southern Laos.

1826–8
Chao Anuvong of Vientiane attempts to re-establish Lao independence but is defeated. In 1828, Vientiane is comprehensively sacked by the invading Siamese.

1870s–1880s
Laos, as far south as Vientiane, is plundered by bands of Yunnanese Chinese known as Haw in the Haw Wars.

The Colonial Interlude

1893–1907
Unequal colonial treaties forced on Siam lead to French control over all Lao territories east of the Mekong.

1900–39
French colonial policy continues traditional Vietnamese policies east of the Mekong. In Laos, as in Cambodia, Vietnamese settlement is encouraged. Laos remains a colonial backwater, of little economic value.

1939–45
World War II ends in Laos with a brief Japanese-inspired declaration of independence, followed by the return of the French.

1949
Laos is recognised as an "Independent Associate State" under French tutelage.

1950–1
The United States and the United Kingdom recognise Laos as part of the French Union. The pro-Communist Pathet Lao rejects this development and forms a government of national resistance.

Laos and the Indochina Wars

1952
The Pathet Lao begins a low-scale insurgency in the northeast of the country.

1953
France withdraws, leaving an independent Laos divided between royalist forces in Vientiane and the leftist Pathet Lao.

1955
Laos is admitted to the United Nations.

1957
Prince Souvanna Phouma leads a coalition government in Vientiane.

1963
The Communist government of North Vietnam begins extensive use of the Ho Chi Minh Trail in Laos. Covert US military activities begin.

1973
US troops withdraw from Vietnam, and the CIA "Secret War" in Laos is wound down.

1975
After the Communist victory in Vietnam, the Lao People's Democratic Republic is established.

The Development of Modern Laos

1975–89
Rigid socialist policies introduced; most of the country's intelligentsia and urban middle classes flee. Communist attempts to weaken the popularity of Buddhism do not work. Former King Savang Vatthana and other members of the royal family die in prison camps. Disaffection grows as poverty increases.

1977
Treaty of friendship and cooperation signed between Laos and Vietnam.

PRECEDING PAGES: Wat Xieng Thong, Luang Prabang. **ABOVE, FROM LEFT:** the flag of French Laos; the Second Indochina War, otherwise known as the Vietnam War; President Choummaly Sayasone of Laos at the global summit on cluster bombs in Vientiane, November 2010.

1989–90
Collapse of the Soviet Union.

1992
Death of Lao president Kaysone Phomvihane. Nouhak Phoumsavanh succeeds him.

1993
A slow start is made in restoring individual liberties; the country begins opening up to tourism.

1994
The "Friendship Bridge" opens across the Mekong, linking Laos and Thailand.

1997
Laos is admitted to the Association of Southeast Asian Nations (ASEAN).

1998
Khamtay Siphandone becomes president.

1999
Laos moves cautiously closer to Thailand as Vietnamese influence diminishes.

2003
Gradual transition to market economy continues.

2006
Choummaly Sayasone becomes president in June.

2009
Rail link with Thailand opened over the Mekong at Nong Kai.

2011
A new stock market opens in Vientiane. Choummaly Sayasone elected for a further five-year term by parliament.

2012
Viet-Lao Solidarity and Friendship Year marks 50 years of diplomatic ties and 35 years of the Vietnam–Laos Friendship Agreement.

THE KINGDOM OF LAN XANG

The early development of Laos was initiated by the southward migration of Tai-speaking peoples, leading to the rise of the kingdom of Lan Xang. The many internal conflicts remained largely unresolved until the 17th-century reign of King Sulinya Vongse.

The Lao people – both the lowland Lao and the various Tai minorities of northern Laos, together with the Thais – are part of the Tai-speaking ethnic group who are thought to have moved south into Indochina around 1,200 years ago. Academic opinion differs as to their origins. Many historians have associated the southward migration with the disintegration of the supposed Tai Kingdom of Nan Chao in southern China; other opinions suggest that pressure from Mongol hordes drove them southwards into the fertile ricelands of mainland Southeast Asia. A more radical school of thought – fascinating, though largely discredited – has the Tai moving northwards and inland from an original home in the Pacific.

It is never easy to be precise about the early history of any people: their origins, early movements and way of life are lost in the mists of time. It is now generally accepted, however, that the first Tai peoples lived in southern China, where they had established small statelets, often no larger than a single valley, called *muang*. From around AD 800 these hardy, independent agriculturalists gradually expanded southwards, not in a wave of conquest of already settled land but into hills and valleys as yet unsettled, or only partially so, by peoples such as the Mon and the Khmer.

Founding two kingdoms

By about 1200, various larger Tai-speaking *muang* were beginning to emerge across a broad belt of land, from the Shan state of Burma

(Myanmar) in the west, through the region which is now northern Thailand, to the forest-clad riverine valleys of upper Laos.

The most significant of these "super" *muang* – which can really be classified as kingdoms – were located in the northern part of mainland Southeast Asia. In the east, in an area rather larger than present-day Laos, the Kingdom of Lan Xang ("One Million Elephants") was established in 1353 by King Fa Ngum. Meanwhile to the west, approximately within the frontiers of present-day northern Thailand, King Mangrai had founded the Kingdom of Lan Na ("One Million Rice Fields") in the late 13th century.

These first major Tai *muang* were destined to be overshadowed by more powerful southern

LEFT: Lan Xang-period Buddha head from Haw Pha Kaew, Vientiane. **RIGHT:** illustration of two early indigenous Tai men.

Fa Ngum made Theravada Buddhism the religion of the new state. The Pha Bang, a golden image of the Buddha from his Khmer neighbours installed at the new capital, Luang Prabang, became the national symbol of the Lao.

Brave new conqueror

In 1353 a Lao warlord, Chao Fa Ngum, captured the important Lao town of Vientiane (literally "City of Sandalwood") with the assistance of 10,000 Khmer troops.

Having grown up in exile at Angkor under the protection of King Jayavarman Paramesvara, Fa Ngum married one of Jayavarman's daughters, before leading mixed forces of Lao and Khmer northwards to conquer not just Vientiane but also the region around the Plain of Jars, parts of northeast Thailand, and finally Luang Prabang.

Having completed these conquests, Chao

neighbours – Sukhothai, Ayutthaya and eventually Bangkok. This does not detract from the grandeur of their achievement, however, and although Lan Na eventually became part of Siam (Thailand), the Kingdom of Lan Xang – albeit battered and bruised by a series of more

powerful neighbours – survives to this day in its modern Lao incarnation.

Very little is known about the early history of Laos before the rise of Lan Na and Lan Xang. Indeed, it seems likely that the various Lao *muang* were little more than a series of vassal states of the powerful but declining Khmer Empire further to the south. Boundaries were inevitably less rigid than they are today, and at the height of its power in the 14th century Lan Na included the Lao *muang* of Luang Prabang within its borders. However, times changed and, as Lan Na found itself increasingly pressured by the growing power of Burma, so Lan Xang (Laos) found itself presented with the opportunity to expand as the Khmer Empire retracted.

Fa Ngum felt able to declare himself the first king of Lan Xang, one of the largest kingdoms in mainland Southeast Asia, with its capital at Luang Prabang. (The role played by Khmer mercenary troops in Chao Fa Ngum's empire building should be noted, however. It has been suggested that the first Lao kingdom was, in essence, a Khmer state.)

Chao Fa Ngum constantly strove to expand the frontiers of his new state. Within a few years his armies had reached the natural barrier of the Annamite Cordillera, which cut Laos off from Vietnam to the north and the Champa kingdom to the south.

Lan Xang was not a state in the modern sense of the word. The king directly ruled and taxed only Vientiane and its immediate area, while the rulers of nearby smaller dependent *muang* raised their own taxes and generally ruled as they saw fit. Their duties to the king were to pay an annual tribute, attend the royal court for major ceremonies, and raise forces to support the king when he waged war. Thus Lan Xang can be thought of more as a loose federation rather than a centralised kingdom with clear boundaries.

Building up a state

Fa Ngum was succeeded by his eldest son, who took the title Phaya Samsenthai ("Lord of Three

Following his death in 1421 at the age of 60, less competent hands took control. Over the next century no fewer than 12 rulers succeeded to the throne of Lan Xang. None has left remarkable records or monuments, but at least the kingdom survived – although by the time of the death of King Wisunalat in 1520, Burma, which was already coming to dominate neighbouring Lan Na, was also knocking at the western gateway of Lan Xang.

Rulers and hill people

King Phothisarat, who took the throne in 1520, was a different character from his predeces-

Hundred Thousand Tai"), who underscored the ties of blood and culture within the various Tai *muang* by marrying a Lan Na princess from Chiang Mai and a Siamese princess from Ayutthaya. He then devoted himself to reorganising and strengthening the state administration of Lan Xang, basing it largely on principles already established at Ayutthaya. He built temples and schools, discouraged foreign military adventures and devoted himself to building up Lan Xang as a trading nation. In this he was largely successful.

ABOVE, FROM LEFT: boat races on the Mekong River; the Pak Ou caves, discovered, it is said, by King Setthathirat in the 16th century.

sors. By the 1540s he had subdued Lan Na and placed his son Setthathirat on the throne there.

In 1548 Setthathirat inherited the throne of Lan Xang, bringing with him the prestigious Pha Kaew (Emerald Buddha). He ordered the building of Wat Pha Kaew to house the new national symbol, and also gave orders for the construction of That Luang, the country's largest and most distinctive stupa (see page 106). Still, apart from these successes, times were dangerous; Lan Xang's control of all but the broad riverine valleys was tenuous, and many of the hill people were still free, proud men who recognised no lowland authority. In 1560 Setthathirat moved the capital from Luang Prabang south to Vientiane, although in reality the two towns functioned almost as joint capitals, with Luang Prabang as the "royal" capital and Vientiane as the "administrative" capital.

In 1571 King Setthathirat's death began another downward cycle for Lan Xang. For 60 years no leader of merit emerged, and this led to long periods of internecine strife and intervention by the forces of Burma. Only in 1637 did a Lao king worthy of the name once more ascend the throne. His name was Sulinya Vongse, and his 57-year rule – the longest of any Lao monarch – is generally considered the Golden Age of the kingdom.

The Golden Age

There is no doubt that Sulinya Vongse (1637–94) was a wise ruler. A good deal is known about this period of Lao history, largely as a result of the peaceful conditions and relative prosperity that distinguished it. Spared the long years of warfare with Burma and courtly struggles with Ayutthaya, the king was able to spend lavishly on temples and Buddhist endowments and on generally embellishing the capital. As a consequence Vientiane acquired a reputation as a centre of Buddhist learning, attracting novices and devotees from as far afield as Burma, Cambodia and northern Thailand.

WESTERN VIEWS OF LAN XANG

Perhaps the most interesting contemporary account of Lan Xang at the time of Sulinya Vongse comes from Giovanni Maria Leria, an Italian Jesuit missionary abroad in the region in the 1640s. Leria notes: "The royal palace, of which the structure and symmetry are admirable, can be seen from afar. Truly it is of a prodigious extent, and so large that one would take it for a town, both with respect to its situation and the infinite number of people who live there. The apartment of the king, which is adorned with a superb and magnificent gateway, and a quantity of fine rooms together with a great hall, are all made of incorruptible timber and adorned outside and in with excellent bas-reliefs, so delicately gilded that they seem to be plated with gold rather than covered with gold leaf."

Another view of King Sulinya Vongse is afforded by Gerrit van Wuysthoff, a merchant in the employ of the Dutch East India Company. Van Wuysthoff travelled to Vientiane in 1641. After a warm welcome he followed a royal procession, led by the king. He reported: "The king is a young man, about 23 years old. Before him marched about 300 soldiers with spears and guns; behind him elephants carried armed men, followed by some groups of musicians. They were followed in turn by 200 soldiers and by 16 elephants carrying the king's five wives (and their ladies in waiting)."

An invaluable source of information about Sulinya Vongse's capital is the extensive diaries and mission reports of Western visitors (see panel), who sought to take advantage of the peaceful conditions for once prevailing in the Middle Mekong. Most of the visiting businessmen were Dutch Protestants. A steady flow of Portuguese Catholic missionaries also provided written accounts of the area.

Sulinya Vongse was an absolute monarch who appears to have ruled justly and wisely, despite his remoteness from his people. Certainly his lengthy reign ensured that Laos enjoyed peace and prosperity for most of the 17th century. He established cordial relations with the Siamese King Narai at Ayutthaya, and this alliance was strong enough to ward off the Burmese and the Vietnamese for many years.

Nevertheless, two unfortunate developments combined to weaken Lan Xang; one of these can be blamed on the king, while the other was effectively beyond his control.

Adultery and isolation

Sulinya Vongse may have had many wives, but he had only one son – Chao Rachabut. This royal heir was essential to the continuity of Sulinya Vongse's line, but when Chao Rachabut was found guilty of adultery with the wife of a palace servant the irascible and unbending old king ordered his son's execution.

The second adverse development was the growing power and influence of neighbouring states such as Burma, Vietnam and, above all, Siam – all of which had the distinct advantage of a coastline. Lan Xang remained an isolated

Under King Sulinya Vongse, Vientiane was endowed with many palaces and temples, becoming a great centre of Buddhist scholarship, with monks coming from Siam and Cambodia to train in its seminaries.

inland entity, wishing and indeed eager to trade with the advancing Western powers but increasingly cut off by its more powerful neighbours, who effectively limited Vientiane's access to

foreign trade. The inevitable results were poverty and backwardness.

King Sulinya Vongse eventually died in 1694, leaving two young prospective heirs, the children of the son he had executed. In an all-too-familiar pattern, no regency was established; the throne was usurped by a powerful minister, who was in turn overthrown six months later. After more than half a century of peace and stability, Lan Xang was fast descending into factionalism and chaos.

Powerful neighbours

On this occasion, however, things were worse

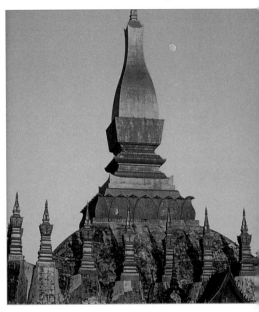

than usual. To the east, Vietnam had expanded hugely in terms of both power and territory. To the west and south, an even more formidable rival had developed in the Siamese Kingdom of Ayutthaya. To the north, albeit more remote from Vientiane, lay the still-powerful Qing Empire of the Chinese.

In these circumstances, factionalism at the Lao court was damaging. For instance, if one faction seized power with tacit Siamese support, its rivals would turn to Vietnam for backing. Both Siam and Vietnam encouraged these manoeuvrings. Siam eyed all Lao territories west of the Mekong and considered itself the rightful ruler of Luang Prabang and Vientiane, while Vietnam coveted the Xieng Khuang

ABOVE, FROM LEFT: an early print of That Luang in Vientiane, the most important national monument in Laos; That Luang today.

region around the Plain of Jars, to which it gave a Vietnamese name, Tranh Ninh, to justify its attentions. To use an antiquated but entirely appropriate Thai phrase, Laos without Sulinya Vongse had become "a bird with two heads" – a weak power paying tribute to two masters, while trying to play one off against the other. This was a bad time for Laos: the ordinary people mired in poverty, the court divided by petty squabbles, and Siam and Vietnam competing for land, people and tax.

Overall, and for obvious geographical reasons, it was the Siamese who tended to be the more powerful of the two overlords. By the

THE STORY OF KHUNYING MO

A popular story recounts how the local population of Khorat was rounded up by Anuvong's men and sent north towards Vientiane. During the march the male prisoners were kept in close captivity, but the women were instructed to act as menials, serving the Lao soldiers their meals and generally "attending to their needs at night". One of the captive women, Khunying Mo, encouraged the soldiers in drunken revelry. When the festivities were at their height she slipped away and released the male prisoners, who made short work of their drunken foes. Two thousand of the invaders were reportedly slain. Mo is still revered by the people of Khorat, with a statue erected in her honour.

beginning of the 18th century Ayutthaya had intervened in the politics of Laos to divide the former Lan Xang into three petty fiefdoms, centred on Luang Prabang in the north, Vientiane in the centre and Champasak in the south. Meanwhile, the inhabitants of Xieng Khuang continued to be effectively dominated by the Vietnamese. By contrast, in the far north, the various *panna* (small states) of Sipsongpanna, territory far removed from even Luang Prabang, paid tribute to China; the question of their partial incorporation into modern Laos would not arise until the advent of French colonialism at the end of the 19th century.

Laos was, however, saved briefly from the growing weight of Siamese power as Ayutthaya itself came under attack from Burma. Unfortunately for Laos, the Siamese made a truly remarkable recovery. Between about 1775 and 1800 King Taksin and then King Rama I established a Siamese hegemony throughout Siam and Laos as well as the greater part of Cambodia. The Burmese had to fall back on their own devices, and the Vietnamese, at least temporarily, were emasculated. Siamese armies occupied both Vientiane and Champasak in 1779, and a few months later King Surinyavong of Luang Prabang opened the gates of the city to their advancing forces.

Nor was it just historical Laos that fell so completely under Siamese hegemony – the various Lao-speaking *muang* of the northeast, which now make up the Thai region of Isaan, were brought fully under Siamese rule for the first time. Henceforth cities such as Si Saket, Ubon Ratchathani, Surin, Roi Et, Mukdahan, Nong Khai and Udon Thani became definitively Siamese, and not Lao, in their political fealty.

Yet, badly defeated though Laos had been, worse was to come. By the beginning of the 19th century three separate Lao kingdoms continued to exist, albeit much curtailed. Separate Lao kings ruled, always under Siamese suzerainty, at Luang Prabang, Champasak and Vientiane. Of these, the first two had lost much of their territory, particularly on the west bank of the Mekong. Vientiane, by contrast, remained a substantial territory. Its major dependencies included Xieng Khuang, Nakhon Phanom, Udon Thani and Mukdahan, the last three extending over much of the Khorat Plateau in present-day Thailand. Vientiane retained political aspirations, too. The last representative of the once great kingdom of Lan Xang did not intend to go quietly.

Vientiane revolt

The first signs of Vientiane's ambitions occurred in 1792. King Nanthasen reinforced his suzerainty over Xieng Khuang by seizing the Phuan prince and putting him under house arrest in Vientiane. He was only released on promising to pay an annual tribute to Vientiane similar to that already paid to Vietnam. Shortly thereafter Nanthasen's forces surrounded Luang Prabang, eventually taking the town by guile.

Next, in 1796, word reached Bangkok of a

fashion – but he soon found that his decision had been unwise.

Inthavong's reign was uneventful, but following his death in 1804 Anuvong took over: the new king was well known at the Siamese court, and trusted by Rama I and Rama II. For the first 20 years of his reign he seems to have had no serious problems with Bangkok. He began his reign in the expected way, by constructing a new palace as well as numerous monasteries, restoring That Luang and generally observing Lao and Buddhist customs. On the other hand – a possible sign of future ambition – Anuvong was quick to recognise Gia Long, the first

plot between Nanthasen and the governor of Nakhon Phanom to throw off Siamese rule. King Rama I, a forceful and active man, moved immediately: Nanthasen and the governor were arrested and escorted to Bangkok.

Bangkok thought – mistakenly – that the Vientiane problem had been nipped in the bud, and appointed two new rulers to govern the troublesome province. Rama's choice fell on two of Nanthasen's younger brothers – Inthavong to reign as first king and Anuvong to reign as *uparat*, or second king, in the Siamese

Nguyen emperor at Hue, by sending tribute.

Things changed in 1825, however, after the death of Rama II. Relations between Anuvong and Rama III seem to have been poor from the start. Anuvong is said to have felt slighted because Rama III treated King Manthathurat of Luang Prabang with more respect than he received himself, and he also resented the Siamese king's widespread use of unpaid Lao labour.

War with Siam

Whatever really happened, Anuvong appears to have returned to Vientiane a changed man, determined to throw off Bangkok's authority and re-establish the glories of the former Lao kingdom. He lost no time erecting new

ABOVE, FROM LEFT: portrait of a Luang Prabang king; an early painting of Wat Mai Suwannaphumaham at Luang Prabang.

defensive works, and called a general council of senior Lao leaders to plan his revolt. It appears that Anuvong felt that Bangkok's power was in decline and the time was right for action. Alas, from a Lao point of view, he was quite wrong. One ally who might have helped him, Vietnam, was not kept fully informed of his plans;

> Both animism and Hinduism were present in Laos before the ascendancy of Buddhism in the 16th century, and traces of these earlier beliefs remain clearly apparent in Laos today.

another potential ally, Burma, was preoccupied in a war with Britain. Not even Luang Prabang could be counted on. The Lao states remained disunited to the end.

Anuvong's plan was to send four armies across the Khorat Plateau to seize Khorat (Nakhon Ratchasima), Ubon Ratchathani and Suvannaphum, gather up the entire population and take everyone back to Vientiane, leaving an unpopulated wilderness between Bangkok and himself. Perhaps he believed that undecided *muang* such as Luang Prabang and even Chiang Mai would join his cause.

The campaign began in December 1826, but

TAX BANDS

An inventive method of distributing tax revenues was introduced in Laos during the 18th century: if people lived in stilt houses, ate sticky rice with their fingers and decorated their temples with images of *naga* (like the Siamese), then they were obliged to pay tax to the representatives of Ayutthaya in Siam; if, on the other hand, they lived at ground level, ate long-grain rice with chopsticks and decorated their temples with dragons (like the Vietnamese), they had to pay tax to the representatives of Hue. This was a complex, if logical, recognition of the age-old fault line between the Indic and Sinitic traditions along which Laos lies.

from the beginning it was apparent that the Siamese were both more numerous and better armed. Despite initial successes – Khorat was seized, as well as numerous smaller towns – the offensive became bogged down, and the Siamese began a swift-moving counterattack.

The defeat of Anuvong

Anuvong, meanwhile, had fled back across the Mekong but, realising there would be no security in Vientiane from the Siamese armies, he left with his family to seek asylum in Vietnam. Within five days Vientiane was in Siamese hands. Palaces and other buildings were burnt and Buddha images were carried off, although monasteries were, by and large, left untouched. Some months later Anuvong returned from Vietnam, apparently in the hope of restoring the status quo, but he was betrayed to the Siamese by Chao Noi, the ruler of Xieng Khuang, whom he had held for four years under house arrest in Vientiane. He was then taken to Bangkok, where he was condemned to a lingering death, exposed in an iron cage over the waters of the Chao Phraya River. The palladium of the Vientiane Kingdom, the Emerald Buddha, was also taken to Bangkok, where it remains to this day.

Thereafter Siamese puppet rulers occupied the Lao throne. Many leading Lao fami-

With the death of Anuvong the dream of a renewed Lan Xang ended, and a new stamp was put on Siamese–Lao relations which has lasted to the present day, although things now seem to be improving. Siam inherited dominance over most of the Tai-speaking world, Laos was relegated to an impoverished and greatly reduced state, and much bitterness was generated. It is not without reason that the present-day government of the Lao PDR refers to the war of 1826–8 as Chao Anuvong's War for Independence, but the official Thai view remains that Anuvong was a rebel troublemaker.

lies were deported and forcibly resettled in Siamese lands. The southern Lao Kingdom of Champassak was also brought under Siamese control, although some of the smaller Lao statelets in the eastern uplands continued to be tributary to the Vietnamese court at Hue. In 1792 the Siamese occupied Luang Prabang, but the ancient capital was treated more kindly than Vientiane had been. It was not looted, it was permitted to keep its palladium, the Phra Bang, and the king kept his throne after due submission to Siam.

ABOVE, FROM LEFT: mid-18th-century group portrait of Lao by Louis Delaporte; a wat mural of water carriers; the ruins of Wat Pha Kaew, Vientiane.

STEALING THE PEOPLE

A significant part of the logistics of and motivation for pre-modern warfare in mainland Southeast Asia rested on the acquisition of people rather than territories. This concept, alien to the Europeans, is based on the effect of warfare on a defeated nation. If Siamese armies penetrated into the traditional territory of Lan Xang – as they often did – they were more likely to withdraw with spoils, including much of the population, than to establish permanent bases. Lao prisoners were, in fact, very much in demand. They were seen as a brother people, obedient, and good farmers. This added to the weakness of Lan Xang, plunging it deeper into despair.

COLONIALISM AND INDEPENDENCE

Complex power struggles between foreign
nations during the early part of the
20th century eventually led to the formation
of the Lao PDR in 1975.

I n the half-century following their conquest of Vientiane in 1827–8 the Siamese continued to expand their influence over the Tai and Lao *muang*, from Sipsongpanna in Yunnan to the remote Hua Phan region of Laos, and even to Sipsongchuthai, which today constitutes the westernmost part of northern Vietnam. For their part, the Vietnamese responded by occupying Xieng Khuang, executing Chao Noi for allegedly betraying Chao Anuvong to the Siamese (see page 52), and incorporating the region into Vietnam as the prefecture of Tranh Ninh, under direct Vietnamese rule. As a consequence of the Siamese–Vietnamese struggle for the spoils of the former Lan Xang, the Lao territories east of the Mekong River suffered serious depopulation through forced resettlement in Siam (Thailand). Xieng Khuang eventually emerged as a joint tributary statelet, though for many years Vietnam continued to hold the upper hand.

The French arrive

And there it might have ended, with Laos effectively partitioned between Siam and Vietnam, but for the arrival of the French in Indochina. French adventurers and priests had been targeting Vietnam and the Indochinese hinterlands since the late 17th century. By the mid-1800s, driven to seek new colonies by their continuing rivalry with the more successful British, imperialist advocates in Paris had determined to establish a colony in the region. The process of colonisation began in

---

LEFT: Social Realist mural depicting Lao wearing traditional clothing, with Socialist construction in background. **RIGHT:** colonial-style homes in Luang Prabang.

1858 when the French seized the Vietnamese port of Da Nang, which was to become their major naval base in Indochina.

By 1862 France occupied most of southern Vietnam; in 1863 protectorate status was imposed on Cambodia, and in 1867 Siam was obliged to accept the new status quo in exchange for the former Cambodian provinces of Battambang and Siem Reap. It was the era of high imperialism and mercantile adventure, and having secured control of the lower Mekong, France now sought a "river route" to China – a route which led through the very heart of Lan Xang.

A solitary French explorer, Henri Mouhot, had penetrated Laos from Siam as far as Luang

Prabang, where he died in 1861. In 1863 his young compatriot Francis Garnier proposed the idea of a voyage up the Mekong, and in 1865 official approval came from Paris. The expedition, led by Doudart de Lagrée and accompanied by Garnier, set out from Saigon on 5 June 1866. It returned just over two years later, having navigated its way up the Mekong, marched through Yunnan and sailed down the Yangtze to Shanghai. From a commercial point of view the mission was a total failure – the "river route" to China was completely blocked by the great Khone Falls on the Lao–Cambodian border – but Garnier did bring back to Europe the first

detailed information on Laos since the 17th century, which he published in 1873 in an extraordinary two-volume publication, complete with paintings and engravings, entitled *Voyage d'Exploration en Indochine*.

This remarkable work makes clear the extent of the devastation which 50 years of war had wrought on Laos. Vientiane, in particular, lay mainly in ruins, semi-deserted by its population, with many buildings overgrown by jungle. In the interests of French imperialism, however, Garnier emphasised the desirability of the region, based on potential mineral and agricultural wealth rather than the disproved possibility of riverine trade. The French, almost without knowing it, were taking a Vietnamese perspective on Indochina.

The Haw Wars

However, a further three decades were to pass before the French inherited the Vietnamese "forward imperative" in Laos as well as Cambodia. In the meantime Laos would have to endure a terrible period of invasion and looting known as the Haw Wars.

"Haw" is a generic name given by the Tai-speaking peoples to the Chinese of Yunnan and southern China. In the mid-19th century this region was torn apart by the Taiping and Yunnan Muslim rebellions. As the Chinese Qing Empire slowly struggled to reassert itself, defeated rebels fleeing Qing reprisals crossed the borders into Laos and northern Vietnam in ever increasing numbers. Armed, ruthless, with nothing to lose, they banded together in so-called "Flag Gangs", which looted and killed at will. In Vietnam the "Black Flags" emerged as

---

BENIGN NEGLECT

The laissez-faire spirit of the former French administration in Laos has been described by Martin Stuart-Fox: "Apart from constructing 5,000km (3,000 miles) of mediocre roads with *corvée* labour, France did virtually nothing either to encourage economic development or to improve social welfare... Ninety percent of the population remained subsistence farmers; there was no industry and a small tin-mining venture benefited only the French and Vietnamese... Health care failed to decrease child mortality... Primary education was left to the Buddhist pagoda schools... Secondary education in French was confined to a tiny minority... French policy in Laos was limited to administering the colony at minimal

cost." No doubt a major part of this easy occupation lay in the fact that the Lao rather welcomed the French, not as liberators, but because they provided an invaluable counterbalance to the external threat of both the Vietnamese and the Siamese. Largely as a result of this there was virtually no opposition to French rule until after the Battle of Dien Bien Phu (in Vietnam) in 1954.

Back in France (as well as in Saigon) Laos would become famous as a land of lotus-eaters, the easiest and reputedly the most dissolute posting east of Suez. But the fact is that at no time did Laos account for more than 1 percent of the exports of French Indochina, and by far the most important part of this was opium, which France made a state monopoly.

an anti-French force, and so enjoyed some rather dubious political legitimacy. In Laos, by contrast, the "Red Flags", "Yellow Flags" and "Striped Flags" were bandits pure and simple. With years of fighting experience behind them, they swept aside local Lao and Vietnamese forces, easily reaching as far south as Tha Khaek. Luang Prabang was threatened, Vietnamese forces were driven from Xieng Khuang, and most seriously, from a Siamese perspective, Vientiane was taken. Everywhere Buddhist temples were sacked.

For Bangkok this situation was intolerable, but defeating the Haw was not going to prove easy. In 1886, angered by the continuing failure of his forces to dislodge their foes, and alarmed by French advances in Indochina, King Chulalongkorn ordered a third, more ambitious expedition to the region. On this occasion the objective was not merely to defeat the Haw but also to annex to Siam all regions formerly subject to Luang Prabang, together with as much of Sipsongchuthai as possible.

This time the Siamese army, together with troops levied from the Lao, at last succeeded in dispersing the Haw. Chulalongkorn's first territorial objective, Xieng Khuang, was seized, and its rulers were escorted to Bangkok to prevent their appealing to Hue – or, even worse, France – for assistance. Next the Siamese turned their

> Vientiane's symbol of nationhood, the gilded spire of That Luang, was thrown to the ground in a frenzied search for gold by the Haw invaders.

attention to Sipsongchuthai, threatened from the east by a major French expeditionary force which had invaded Tonkin in 1883. Muang Thaeng (better known today by its Vietnamese name, Dien Bien Phu) was taken, and three princes of the Sipsongchuthai ruling family were seized and sent to Luang Prabang as hostages in a bid to ensure the submission of their brother, the White Tai chieftain Kham Hum.

This was the high point of Siam's control in the region. Had Chulalongkorn's bold move succeeded, not only Laos but also a sizeable

ABOVE, FROM LEFT: Lao prince on his way to the temple (c.1910); French and local authorities in Luang Prabang.

portion of northern Vietnam might have been incorporated within Siam. Kham Hum, however, chose not to submit and, allied with Haw bands, advanced on Luang Prabang, which had been left largely undefended. On 7 June 1887 the Lao royal capital was seized and sacked; the elderly ruler, King Unkham, barely escaped with his life. As luck would have it, he was accompanied by the French vice-consul, Auguste Pavie, from whom he requested formal protection. Six years later, in 1893, this appeal would be used as legal justification for the French annexation of Laos, resulting in Siam's permanent loss of control over the region.

Land of the lotus-eaters

Through a succession of treaties essentially forced on Bangkok by Paris using military strength, or the threat of it, between 1893 and 1907, Siam gradually relinquished control of all territories east of the Mekong, the islands in the great river, and the territories of Sainyabuli and part of Champasak on the west bank. The French Indochinese administration united all former Lao principalities within a single colonial territory which they called "Laos". The word was, in fact, a misnomer which has stuck, since in the Lao language both country and people were, and remain, simply "Lao".

In 1900 France chose Vientiane as the administrative capital of this newly created entity, and began the establishment of a simple colonial administration. By 1904 a mere 75 French officials were administering the whole of Laos, and by 1940 no more than 600 French citizens were resident there. Most administrative officials under the new regime were Vietnamese.

In fact, the brief French presence in Laos may be seen as a fleeting interruption of the social and political relationship between the Lao and the Vietnamese, with France representing traditional Vietnamese interests. Initially there were plans for a railway from Da Nang to Tha Khaek, and for extensive Vietnamese migration to farm the underpopulated lands of the eastern Mekong Valley. Had these come to fruition, Laos might eventually have become entirely absorbed within Vietnam. But the railway was not built, and the many Vietnamese who settled in Laos chose to do so not as farmers but as city-dwellers: members of the civil service, jewellers, tailors, hairdressers, restaurateurs and so on. By 1945, as a result of this immigration, Viet Kieu (migrant Vietnamese) communities dominated all the major Lao towns except Luang Prabang, accounting for more than 50 percent of the inhabitants of the capital, Vientiane, and as much as 85 percent of the second city, Tha Kaek.

THE RED PRINCE

Souphanouvong, a member of the royal house of Luang Prabang, revolutionary nationalist and founding member of the Lao Communist movement, was born in 1912, one of 23 children sired by the Luang Prabang viceroy, or second king, Boun Khong. Due to his privileged birth, Souphanouvong automatically acquired the status of a royal prince. He and his three elder half-brothers would go on to play important roles in the government of post-1953 independent Laos.

As a young man, Souphanouvong studied in Hanoi and France, later marrying a Vietnamese and becoming involved in the anti-colonial movement. Under the guidance of Ho Chi Minh, he set up the Pathet Lao (Lao People's Liberation Army) in 1951. With his half-brothers serving in the French-supported Royal Lao government in the years 1953–75, Souphanouvong took to the jungle in pursuit of the revolutionary goals which earned him the sobriquet "the Red Prince".

He did not enter Vientiane again until 1974, by which time the Communist victory throughout Indochina was assured. His return was greeted with great enthusiasm by the people, and after the establishment of the Lao PDR in 1975 he was appointed president, a post he retained until the Fourth Party Congress in 1986, when he retired because of ill health. Until his death in 1995, Souphanouvong remained popular with ordinary Lao people.

The lowland Lao mostly accepted the status quo, though they chafed under the pressure of rising Viet immigration, French taxation and French-imposed *corvée* (unpaid labour). What nationalist opposition there was to French rule came mainly from the highlanders and the Vietnamese of the cities, although the concern of the latter was almost exclusively for their homeland, of which they saw both Laos and Cambodia as future appendages. Only a few lowlanders paid any attention to the rise of Vietnamese nationalism, and these were almost exclusively children of the Lao elite studying in Hanoi or Saigon. Communist ideals, similarly, took no root in

Japanese interference in Indochina, where the colonial administration supported Vichy.

In 1941, under the military ruler Phibun Songkhram, Thai forces fought a series of battles with French Indochinese troops for control of the Lao territories of Champasak and Sainyabuli on the west bank of the Mekong. Though the struggle was indecisive on land (the Thais suffered defeat at sea), Japan intervened and imposed an armistice. As a result of this agreement France ceded all Lao west-bank territories to Thailand. The French, though humiliated, were to retain nominal power in Indochina for a further four years, but on 9 March 1945 the

Laos, Marxists being limited to Viet Kieu followers of Ho Chi Minh who were constantly harassed by French security police. The Indochinese Communist Party was formed, under Vietnamese auspices, but only one ethnic Lao is known to have joined before World War II.

Japan intervenes

The period of "lotus-eating" came to an abrupt end in 1940 with the German defeat of the French in World War II, the establishment of the collaborationist Vichy regime in France, and increasing

---

ABOVE, FROM LEFT: anti-French painting in the Lao Revolutionary Museum, Vientiane; Pathet Lao leadership.

Japanese, sensing defeat by the Allied forces, staged a coup against the Vichy administration and forced the pro-French Lao monarch, King Sisavang Vong, to declare independence. Despite this confidence, within months Japan had surrendered, and the first French paratroopers had landed in southern Laos.

Free Lao movement

The French were opposed by Prince Phetsarath, the wartime prime minister, and by the small Lao Issara ("Free Lao") underground movement which had grown up in protest against both French and Japanese rule. For six months, from October 1945 to April 1946, a Lao Issara government, backed by the Viet Minh government of

Ho Chi Minh, attempted to set up a functioning administration. A small defence force was set up under Phetsarath's half-brother, Prince Souphanouvong (who later became famous as "the Red Prince" – see panel), and negotiations were entered into with the French, but to no avail. In March 1946 French forces moved north. Lao Issara forces, supported by resident Viet Kieu, attempted to make a stand at Tha Khaek but were roundly defeated.

Although Laos was back in French hands by the end of May, within months the restored colonial authority indicated a willingness to concede autonomy. This offer caused the Lao

Issara to become hopelessly split. One faction, led by Prince Phetsarath, set up a government in exile in Bangkok; a second faction, led by Prince Souphanouvong, favoured an alliance with Ho Chi Minh and the Vietnamese Communists; while a third faction, led by Prince Souvanna Phouma, another half-brother, favoured a deal with the French. As a consequence, France proceeded without Lao Issara cooperation, and in 1949 recognised Laos as an "Independent Associate State" of the French Union. This unilateral move caused the breakup of the Lao Issara movement, but in 1951 Prince Souphanouvong announced the formation of the Neo Lao Issara, or "Free Lao Front" – a pro-Communist organisation later known as the Pathet Lao, or "Land of the Lao".

Independence and Communism

Souphanouvong was given the full backing of the Viet Minh authorities in Hanoi. The consequence would be some 25 years of armed struggle, during which Laos would become inextricably bound up with the war in Vietnam, culminating in the establishment of the Lao People's Democratic Republic (Lao PDR) in 1975. For the moment, however, the Pathet Lao remained a tiny force, with their Viet Minh allies doing most of the fighting against France on Lao soil.

France, being fully caught up in its punishing war of attrition with the Viet Minh, continued largely to ignore Laos. As a consequence, in 1953, with the decisive battle of Dien Bien Phu looming, Laos was granted full sovereignty and independence as a constitutional monarchy known as the Kingdom of Laos.

Following the French withdrawal from Indochina in 1954 the United States, anxious to counter rising Communist influence in Laos, began to fill the coffers of the Royal Lao government in Vientiane. During the same period the Pathet Lao established secure bases in the northeastern provinces of Hua Phan and Phongsali, within easy supply distance of Hanoi. There followed years of complex political and military manoeuvring, with a royalist-Pathet Lao coalition in 1957–60, followed by a series of neutralist and royalist coups and counter-coups until 1964.

The most violent episode was the so-called battle of Vientiane, which took place in December 1960 between neutralist and "rightist" forces. The "leftist" Pathet Lao delegation

MOUNTAIN WARRIORS

The Hmong have long been celebrated – and feared – warriors in Laos. As the main ally of the USA in the CIA "Secret War", many refused to surrender when the Communists seized power in 1975, but took to the remote mountain tops, where they harassed the Communist authorities in a low-key but long-running insurgency. Meanwhile, they were supported financially and politically by Hmong refugees who had resettled in the United States. As recently as 2004 two Swiss tourists were killed when they ran into an exchange of hostilities, but after a large group of insurgents surrendered in 2006, the Hmong military struggle seems all but to have ended, and the roads safe for travel.

> At the time of the 1957 coalition the Communists controlled a mere two of the country's 13 provinces; by 1973 this equation had been almost precisely reversed.

swiftly left town to avoid becoming caught up in the fighting, and Pathet Lao forces stationed at Na Khang, some 60km (37 miles) to the north, did not intervene. A massive display of firepower by the rightist forces resulted in the deaths of 400 to 500 civilians in the town, mostly Vietnamese residents, and the wounding of another 1,000 to 1,500 civilians. The neutralist troops only lost 17 killed. Rightist armour rolled into town and the victorious commander, Phoumi, installed a royalist, Prince Boun Oum, as premier in the new administration. The Boun Oum administration survived until 1962, and was then replaced by the royalist government of Prince Souvanna Phouma. After the Communist seizure of power in 1975, Phoumi Nosavan fled to Bangkok, where he died in 1985. Boun Oum died in France in 1980. From the time of the battle in 1960, the Pathet Lao refused to participate in any negotiations, believing correctly that it would eventually seize power through military means.

Between 1964 and 1973 the Pathet Lao areas of Laos suffered massive bombing by the United States (see page 63) but nevertheless continued inexorably to expand. In 1973, when the US eventually negotiated its way out of direct military involvement in Vietnam, a ceasefire was negotiated in Laos. This time the Pathet Lao was clearly the dominant party. In 1975 first Phnom Penh, then Saigon, fell to the Communists. The writing was on the wall in Vientiane, and a mass exodus of royalist ministers and generals across the Mekong to Thailand began. The subsequent takeover was bloodless, with the Lao PDR formally established on 2 December 1975.

For the next five years Communist policy was extremely harsh, particularly by the usually relaxed standards of the Lao people. Buddhism was curtailed, links with Thailand were

---

ABOVE, FROM LEFT: portrait of Lenin on a children's book cover; King Savang Vatthana reigned for 17 years from 1959–76 before being ousted by the Pathet Lao.

practically cut, and a vicious campaign was mounted against the Hmong minority, many of whom had refused to accept the Lao PDR or to lay down their arms. Tens of thousands of people were arrested and sent for "re-education" to camps known as *samana* in the remote northeast. These arrests covered all levels of society, from the prostitutes and pickpockets of Vientiane through small businessmen and landholders to members of the former ruling elite. In 1977 King Savang Vatthana, who had abdicated, joined this group, together with his family; they reportedly died of malnutrition in a remote part of Hua Phan.

New Thinking

By 1979 these policies had aroused fierce resentment among the Lao peasantry, the traditional power base of the Pathet Lao. It was also becoming painfully apparent that Communist economic policies were failing to deliver positive results as Laos slumped far behind its rich Thai neighbour. This resulted in perhaps as many as 400,000 people (about 12 percent of the population) taking the relatively easy option of crossing the Mekong to Thailand, where many simply blended in with their fellow ethnic Lao. Laos was losing many of its brightest and best-qualified citizens.

As a result, younger, less hardline party members, together with non-party members,

Unexploded Ordnance (UXO) remains a problem in Laos despite the best efforts of international de-mining groups. Most populated areas are safe, but in the uplands by the Vietnamese border, much UXO still remains lethally concealed.

increased pressure on the old, pro-Vietnamese leadership of the Lao PDR – particularly since Communist economic policies in Vietnam were manifestly failing too. Eventually, in 1989, this led to the introduction of *jintanakan mai*, or "New Thinking", an economic and

political liberalisation which in some ways closely paralleled the process of *perestroika* in the former Soviet Union, and went beyond the supposedly parallel process of *doi moi* in Vietnam. During the 1990s this process continued, particularly after the death of the Lao PDR president and the Communist hardliner Kaysone Phomvihane in 1992. Restrictions on individual liberties were slowly lifted, Lao émigrés (especially businessmen) were encouraged to return home, and the country was gradually opened to tourism. Relations with Thailand improved dramatically, symbolised by the opening of the "Friendship Bridge" in 1994 and the official visit of then-President Nouhak Phoumsavanh to Thailand in 1995. As a direct

result of these reforms, the Lao PDR joined ASEAN in 1997.

Unfortunately, in the same year, the Asian economic crisis brought about the collapse of the Thai baht, dragging down the value of the Lao kip. The government reintroduced currency controls in an effort to control the situation, but it would be four years before the kip stabilised again.

This state of relative stability was still occasionally disturbed. In 2000, for example, a series of minor bombings took place in Vientiane, Savannakhet and Pakse involving hand grenades and small handmade explosives. The bombings were suspected to be the work of a group called the Underground Government in Exile. There was an additional bombing incident in October 2003. Today, however, the process of reform is so far advanced that it would be impossible to turn back the clock, and the Lao people continue to enjoy peace and an improving standard of living.

In March 2006, Choummaly Sayasone took over from Siphandone as leader of the ruling Communist Party. He also officially replaced Siphandone as president in June that year. In December 2006, a group of 400 ethnic Hmong insurgents who had been waging a low-level insurgency against the Lao authorities since 1975 surrendered. Subsequently, in June 2007, US prosecutors charged nine US residents – including the former royalist Hmong general Vang Pao – with planning a coup against the Lao authorities. These events, taken with the country's application to become a full member of the World Trade Organization (WTO) in January 2008, seem indicative of improving ethnic relations within Laos and the adoption of a generally less authoritarian attitude by the Lao authorities. Links with outside nations other than Vietnam continued to improve, too, with the construction of a fully sealed road between Xhiang Khong in Thailand and Boten on the Chinese frontier, as well as the opening of a rail link across the Friendship Bridge between Thailand and Laos in 2009. In January 2011, former general Vang Pao died in California, bringing a symbolic closure to the CIA "Secret War". In June of the same year Choummaly Sayasone was confirmed in office as President of the Lao PDR for a further five-year term, strengthening the reform process under way in the country.

LEFT: Hmongs in Laos.

The Secret War

Caught up in the global struggle between Communism and the USA, strategically located Laos was the setting for a covert war in the 1970s.

For more than 10 years, between 1963 and 1973, Laos was the hidden arena for a "Secret War" that most of the world knew little or nothing about. Under the Geneva Accord of 1962 Laos was officially recognised as a neutral state in which no foreign military personnel might be stationed, but in practice this was ignored by all sides. The greatest violator of Lao neutrality was North Vietnam. The Communists had used northeastern Laos as a springboard for attacks on the French during the First Indochina War and never subsequently withdrew. By 1970 an entire North Vietnamese division – the 316th – was deployed in Laos, fielding a total of more than 75,000 troops. Other areas of eastern Laos, too, were crisscrossed with a network of hidden tracks comprising the notorious "Ho Chi Minh Trail" *(see page 158)* for resupplying Communist units in Cambodia and South Vietnam.

Communist China, too, maintained an area of special interest in the far northwest of Laos at this time, arming and supplying leftist opponents of the Royal Lao government in Vientiane, not least to off-set the predominance of Vietnamese influence over their Pathet Lao allies. This policy reached its zenith during the 1960s and early 1970s, when the People's Liberation Army built a network of roads throughout Phongsali and Luang Nam Tha, reaching as far south as Pakbeng in Udomxai province. This road-building programme owed its origins to an agreement reached between Chou En-lai and the Lao premier, Prince Souvanna Phouma, at Beijing in January 1962. By the mid-1960s, however, Vientiane could only watch helplessly as the Chinese, without consultation, built roads throughout the far north-west. At the height of the programme as many as 10,000 labourers toiled under the protection of Chinese armed sentries and anti-aircraft units.

Meanwhile the USA was equally active. Although it was legally prohibited from intervening in support of the royalist forces, US "technicians" appeared in Laos as early as 1959, when they began training the Royal Lao army and building up a Hmong hill-tribe army under the

RIGHT: sitting on a bomb dropped by a US B-52.

leadership of Vang Pao. By 1962 this US-equipped secret army had reached a strength of around 10,000, centred on Vang Pao's headquarters at Long Tien in the Plain of Jars. So secret was this US involvement that the name Laos was never used in official communications – the country was known simply as "The Other Theatre", and Long Tien as "Alternate".

Civil war

Meanwhile, as Laos was torn apart by civil war, involving Vietnamese, Chinese and US-backed forces, the USA resorted increasingly to air power in an attempt to defeat the leftist forces. By 1973 nearly 600,000 sorties had been flown over the

country, dropping an average of one planeload of bombs every eight minutes, 24 hours a day, for nine years. In the end, almost 2 million tonnes of bombs had been dropped on Laos – about half a tonne of explosives for every person in the country. And every year, around 300 people are killed or maimed by the lethally hidden remaining bombs.

And yet it was to no avail. The Hmong secret army and Royal Lao forces were consistently out-manoeuvred by the North Vietnamese and their Pathet Lao surrogates. The single most expensive covert para-military operation ever conducted by the USA ended in failure with the Communist takeover of Vientiane in December 1975. And yet, despite the bombing, bloodshed and years of brutality on both sides, the US Embassy was shut for a total of just one day.

POPULATION, SOCIETY AND ECONOMY

The population of Laos is a broad ethnic mix, the product of an uneasy history, but past hostilities are giving way to mutual cooperation.

With around 6.2 million inhabitants, Laos has one of the lowest population densities in Asia – just over 22 people per sq km (9 per sq mile). Outside a handful of relatively large towns in the Mekong Valley, most Lao – around 85 percent – live in rural areas and lead agricultural lives.

In fact, only around 50 percent of the country's population is ethnically Lao, the rest being divided between numerous tribal groups, although the methods of classification for these are varied and frequently contradictory.

The Lao government divides the population into three main ethnic categories, ostensibly according to the altitude at which they live: Lao Soung (higher mountain), Lao Theung

> It's common in Laos for shows to be put on of Lao Loum, Lao Theung and Lao Soung women dancing together in harmony in their diverse ethnic clothing. In reality, all the dancers are usually Lao Loum lowlanders.

(lower mountain) and Lao Loum (lowland). Some 50–60 percent of the population are Lao Loum, 20–30 percent are Lao Theung and 10–20 percent are Lao Soung. This is, however, a somewhat arbitrary categorisation, as there are at least 49 different ethnic groups in Laos, each with its own linguistic, religious and culinary traditions.

PRECEDING PAGES: monks at Wat Nam Kaew Luang, Luang Nam Tha. **LEFT:** Hmong mother and baby.
RIGHT: a resident of Phongsali.

Lao Loum

In general, the Lao Loum live in the Mekong River Valley, subsist on wet-rice cultivation and practise Theravada Buddhism. These are the people of the Mekong Valley lowlands who predominate in the provinces of Luang Prabang, Vientiane, Tha Kaek, Savannakhet and Pakse, and who have traditionally controlled Lao government and society. The Lao Loum are closely related to the Lao-speaking inhabitants of neighbouring northeastern Thailand and, slightly more distantly, to the central Thai or Siamese. The distinction between Lao and Thai is rather indistinct and something of a new (and politically motivated) phenomenon. Certainly the two groups are part of the same family, something both sides will happily accept – yet the Lao can be irritated by the rather arrogant and frequently stated Thai contention that the Lao are their "little brothers".

Lao Theung and Lao Soung

Next there are the Lao Theung, or "approaching the top of the mountain Lao", a loose affiliation of mostly Mon-Khmer-speaking people who live at moderate altitudes and are generally animists rather than Buddhists. Formerly known to the ruling Lao Loum by the pejorative term *kha*, or slave, this group constitutes a further 15–20 percent of the population, and makes up

> The European expat community in Laos remains small (less than 3,000), and is mostly made up of employees of international aid organisations in Vientiane, as well as hoteliers and restaurateurs, especially from France.

Tai), all ethnic Tai sub-groups. All these groups are closely related to the Lao Loum.

Laos is also home to sizeable and very significant ethnic Vietnamese (Viet Kieu) and ethnic Chinese (Hua Jiao) communities. In the past decade Hua Jiao have increased mark-

by far the most economically disadvantaged section of Lao society.

Finally, on the distant mountain tops live – as might be expected – the Lao Soung, or "High Lao", people whose communities are at altitudes of more than 1,000 metres (3,200ft) above sea level. Representatives of this group are also to be found in northern Thailand, northwestern Vietnam and southern China, and include Hmong and Mien, together with smaller numbers of Akha, Lisu and Lahu. The Lao Soung have traditionally relied on the cultivation of dry rice and opium. An estimated 20 percent of these upland dwellers comprise Tai-speaking minority groups such as the Tai Dam (Black Tai), Tai Daeng (Red Tai) and Tai Khao (White

edly, as overland Chinese from Yunnan and Guangdong have migrated to Vientiane and other cities, where they are overwhelmingly engaged in business. Viets also make up an influential portion of the traders and small business owners in Laos – not to mention the continuing Vietnamese military presence in some provinces. Both groups are largely urban-based, the Chinese more in the north of the country and in Vientiane, the ethnic Viets in the Mekong Valley towns like Tha Khaek and Savannakhet. The Vietnamese, in particular, settled in Laos during colonial times, and were employed by the French authorities as teachers and civil servants and at lower levels of administration.

Relations between Lao and Viet have not always run smoothly. In terms of their traditions the two peoples live on opposite sides of the great cultural fault line that divides mainland Southeast Asia into Indic and Sinitic zones. In geographical terms, too, they are largely divided by the mountainous Annamite Cordillera, which separates the two countries along the ridges of a shared 1,950km (1,220-mile) border. A number of folk aphorisms exist which supposedly sum up the ethnocentric views which the two peoples have of each other. "Lao and Viet, Cat and Dog" is an old Lao proverb which indicates the difficulties of mutual co-existence,

The hostility of the Lao to the Vietnamese on an ethnic basis has perhaps dulled over the years, yet the failure of Vietnam's socialist economic system has inevitably affected Lao thinking; Thailand, whose economy for decades far outperformed that of Vietnam, is now generally regarded as a better model for economic (but not social) development for the Lao PDR, even though Vietnam is now catching up fast.

Thai migration

One other important immigrant community is the Thai – though it's difficult to know quite where new Thai migration begins and old Lao

while another old saying claims: "The Viets plant the rice, the Khmers watch them planting, but the Lao listen to the rice grow."

Today a small but flourishing Viet Kieu element survives in Vientiane, although it is rapidly being outnumbered by incoming Thai entrepreneurs and Chinese business people. In the last decade, the sheer numbers of the incoming Chinese, coupled with their relative wealth and political influence, have made the local population suspicious of, and even hostile to, further Chinese immigration.

ABOVE, FROM LEFT: Laos has a small Muslim community; out and about in Vientiane; a time for prayer and reflection at Wat Phu, Champasak.

Still deeply suspicious of outside influences, authorities restrict marriages between Lao nationals and overseas visitors. Foreigners require special permission, and a reference from their embassy, before they can wed a Lao citizen.

re-immigration ends. This is because of the almost identical linguistic and ethnic character of the lowland Lao and the people of northeastern Thailand (also known as Isaan), who also quite happily call themselves "Lao". They are, in fact, one and the same people. Thai immigrants from Bangkok are easier to identify, as they speak Central Thai rather than Lao. They, too, are appearing in increasing numbers, especially in the main towns of Laos, where their longer acquaintance with capitalism, business savvy and access to financial capital combines to give them a distinct business advantage. As with the ethnic Chinese, this leads to a degree of suspicion and even envy on the part of the Lao – but the fact remains that Lao and Thai are ethnic and cultural kin, speaking almost identical languages, and both devout Theravada Buddhists. This means that hostility levels to the Thai incomers is substantially less than towards the Han Chinese. The former may be seen as "city slickers" and "wide boys", but the

latter are considered to pose a more significant threat to the Lao identity in the long term.

The economy

Laos remains one of the world's poorer countries, its economy heavily propped up by extensive foreign aid, which currently accounts for 25–30 percent of the annual budget, down from around 50 percent in the late 1990s. Important exports include wood, wood products and electricity. Laos is rich in minerals; tin and gypsum are the most important, but copper, gold, iron and zinc are also present. As yet these natural resources remain largely untapped, although

THE MUSLIMS OF LAOS

Chinese Muslims from China's southwestern province of Yunnan once carried on much of the traditional trade in the mountains of Laos. Known to the Lao and Thais as Chin Haw, these pioneering caravaneers drove their mule trains south to Luang Prabang and beyond. In the late 19th-century Haw Wars (see page 56), outlaw bands of Haw sacked Vientiane, where they tore the spire off That Luang in search of buried gold. Some Haw Muslims still live in the mountains, acting as middlemen in the trade between lowlanders and hill people.

There is also a small South Asian Muslim community in Vientiane, centred on the Jamia Masjid behind the central Nam Phu fountain. Signs inside the mosque are

written in five languages – Tamil, Urdu, Arabic, Lao and English. This unexpected Tamil influence derives from Pondicherry, France's former Tamil toehold on the coast of India, which sent many Chulia or Tamil Muslim businessmen to Indochina during the period of French rule. Most of Vientiane's South Asian Muslims are businessmen, involved in the manufacturing of textiles, in various branches of import-export, or serving their community as butchers and restaurateurs.

There is also a minuscule Cham Muslim community in Vientiane, with its own mosque. Refugees fleeing Pol Pot's Cambodia arrived in the 1970s, to be joined over the years by small numbers of relatives.

several companies are engaged in oil exploration. Secondary manufacturing industry is slowly developing, with some clothing now being exported, but investment is needed in education to increase the skills of the workforce before more sophisticated manufacturing concerns move in. Some basic products are already produced in local factories, helping to keep imports low.

When the current government took control in 1975 it implemented a brief, disastrous programme of nationalisation and collectivisation of agriculture. In 1979 it abruptly reversed course and embarked on a process of reform in

agriculture, monetary policy and commodity pricing that still continues today. The economies of urban centres like Vientiane have been transformed since the mid-1980s, when restrictions on private enterprise and ownership of private property began to be lifted, and the economy is now "socialist" in name only.

Laos now has a liberal foreign investment which allows 100 percent foreign ownership for government-approved projects. Thailand, the USA and Australia now top the list of foreign investors.

ABOVE, FROM LEFT: ethnic Vietnamese (Viet Kieu); relations between Laos and Vietnam have not always been harmonious.

However, Laos remains one of the poorest nations in Asia. Eighty-five percent of the population work in agriculture, fishing and forestry, and 10 percent in the armed forces or the civil service. Industry is almost non-existent, and the economy is overwhelmingly dependent on foreign aid from bodies like the UN and the World Bank. Annual per capita income hovers just over US$1,000. The Asian economic crisis of the late 1990s, particularly the currency woes in Thailand, sent the kip on a free-fall. Civil service salaries did not keep pace with the resulting inflation, and were rendered almost worthless. Today the authorities in Vientiane are watching the current world recession anxiously, fearful of another Asian financial meltdown.

The currency, while not convertible outside the country, has been allowed to float according to market forces, largely eliminating a once-thriving black market in the kip. In a sign of continuing economic and fiscal weakness, however, the US dollar and also the Thai baht are generally preferred to the local currency.

The best hope for future economic growth seems to lie in the many hydroelectric projects under discussion or development – despite the environmental concerns surrounding them, as well as the forestry and mining potential. Thai, American, French and Australian as well as Lao companies have poured money into these developments, secure in the knowledge that the regional market for electricity, particularly in Thailand and Vietnam, will continue to grow rapidly. A possible by-product of hydroelectric projects is the fish which can be farmed in the new lakes, for which there is a

TOURISM'S INFLUENCE ON SOCIETY

Tourism is, inevitably, having an increasing impact on Lao society – and not all of it good. The Lao leadership looks askance at some aspects of tourism in Thailand, not least in terms of public morals; and while Vientiane may want the foreign exchange that international tourism brings, the free-wheeling alcohol, sex and drugs scene now developing among young Westerners at Vang Vieng is attracting increasing criticism. The Lao authorities initially tried to control tourism by attempting to limit visitors to "top end" tour groups, but to no avail. Laos is a near-perfect destination for budget tourists and it is this sector that is currently expanding fastest.

ready market both in Laos and in neighbouring countries.

Several international companies, Non-Governmental Organisations and local government offices have been upgrading the road network throughout the country in order to provide a more workable infrastructure for economic development and tourism. New highways and bridges linking Laos to its neighbours and putting it at an economic crossroads have been – or are being – built. With improved communications, investors are looking to develop southern towns, especially those on the Thai border and the cross-country

routes to Vietnam. China, too, is very active in the transport development stakes, and a new bridge across the Mekong between Huay Xay in Laos and Chiang Khong in Thailand, jointly financed by China and Thailand, is scheduled to open in mid-2013. This project will link China with Thailand by road across northern Laos, and a future rail link is also planned.

Education

Public education in Laos involves five years of primary school, three of middle school and three of high school. The National University in Vientiane provides what is really the only

THE GOVERNMENT

The Lao People's Democratic Republic (Lao PDR) was formed on 2 December 1975, when the Communist Lao People's Revolutionary Party (LPRP) took over from the Royal Lao government in the wake of the Second Indochina War. To this day the LPRP remains the primary ruling institution in the country, exerting considerable influence on people's everyday lives. Power within the LPRP lies in the nine-member Politburo, the 49-member Central Committee and the Permanent Secretariat. The Secretary General of all three bodies was President Khamtay Siphandone until 2006, when Choummaly Sayasone took over as the head of the LPRP and also succeeded Siphandone as president.

State administration is made up of the Council of Government, which includes the 12 ministries, the Office of the Prime Minister and the National Planning Committee. The National Assembly is the nation's sole legislative body. Representatives, almost all of whom are party members, are elected by the public and meet once a year to rubber-stamp Central Committee decisions and prime ministerial declarations.

Laos is divided into 16 different provinces *(kweng)*, one municipality, Vientiane, and one "Special Zone", Saisomboun, which continues to be administered by the Lao military. Each province is further divided into district, subdistrict and village levels.

opportunity for higher education inside the country. Most rural Lao complete less than three years of formal education. Public-school teachers are notoriously under-educated and underpaid, and educational facilities throughout the country are still extremely poor. The government has upgraded existing schools, built new ones and expanded adult education, but it still cannot afford to pay teachers or to provide textbooks. School buildings are inadequate both in facilities and numbers, and most Lao children (as in neighbouring Vietnam) are obliged to attend school on a shift basis – one group in the morning, another in the afternoon.

Laos is still considered a francophone nation by the French – but not by anyone else. As in neighbouring Vietnam and Cambodia, English is popular as a second language, taught in schools as the international tongue.

French-speaking Lao are few in number and increasingly elderly.

After the revolution in 1975 there was a marked decline in the quality of public education. While the number of schools expanded rapidly, the limited facilities served as little more

than centres for political indoctrination. Lack of funding for buildings and books, and a serious lack of qualified teachers (most of the educated population fled after 1975), plague the system to this day. The country still loses around 35 percent of its educated youth to migration.

During the Cold War, Laos's best students completed their education abroad, usually in Eastern Bloc countries. Most of these Lao later struggled to replace whatever largely irrelevant language they learnt overseas with English. Today, however, very little English is spoken except in tourist areas and aspiring Lao students want to learn English and Chinese. The second language will remain Thai, however, especially in urban areas – an indication of the power and influence of Thai TV and radio.

Almost all Lao men spend at least a part of their youth studying at the local wat, or Buddhist temple; for Lao boys in rural areas, the wat might offer the only chance to obtain an education and to work their way up in society.

Public education was introduced into Laos under the French in 1902, when the first public elementary schools were opened in Vientiane and Luang Prabang. Children of the Lao upper classes would study at French *lycées* in the country's urban centres, while royalty were sent off to study in France. Today, however,

ABOVE, FROM LEFT: body-building contest in Vientiane; many Lao schoolchildren – here in a classroom in Champasak – must attend school on a shift basis.

Neighbourly Relations?

Throughout its history, Laos has been hugely influenced by its three powerful neighbours – Vietnam, China and Thailand.

Traditional antagonisms between Lao and Viet are rooted in their disparate cultural godfathers, India and China, and the widely divergent Brahmin and Mandarin world-views – but they have also been sharpened by practical realities. To begin

with, and most importantly, there are a great many more Vietnamese than there are Lao, making the former of necessity an expansionist people. Fortunately for the Lao, their homeland is protected by the jagged mountains of the Annamite Cordillera, so they have escaped the full weight of Vietnamese expansion.

Instead, the territorial imperative of the Viets has been channelled south, to the former Kingdom of Champa, the Mekong Delta and Cambodia. For this reason anti-Vietnamese feeling is much stronger in Cambodia than in Laos. Still, an inherent suspicion of their serious, hard-working and disturbingly numerous Viet neighbours runs deep in the psyche of most Lao.

During the half-century which elapsed between France's acquisition of Laos in 1893 and the

subjugation of Indochina by the Japanese, the French actively encouraged the migration of Vietnamese to Laos. These immigrants, who totalled more than 50,000 people by the outbreak of World War II, included technicians, artisans, lower-ranking officials, schoolteachers, doctors, dentists and other professionals. By 1939 the public services of Laos were all largely staffed by Vietnamese, and the urban population, too, was predominantly Viet Kieu (migrant Vietnamese settlers).

When Laos eventually achieved independence from France in 1953, the traditional ethnic balance of the country had changed almost beyond recognition. Viet Kieu made up 7 percent of the total population, and ethnic Chinese (primarily from Fujian and Guangdong) a further 2–3 percent. In urban terms the contrast was startling: between them the two non-indigenous peoples dominated urban Laos, constituting 57 percent of the population of Vientiane, 89 percent of that of Tha Kaek and 85 percent of that of Pakse.

During the Indochina Wars which followed France's withdrawal, much of the hostility of the Royal Lao government and the general urban populace towards the Vietnamese stemmed from this colonial experience. By contrast the Chinese, who were involved almost exclusively in trade and had eschewed government service under the French, were generally accepted by the Lao.

Political links with Vietnam

Meanwhile, in the mountain fastnesses of Sam Neua and Phongsali in the far north, opponents of the Royal Lao regime – dissident Lao, who enjoyed strong links with Vietnam – set up the Lao Issara, or Free Lao, which subsequently became known as the Pathet Lao. Given the special links between the Pathet Lao leadership and the Viet Minh, strengthened by 30 years of mutually supportive armed struggle, it was widely expected that, following the Pathet Lao victory and the establishment of the Lao PDR in 1975, Vietnamese migration to Laos would resume in a big way. This did not prove to be the case, however. During this time the special relationship between the governments of Laos and Vietnam was described by the Lao as "closer than the lips and the teeth" and by the Viets as "deeper than the Mekong River".

After 1975 the relationship between the Lao PDR and the Socialist Republic of Vietnam was marked more by continuing military cooperation, and the presence in Laos of Vietnamese advisers and specialists at all levels, than by the return of Viet Kieu settlers. For example, at the height of the Sino-Vietnamese hostilities of the early 1980s, following China's "lesson" to Vietnam, between 50,000 and 80,000 Vietnamese troops were moved into northern Laos to deter further Chinese attack. Yet as tension declined these troop levels were reduced.

Some migration – or re-migration – of Vietnamese people to Laos took place through the late 1980s and early 1990s, but this was at a time when both Thai and Western influence was markedly on the increase in the Lao PDR. A census of the Vientiane population found 15,000 Vietnamese living illegally in the capital. Most of them were promptly deported back to Vietnam.

China

Following the fall of Saigon in April 1975, and the establishment of Communist rule over Laos in December of the same year, the new Lao authorities did their best to keep on good terms with both Hanoi and Beijing. Vietnam was undoubtedly the dominant power in Indochina, but China was invited to stay on and to continue road-building and other developmental aid in the northwest of the country as far south as Luang Prabang.

During the early 1980s, however, relations between Laos and China deteriorated. The Lao Communist leader Kaysone Phomvihane publicly accused Beijing of "dark and extremely cruel schemes against Laos", and Beijing responded with a warning that "criminal Vietnamese schemes to intensify their control over Laos will only invite stronger opposition from the Lao people". Many ethnic Chinese residents fled Laos during this period, and were eventually resettled on Hainan Island.

By the mid-1980s, however, as the conflict between Vietnam and China gradually died down, Laos wasted little time in discreetly re-establishing

amicable relations with Beijing. Since that time Beijing has hardly looked back, and today China's political and economic influence over northwestern Laos is paramount.

In time, no doubt, the people of northwestern Laos will benefit substantially from political and economic developments. Certainly standards of living are already rising for the residents of Luang Nam Tha and Bokeo, strategically located between the fast-expanding economies of China and Thailand, as they begin to feel the benefits of free trade. In economic terms the area is rapidly becoming more closely tied to China than it has been at any time since the French annexation in 1896.

Thailand

Meanwhile the third and culturally closest of Laos's big neighbours, Thailand, is making a significant comeback in the friendship stakes. Thai cultural influences permeate Laos, and Thai television and radio – readily comprehended by most Lao in a way that simply doesn't hold true for either Vietnamese or Chinese – are watched avidly throughout the country. It seems that, at long last, the legacy of Lao suspicion of its brasher, larger and stronger neighbour to the west of the Mekong is disappearing. Road – and now rail – bridges are springing up fast, and many Lao, both in government and ordinary citizens, now see Thailand as a useful counterweight to their Vietnamese and Chinese neighbours, as well as an economic role model to follow in the future.

ABOVE, FROM LEFT: Pathet Lao forces take power, 1975; bridging the gap to Thailand.

ETHNIC MINORITIES

Highland areas in both Laos and Cambodia are home to a rich assortment of ethnic-minority peoples.

Laos is ethnically very diverse. The majority Lao – **Lao Loum**, or "Lowland Lao" – constitute around half of the population, while the remainder is made up of various "hill peoples", as well as urban-dwelling Viets and Chinese.

In all, there are 49 officially recognised nationalities. The **Lao Theung** ("Approaching the top of the mountain Lao") traditionally live at moderate altitudes and include the **Khamu** and the **Htin**. They are largely descended from Mon-Khmer groups living in the region before the southward migration of the Lao from the 8th century. These ethnic groups no longer wear particularly distinctive costumes – the "Lao Theung" dancers you will see at cultural shows in Vientiane and Luang Prabang are generally lowland Lao wearing idealised costumes.

The most distinct minorities are found in the north. The **Lao Tai**, the Tai-speaking groups, including the **Tai Dam** (Black Tai), are identifiable by the unusual, multicoloured headdresses worn by the women. They form part of the **Lao Soung** ("Highland Lao") and include the **Hmong**, **Akha**, **Lanten** and **Mien** (**Yao**).

Cambodia is much more ethnically homogeneous than Laos, though the government's claim that ethnic **Khmer** make up around 95 percent of the population is certainly on the high side. Other urban lowland-dwellers such as the ethnic Chinese and Vietnamese aside, Cambodia's most distinctive and accessible minority are the lowland-dwelling **Cham Muslims**, whose extensive communities north and west of Phnom Penh are easily visited. Other **Khmer Loeu** or "Upland Khmer" minorities live much further off the beaten track, chiefly in the northeastern provinces of Rattanakiri and Mondolkiri (the **Tompuon**, **Pnong**, **Kreung**, **Brau** and **Jarai**), whose women tend to wear heavy jewellery, especially earrings, and to smoke pipes, as well as the truly remote **Pear** and **Saoch** of the Cardamom Mountains in southwestern Cambodia, whose costume is – well, very little clothing at all.

ABOVE: the Lowland Lao are the traditional rice farmers of the Mekong Valley. They first arrived in the region as part of a larger migration of Tai-speaking peoples from southern China in the 8th century and are now a majority in much of northeastern Thailand.

ABOVE: Hmong children; the Hmong have been persecuted in Laos due to their links with the US during the Vietnam War years.

LEFT: a village elder smokes a waterpipe in Longloa.

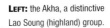

LEFT: the Akha, a distinctive Lao Soung (highland) group.

BELOW: a Lao Theung woman gathers firewood in Udomxai province. The various Lao Theung groups have been historically disparaged as backward by the lowland Lao majority.

MINORITY POLITICS

The Lao authorities are very keen both to promote good inter-ethnic relations and to portray the Lao PDR as a happy family of equal nationalities. In fact, power tends to lie with the Lowland Lao population, as it has done for centuries. To be fair to the Lao government, however, it must be said that the position of minority groups has probably never been better, both in terms of representation and standard of living. One continuing problem for the government have been the Hmong. The authorities wish to see the Hmong settled, with schools teaching their children Lao. Some Hmong, however, would prefer to stay on their distant mountain tops, remote from government authority.

ABOVE: Lanten woman and child.

Cambodian government policy towards minorities is less clear-cut and less legally codified. In theory, all nationalities living in Cambodia are equal, though the Khmer majority is clearly predominant. The Cham and the ethnic Chinese are generally well treated, as are – in a rather paternalistic manner – such indigenous groups as the Brau, Jarai, Pnong, Pear and other minorities. A major exception are the ethnic Vietnamese, thought to be the largest minority group in Cambodia, but generally mistrusted by most Khmers, whether urban elite or rural peasantry. Cambodia's ethnic Vietnamese, generally readily distinguishable by the all-but-ubiquitous *non la* conical hat worn by the women, continue to suffer widespread de facto discrimination.

RIGHT: a colourfully clad Mien woman in northwestern Laos. The Lao Soung highland peoples are relatively recent arrivals, having only migrated into the region (mostly from China) in the past 200–300 years.

CULTURE, ART AND ARCHITECTURE

Lao culture, like that of neighbouring
Cambodia, suffered under the Communists;
but traditional art forms have survived
and are re-emerging into daily life.

The traditional art and culture of Laos are closely related to those of neighbouring Thailand, and especially to those of Thailand's Lao-speaking northeastern provinces. The very close relationship between Lao and Thai culture is immediately apparent to anyone crossing the Mekong River between the two countries.

Yet the 15 years of rigid Communist domination and isolation behind the "bamboo curtain" between 1975 and 1990 have had a lasting impact which, given the slow-moving pace of Laos, is unlikely to disappear completely for some years to come. Some of the most interesting aspects of contemporary Lao cultural arts are directly related to the brief period of Communist ascendancy.

Literature

The most popular and enduring epic in Lao literature is the *Pha Lak Pha Lam*, the Lao version of the Hindu *Ramayana* (see page 229). This classic is thought to have come to Laos about 1,000 years ago, when the southern part of the country was dominated by the Hindu Khmer Empire. Also derived from Indian tradition are the *jataka*, the stories of the life cycle of the Buddha, called *saa-tok* in Lao. Traditionally, religious texts and other literature were written by hand on palm leaves.

Music and dance

Traditional Lao music is much less complex than that of Vietnam and Cambodia. When sung it is always memorised, and improvisation is popular.

The main Lao instrument is the flute-like *khene*, which is made of bamboo. There are two types of orchestra, the *seb gnai* which uses large

State-sponsored dances in both Laos and Cambodia generally feature smiling minorities dancing in unison with the dominant Lao or Khmer ethnic group. It's likely that few of the performers are really from minority ethnic groups.

drums and wind instruments to play religious music, and the *seb noi* which employs *khene*, flutes called *khuy*, a two-stringed instrument called the *so*, and the *nangnat*, which is a form of xylophone. To this is generally added the music of the *khong vong*, a semicircular instrument made from cane which carries 16 cymbals around its periphery.

Modern popular Lao music is often based on *khene* music. However, most Lao living in the Mekong Valley tend to tune in to Thai radio stations and watch Thai TV programmes, and in Thailand's Isaan provinces the influence of Thai popular music culture is predictably great.

Lamvong, the Lao equivalent of Thai *ram-wong* dancing, is extremely popular. At its best this is performed by graceful female dancers who use their arms and hands to relate stories from the *Ramayana* and other epics. In general, though, *lamvong* may be performed by anyone of either gender, spontaneously at parties and festivals.

Contemporary Lao socialist art

With Social Realism established as the sole legitimate art form in both the Soviet Union and Communist China, it followed naturally that the genre was introduced throughout Vietnam following the Communist victory in 1975. The Lao Communists, always strongly influenced by their Vietnamese "elder brothers", had long applied Social Realist standards in their northeastern base in the provinces of Hua Phan and Phongsali. Following the establishment of the Lao PDR in December 1975, the highly formalised style was extended to the rest of the country as a matter of course – as usual, brooking no rivalry.

In easy-going non-industrialised Buddhist Laos the results of this policy seemed particularly incongruous. Images of heroic peasants shooting down marauding US planes with AK47 assault rifles alternated with images of massively muscled Lao "shock workers" building steel mills for the socialist society. Other unlikely images included, for example, Lao hill tribes demonstrating their unshakeable solidarity with Cuban forces in Angola.

In Eastern Europe and the Soviet Union, following the collapse of Communist power, Social Realism was abandoned almost overnight as people celebrated their new-found cultural freedom. Some countries of the former Soviet Bloc even established museums to house especially lurid examples of totalitarian kitsch. In cautious, sleepy Laos, by contrast, change has been rather more gradual.

Today, militant images celebrating the anti-imperialist struggle have all but disappeared

– except from the walls of the People's Museum of the Lao Army, which is, in any case, generally closed to visitors. By contrast, hoardings celebrating the more pacific side of Communist aspirations – mass inoculation campaigns, the construction of heavy industry, and the "bumper harvest" – still survive. A revealing change around the start of the new millennium was the introduction of two previously uncelebrated elements of Lao society: the monk and the businessman. In downtown Vientiane these formerly shunned figures have joined those stalwarts of Lao Social Realism, the peasant, the soldier and the worker, in hoardings celebrating the achievements of the

ABOVE, FROM LEFT: the *khene*, a traditional flute made from bamboo; happy faces in the Social Realist style.

FOLK THEATRE

Maw lam khuu is a traditional music drama during which a man courts a woman by singing love songs. The songs involve question-and-answer "dialogues". By contrast, *maw lam dio* is a popular form of folk theatre sometimes used as a propaganda vehicle for government doctrines, although in the past – and, increasingly, again today – it was used to teach or promote religious concepts. It is always performed by a single person. *Maw lam luang* is a popular and more light-hearted form of Lao musical drama, while *maw lam chot* is a form of folk theatre where two performers of the same sex will either discuss or argue about a particular subject.

government. In the Lao PDR the writing is, literally, on the wall – Buddhism and private enterprise are both back in style.

Architecture

Laos is blessed with a surprisingly rich range of temple styles, with most traditional Lao architecture relating directly to Theravada Buddhism. A Lao wat complex will typically consist of several structures including a *sim*, or building where *phra* – that is, monks – are ordained; a *haw tai*, or library; *kuti*, or monks' dwelling places; *that*, or stupas; and generally a *haw kawng*, or drum tower.

The classic temple style of Vientiane and the lower Mekong differs from that of the north. The *sim* is generally narrower and higher than in the north of the country, with heavy columns and much steeper eaves, and is often distinguished by an elaborately carved wooden screen over the front entrance porch. Figures in such carvings may represent the Buddha or be mythical figures such as the *garuda* (a fierce half-bird, half-human creature from Hindu and Buddhist mythology) or the *kinnari* (a female creature with a human upper torso but the wings and legs of a bird). The main part of the *sim* is generally made of brick and stucco. Roofs

TEXTILES AND JEWELLERY

Weaving is an ancient and honoured craft throughout Laos, but especially among the lowland ethnic Lao. Both silk and cotton fabrics are woven, generally as a cottage craft beneath the stilt houses of villagers by the banks of the Mekong River and along its tributary valleys. Patterns comprise repeated geometric shapes, or feature animals and flowers. The most common item manufactured is the traditional *phaa nung*, or tube-skirt, which forms part of the Lao female national dress. Weaving is also practised among upland peoples and among the Mon-Khmer minorities of the southern uplands.

Gold, jewellery and silverware are all manufactured to a high standard in Laos and are for sale, notably at Vientiane's *talaat sao* (morning market). The highest standards of craftsmanship are attained by the Lao silversmiths, whose intricate belts complete the traditional costume of Lao women. Fine handbags and other decorative items are also manufactured, as well as equally fine rings, bracelets, necklaces and various vessels. Lao silverware is closely related to that of Chiang Mai in Thailand; this probably dates from the time when the two independent kingdoms of Lan Na and Lan Xang were neighbours, and their respective courts exchanged cultural gifts and skilled artisans.

are high-peaked and culminate in characteristic *jao faa* or upward-sweeping hooks. The architectural school in evidence here is Rattanakosin, from Bangkok in central Thailand, and quite different to the various northern schools – it's grander, certainly, but less intimate.

Luang Prabang temples differ quite markedly in style from those of Vientiane. The north of the country shares cultural and artistic links with the ancient northern Tai Kingdom of Lan Na, now the region around Chiang Mai, as well as the Thai Lu principalities of Sipsongpanna, now at the heart of China's Xishuangbanna Dai Autonomous Region. Part of the sophisticated

Khuang after the old Phuan capital – resembled the Luang Prabang temple style but with single rather than tiered roofs. Unfortunately the unrestrained bombing of the Plain of Jars during the Vietnam War resulted in the total destruction of all Xieng Khuang temples in their native Phuan region. Fortunately, however, a few still survive in Luang Prabang, adding to the richness of the architectural heritage of the northern capital – Wat Sop on Thanon Xieng Thong is the best such example.

The pre-eminent religious building in the country is That Luang in Vientiane – effectively the symbol of Lao nationhood (see page 106).

Tai Lu architectural heritage lies in Laos, notably at Muang Singh in the far northwest.

The temples of Luang Prabang are lower and broader than those of Vientiane, with sweeping, multi-tiered roofs and "eyebrow" pelmets, the *sim* being reached by a narrow flight of *naga* (river snake spirit) -lined stone steps. Wat Xieng Thong, with its spectacular roofs and liberal use of gold, is probably the best example of this style (see page 124).

There was once a third Lao temple style, that of the ancient Phuan Kingdom centred on the Plain of Jars. This style – known as Xieng

It is part of a distinctive style associated with Vientiane and the northeast, distinguished by tall, gilded *chedi (that)*, reliquaries for venerated Buddha relics. That Phanom, just across the Mekong in Thailand, is similarly impressive and is sacred to the Lao people of northeastern Thailand.

There are other religious traditions present in Vientiane and the central Mekong Valley – French colonial-period churches and chapels, and even a tiny mosque in central Vientiane – while the architectural treasures of southern Laos are in fact Cambodian, and are best represented by Wat Phu in Champasak (see page 168), which was founded in pre-Angkorean times, but also has later Angkor-era structures.

ABOVE, FROM LEFT: traditional Lao textiles; Wat Xieng Thong typifies the Luang Prabang temple style.

LAO FOOD

Lao cuisine is similar to that of Thailand and has grown in popularity, though the country dishes of raw meat may not appeal to all.

L ao cuisine, although distinctively and unmistakably "Lao", is by no means confined to Laos. Just across the Mekong River in northeastern Thailand (known as Isaan) there are perhaps six times as many ethnic Lao as there are in Laos itself, while the number of Lao-speaking inhabitants flocking to Bangkok means that there are now far more ethnic Lao in the Thai capital than in any other city, Vientiane included. As a consequence, Lao cuisine has gained in fame and popularity, being enjoyed throughout Thailand and even having a chain of fast-food restaurants developed to serve it called "Isaan Classic".

Lao cuisine may be seen as the cooking tradition and style of the entire Lao ethnic group and is based on the consumption of sticky rice as a staple. Other essential ingredients include *kha*, or galangal (a ginger-like rhizome with a peppery flavour), and *nam paa* (fish sauce). Lao cuisine has numerous regional variations, but that of Vientiane, the capital, is generally considered the most sophisticated.

Staple diet

In common with neighbouring Southeast Asian countries, the Lao diet is based on rice. This isn't the long-grain rice that Viets, Central Thai and most Westerners are used to eating, however, but *khao niaw*, or glutinous "sticky rice", deftly rolled into a neat, small ball and eaten with the hand. In Vientiane, as indeed in all other large towns, long-grain rice, or *khao jao*, is readily available, but *khao niaw* remains the basic staple of the Lao people and is the single most distinctive

feature of the cuisine. Along with it there is another vital ingredient, *paa daek*, a highly pungent fermented fish paste. On the back veranda of virtually every Lao peasant's house you will find an earthenware jar of *paa daek*.

Sticky rice is generally accompanied by a selection of dips, parboiled vegetables, salads, soups and various curried meat or fish dishes. The rice is usually served in a simple but attractive woven bamboo container called a *tip khao*. It's considered bad luck not to replace the lid on top of the *tip khao* at the end of the meal. When Lao go off to work in the fields or elsewhere you will often see hanging at their sides small woven baskets in which they carry supplies of sticky rice and perhaps small amounts

LEFT: keeping the vegetables fresh.
RIGHT: transplanting rice.

of fish or meat which will serve as their midday meal. While sticky rice is eaten by hand, long-grain rice is always eaten with a spoon and fork. Chopsticks are reserved for Chinese-style noodle dishes or for use in Chinese and Vietnamese restaurants.

Dishes are generally cooked with fresh ingredients that include vegetables, poultry (chicken, duck), pork, beef and water buffalo. Fish and prawns are readily available but, with Laos being a landlocked country, are nearly always of the freshwater variety. Mutton is not eaten except by the country's small South Asian Muslim population, nearly all of whom live in Vientiane.

> *Soup is considered a necessary part of any Lao meal. Visitors should look out for kaeng no may, fresh bamboo-shoot soup, and kaeng het bot, made with a variety of fresh mushrooms.*

and innards used in *laap* are finely chopped and spiced with onion, chillies and other herbs such as mint. Lao *laap* is generally cooked, unlike *laap dip* in northern Thailand, but can be raw. If you are concerned about this, ask for *laap suk* (cooked *laap*). Many rural Lao prefer

Upcountry, particularly in the north, jungle foods and game are more in evidence. Besides wild boar and deer these include such unlikely animals as pangolin, monitor lizard, civet, wild dog and field rat.

Popular dishes

Popular Lao dishes include *tam som* – the equivalent of Thai *som tam* – a spicy salad made of sliced green papaya mixed with chilli peppers, garlic, tomatoes, ground peanuts, crab, lime juice and fish sauce. This is often eaten with sticky rice and *ping kai* (grilled chicken). Another standby is *laap*, a spicy dish of minced meat, poultry or fish mixed with lime juice, garlic, chilli pepper, onion and mint. Meats

laap seua, or "tiger *laap*", which is raw chopped meat. Visitors will usually be served cooked *laap*, especially in restaurants.

Other dishes include *tom khaa kai* (chicken soup with galangal and coconut milk), *kaeng jeut* (mild soup with minced pork and bitter gourd), and *khao laat kaeng*, or curry, served on a bed of *khao jao* long-grain rice – all virtually identical to Thai dishes of the same name served on the other side of the Mekong. Then there is rice vermicelli, or *khao poun*. This is served cold with a variety of raw chopped vegetables, on top of which is placed coconut-milk sauce flavoured with meat and chillies. This is considered an auspicious dish at weddings and other celebrations, and is usually a favourite with foreigners. A popular regional dish is *or lam* from Luang Prabang. Lemon grass, dried buffalo meat and skin, chillies and aubergine along with *paa daek* are slowly stewed together, then eaten with crisp-fried pork skin and sweet basil.

Other popular cuisines available include Italian and French (especially in Vientiane and Luang Prabang), and South Asian (in Vientiane). Laos is an excellent place for breakfast, chiefly because of the French colonial legacy. French bread or *khao jii* is freshly baked each day and served with pâté, fried eggs and omelette. Good coffee, grown in the hills of southern Laos, is

Hokkienese, though some Yunnanese food is sold in Vientiane.

Country cuisine

Travelling upcountry away from the "big cities" is a rather different experience, and not necessarily to every visitor's liking food-wise. Upcountry Lao cuisine is very definitely an acquired taste. Raw meat is common, served with a salad of chopped jungle leaves and herbs, usually washed down with fiery home-made rice whisky. Many people live near to forests where hunting and gathering of food remain a

also available; you can start the day with coffee and croissants in the major urban centres, though upcountry the croissants may have to be replaced with *pah thawng ko*, or deep-fried Chinese dough sticks.

Also popular at breakfast, or as a snack at any time, is Vietnamese *pho* (noodle soup) and *yaw jeun*, deep-fried spring rolls. For a variant try *yaw dip* or fresh spring rolls. Vietnamese food is good and plentiful, especially in Vientiane and the larger cities. The same is true of Chinese food, which is generally Cantonese or

ABOVE, FROM LEFT: the galangal root and other seasonings; waffles stacked high at the Km 52 market, near Vientiane; a glutinous dessert.

LAO DINING STYLE

In traditional Lao society, eating is communal and an important social occasion. Diners, whether members of the same family or neighbours, will sit together at floor level on reed mats surrounding a raised rattan platform called a *kantoke*. Each *kantoke* will bear several communal dishes of laap, or curry, as well as small woven baskets of sticky rice – the essential wherewithal, without which Lao people often feel that they have not eaten. Traditionally, as in northern Thailand, sticky rice and curries are eaten by hand. Spoons are used for soup and for long-grain rice, but only noodles, a Chinese cultural and culinary import, are eaten with chopsticks.

way of life. When a deer is shot it is carried back to the village; there the whole animal is prepared for *laap*, to be eaten at once (partly because there are very few refrigerators in these areas), and so the family's friends and neighbours come to join in the feasting and drinking.

Haute cuisine

The haute cuisine once served at the royal court of Luang Prabang is worlds away from the "peasant food" described above, and it has long been absent from most Lao dining tables. As Laos increases in prosperity, and as

tourist demand rises, this distinguished form of cooking is making a return. Fortunately its secrets have been kept alive in a book published in Lao and English called *Traditional Recipes of Laos*. The author, Chaleunsilp Phia Sing, was born at Luang Prabang in 1898. According to Alan Davidson, a former British Ambassador to Laos, Phia Sing was both the master chef at the royal palace in Luang Prabang and the Royal Master of Ceremonies. Davidson describes him as a "sort of Lao Leonardo da Vinci... at a court of many and beautiful ceremonies, a physician, architect, choreographer, sculptor, painter and poet". His last years were devoted to compiling a detailed account of his experiences as a royal chef, listing 114 recipes in all. They have since been painstakingly translated and annotated.

Fruit and drinks

There is plenty of fruit in Laos, although – as with food in general – the range and quality is much better in the Mekong Valley than upcountry and in the hills. In the appropriate seasons, and especially towards the end of the hot season in May, markets overflow with a wide variety of exotic fruits including mango, papaya, coconut, rambutan, durian, custard apple, guava, mangosteen, starfruit, pineapple, watermelon, jackfruit and bananas.

It is always advisable to drink bottled water in Laos. Beware of ice of dubious origin, particularly upcountry or at street stalls. Soft drinks are available everywhere, as is canned and bottled beer. The real treat to look out for is the excellent and cheap local product, Beer Lao, which comes both bottled and draught. Imported wine – a reminder of Laos's colonial past – is available in major towns.

Caution should be exercised with fresh fruit juices and sugar-cane juice, but cartons and cans of fruit juice, milk and drinking yoghurt are available in supermarkets in Vientiane and Luang Prabang.

Good coffee and tea are generally available throughout the country. Chinese tea is often served free as an accompaniment to meals or with the thick strong Lao coffee.

LAO DINING ETIQUETTE

Lao meals typically consist of a soup dish, a grilled dish, a sauce, greens and a stew. The greens are usually fresh raw greens, herbs and other vegetables, though depending on the dish they accompany, they could also be steamed or, more typically, parboiled, and are therefore very healthy. Dishes are not eaten one after the other, but at the same time; the soup is sipped throughout the meal. When guests are present, the meal should always be a feast, with food made in quantities sufficient for twice the number of diners. For a host, not having an abundance of food for the guests would be considered excruciatingly embarrassing.

LEFT: watermelon makes a juicy snack.
RIGHT: spice market stalls.

LAOS: PLACES

A detailed guide to the entire country, with principal sites clearly cross-referenced by number to the maps.

aos is often described as a tiny, landlocked country. It is true that the population of around 6.5 million is not large, especially set against those of nearby China and Vietnam, but at 236,800 sq km (91,400 sq miles) Laos is almost exactly the same size as the United Kingdom, and has many spectacular rivers and mountain ranges for the visitor to explore.

The outstanding destination in this little-known Southeast Asian backwater must be the ancient royal capital of Luang Prabang, set amid beautiful scenery on a bend of the mighty Mekong River. Now a World Heritage Site, it is the most perfectly preserved traditional capital in Southeast Asia. It is difficult to exaggerate the tranquillity of the atmosphere and the exquisite distinction of the architecture in this elegant little town. Further down the Mekong there is the capital, Vientiane, the region's smallest and quietest, a hybrid, French-influenced city which combines the best of both Lao and French architectural traditions, as well as Sino-Vietnamese temples and shophouses.

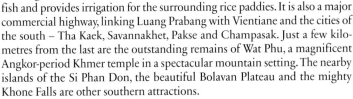

Winding through the country from north to south, the Mekong serves as a source of nutrition in the form of plentiful fish and provides irrigation for the surrounding rice paddies. It is also a major commercial highway, linking Luang Prabang with Vientiane and the cities of the south – Tha Kaek, Savannakhet, Pakse and Champasak. Just a few kilometres from the last are the outstanding remains of Wat Phu, a magnificent Angkor-period Khmer temple in a spectacular mountain setting. The nearby islands of the Si Phan Don, the beautiful Bolavan Plateau and the mighty Khone Falls are other southern attractions.

Laos has long been isolated from the outside world by poor communications and an inward-looking, rather secretive government. Things are changing, however. Three new highways are set to link southwestern China with Thailand and Vietnam, putting Laos at a crucial crossroads. A high- speed rail link between China and Thailand running across northern Laos is also being considered. Yet, for now at least, this Buddhist country remains a sleepy anachronism, offering a tantalising glimpse of a fast-disappearing world.

PRECEDING PAGES: the Plain of Jars; along the banks of the Mekong River, Vientiane. **LEFT:** working elephant in the hills north of Luang Prabang. **ABOVE, FROM LEFT:** Wat Phu, near Champasak; That Ing Hang Stupa, near Savannakhet.

Nanning Qinzhou

Tiandeng Longzhou Chongzuo Chengzhong Dinh Lap Ha Dong Cam Pha Ha Long Hai Phong

Lang Son Ban Re Vinh Bac Bo (Gulf of Tonkin)

Debao Jingxi Cao Bang That Khe Thai Nguyen Bac Giang Bac Ninh Thai Binh

Na Phac Giang Tien Kep Hat Duong Nam Dinh

Ha Giang Tuyen Quang Phu Tho Ha Noi (Hanoi) Phu Ly Ninh Binh Tam Diep Vinh

Lang Cay Yen Bai Viet Tri Hoa Binh Thanh Hoa Dien Chau

Poun Loung Ba Khe Phu Yen Lang Chanh Tuong Duong

Nam Bai Moc Chau Quan Hoa Lam Son Con Cuong

Kunming Lao Cai Son La Nam Son Ban Kaewkut Ky Son

Muang Et Xieng Khaw Sam Neua Nam Sam NBCA Sam Tai Hong Haet

Jinping Tuan Giao Dien Bien Phu Phu Leuy 2062 Nam Noen Ban Phiangdang Muang Kham Phou Samsum 2621

Nam Cum Muang Lay Phu Et NBCA Vieng Thong 6 Xai Phu Restricted

Wenshan Ban Huaypchat Pak Xeng Phu Loei NBCA Muang Sui Phonsavan Xieng Khuang Muang Khun (Xieng Khuang) Ban Naluang

Phongsali Ban Phonsana Vieng Kham 1 Muang Ngoi Xaysomboune

Mojiang Ban Xiangeo Muang Khua Muang Ngoi Louangphrabang Xieng Ngeun Muang Phu Khoon Ban Phatang Yang Vieng

Phu Den Din U Tai Ban Hat Sa Ban Buntai Muang La Pak Ou Viangchan 13 Kasi

Simao Yunjinghong Ban Bun Neua Phongsali Ban Sinxai Nam Bak Ndng Khiaw Louangphabang (Luang Prabang) Muang Ban Paksi Phiang

Na Toei Na Mo 4 Muang Xay (Udomxai) Ban Khokpho Xainyabuli Dol Lo 2070

Mengla 3 Nam Tha NBCA Udomxai Hong Sa Ban Naphun

Ban Say Muang Sing Luang Nam Tha Ban Donchai Pakbeng Xieng Hon Xainyabuli Nan

Meung Luang Nam Tha Khop Chiang Kham Tha Wang Pha

Dali Huay Xai Bokeo Chiang Khong Chiang Muan

BURMA (MYANMAR)

CHINA VIETNAM LAOS

0 50 miles 50 km 0

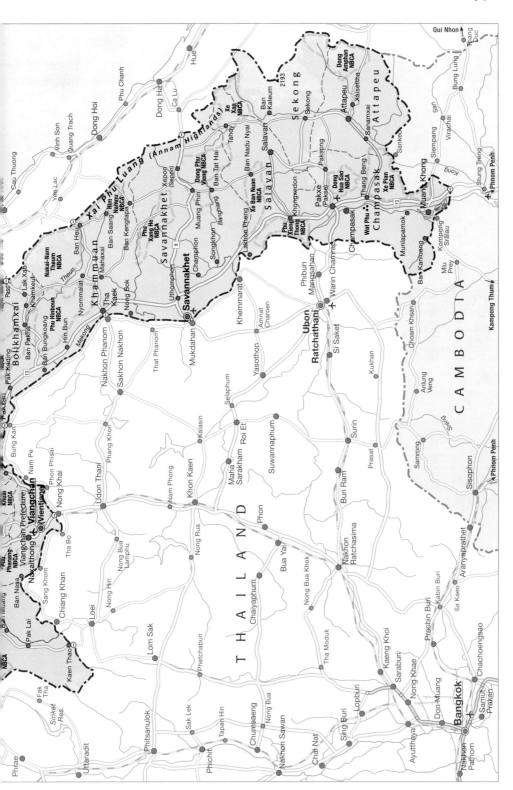

VIENTIANE

This small city on the Mekong is lethargic in comparison with other Asian capitals, and its air of decaying charm adds to this relaxed ambience.

"**V**ientiane is exceptional, but inconvenient," wrote Paul Theroux in 1975. "The brothels are cleaner than the hotels, marijuana is cheaper than pipe tobacco, and opium easier to find than a cold glass of beer." Though much has changed in Laos since Theroux's romp through Southeast Asia, after almost 40 years of Communist rule Vientiane still retains a bit of its old frontier-town spirit: a city where almost anything goes, but not quite everything works. For a capital city, it is remarkably quiet, laid-back and, above all, petite – the population of the entire metropolitan area is less than 750,000 (although it is still comfortably the largest city in Laos).

Sometimes spelled Vieng Chan, Viengchan or Viangchan (the name "Vientiane" is a French romanised version), the city has been controlled at various times by the Vietnamese, the Siamese, the Burmese and the Khmers – and, more recently, the French. A positive result of all this outside intervention is that the streets are a compelling mélange of Lao, Thai, Chinese, Vietnamese, French and even Russian influences in architecture, cuisine and culture. It is home to a little over 10 percent of the country's population, but a far larger share of its wealth.

As a result of rapid modernisation in recent years, today's Vientiane is a far cry from the time immediately after the Second Indochina War, when the author Norman Lewis found that light bulbs only worked occasionally – and never at night. Today not only is electricity reliable but there is also ready access to the internet and, in more expensive hotels, to BBC and CNN news networks.

Downtown Vientiane

Vientiane owed its early prosperity to its founding on the fertile alluvial

Main attractions
MEKONG RIVER
NAM PHU
HAW PHA KAEW
COLONIAL ARCHITECTURE
WAT SI MUANG
PATUXAI
THAT LUANG

PRECEDING PAGES: scenery at Vang Vieng. **LEFT:** a tuk-tuk hits the streets. **RIGHT:** French architecture in Vientiane.

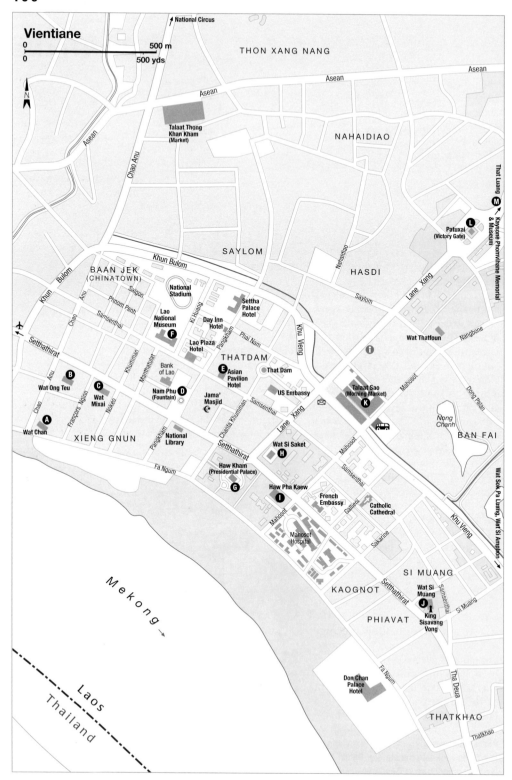

Vientiane

0 ———————— 500 m
0 ———————— 500 yds

N

→ National Circus

THON XANG NANG

Asean

Asean

Asean

Talaat Thong
Khan Kham
(Market)

NAHAIDIAO

Chao Anu

That Luang

Kaysone Phomvihane Memorial & Museum

M

L Patuxai
(Victory Gate)

Khun Bulom

SAYLOM

HASDI

Lane Xang

BAAN JEK
(CHINATOWN)

Bulom

Anu

Saigon

National
Stadium

Settha
Palace
Hotel

Phai Nam

Saylom

Wat Thatfoun

Nangbone

Khun

Chao

Phnom Penh

Samsenthai

Ki Huang

Lao
National
Museum **F**

Day Inn
Hotel

Pangkham

Khu Vieng

✈

Setthathirat

Khunman

Mantatulat

Lao Plaza
Hotel

THATDAM

ℹ

Dong Palan

Mahosot

Wat Ong Teu **B**

C

Bank
of Lao

E Asian
Pavilion
Hotel

That Dam

US Embassy

Talaat Sao
(Morning Market)

K

Nong
Chanh

BAN FAI

Anu

Chao

Françoys Ngin

Wat
Mixai

Nokeo

Nam Phu
(Fountain) **D**

A

Wat Chan

XIENG GNUN

Pangkham

National
Library

Chanta Khumman

Jama'
Masjid
☪

Samsenthai

Lane Xang

✉

🚌

Wat Sok Pa Luang, Wat Si Amphon

Fa Ngum

Setthathirat

Wat Si Saket **H**

Mahosot

Samsenthai

Khu Vieng

Haw Kham
(Presidential Palace)

G

Haw Pha Kaew

I

French
Embassy

Galliéni

Catholic
Cathedral

SI MUANG

Mahosot

Mahosot
Hospital

KAOGNOT

Sakarine

Setthathirat

Wat Si
Muang
J

King
Sisavang
Vong

St Muang

Samsenthai

M e k o n g →

PHIAVAT

Don Chan
Palace
Hotel

Fa Ngum

Tha Deua

Laos

Thailand

THATKHAO

Thatkhao

plains on the banks of the Mekong River – as good a place as any to begin your exploration of the city. Named after the founder of the Kingdom of Lan Xang, **Fa Ngum Road** is a pleasant riverfront boulevard that runs right along the Mekong at the southern edge of the town. Head for the path on top of the reinforced dyke – actually the site of the old town wall, built as a line of defence against invading armies and overflowing waters – for a pleasant stroll with a view across the river to Thailand. Many outdoor cafés and small restaurants line the riverfront, offering food, fruit shakes and beer.

A few small streets run through the neighbourhoods between Fa Ngum Road and **Setthathirat Road**, named after the king who consolidated the move of the capital of Lan Xang from Luang Prabang to Vientiane in 1560. **Chao Anu Road** is a reminder of Chao Anuvong, the ruler of the Kingdom of Vientiane from 1805 until 1828. In 1826 Anuvong launched an ill-fated attack on neighbouring Siam which prompted a fierce response, resulting in the partial destruction of

the city in 1828. The Siamese resettled large numbers of local residents in northeastern Thailand (even today there are around six times more ethnic Lao living in Thailand than in Laos), and captured Anuvong, bringing him to Bangkok, where he was executed.

This area of the town is dotted with temples that were restored after their abandonment following the 1828 Siamese invasion. The *sim* of **Wat Chan** **A** (daily; free/voluntary donation), located at the intersection of Chao Anu and Fa Ngum roads, houses a large bronze seated Buddha that survived the destruction, in addition to a series of beautifully carved wooden panels. **Wat Ong Teu** **B** (daily; free/voluntary donation), a short distance to the north on Setthathirat Road, is named after the large 16th-century "Heavy Buddha" found at the rear of the *sim*. Home to the Buddhist Institute, a school for monks who come from all over Laos to study here, Wat Ong Teu is one of the most important religious centres in the country. **Wat Mixai** **C** (daily; free/voluntary donation), east of Wat Ong

DRINK

When staying in Vientiane – which is, in any case, a very relaxed and laid-back city – the visitor can do no better, towards dusk, than take a stroll north along the banks of the Mekong to one of the city's celebrated "sunset bars". The views across the Mekong to Thailand are memorable.

BELOW: Wat Mixai and one of its attendant giants.

Jumbos or tuk-tuks are a good way to get about town, but agree the fare before you start your journey.

BELOW: Lamvong traditional dance enacts scenes from the Ramayana.

Teu on Setthathirat Road, is built in the Bangkok style with a surrounding veranda. Two guardian giants stand to attention outside the heavy gates.

Continuing east on Setthathirat Road you will see **Nam Phu** , the central fountain at the heart of Vientiane's downtown area, built in the late 1960s on the site of an old roofed market. Across the street from Nam Phu, and lined with a row of beautiful frangipani trees (*dok champa*, Laos's national flower), is the **National Library** (daily 8am–noon and 1–4pm, closed 29th of every month), built by the French as a police headquarters. Just to the east is the **Vientiane Jama' Masjid** (closed to non-Muslims during prayer times; free), the hub of the city for the small Tamil Muslim community (see page 21). The even smaller Cham Muslim community uses the Azhar Mosque in the north of the city. These are the only two mosques in the entire country.

Lao and Chinese commerce

North of the Nam Phu fountain is **Samsenthai Road**, the main route through Vientiane's prosperous commercial district. As recently as the mid-1990s this area was something of a ghost town: most of the shops were shut, as the government had yet to initiate economic reform or to open up Vientiane to foreign investment. Things have changed a good deal since then, and the imposing Thai-owned **Lao Plaza Hotel** is a monument to the city's recent economic growth. The nearby **Asian Pavilion Hotel** was popular with the press corps during the Second Indochina War, when it was known as the Hotel Constellation; journalists sat out the 1960 battle of Vientiane in the lobby while, outside, 500 people died during the fighting that followed a coup by the neutralist general Kong Le.

Just to the northeast, off Samsenthai Road, is **That Dam**, the Black Stupa, which dates to the early Lan Xang period. According to local legend, it is home to a seven-headed dragon that came to life and protected Vientiane residents during the 1828 Siamese invasion. Nearby is the sprawling **US Embassy** complex, once one of the largest in

City of Sandalwood

Accurate according to the Lao interpretation of the Indian *Ramayana*, the *Phra Lak Phra Lam*, Vientiane – which means "City of Sandalwood" in Lao – was founded by the legendary Prince Thattaradtha in the mists of time. Most historians, however, take a rather more prosaic view, considering the embryonic city on the Mekong to have developed as an early Khmer settlement clustered about a Hindu temple. The Phra That Luang stupa would eventually replace the temple as the focus of the city as Buddhism became the state religion. After 1354, when King Fa Ngum established the Kingdom of Lan Xang, Vientiane became the main administrative centre of Laos and most important city in the realm, a position traded with Luang Prabang over the centuries but re-established in the present day.

the world (now far outstripped by the US Embassy in Baghdad); the embassy remained open even at the height of the Indochina Wars and after a two-day closure, following the Communist takeover.

West on Samsenthai Road, adjacent to the **National Stadium**, is the **Lao National Museum** ❻ (daily 8am–noon and 1–4pm; charge). Built in 1925, this elegant structure was once the French governor's residence, and was used by the Lao government as an administrative building before being converted into a museum in 1985. The permanent exhibition provides a selective history of Laos's struggle for independence, leaving out major details like the heavy Vietnamese involvement in the "revolution". But it is filled with interesting artefacts from the war, particularly the weapons, clothing and supplies of key revolutionary figures.

Continuing west on Samsenthai you will enter **Baan Jek**, Vientiane's **Chinatown** district, home to the city's growing ethnic Chinese population and one of the capital's most vibrant areas. North of Chinatown, at the corner of Thong Khan Kham Road (Chao Anu) and Dong Miang Road (Asean), is **Thong Khan Kham Market**, the largest produce market in Vientiane, selling just about everything. It is also one of the best places in the town to buy traditional Lao baskets and pottery. Laos's **National Circus**, built by the Soviet Union at the height of the Cold War, is located nearby. The national circus troupe offers irregular performances, and occasional pop and classical music performances also take place here.

Royal and Buddhist headquarters

Heading east from Nam Phu fountain on Setthathirat Road, past a series of restored French colonial villas, you soon arrive at the **Presidential Palace** ❼ (Haw Kham), originally built as the French colonial governor's residence. The French took control of Laos in 1893 and administered the territory directly through the *résident supérieur* in Vientiane. After independence, King Sisavang Vong and, later, his son Savang Vatthana used the palace as a residence when visiting Vientiane from the royal seat in Luang Prabang. It is

The chest expander used by Kaysone Phomvihane, leader of the Lao Democratic Republic from 1975 to his death in 1992, is exhibited in the Lao National Museum.

BELOW: the Presidential Palace.

Wat Si Saket, probably the oldest original temple in Vientiane.

BELOW: prayers at the main city mosque.

now used for hosting foreign guests of the Lao government and for meetings of the presidential cabinet – the president himself does not live here. The building is not open to the public.

Across the street from the Presidential Palace is **Wat Si Saket** (daily 8am–noon and 1–4pm; charge), built in 1818 by Chao Anuvong. The temple was designed in the early Bangkok style, which possibly explains why it was left relatively untouched when the Siamese destroyed the city in 1828. Wat Si Saket is probably the oldest original temple in Vientiane – all the others were either constructed after this one or were rebuilt after the invasion.

The interior walls of the cloister surrounding the central *sim* of Wat Si Saket are filled with small niches containing more than 2,000 miniature silver and ceramic Buddha images, most of them made in Vientiane between the 16th and 19th centuries. On the western side of the cloister is a pile of broken and melted-down images, relics of the 1828 war and intended as a reminder of past Thai aggression. Behind the *sim* is a long wooden trough resembling a *naga*, or river-snake spirit, used during the Lao New Year celebrations to pour cleansing water over the temple's Buddha images. To the left of the *sim* is a raised Burmese-style structure that was once a library containing Buddhist scriptures, which are now housed in Bangkok. Today Wat Si Saket is home to the head of the Lao *sangha*, the order of Buddhist monks.

Home of the Emerald Buddha

Haw Pha Kaew ❶ (daily 8am–noon and 1–4pm; charge), the former royal temple of the Lao monarchy, is next door to the Presidential Palace and just across the street from Wat Si Saket. King Setthathirat built the original in 1565 to house the Emerald Buddha which he brought with him when he moved to Vientiane from Lan Na (the former Kingdom of Chiang Mai) following the death of his father, King Phothisarat. During the Siamese invasion of 1779, Vientiane was looted, and a host of sacred images was carried off to Bangkok along with members of the Lao royal family; today the Emerald Buddha sits in Bangkok's own Wat Phra Kaew.

The current structure is the result of a 1937–40 restoration under the supervision of Prince Souvanna Phouma, a Paris-educated engineer and, later, prime minister of an independent Laos. While Haw Pha Kaew is no longer used as a temple, bus-loads of Thai tourists often visit here. The museum contains a gilded throne, Khmer Buddhist stelae, and bronze frog drums of the royal family. The two main doors contain the only remnants of the original temple – sculptured wooden panels with images of the Buddha in nature, while the garden, a peaceful retreat from the dust and heat of Vientiane, contains a small jar from the Plain of Jars in Xieng Khuang province.

The surrounding area was once the administrative centre of French colonial rule, and in this neighbourhood are the spectacular **French Embassy** and residential complex, the Roman

Catholic **Cathedral**, built by the French in 1928 and still offering daily services, and a number of administrative and residential buildings. Considering it was the capital of a colony that ran at a financial loss – the French made up for Laos with profits from operations in Cambodia and Vietnam – Vientiane experienced a fair amount of construction under French rule.

The lucky temple

Wat Si Muang ❶ (daily; free), one of the most active temples in Vientiane, is located to the southeast of the French Embassy on Setthathirat Road. After the temple site was selected in 1563 by a group of King Setthathirat's advisers, a large hole was dug to receive the *lak muang*, or city pillar, which contains the city's protective deity. Legend has it that, on the day the temple was dedicated, the *lak muang* was suspended over the hole with ropes as the authorities waited for a volunteer to jump in. A pregnant woman (or a virgin, depending on whom you ask) finally did, and the ropes were severed, the woman's sacrifice bringing good luck

to the new capital. The *sim* was constructed around the *lak muang*, which is wrapped in sacred cloth. However this did not prevent Wat Si Muang from being destroyed by the Siamese in 1828. It was reconstructed in 1915.

The temple is filled with Buddha images, at least one of which dates from before the 1828 invasion; partially damaged, it sits on a pillow in front and to the left of the main altar. Worshippers believe that the image has the power to grant wishes and answer important questions about the future. The platters of fruit and flowers scattered throughout the *sim* are evidence of the popularity of this belief (offerings are brought to the temple when a wish is granted), as are the votive flowers, candles and other offerings sold at the small market across the street.

Just to the south is a small public park surrounding a statue of **King Sisavang Vong**, a somewhat unlikely prewar gift from the Soviet Union. In his outstretched hand the king holds a palm-leaf manuscript of the country's first legal code.

The museum at Haw Pha Kaew houses some excellent examples of the three Buddhist sculpture types common in Laos: "calling for rain", with hands straight at the sides; "offering protection", with palms stretched out in front; and "contemplating the Tree of Enlightenment", with hands crossed at the wrist in front.

BELOW: the gilded city pillar at Wat Si Muang contains Vientiane's protective deity.

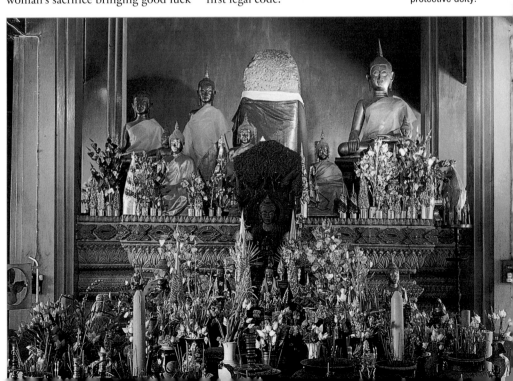

On the way up to the top of Patuxai you will pass an array of shops selling T-shirts and souvenirs.

BELOW: the view towards the Presidential Palace from Patuxai.

North to Patuxai

Arrowing northeast from the Presidential Palace is **Lane Xang Avenue** ("Avenue de France" under the French), which runs past the **Talaat Sao** Ⓚ (Morning Market). The market, despite its name, is open daily from 6am to 6pm and is a maze of individually owned stalls selling everything from antique textiles and carvings to household appliances. You will probably see stalls selling tickets for the immensely popular National Lottery, which is a central preoccupation of Vientiane residents, many of whom will consult monks or nuns before choosing a lucky number.

Lane Xang Avenue ends at a traffic circle resembling the Etoile in Paris, at the centre of which stands **Patuxai** Ⓛ, Vientiane's own Arc de Triomphe. Patuxai (Victory Gate) was completed in 1969 in memory of the Lao killed in wars before the Communist revolution. It is also known as the "vertical runway", as the project was finished with cement paid for by the Americans and intended to be used for the construction of a new airport in Vientiane. Despite the French inspiration, uniquely Lao elements are evident: Buddhist imagery is present in the Lao-style mouldings, and the frescoes under the arches represent scenes from the *Ramayana*. Climb the winding staircase to the top of the monument for a panoramic view of the low-rise city (Mon–Fri 8am–4.30pm, Sat–Sun until 5pm; charge).

That Luang – symbol of Laos

Around 2km (1.2 miles) northeast of Patuxai is the shining, 45-metre (146ft) **That Luang** Ⓜ (daily 8am–noon and 1–4pm; charge), the Great Sacred Stupa. It is a striking sight, and of great spiritual significance for the Lao people, considered the symbol of Lao independence and sovereignty ever since it was built in the mid-16th century. It is a strange and exotic structure, combining the features of a Buddhist temple with the mundane requirements of a fortress. According to legend, That Luang was first established in the 4th century BC, when five Lao monks who had been studying in India returned

home bearing the breastbone of the Buddha, and a stupa was duly built over the sacred relic. It is commonly believed that this, the earliest stupa at That Luang, is enclosed within the present structure.

The second historic establishment of That Luang was undertaken by King Setthathirat the Great, who consolidated the move of the Lao capital from Luang Prabang to Vientiane begun by his father, King Phothisarat. Construction of the great stupa began in 1566, on the site of the former Khmer temple, and in subsequent years four smaller temples were built at the cardinal points around the central *that*.

Today the great edifice still retains a very fortress-like appearance. It is surrounded by a high-walled cloister, which is pierced by tiny windows, and access is by way of finely gilded red-lacquer doors which add to the impression of a medieval keep. Close up, however, the sacred character of the structure is unmistakable because of the abundant religious imagery. *Naga* serpents – those characteristic insignia of Theravada Buddhism – compete for space with gilded figurines of the Buddha and stylised lotus flowers. The cloister's tiny windows were added by Chao Anuvong as a defence against attack, but they were of little use during the Siamese, Burmese and Chinese invasions of the 18th and 19th centuries, which left That Luang in ruins. Serious restoration work didn't begin until the French initiated a project in the 1930s.

That Luang originally faced east, with its back to Vientiane (Buddhism divides the world between East, the sphere of illumination, and West, the sphere of inauspiciousness), but the restoration authorities failed to respect this orientation, so the temple now faces west. The surface of the stupa was regilded in 1995, the 20th anniversary of the founding of the Lao People's Democratic Republic.

Of the four temples that King Setthathirat originally had built to surround That Luang, only two remain: **Wat That Luang Neua** to the north and **Wat That Luang Tai** to the south; both are open daily (free).

Northern suburbs

Further north from That Luang is the **National Assembly** building, and beyond, on Phon Kheng Road, the **Unknown Soldiers Memorial**. This white stupa-like monument is dedicated to Pathet Lao soldiers who died during the Second Indochina War.

Phon Kheng Road takes you northeast from Patuxai to the **Kaysone Phomvihane Memorial and Museum** (Tue–Sun 8am–noon and 1–4.30pm; charge), at Km 6. The exhibits detail Kaysone's childhood in Savannakhet province, his role in the Communist revolution, and his leadership of Lao PDR from 1975 until his death in 1992. Certainly the most interesting portion of the museum is the tour of Kaysone's private living quarters, a small house among a series of identical structures inside the compound, reminiscent of post-war suburban America (the museum is on the site of the former USAID/CIA compound).

Ancient Buddha statue in Wat Si Saket, whose cloister wall niches reveal a multitude of miniature Buddhas.

BELOW: That Luang, Vientiane's golden icon.

FRANCE ON THE MIDDLE MEKONG

The Gallic lifestyle influenced the Lao urban elite throughout the French colonial period, and has left its mark to this day.

One of the most pleasant surprises awaiting the visitor to Vientiane is the French cultural influence surviving in the city. It is a pleasure to enjoy a breakfast of croissants and *café au lait*. Lunch may well comprise freshly baked baguettes and pâté accompanied by a carafe of wine. In the evening, excellent French cuisine is available at upmarket restaurants, following years of socialist austerity.

This agreeable ambience aside, Vientiane's most notable memorial to the French influence must be its architecture. There are numerous small residences, and not a few mansions, built in the style of the former colonial power. Many of these may be found in the older part of the town, along the riverside appropriately designated Quai Fa Ngum. Here, as by the shaded boulevards in the vicinity of That Dam and along Lane Xang Avenue, the "Champs Élysées" of Vientiane, may be found fine examples of colonial French architecture, complete with shutters and red-tiled roofs, which would not be out of place in a French provincial city like Dijon or Tours. A decade or so ago, many of these former private residences were in stages of advanced decay, and some were clearly beyond saving. In recent years, however, many have been painstakingly restored – clearly, as the authorities came to realise the potential value to tourism of this unique architectural legacy, not to mention the inherent charm of the Lao capital, preservation rather than demolition became the order of the day.

ABOVE: baguettes on sale in Vientiane – and across most of the country – are one of the most visible reminders of the French influence. Stock usually runs out by lunchtime.

BELOW: the restored facade of the National Library in Vientiane, originally built in the colonial era as a police station.

LEFT: French still appears alongside Lao on local letterboxes.

ABOVE: *le petit déjeuner* – watch the world go by and start the day the French way with a (Lao) coffee and croissant at a Vientiane café.

THE FACE OF FRANCE IN LAOS

Born in France in 1847, Auguste Pavie was a French explorer and diplomat who almost single-handedly brought Laos under French control. Pavie had a gift for languages and learned to speak Vietnamese, Khmer, Thai and Lao. In 1886, he became the first French vice-consul in Luang Prabang, the Lao capital. During the next five years he travelled throughout northern Laos and gained the friendship of local rulers for France, frustrating Bangkok's attempts to bring the region fully under Siamese control. Arguing that the Lao states had been vassals of Vietnam and that France had succeeded to Vietnam's rights in Laos, Pavie justified regional military movements, provoking a crisis that resulted in Laos becoming a French protectorate in 1893.

LEFT: one of the less attractive aspects of French colonisation: Lao *corvée* (unpaid) workers on road construction duties.

LEFT: a familiar name for a tailor shop in Vientiane.

RIGHT: the 19th-century explorer Auguste Pavie opened up the interior of IndoChina to the French.

VIENTIANE ENVIRONS

Beautiful river and lake scenery and a national park are some of the attractions within easy reach of the capital. Further north are the stunning landscapes and adventure sports of Vang Vieng.

ost visitors to Laos end up staying in **Vientiane** (**Viangchan**) ❶ for only a few days, and relatively few visitors take time to explore the area around the city. This is a pity, as there is a great deal to see in the districts surrounding the capital; you don't have to go far from the capital to find beautiful natural areas and simple village life. Most of the attractions surrounding Vientiane lie along a loop just to its north; we will follow Route 13 northwards as far as Ang Nam Ngum, and then return to Vientiane in a southerly direction via Route 10. The final section of this chapter highlights the attractions of Vang Vieng on Route 13 north towards Luang Prabang. Vang Vieng is known for its beautiful scenery, "tubing" on the Nam Song River, and increasingly wild party life.

North to Ang Nam Ngum

About 25km (16 miles) north of Vientiane, just off the main road to Luang Prabang (Route 13), lies the **Nam Tok Tat Son** ❷ waterfall. Created by the construction of a dam in the 1970s, the "waterfall" is really a series of modest rapids. A recreational area with restaurants, picnic facilities and caged animals surrounds the falls. Walk away from the rest area for about

200 metres/yds and you'll find a peaceful rock upon which sits a simple altar with primitive Buddhist statues; the shaded spot overlooks the surrounding forest.

More rewarding is the area near an incomplete temple, **Wat Lansoun** (free), 2km (1.2 miles) beyond Nam Tok Tat Son at the end of a dirt road. Too isolated to have resident monks, the temple sits upon a hill among ageing Buddha images and caves. Some of the imposing rock formations are marked by Buddhist stele inscriptions.

Main attractions

NAM TOK TAT SON WATERFALL
ANG NAM NGUM LAKE
PHU KHAO KHUAI
VANG VIENG

LEFT: bridge across the Nam Song at Vang Vieng. **RIGHT:** watering crops on the banks of the Mekong.

An Indochinese tiger surveys his domain from the water.

The panoramic view of the valley below is one of the most breathtaking in central Laos.

Continuing along Route 13 will bring you to the **Talaat Lak Haa-Sip Sawng** (Km 52 Market) in the village of Ban Lak Haa-Sip Sawng, a large daily market offering wild foods (including some rare and endangered species, much to the chagrin of environmental organisations working in Vientiane) and minority handicrafts, frequented by Hmong and other local ethnic minorities.

Further north, near the town of Phonsavang, is **Vang Sang ❸** (free), or "Elephant Palace", a supposedly Mon sanctuary featuring 10 sculptures of the Buddha on cliffs. The site dates as far back as the 11th century, and may have been a stopover for Buddhist worshippers heading north from Mon-Khmer city-states in today's southern Laos. The name refers to an elephant graveyard that was once found nearby. Another small cluster of images can be found about 20km (13 miles) away from the main site.

BELOW: Logging trucks.

Ang Nam Ngum ❹, about 90km (55 miles) from Vientiane, is a large reservoir created in 1972 when the Nam Ngum was dammed and the entire area flooded. The dam remains a symbol of development, generating enough electricity both for Vientiane and for export to Thailand. When the lake was created, 250 sq km (100 sq miles) of forest were submerged, although some areas of higher land remain visible as hundreds of small islands. Prostitutes, drug addicts and petty criminals were sent to the islands following the Communist takeover in 1975, and two – one for women and the other for men – are still used as prisons to this day.

To reach the reservoir, turn off Route 13 at the town of Phon Hong and head east to **Thalat**, where the central market – as at the Km 52 Market mentioned above – specialises in deer, rats and assorted insects for local consumption.

An easily arranged boat cruise from the main pier in **Na Keun**, beyond Thalat, will allow you to explore the lake and to view the beautiful scenery.

Waterfront restaurants offer tasty lunches featuring fresh fish from the lake: grilled fish, fish *laap*, fish soup – all the dishes are generally excellent.

Most visitors come to Ang Nam Ngum on day trips, but there are a few guesthouses in the villages at the northern end, such as in Ban Thahua, which is on the main Route 13 north. There is also a resort – the **Dansavanh Nam Ngum Resort** (tel: 21-223 782/3/4; www.dansavanh.com) – on the southern shore of the lake for those with a larger budget. Built by Malaysian developers, this US$200 million casino and lakeside resort on Ang Nam Ngum offers hang-gliding, powerboat cruises, an "island floating shopping network", a golf course, a disco and, unusually, an insect museum. The Gaming Centre offers gamblers roulette, baccarat and blackjack as well as the usual slot machines. Most customers are from Thailand, China, Vietnam, Taiwan and Malaysia; Lao citizens are forbidden by law to gamble and may only enter the casino to work there. The resort can be reached by boat in about 20 minutes from the lakeside at Na Keun, but is more usually accessed by a small side road north of Highway 10 just beyond Ban Keun and Thulakhom Zoo.

Around Ang Nam Ngum Lake

Heading back southwards towards Vientiane from the reservoir on Route 10, you will soon come to **Ban Keun ❺**, a bustling town on the banks of the Nam Ngum, which means Silver Water. The remaining French colonial buildings and riverfront scenery are worth a short stroll, as is a visit to the local market place, which is quite different to the larger markets of Vientiane. Here you can see rural Laos at its most picturesque, though be warned that you may well see local "bush meat" for sale – wild animals such as deer, squirrel and pangolin are brought here to be sold as food.

Just beyond Ban Keun, about 60km (40 miles) from Vientiane, lies the **Thulakhom Inter Zoo** (daily 8am–-4.30pm; charge), a complex of animals kept in surprisingly humane conditions. The zoo, also known as

BELOW: sunset on the Nam Song River, Vang Vieng.

Vang Vieng–Luang Prabang

It's a long and rather tortuous 168km (105-mile) journey between Vang Vieng and Luang Prabang. Closed for many years due to the insurgency from the Hmong rebels, the road is extremely winding, and if you suffer from car sickness it's best to stock up on motion-sickness pills. This area is the very heart of mountain Laos, with switchback roads leading over and past spectacular karst outcrops. There are many minority villages in the area, but few are as yet developed in any way, and there are few or no facilities for overnight stays. The small town of **Kasi**, 55km (35 miles) north of Vang Vieng, is certainly the best place to break for a lunch stop en route to Luang Prabang, but accommodation is basic at best, and it's best to press on to your destination.

Go for a guided jungle trek on Phu Khao Khuai for a chance to spot wildlife such as the rare clouded leopard.

BELOW: statue at Xieng Khuan.

the Vientiane Zoological Gardens, has tigers, sun bears, a white elephant, emus and camels. A botanical garden and an aquarium are additional attractions. The zoo is a popular weekend destination for families from Vientiane – it's best to visit during the week if you want to avoid the crowds. Further along Route 10 is the beautiful **Nong Nok** (bird lake) at Ban Sivilay village. A seasonally flooded wetland, it is home to a great variety of birds – including the Chinese pond heron, black crowned night heron, common kingfisher, cattle egret and little egret. In the latter stages of the dry season more than 1,200 whistling teal roost in the wetland. The lake is used by the villagers for commercial fish-breeding; fish are released annually during the wet season, and then from February to April they are caught and sold to nearby communities and in Vientiane. Nong Nok is a good example of a community-managed ecosystem, and the villagers work to maintain an ecological balance: regular guards ensure that birds are not killed and fish are not poached. Income from fish is evenly distributed in the village, which now has more than 225 shareholding householders.

At the moment there are very limited tourist facilities at Nong Nok, but the Lao government has plans, dependent on outside funding, to improve transportation to the lake and to develop the area as an ecotourism site. The plans involve building birdwatching hides, a guard facility and a parking area. It's already possible to camp at a government-approved site by the lake.

Mountain reserve

Further south along Route 10 is the turning for the conservation area of **Phu Khao Khuai** (Water Buffalo Mountain) ❻, a pine-forested plateau surrounded by 2,000-metre (6,500ft) peaks. One of the country's National Biodiversity Conservation Areas (NBCA), the 2,000-sq-km (770-sq-mile) Phu Khao Khuai is rich in wildlife, with elephants, black bears, tigers and clouded leopards. Seventeen NBCAs, totalling 24,600 sq km (9,500 sq miles), or about 10 percent of the country, were designated by the Lao government in 1993. While this marked a positive step forward for environmental protection in Laos, the familiar story of corruption, lax enforcement and inadequate planning and management have combined to plague the NBCA initiative.

Inside the reserve there is a pleasant picnic area by the Nam Ngum from which you can take short nature walks, while a telecommunications centre on the top of the mountain provides a good view of Vientiane and the surrounding districts. In the years following the Communist victory in 1975, foreigners were not allowed into this area as it contained a military base – the old airstrip is still visible today. Phu Khao Khuai offers a cool retreat from the heat of Vientiane during the hot season; at other times of the year it can be cold and misty, so it is a good idea to bring extra clothing with you for the evenings. Visitor facilities are lacking, so it is also advisable to bring food with you.

Back on Route 10, you will cross a small toll bridge at the village of **Tha Ngon**. Just under the bridge are a number of floating restaurants where you can sit and watch the Nam Ngum flow past as you eat some of the freshest fish and stickiest rice in the area.

One of the best-kept secrets in the vicinity of Vientiane is the **Houei Nyang** forest reserve, just off Route 10 about 20km (12 miles) from the centre of the city. The field centre was built with funding from the Swedish government, and offers an English-language guide to the Mai Te Kha nature trail. The nature walk lasts about two hours, leading you past numbered points of interest described in the trail guide. You won't find any large animals in Houei Nyang, but smaller species such as mouse deer, porcupines and wild cats thrive here (although they are difficult to see). A variety of birds and beautiful butterflies can easily be seen, however (and, in the case of the former, heard). The reserve is probably of greatest interest to plant-lovers – the forest has experienced considerable disturbance from agriculture and other human involvement over the years, and thus provides opportunities for a good look at the stages in the development of an old-growth forest.

East of Vientiane

Located on the Nam Ngum River about 50km (30 miles) northeast of Vientiane, **Ban Pako** (tel: 030-988 4611; www.banpako.com) is an eco-friendly resort built using local materials and techniques. Owned and run by an Austro-German couple, the resort includes a longhouse with three double rooms with private bathrooms; a seven-bed dormitory with shared bathroom; separate bungalows, each with a two-bedded room and bathroom; and a veranda for sleeping under the stars (mosquito nets are available). Ban Pako also offers a bar and restaurant serving relatively expensive but tasty and good-quality Lao food, although there are barbecues at weekends. It has long been popular with the Vientiane expat community.

Along the Mekong

If you are only in Vientiane for a short while, it is still possible to make afternoon or day trips just outside the city to other attractions. South of the city centre, Tha Deua Road runs alongside the Mekong and leads to

BELOW: Containers for the ubiquitous Lao sticky rice are fashioned from bamboo.

TIP

Vang Vieng may be the most "happening" place in Laos, but it is also officially the most dangerous, at least for visitors. In 2011 no fewer than 27 travellers died here from various forms of excess or dangerous revelry, while many more were injured. It's also the place you are most likely to be robbed while in sleepy Laos, usually by some other traveller.

BELOW: more outsize creations at Xieng Khuan.

the **National Ethnic Cultural Park** (daily 8am–6pm; charge), at Km 18 (about 2km/1.2 miles before the Friendship Bridge). Built in 1994, the park features mock houses in the style of the Lao Loum, Lao Theung and Lao Soung ethnic groups. The concrete structures are not at all authentic, but the place gives you some idea of the way in which the current government is attempting to combine the diverse ethnic groups of Laos into a unified Lao people. The park also includes a small zoo (with a few very depressed specimens) and life-size replicas of dinosaurs. The riverside restaurants along the Mekong are the main attraction for Vientiane families, who often spend a day here at weekends.

Beyond the National Ethnic Cultural Park, still on Tha Deua Road, is the **Thai–Lao Friendship Bridge** ❼, completed in 1994 at a cost of about US$30 million; it was funded by the Australian government. Some 1,240 metres (0.7 miles) long, it connects Nong Khai in Thailand to Vientiane, and is symbolic of the opening of Laos to outside (and

especially Thai) influences. A railway line has recently been built across the bridge but has not yet been extended to nearby Vientiane. Since the terrain between the current rail terminal at Thanaleng Railway Station, Dongphosy Village, just 20km (12.5 miles) east of Vientiane, is completely flat and without natural obstructions of any kind, this is something of an anomaly, and it can only be a matter of time – or perhaps international aid – before the line is extended all the way to the Lao capital.

Prior to 1994 there were no bridges across the Mekong between Laos and Thailand; a second bridge was built near Savannakhet in 2006, and a third opened between Thakek and Nakhon Phanom some 100km (60 miles) further north on 11 November 2011. In a sign of the times, a fourth Thai–Lao Friendship Bridge between Chiang Khong in Thailand's northernmost Chiang Rai Province and Ban Houaxay in Laos is currently under construction. This will provide a direct road link across Laos between Thailand and China via Boten – as well as, if current

plans go ahead, a high-speed rail link between Kunming in China and the Thai capital Bangkok. In this case isolated, landlocked Laos will become a key linchpin in the Southeast Asian road and rail network.

Still further along Tha Deua Road, 3km (2 miles) east of the bridge, is the odd yet interesting **Xieng Khuan** ❽, or Buddha Park (daily 8am–6pm; charge), which features a Tim Burtonesque collection of Buddhist and Hindu sculptures built in 1958. The park was constructed by Bunleua Sulitat, a priest-shaman who merged Hindu and Buddhist traditions to develop quite a following in Laos and northeastern Thailand; he left Vientiane in 1975 and moved across the river to Nong Khai, where he built a second Buddha Park. The oversized concrete statues – images of Shiva, Vishnu, Buddha and even a few secular Lao figures – give the place an air of fantasy which is emphasised by the massive pumpkin-shaped structure that dominates the park. This has three levels, representing hell, earth and heaven, and there is a good view from the very top, which is reached by a spiral staircase. Xieng Khuan is now a popular public park, complete with riverfront food stalls, and the whole place makes an enjoyable half-day out of town, though the atmosphere is more kitsch than religious to most visitors.

Vang Vieng

Located close to the midway point between Vientiane (156km/116 miles south) and Luang Prabang (168km/ 105 miles north), the tiny settlement of **Vang Vieng** ❾ is a convenient place to break the journey between these two towns in either direction. Set by the banks of the Nam Song, amidst a startlingly beautiful natural terrain of limestone karsts, Vang Vieng was once a little backpacker haven, a relatively inexpensive, relaxed destination, with all the usual budget-traveller restaurants and bars – as well as a burgeoning and rather dangerous drug scene. The Lao authorities are reportedly increasingly on the alert for narcotics violations – even a small amount of hashish or marijuana – and penalties are severe.

Today Vang Vieng has developed into Laos's most popular, most accessible and most reasonably priced adventure destination, with tubing and kayaking on the river, caving in the surrounding hills, and climbing on the precipitous limestone karst faces. Other popular activities include mountain biking, trekking, rafting and freshwater swimming in the Nam Song River. For those not interested in caving or tubing, there are cultural attractions as well. There are three small temples in the area which merit visiting, as well as two Hmong villages, the resettled inhabitants of which are a colourful addition to Vang Vieng market – though whether they have settled comfortably into their new lowland environment, with its strange foreign visitors and systematic government surveillance, remains a moot point.

The many caves around Vang Vieng are often spectacular, vast and filled

BELOW: The forests and grasslands of Laos are home to dozens of species of butterfly, with new species being discovered each year.

TIP

If you have had enough of backpacker Vang Vieng and wish to experience something a little more authentic, head out west on a hire bike or motorbike to Ban Na Som and several other tiny villages in the heart of the karst country. It's just a half-day's excursion from Vang Vieng, and you can be back in town for *laap*, pizza or burritos by dusk.

BELOW: hanging out near Vang Vieng.

with wildlife of all kinds, from swiftlets and bats to centipedes and blind fish. At the same time they remain largely unexplored, often slippery, dank, dark – and dangerous. It's better to explore these caverns in a group, preferably with a guide, and carrying a flashlight.

Because of its popularity, Vang Vieng has attracted an increasing number of backpacker-oriented restaurants, serving all the usual budget-travel dishes from banana pancakes and fruit smoothies to Mexican chilli con carne – in addition to hallucinogenic "magic mushrooms" and marijuana-laced pizza. It's quite a scene, and one that the Lao authorities are viewing with increasing displeasure.

In fact in recent years Vang Vieng has acquired a growing reputation for drugs, drunkenness, sexually permissive behaviour, improper dress and just plain bad manners. It's also recognised by foreign embassies as increasingly dangerous, with a disturbing number of young visitors dying of drug and alcohol excess, drowning and diving into shallow water only to hit the rocks. No doubt it's a great place to hang out, but visitors should bear in mind that Laos is a conservative, traditional place, and quite apart from the damage that unrestrained drinking, drug-taking and even unrestrained diving can do to the unwary, Lao perceptions of foreigners – in fact mainly if not exclusively Westerners – are being seriously damaged by such displays of intoxication and excess. One of the great charms of Laos, if not its greatest, is the accommodating manner and polite tolerance of its gentle populace; if this is abused, much that is unique about this charming backwater will be lost.

About 40km (25 miles) north of Kasi on the road between Vang Vieng and Luang Prabang, Muang Phu Khoun is a rather melancholy reminder of the former French presence in colonial Laos. Today there is little to see beyond a few shophouses and a small hotel – but in times past this was an isolated but important French garrison on the key route between the administrative and royal capitals.

Cycling in Laos

Laos has plenty to draw the cyclist, from world-famous heritage sites to its caves and jungles. Its quiet roads and friendly welcome make Laos an exciting destination for cycle touring.

Cyclists in Laos have many options open to them; there are the hills and mountains of north Laos or the laid-back charms of the flat south. The main transport spine, Route 13, runs north to south and covers the full length of the country.

A major draw for cyclists to Laos is the amount of accommodation that has become available in recent years. Every small town now has a guesthouse, making it easier for cyclists to negotiate the roads of Laos without heavy camping equipment. Where accommodation is not available, cyclists have found local homestays and temples are very happy to put up a weary traveller, thus enhancing the cultural experience.

Cyclists will find the north challenging for its topology, while the south will be more challenging for the distance covered between towns (and accommodation), and the country in general will be challenging on account of its heat. Laos is a popular place to cycle because of its variety and its relative freedom.

When cyclists come to Laos, there are two major starting points, and a whole host of minor ones. Most begin their journeys in Vientiane or Luang Prabang. Vientiane is situated close to Thailand and its transport network, allowing easy access to Laos and its mysterious tourist delights. Many cyclists fly into Bangkok and catch the train up to Nong Khai and enter Laos over the Friendship Bridge. There is a simple 20km (12.5-mile) cycle into the heart of Vientiane and the gateway to the north and south of Laos. For Luang Prabang, cyclists can either choose to fly in or take the boat down the Mekong from the Chiang Khong/Huay Xai border point.

Popular routes

To cycle all the roads and see all the sights of Laos would potentially take the cycle tourist many months; however, most cyclists choose to see as much as possible in a few weeks or a month. There are a number of main routes to choose from that can be taken to see the major highlights on offer. Probably the most popular route and one of the shorter journeys in Laos is the road between Luang Prabang and Vientiane. This is a short trip of between 4 and 5 days; however, it does offer some of the best combinations of delights that Laos has to offer the cyclist. From the UN-sponsored religious chic of Luang Prabang's old town and the hills of Northern Laos, to the flat plains and quiet charms of Vientiane and its surroundings, this route dominates as a classic. This route is principally responsible for the explosion in the numbers of cyclists over the last 10 years.

Other popular routes in the country include the east-to-west route through Northern Laos. The starting point is usually Vietnam and there is a choice of roads through some of the most glorious hills that Southeast Asia has to offer. Additionally, this route offers the wonder of Phonsavan and the Plain of Jars, the caves at Vieng Xai and the trekking delights of the far north in Pongsali.

The final main route is the ride through the south. Leaving from Vientiane, cyclists head down Route 13 alongside the Mekong, taking in the flat plains of Southern Laos and the pleasures of the Bolaven Plateau, eventually ending up at the Laos/Cambodia border.

RIGHT: a tour group of mountain bikers cycle along a dirt road beside the Mekong River.

LUANG PRABANG

The temples and culture of Luang Prabang, capital of Laos and seat of the monarchy until the 16th century, have been so well preserved that the city is now a World Heritage Site.

Main attractions
ROYAL PALACE MUSEUM
MOUNT PHU SI
WAT XIENG THONG
MEKONG WATERSIDE RESTAURANTS
  AND BARS
WAT PAA PHON PHAO
PAK OU CAVES

With its splendid natural setting amid forested hills at the confluence of the Mekong and Nam Khan rivers, and a long, illustrious history as a royal capital, **Luang Prabang ❶** (Louangphabang) is one of the most intriguing, magical and romantic cities in Asia. Added to Unesco's World Heritage List in 1995, the city is filled with fine old temples, and its quiet streets are lined with handsome colonial buildings.

For centuries before the city was founded, the area around played host to various Thai–Lao principalities in the valleys of the Mekong, Khan, Ou and Xuang rivers. In 1353 King Fa Ngum consolidated the first Lao Kingdom, Lan Xang (see page 45), on the site of present-day Luang Prabang. At the time the city was known as Xawa, possibly a local form of Java, but it was soon renamed Meuang Xieng Thong (Gold City District). A little later, Fa Ngum received from the Khmer sovereign the gift of a Sinhalese Buddha image called Pha Bang, from which the city's modern name derives.

Two centuries later, King Phothisarat moved the capital of Lan Xang to Vientiane, but Luang Prabang nonetheless remained the royal heart of the kingdom. After the collapse of Lan Xang in 1694 an independent kingdom was established in Luang Prabang, which co-existed with kingdoms based in Vientiane and Champasak further south. Kings ruled Luang Prabang until the monarchy was officially dissolved by the Pathet Lao in 1975, though they were at various times forced to pay tribute to the Siamese and the Vietnamese and, later, to submit authority to the French. The last king and queen were imprisoned in a cave in the northeast of the country, where they died in the early 1980s.

LEFT: monks pay a visit to the Pak Ou caves. **RIGHT:** That Makmo stupa.

Lavish detail on the facade of the Royal Palace Museum.

The Royal Palace Museum

In the centre of the city, between Mount Phu Si and the Mekong, is the **Royal Palace Museum** (Haw Kham; Thanon Sisavangvong; daily 8–11am and 1.30–4pm; charge), which offers an insight into the history of the region. The palace was constructed from 1904 as the residence of King Sisavang Vong, and is a pleasing mix of classical Lao and French styles, cruciform in layout and mounted on a multi-tiered platform. In a room at the front of the building is the museum's prize, the famed Pha Bang Buddha image after which the city is named. The 83cm (32-inch) -tall image, in the attitude of Abhayamudra, or "dispelling fear", is almost pure gold. Legend says that it originated in Sri Lanka in the 1st century AD; it was presented to the Khmers, who gave it to King Fa Ngum. The image was twice seized by the Siamese before finally being returned to Laos in 1867.

The Pha Bang Buddha shares a room with several beautifully embroidered silk screens and engraved elephant tusks, while the rest of the museum houses a fairly substantial collection of regalia, portraits, diplomatic gifts and art treasures, friezes, murals and mosaics.

In the southeastern area of the same compound is the **Royal Ballet Theatre**, formerly a palace building. Performances by local dancers are scheduled every Monday, Wednesday, Friday and Saturday at 6pm, and include a traditional ballet performance of an extract from *Phra Lak Phra Ram* (the Lao version of the Indian epic *Ramayana*). Tickets are available at the door on the evenings of the performances.

To the southwest of the Royal Palace is **Wat Mai Suwannaphumaham** (Thanon Sisavangvong; daily 8am–5pm; charge). Dating from the early 19th century, this temple was once the residence of the Sangkhalat, the supreme patriarch of Buddhism in Laos. The *sim* is wooden, with a five-tiered roof in classic Luang Prabang style (see page 81). The main attraction is the gilded walls of the front veranda, the designs of which recount scenes from the *Ramayana* and the Buddha's penultimate incarnation. For the first half of the 20th century the Pha Bang was housed inside, and it is still put on display here during the Lao New Year celebrations. Within the compound are two longboats, kept in their own shelter, which play a part in the celebrations at New Year.

Mount Phu Si

On the other side of Thanon Sisavangvong rises **Mount Phu Si**, the rocky 100-metre (330ft) hill that dominates the centre of Luang Prabang. At its foot stands **Wat Paa Huak** (daily 6.30am–6.30pm; charge), which features well-preserved 19th-century murals showing Mekong scenes. From this temple 328 steps wind up the forested slopes to the 24-metre (79ft) **That Chom Si** on the summit, which has an impressive gilded stupa in classical Lao form, as well as a rusting

BELOW: family posing on top of Mount Phu Si.

anti-aircraft gun. There are magnificent views across the ancient city, best at sunset, with the Mekong and Nam Khan rivers encircling the historic Unesco-protected peninsula that lies at the heart of old Luang Prabang.

The path continues down the other side of Phu Si to **Wat Tham Phu Si**, a cave shrine housing a Buddha image of wide girth, in the style known locally as *Pha Kachai*. Close by the main road is **Wat Pha Phutthabaat D** (free), a temple containing a 3-metre (10ft) Buddha footprint dating from the late 14th century.

Along the peninsula

Heading northeast along Thanon Sisavangvong from the foot of Phu Si towards the confluence of the Nam Khan and the Mekong you pass a string of glittering temples, interspersed with evocative colonial buildings. **Wat Paa Phai** (Bamboo Forest Temple; daily; free) on the left is noteworthy for its 100-year-old fresco and carved wooden facade depicting secular Lao scenes. Further along the street, also on the left, is **Wat Saen E** (One Hundred Thousand Temple; daily; free), whose name refers to the value of the donation with which it was constructed. This temple is different in style from most others in Luang Prabang, and the trained eye will immediately identify it as central Thai in style. The *sim* was originally constructed in 1718 but was restored twice in the 20th century.

Luang Prabang's Mae Nam Khan, or "Crawling River" – perhaps named because it flows slowly compared with the nearby Mekong – is a source of fresh-water seaweed which, when dried and eaten with peanuts and other condiments, is a popular and enduring snack best taken with a Beer Lao at sundown.

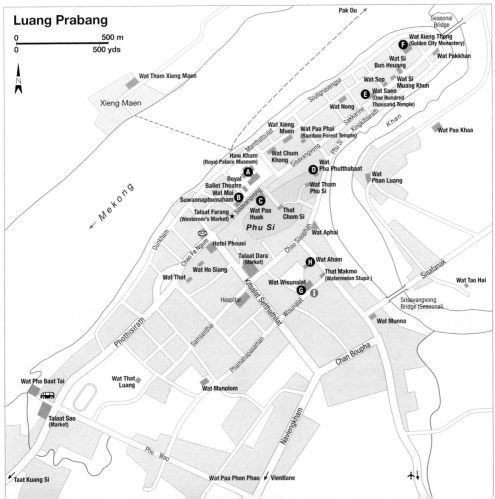

Luang Prabang

Mosaic detail in the Red Chapel of Wat Xieng Thong.

Wat Xieng Thong

Close to the tip of the peninsula, on the banks of the Mekong, reminding the visitor of the importance of river transport in Laos, is Luang Prabang's most renowned temple, **Wat Xieng Thong** ❻ (Golden City Monastery; Thanon Sakkarine; daily 6am–6pm; charge). This temple, with its low sweeping roofs epitomising the classic Luang Prabang style, was built in 1560 by King Setthathirat (1548–71) and was patronised by the monarchy right up until 1975. Inside the *sim* the eight thick supporting pillars, richly stencilled in gold, guide the eye to the serene golden Buddha images at the rear, and upwards to the roof, which is covered in *dhamma* wheels. On the outside of the *sim*, at the back, is an elaborate mosaic of the Tree of Life set against a deep red background. Throughout, the combination of splendid gold and deep red gives this temple a captivatingly regal atmosphere.

Adjacent to the *sim* is a smaller building, dubbed by the French *La Chapelle Rouge*, containing a unique

reclining Buddha figure. What makes the image so unusual is the Lao proportions, especially the robe curling outwards at the ankles, and the graceful position of the hand supporting the head. This figure was displayed at the Paris Exhibition in 1931, but happily returned to Luang Prabang in 1964 after several decades in Vientiane. The chapel itself is exquisitely decorated. On the outside of the rear wall is a mosaic showing rural Lao village life, executed in the 1950s in celebration of two and a half millennia since the Buddha's attainment of Nirvana.

Also in the Xieng Thong compound are various monks' quarters, reliquary stupas and a boat shelter. Close to the east gate is a building housing the royal funeral carriage; the interior decoration is only half-finished, as work ceased after the Communist victory in 1975.

It is a very pleasant stroll back towards the Royal Palace along the Mekong. Nothing appears to have changed in the past 30 years, nor is it likely to under the present Unesco regulations. Boutique restaurants have

BELOW: inside the Wat Xieng Thong compound.

largely replaced the scruffy old sticky-rice places, while the colonial-style buildings have been painstakingly restored or rebuilt.

Southeast of Phu Si

Back in the vicinity of Mount Phu Si, another temple of note is **Wat Wisunalat** Ⓖ (Wat Vixoun; Thanon Wisunalat; daily 6.30am–5pm; voluntary donation). Built by King Wisunalat (1501–20) between 1512 and 1513, this is the oldest temple in the city still in use. The *sim*, rebuilt a decade after the original wooden structure was destroyed by fire in 1887, is unique in style, with a front roof sloping down over the terrace. Sketches by Louis Delaporte of the original building exist from the 1860s, and confirm what a later visitor wrote: "[Wat] Visunalat is shaped like a boat, the same shape that Orientals give to their coffins. The wooden walls are sculpted with extreme refinement and delicacy." Though the wood has gone, the builders who performed the restoration attempted to capture the shapes

of the original wood in the stucco work. Inside is an impressive collection of Buddhist sculpture.

In the temple grounds is That Pathum, or Lotus Stupa, which is affectionately referred to as That Makmo, or Watermelon Stupa, and which is just as distinctive as the temple itself. The stupa is over 30 metres (100ft) high, and was constructed in 1503–4, at which time it was filled with small, precious Buddha images. Many of these were stolen by Chin Haw marauders from Yunnan in the 19th century – the rest are now safely on display in the Royal Palace Museum.

Next to Wat Wisunalat is the peaceful **Wat Aham** Ⓗ (daily 6.30am–5pm; voluntary donation), formerly – before Wat Mai took the honour – the residence of the supreme patriarch of Buddhism in Laos. The temple's red facade combines with striking green *yak* temple guardians and mildewed stupas to create an atmosphere of extreme tranquillity. The temple rarely has many visitors, other than those quietly making offerings at an

BELOW: shopfront in Luang Prabang.

Perhaps the most remarkable sight to be seen in Luang Prabang is the early morning sai baat, when devout citizens (and foreign photographers) gather at dawn to greet lines of saffron-clad monks receiving their alms. Lines of as many as 400 monks wend their way around the narrow streets on a daily basis.

BELOW: the multi-tiered Kuang Si Waterfalls.

important shrine at the base of the two large old pipal trees.

Outside town

Across the Mekong from Luang Prabang, in Xieng Maen district, are no fewer than four more temples set in beautiful surroundings. Boats depart from the pier behind the Royal Palace, or you can charter a vessel from the pier 500 metres (yards) further north. **Wat Tham Xieng Maen ❷** is situated in a 100-metre (330ft) -deep cave. This is generally kept locked, but the keys are held at nearby Wat Long Khun, the former retreat of kings awaiting their coronation. A small donation is requested for access to the cave temple.

Close to the southern edge of the city is a forest retreat, **Wat Paa Phon Phao ❸**, comprising a three-floor pagoda (daily 8–10am and 1–4.30pm; voluntary donation), complete with an external terrace near the top which affords excellent views of the surrounding countryside. The *chedi* is a popular destination for locals and visitors alike.

Further out, about 4km (2.5 miles) beyond the airport, is the Tai Lü village of **Ban Phanom ❹**, renowned as a silk- and cotton-weaving village. At weekends a small market is set up for those interested in seeing the full range of fabrics produced. There are also a number of well-stocked shops that open on a daily basis. All weaving and dyeing is done by hand using traditional techniques, a fascinating process to watch. In the vicinity, a few kilometres along the river, is the tomb of Henri Mouhot, the French explorer who took the credit for "discovering" Angkor Wat in 1860. He died of malaria in Luang Prabang in 1861, though his tomb was not rediscovered until 1990.

A two-hour (by long-tail boat), 25km (15-mile) journey upriver from Luang Prabang is the confluence of the Mekong and the Nam Ou. Opposite the mouth of the Nam Ou, in the side of a large limestone cliff, are the **Pak Ou caves ❺** (daily; charge). Legend maintains that King Setthathirat discovered these two caves in the 16th century, and they have been venerated ever since. Both caves are full of Buddha images, some of venerable age. The lower of the two caves, Tham Ting, is easily accessible from the river. The upper cave, Tham Phum, is reached by a staircase, and is considerably deeper, requiring a torch for full exploration. There is a pleasant shelter between the two caves, an ideal spot for a picnic lunch.

On the way to Pak Ou, boats will stop by request at **Ban Xang Hai ❻** (Jar-Maker Village), named after the village's former main industry. Jars still abound, but they are made elsewhere, and the village devotes itself to producing *lao-lao*, the local moonshine rice spirit. Archaeologists digging around the village have unearthed jars dating back more than 2,000 years. Opposite, at Ban Thin Hong, close to Pak Ou village, recent excavations have uncovered even

earlier artefacts – tools, pottery and fabrics – around 8,000 years old. As yet the site hasn't been developed as a tourist attraction.

Several waterfalls are in the vicinity of Luang Prabang which can make for attractive half-day or day excursions, perhaps combined with stops in some rural villages along the way. About 30km (20 miles) south of the town are the multi-tiered **Kuang Si Waterfalls**, replete with beguiling limestone formations and crystal-clear pools. Food vendors keep most of the local visitors at the lower level of the falls, which can be very crowded during holidays. Up a trail to the left of the lower cascade is a second fall with a pool which makes for good swimming and is generally quieter. The trail continues to the top of the falls, though after rain it can be dangerously slippery.

Taat Sae 7, also south of town, is closer to the city (15km/9 miles away), and hence more crowded at weekends. The falls here have more pools and shorter drops. They can be reached by boat from the delightful village of Ban Aen on the Nam Khan.

Festivals in Luang Prabang

Because of Luang Prabang's long status as the chief royal city of Laos – a status surpassing that of the less princely cities of Vientiane and Champasak – it is richly associated with festivals. The re-emergence of festivals in recent years, after a period of decline, is both a result of Unesco World Heritage Site status, and because the Lao authorities are keenly aware of the potential appeal such traditions can bring to the expanding tourist market. It is also explained by the simple fact that the Lao people delight in festivals and festivities.

The most exciting event is the **Lao New Year** (Boun Pi Mai), celebrated each April full moon to mark the beginning of the agricultural year. In times past, celebrations lasted for around three weeks as the entire population of the city indulged in an apparently endless round of ceremonies, rituals, games and processions. These days the New Year is celebrated with great vigour all over Laos, but most extensively at Luang Prabang. Boat races are held on the Mekong, and much water is thrown and poured over the celebrants.

BELOW: one of the royal guardian deities, or *devata luang*, of Luang Prabang.

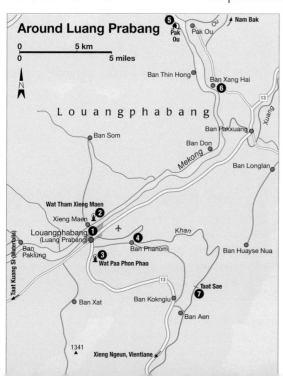

Around Luang Prabang

0   5 km
0   5 miles

N

Louangphabang

Pak Ou
Pak Ou
Nam Bak
Ban Thin Hong
Ban Xang Hai
Ban Som
Ban Pakxuang
Ban Don
Xuang
13
Mekong
Ban Longlan
Wat Tham Xieng Maen
Xieng Maen
Louangphabang (Luang Prabang)
Khan
Ban Paklung
Ban Phanom
Ban Huayse Nua
Wat Paa Phon Phao
Taat Kuang Si (Waterfalls)
13
Taat Sae
Ban Xat
Ban Kokngiu
Ban Aen
1341
Xieng Ngeun, Vientiane

NORTHEASTERN LAOS

One of the most memorable sights in Laos, the ancient Plain of Jars, brings tourists to the far-flung northeast of the country. Other highlights include the secret caves of Vieng Xai.

The northeastern provinces of Xieng Khuang and Hua Phan owe much of their history and character to their proximity to Laos's eastern neighbour, Vietnam; indeed, both of these provinces have existed more often as independent statelets, or vassal states, of Vietnam than as part of a Lao political entity. In the post-colonial era the Pathet Lao forces chose the area as their headquarters for its close strategic position to their North Vietnamese allies. This attracted the attention of the Americans, who pounded both provinces from their B-52s during the Vietnam War, obliterating dozens of towns and villages and forcing the population, both military and civilian, to make their homes in the region's plentiful caves. It should be noted that the North Vietnamese also took part in the destruction, attacking areas under control of the royalist forces with heavy artillery.

Although the scars of war remain, northeastern Laos has much to offer the visitor. The local people have put the past behind them and bear no ill will to foreigners. Fascinating – and as yet not fully explained – archaeological sites, rugged mountainous terrain (particularly in Hua Phan province), a relatively benign climate and a plethora of ethnic minorities make this remote, sparsely populated region well worth a visit.

Exploring the northeast

The following pages take the reader from Phonsavan, the capital of Xieng Khuang province, to Sam Neua, the capital of Hua Phan province, and to the limestone mountains and caves beyond.

Lao Airlines operate regular flights between Vientiane and Xieng Khuang, and sometimes schedule flights between Luang Prabang and Xieng

Main attractions

PLAIN OF JARS
MUANG KHUN
NAM NGUM RIVER SPRINGS
SUAN HIN
SAM NEUA MARKET
VIENG XAI CAVES

LEFT: pedal power. **RIGHT:** bomb cases from the war are scattered throughout the region.

CHINA

Dali

Ban Ngay Nua

Ban Hat Sa

Sa Pa

Ban
Na Pheo

Mengyuan

Phu
Den
Din
NBCA

Luan Chau

Phongsali ⓫

Ban Bun Neua

Tuan Giao

Mengla

Mengpeng

Ban Pakha

Phongsali

Ban Bun Tai

Ban Sam Phan

Ban Veng

Ban Lon

Loi

Ban Sav

Muang Taung

MYANMAR

Mönj Yawng

(BURMA)

Ban Sakamdeng

Muang Sing ⓮

Boten

Ban Finho

Ban Namaek

Na Toei

Ban Sinxai

Ban Hatnga Nua

Ban Huayphuk

Muang Mai

Ban Cong Deng

Dien Bien Phu

Ban Khoa

Ban
Khoa

Sop
Houn

Muang Khua ⓰

Ban Nam Bok

Muang Long

Ma

Luang Nam Tha ⓭

Luang
Nam Tha

Ban Sopkai

Ban Viangxai

Ban
Phonsana

Muang Long Kok

Ban Xieng Kok

Ban Xiangdao

Meung

Vieng Phukha

Nam Ha
NBCA

Ou

Ban Xang

Ban Kiulai

Ban Huaypacha

H

Ban Ko Noy

Muang La

Muang
Ngoi Neua

Wan Pai

Bokeo

Ban Huayhi Nyai

★ Gibbon
Experience

Ban Namngeun

Ban Donchai

Udomxai
(Muang Xay) ⓬

Ban Pakmong

Nam Bak

Nong Khiaw ⓽

Ban Muam

Ban Namngiu

Ban Napa Tai

Ban Ne

Louangphabang

Top
Pheung

Ban Namgiu

3

★⓯ Huay Xai

Ban Kho

Beng

Muang Beng

Ban Muangxun

Pak Xeng

Ban Sakok

Chiang
Khong

Ban Keun

Tha

Ban Khoknang

Ban Buamphaxeng

Vieng Thong

Thung
Sang

Pak Tha

Udomxai

Muang Houn

Ban Khokpho

Pak Ou

Ou

Ban Nong

Phu
Loei
NBCA

Khop

Pakbeng ⓰

Ban Namko

Ban Bo

Louangphabang
(Luang Prabang)

Pak Ou

Ban Pakxuang

Ban Don

Ban Vanglom

Mekong

Ban Thaxoang

1804

Ban Xom

Thoeng

Ban Sop Luang

Xieng Hon

Hong Sa

Ban Paksi

Xainyabuli

Ban Phonxai Nyai

Xieng Ngeun

Khan

Tran Ninh Highlands

Mu

Tham Pi

Chiang Kham

Ban Siphom

Kuang Si ★

Muang Nan

Ban Kengkung

Ban Kiukacham

Ban Udom

Muang Sui

Nong Pet ★

Ban Theun

⓵ Phonsavan

Thung
Chang

Na Rai
Luang

Dok Lo
2070▲

Xainyabuli

Muang
Phu Khoun ★

Plain of Jars
Thong Hai Hin Site 1

Hai Hin Phu Salato Site 2 ★

Hai-Hin Laat Khai Site 3

⓶

⓷

Muang Khun
(Xieng Khuang)

Bar

Xieng Kh

Pong

Tha Wang Pha

Phiang

Ban Phatonglom

7

Phu Xao
2590▲

Chiang Muan

Nan

Feuang

Kasi

Ban Jiang

Ban Phatang

Xaysomboune

Phu Bia
2819▲

Ban
Thaviang

Ban
Luang

Ban Nampuy

Ban Naphun

Vang Vieng

Ban
Naluang

Special

THAILAND

Song

Wi Ang Sa

Phu
Phanang
NBCA

Ban Paknyan

Ban Sammun

Ban Thahua

Ban Namphao

Ang Nam
Ngum

Zone

Ban Hath

Muang Longsan

Na Noi

Ban Hinhup Tai

Viangchan

Ban Namching

Rong Kwang

Ban Suvannaphun

Ban Muang

Phon Hong

Phu
Phanang
NBCA

13

Phu Khao
Khuai
NBCA

Tha Phabat

Sali

Phrae

Ban
Namxong

Pak Lai

Ban Naxong

Ban
Nasa

10

Ban Keun

Ban Cheng

Pak Kad

Ban Khok

Fak Tha

Ban
Kengsao

Xanakham

Pak Chom

Sangkhom

Naxaithong

Viangchan Prefecture

Ban Naxon

Nam Pe

Phon Phisai

Siriket Res.

Viangchan
(Vientiane)

Nong Ka

Nan

Nam Pat

Kaen Thao

Tha Li

Si Chiang Mai

Tha Bo

Chiang Khan

Nong Khai

Na Haeo

Muang
Boten

Loei

Ban Phu

THAILAND

Ngoi

Sawang
Daen Din

Phu Rua

Udon Thani

Khon Kaen

▼ Phitsanulok, Bangkok

Khuang as well, especially during the high seasons. Their flight schedule changes frequently, so it is necessary to check prior to travelling (www.laoairlines.com). Travel by land to Xieng Khuang is also possible via Route 13 and the now-sealed Route 7. Daily buses from Vientiane take around 11 hours to reach Phonsavan, while buses from Luang Prabang take about 10 hours. Vang Vieng is 6 hours away. Sam Neua is a further 8–10 hours from Phonsavan.

Those with less time and/or less inclination to endure long journeys on bone-shaking buses should take one of the flights that operate most days from Vientiane or Luang Prabang to Phonsavan, travel by land from there to Hua Phan province, enjoying the various sights en route, and return to Vientiane by air. For the hardy, and those not wishing to double back to Vientiane, fly into Sam Neua, then travel by land to Phonsavan.

Xieng Khuang province

Home to a proud and independent people, Xieng Khuang province has often been something of a battleground. This was possibly due to its strategic location equidistant between the Lao and Vietnamese capital cities, or to its agriculturally fertile, temperate plain. Attempts to exist as an independent state have largely failed, and although it was only briefly subsumed into the Lao Kingdom of Lan Xang (see page 45), the region has spent long periods under Siamese and Vietnamese control. Indeed, during the 1830s it was formally a part of Vietnam, and the local inhabitants were forced to dress and behave according to Vietnamese custom.

In the centre of the province, the present-day provincial hub, **Phonsavan ❶**, was established after the former capital (which was called Xieng Khuang), located to the southeast, was obliterated during the Vietnam War (it has now been rebuilt

Travellers who wish to break their journey between Vientiane or Luang Prabang and the northeast can do so at Muang Phu Khoun, the town at the point where Route 7 turns off from the main north–south Route 13. Muang Phu Khoun is the site of a former French garrison and its strategic location was constantly fought over during the Second Indochina War. Alternatively, for those coming from Vientiane, the backpacker centre of Vang Vieng makes a good stopover

The origin of the huge jars on the Plain of Jars remains a subject of debate among archaeologists.

BELOW: at Muang Khun, the ravages of war are plain to see.

and renamed Muang Khun). With a large number of bland modern buildings housing a rapidly expanding population (now exceeding 65,000), it is not the most attractive place in Laos; nonetheless, there are some reasonable hotels, and its proximity to some of the Plain of Jars sites makes it a good base for exploring the region.

A large market in the middle of town offers tribal handicrafts as well as the standard range of goods that sustains the local population. Other handicraft shops on the main street of Phonsavan offer interesting local textiles and silver wares. Recently, due to increased trade with nearby Vietnam, Vietnamese ceramics, woodcarvings, reproduction opium pipes and even *non la* conical hats have also appeared for sale.

The Plain of Jars

The **Plain of Jars ❷** is Xieng Khuang's major attraction. Huge stone jar-shaped vessels are scattered over a dozen locations on the lonely plateau around Phonsavan, fascinating and mysterious. Key questions remain unanswered. What exactly are these ancient megaliths? Who constructed them? When did they build them, and why?

Three major sites are easily accessible from Phonsavan, and have been cleared of unexploded American bombs (UXO), although it's still best to stay on the main paths. **Site 1** or **Thong Hai Hin** (Stone Jar Plain) is located 15km (9 miles) southwest of Phonsavan (daily; charge). This site has the biggest collection of jars, numbering over 250, and also the largest jar, which according to local lore is the victory cup of the legendary Lao king Khun Jeuam, who is said to have liberated the local people from an oppressive ruler. On nearby hillsides are odd bottle-shaped excavations; the locals use these as bird traps. Although the site is impressive, the presence of a nearby Lao air force base and some buildings erected for the visit of Thailand's crown prince a decade or so back detract from the overall atmosphere.

Another jar site, known locally as **Hai Hin Phu Salato** (daily; charge), or **Site 2**, is located 25km (16 miles)

south of Phonsavan. Here about 100 jars are spread across two adjacent hillsides. The view from the top is worth the short climb.

The most attractive site is a further 10km (6 miles) south from Site 2, and is called **Hai Hin Laat Khai** (daily; charge), or **Site 3**. Here about 150 jars are located on top of a small hill from which one can enjoy great views not only of the surrounding plains, but also of the relatively prosperous farming community of Ban Sieng Dee, set on an adjacent hillside. This Lao village, another 2km (1.2-mile) walk from the jar site, has a small Buddhist temple and visitors are welcome. (For more information on the Plain of Jars, see page 138.)

Time permitting, you could also visit old Xieng Khuang, now known as **Muang Khun ❸**, located 30km (18 miles) southeast of Phonsavan, about 10km (6 miles) beyond Site 3. This town was once a royal capital, the centre of the Phuan Kingdom. This period ended when Vietnamese invaders abducted the king, Chao Noi Muang Phuan, in the mid-19th century. The town was heavily bombed during the war and its once beautiful temples pulverised (see panel). The palace of the French legation, though badly damaged by the bombs, still stands. The authorities' decision to relocate the provincial capital, and leave the destruction visible, makes Muang Khun a memorable but painful place to visit.

East to the Vietnam border

The comparatively well-surfaced Route 7 runs east from Phonsavan to the market town of **Nong Haet** and the border with Vietnam, where the crossing is open to international travellers. En route you can visit a variety of local attractions, each of which, in its own way, offers an insight into the history and everyday life of the Xieng Khuang region.

About 25km (15 miles) east of Phonsavan, the Nam Ngum River begins its journey south to the Ang Nam Ngum (see page 112). Known as **Nong Pet**, this tranquil spring is a pleasant picnic or swimming spot. A few kilometres further, on the south side of Route 7, is **Baw Noi**, a hot

TIP

If you plan to visit only Site 1 on the Plain of Jars, a jumbo (motorised trishaw) chartered in Phonsavan will suffice, but for visiting all three sites hardier transport, for example a jeep, is recommended. Any of the hotels or travel agencies in Phonsavan can make the necessary arrangements. Hmong villages are located in the vicinity of Phonsavan and can be included in the itinerary.

BELOW: overgrown temple ruins at Muang Khun.

The Lost Temples

Before the destructive bombing of the Vietnam War, the northeastern region boasted its own unique and beautiful temple architecture, generally called the "Xieng Khuang style". Xieng Khuang temples had sweeping, low-eaved, single-tiered roofs with gracefully curved pediments. Unfortunately, almost every temple in the region was destroyed during the aerial onslaught, along with just about all of the secular buildings in Xieng Khuang town (now Muang Khun). Fortunately a few examples of Xieng Khuang temple style have managed to survive, most notably at Wat Xieng Muang in Luang Prabang, as well as in French colonial photographs and architectural drawings. Hopefully in future, as both Laos and Xieng Khuang develop, some of these lost temples can be recreated from these examples.

The ubiquitous two-stroke motorbike, main form of transport the length and breadth of Laos.

BELOW: children supervising a grazing buffalo.

mineral spring which makes another pleasant spot for a dip – especially when the weather is cool. A further 5km (3 miles) brings you to the turn-off for **Baw Yai ❹** (daily; charge), another mineral spring, larger than Baw Noi, which has now been developed as a resort, with bungalows and bathing facilities. The resort was originally open only to the Party elite, but is now open to the public.

At **Muang Kham**, 50km (30 miles) and a two-hour drive from Phonsavan, the road forks. The left fork becomes Route 6, heading north into Hua Phan province, while the right continues to the Vietnamese border.

Muang Kham itself is no more than a crossroads trading village, but there are guides who will take you to nearby **jar sites** or on to **Tham Piu ❺**, a cave a few kilometres northeast of town. Tham Piu is another Vietnam War site, where in 1969 a single rocket fired from a royalist (or American, depending on the version you choose) aircraft caused the death of hundreds

of people who had taken refuge in the cave. Controversy still exists about whether these were Lao locals or, in fact, Vietnamese who had set up a makeshift hospital in the cave.

For those who might wish to avoid another reminder of the region's troubled past, it is still worth making the trip to Tham Piu to enjoy the beautiful scenery and the tribal villages in the vicinity. Another cave, **Tham Piu Song**, which was spared the bombing, can also be visited. Although the caves are only a few kilometres from the main Route 7, a guide is recommended, as the trails are not clearly marked and, as always in this area, the risks posed by UXO remain real. It is best to hire guides in Phonsavan, where you can arrange an itinerary to include a visit to the mineral springs as well as the caves and a minority village.

Hua Phan province

Lying northeast of Xieng Khuang province, Hua Phan province shares a similar history. It has, for the past several hundred years, been alternately a vassal state of Vietnam, known as Ai Lao, owing to

its position close to Hanoi, or an independent kingdom. Even more remote than Xieng Khuang from the traditional Lao capitals of Luang Prabang and Vientiane, it was in fact only fully incorporated into the Lao polity during the French colonial period.

Hua Phan currently has a population of approximately 285,000 people. More mountainous than Xieng Khuang, it is home to over 20 ethnic minorities, most of whom are Tai-speaking. The weather up here can become quite cold during winter, especially for those accustomed to the adjacent lower-lying tropical regions.

To reach Hua Phan from Xieng Khuang province, travel northeast to Muang Kham via Route 7, bear left onto Route 6, and continue to Nam Noen, which is about a four-hour trip in total. Past Nam Noen the road is well graded but ceases to be paved, and starts to climb through beautiful mountain scenery with many tribal villages in evidence. About 20km (12 miles) beyond Nam Noen is the village of Hua Muang, where, unless you already have a guide, it is possible to obtain directions to

Suan Hin 6, literally meaning "Stone Garden" in Lao. This site is an earlier manifestation of the civilisation that built the jars of Xieng Khuang. Here, rather than jars, one sees several groupings of upright stone pillars, ranging in height from 1–3 metres (3–10ft).

Adjacent to the pillars are small underground chambers, believed to be burial crypts. This site was also researched in the 1930s by the French archaeologist Madeleine Colani (see page 138). It was inhabited before the Plain of Jars, as witnessed by the fact that only stone and not iron cutting tools were used to produce these pillars, which Colani called "menhirs". The site calls to mind a miniature Stonehenge, and Colani also hypothesised the existence of a sun cult among the prehistoric inhabitants of the region.

The menhirs of Suan Hin are several kilometres off the main Route 6, but are now accessible by vehicle. An American government opium-suppression project built a road to some nearby Hmong villages, hoping to give the inhabitants access to local markets with the produce they were

The indigenous Lao people of Xieng Khuang are known as the Lao Phuan. During 19th-century wars with Siam, many were carried off and resettled in Thailand. Today substantial communities that still call themselves Phuan live in Thailand, notably at Suphanburi just to the north of Bangkok.

BELOW: the menhir-strewn landscape of Suan Hin.

One of the many caves used to shelter the Pathet Lao forces from US bombing.

to grow instead of opium. Unfortunately, the road passes dangerously close to the main grouping of stelae, and this has caused some to collapse. Local villagers have carted the smaller pillars away to use as tables. Nonetheless, the menhirs of Suan Hin are an impressive and mysterious sight, spread over several adjacent hillsides. Constructed of stone containing silica-like chips, they sparkle in the afternoon sun.

Sam Neua ❼, the capital of Hua Phan, is 45km (28 miles) northeast of the Suan Hin site. Its setting in a verdant valley at an altitude of 1,200 metres (3,900ft) is more attractive than the town itself, although Sam Neua's **market** is thriving as the largest in the region, and is a good spot to observe the many ethnic minorities, including Hmong, Tai Daeng and Tai Lü, who come here for supplies. Sam Neua's famous handwoven textiles, as well as handmade silver jewellery, are sold in some of the small shops and market stalls. Cutlery said to be made from

downed aeroplanes can also be found, as well as ceramics and other cheap souvenirs imported from nearby Vietnam (Sam Neua is only 150km/90 miles from Hanoi by road, although there are no buses between the two).

Although Sam Neua remains one of the least visited towns in the country, basic accommodation is readily available. Two kilometres (1.2 miles) from Sam Neua's market is **Wat Pho Xai**, a tiny monastery with only five monks in residence. A 1979 independence monument, mounted on a red star, is situated on a hill on the outskirts and has views over the town.

Vieng Xai and the Pathet Lao caves

The heart of Hua Phan's significance is the district of **Vieng Xai ❽** (a recent appellation meaning "City of Victory"), some 30km (20 miles) east of Sam Neua close to the Vietnam border. It was here that the Pathet Lao leadership established its headquarters during the 20-year struggle for supremacy in the Second Indochina War. The area was chosen for its

BELOW: returning from the maize fields.

proximity to Vietnam and also for the abundance of caves which afforded shelter from American bombs. Not coincidentally, this is a wild, remote area, and the karst and jungle scenery is spellbinding. Combined with the historical significance, it all adds up to make a visit to this inaccessible corner of Indochina a memorable experience.

The authorities have an ambivalent attitude towards allowing foreigners to visit these sites. On the one hand, they are proud of their tenacious struggle and resourcefulness in surviving in these conditions; on the other hand, they still consider the area to be a high-security military zone. An explanation for their reticence to allow visitors free access to the area is no doubt the legacy of *samana*, the re-education camps of the Pathet Lao gulag.

After the Pathet Lao victory in 1975 thousands of Lao were sent to camps for lengthy "re-education" under extremely harsh conditions, including isolation, forced labour and political indoctrination. Many did not survive. The camps that held the higher officials (including the Lao royal family and former ministers) were located in Vieng Xai and nearby Sop Hao. Most camps were closed by 1989, but there is a belief that at least one camp still exists.

The caves of the Pathet Lao leaders, of which there are estimated to be about 100, are within walking distance of Vieng Xai. Located in an impressively steep and narrow limestone valley, the caves are treated as a serious historical monument by the military "guides" who must accompany all visitors. Tours take in three or four caves and last a couple of hours. The first cave, which one must visit to register, pay a nominal fee and be assigned a guide/guard, is **Tham Thaan Souphanouvong**. This was the home and office of the famous "Red Prince", Souphanouvong, a member of the Lao royal family who sided with the revolutionaries (see page 58). Befitting his royal background, this cave is well appointed, with wooden walls and

floors dividing it into different working areas. A comfortable house was constructed for the Red Prince outside the mouth of the cave after the 1973 Paris accords brought an end to the American bombing.

Tham Thaan Kaysone was the cave residence and headquarters of the Pathet Lao supremo and first president of the Lao People's Democratic Republic, Kaysone Phomvihane. Larger and more office-like than the Red Prince's cave, it extends down to a depth of around 150 metres (490ft), including a meeting room and library, and has an exit at the back which leads to an outdoor meeting area and a kitchen. An attractive house stands in front of the cave. One of the deepest caves, **Tham Xieng Muang**, was used as a temporary military hospital.

The remote border crossing on Route 6B east of Vieng Xai is open to travellers, although there are no buses either side of the border, only *songthaews* (pick-up trucks) and motorbikes. A visa on arrival has been available at this border crossing for a number of years.

Sets of cutlery for sale around Sam Neua may or may not have been made from shot-down aircraft. On balance, it seems unlikely, not least because Lao people generally eat with their fingers! But evidence of recycled UXO, especially bomb cases, is not hard to find. They are used for everything from temple gongs and school bells, through planting pots, to stilts to hold up houses.

BELOW: several of the cave sites in the hills around Vieng Xai are open to visitors.

MYSTERIOUS JARS

Strewn across the rolling plateau around Phonsavan are clusters of large stone jars of obscure origin. The remote setting and sense of mystery make for a memorable experience.

One of the best-known sights in Laos, the jars of Xieng Khuang province are ranged across three separate sites (see page 132) in the vicinity of Phonsavan.

A French archaeologist, Madeleine Colani, undertook a comprehensive study of the jars during the 1930s. Colani spent three years in the region, travelling mainly by elephant. Her work, *Mégalithes du Haut-Laos*, published in Paris in 1935, details the history of both the jars and the upright stone pillars found in Hua Phan province. Colani conclusively linked the two sets of monuments to a single civilisation which she believed flourished in the area between 300 BC and AD 300, postulating that both the jars and what she called the "menhirs" of Hua Phan were funerary monuments (see opposite page).

Other artefacts found in and around the jars included beads from China, bronze figurines from Vietnam and ornaments associated with Tai culture. This allowed Colani to conclude that the civilisation that produced these monuments was highly developed and had trading links throughout the region. She drew no direct conclusions as to the origins of the civilisation, but more recent researchers have attempted to trace them alternatively to the Cham of Vietnam or to some of the Lao Theung groups which now inhabit Attapeu province in southeastern Laos. No researcher has yet offered a convincing explanation for the civilisation's demise.

The traditional local explanation for the jars is that a Lao king, Khun Jeaum, deposed the sadistic local chief of the region in the 6th century. To mark his conquest, he ordered a huge quantity of rice wine to be made and the casting of thousands of stone jars in which to store it.

ABOVE: the largest jars weigh several tonnes. Some are made from granite, others from limestone, but the majority from a sandstone-like conglomerate called molasse. Each jar is thought to have been cut from an individual boulder.
BELOW: celebrating the ancient Rocket Festival (Boun Bang Fai; see page 330) at Site 1.

LEFT: this small Buddha statue was excavated at Site 3 and is on view at the Unesco office in Phonsavan.

Above: a bomb-clearance operation uses coloured sticks to mark unexploded ordnance. Although the tourist sites have been largely cleared of explosives from the Vietnam War, other areas remain dangerous – stick to the paths.

But What Were They For?

The jars of Xieng Khuang average about 1.5 metres (5ft) in both diameter and height, although some are considerably larger. The largest weighs an estimated 15 tonnes. Most were carved from the local sandstone, using iron implements. Madeleine Colani established her hypothesis that the jars were funerary monuments by recovering charred human bone fragments from them, and she also discovered what appears to be a central crematorium at the village of Ban Ang on the Xieng Khuang Plateau. The round discs which are now scattered in the vicinity of the jars were not lids, as one might logically suppose, but were placed, decorative side down, over ritual objects such as stone axes. It is sometimes suggested, especially by her detractors, that the jars were in fact used for storing rice wine (this is the traditional Lao story – see opposite page). The obvious problem here is that bamboo, wooden or ceramic rice containers would have been far cheaper to produce and, crucially, portable. The counter-argument is that they may have been used for storing these foodstuffs for ritual offerings.

Above: all of the jars are uncovered, but there is disagreement about whether they were originally built with stone lids. The disc-shaped objects alongside a few of the jars do appear to be lids, but are generally believed to have had a different function related to ritual objects. Many of the smaller jars, being more easily moved, have long since been carted off, but several hundred remain – Site 1 alone has around 250.

Right: the plateau is home to a large Hmong minority.

NORTHWESTERN LAOS

The remote northwestern districts of Laos are where the borders of China, Thailand and Burma converge. The scattered towns and villages give a glimpse into the lives of the numerous ethnic minorities.

Laos's wild and mountainous northwest shares frontiers with Thailand, China and Burma. The region has long been a natural path of migration, generally from north to south, for a wide variety of peoples; many of them – intentionally or otherwise – ended their peregrination in these hills. The cultural and ethnic ancestors of the Lao people, the Tai, originated just to the north in the area of China's Yunnan province known as Sipsongpanna (Xishuangbanna in Chinese), while the greatest of the Lao kingdoms, Lan Xang, traces its origins to the early *muang* (city-states) which originated here (see page 45).

In addition to the Tai, northwestern Laos is home to a large number of colourful Tibeto-Burmese peoples, such as the Yao, Hmong and Akha. The Lao government now collectively refers to these groups as Lao Sung or "High Lao", a reference to the mountain tops that they have historically chosen to inhabit. In Luang Nam Tha province these "ethnic minorities" are in fact a majority, outnumbering the Lao by two to one.

Malefactors and opium

Being a frontier region is not without dangers, and the area's history is characterised by periods of violence. The depredations of the Haw, "Overland Chinese" freebooters, accompanied by Vietnamese mercenaries and French deserters who terrorised Laos at the end of the 19th century, were particularly brutal here. More recently the area has become known as part of the infamous "Golden Triangle", where an ever-changing parade of malefactors of various nationalities has chosen to profit from one of the local people's traditional crops, opium. Although it was spared the heavy American bombing which devastated northeastern Laos during the 1970s, the

Main attractions
NAM OU BOAT TRIPS
NONG KHIAW
PHONGSALI
LUANG NAM THA
MUANG SING
GIBBON EXPERIENCE

LEFT: Yao-minority boy, Muang Sing. **RIGHT:** floating down the Nam Ou.

A small cargo boat hoisted onto stilts and used as a home.

BELOW: loading up the riverboats.

northwest was heavily involved in the strife, largely because the Hmong, supported by the American CIA, resisted the Communist Pathet Lao forces which had major bases in Luang Nam Tha province. Air America, the CIA airline, based many "training forces" here, and once again the lure of opium as a source of financing military activities raised its ugly but profitable head.

Towards the end of the Vietnam War the northwest was "liberated", and the Chinese allies built a network of paved roads connecting Mengla in China with Udomxai, Nong Khiaw on the Nam Ou and Pakbeng on the Mekong. Currently undergoing widespread and thorough upgrading, these roads continue to provide the major land thoroughfares of the region. With the rapid reopening of Chinese borders in recent years, road-building soldiers have been replaced by a variety of traders and skilled labourers from the neighbouring provinces of China. Sometimes trading only in Laos, sometimes en route to and from Thailand, they add another interesting dimension to this multifaceted cultural environment. This ethnic potpourri, combined with the mountainous geography and possibility of river travel, makes this region well worth the sometimes arduous conditions.

Along the Nam Ou

Indeed it is travel by river, not only the mighty Mekong but also large tributaries such as the Nam Ou, which offers the visitor a truly Lao experience. Nonetheless, with the roads improving, slow riverboats are becoming a less cost-effective way for the Lao to travel and their future is uncertain. Since for most villages the river is the focus of many daily activities, social and domestic, travel on a riverboat will, for now at least, provide glimpses of Lao rural life that you simply cannot get from road travel.

The Nam Ou, a major tributary of the Mekong, flows south from the mountains of China's Yunnan province through the Lao provinces of Phongsali and Luang Prabang before reaching the Mekong 20km (12 miles) upstream from Luang Prabang. It is possible to travel along the Ou by boat

from its confluence with the Mekong way up north to within a few kilometres of the mountain-top town of Phongsali (see page 145).

One can negotiate directly with the boatmen for a charter from Luang Prabang as far as Nong Khiaw or points further north. Since the completion of the road (Route 13) north to Pakmong (and on to the Chinese border), the locals have understandably chosen to forgo the river in favour of the usually faster (journey time around four hours) and cheaper buses, so there are no regular ferries and travellers must rely on charters. Rates vary according to water level and demand, but US$70–80 should secure a worthy craft. These boats can take up to 10 passengers, so sharing with others makes the cost quite reasonable. Water levels are low from January to June, and at times may be low enough to prevent boats (particularly speedboats) sailing up the river. Journey times vary, but four to six hours is typical. Speedboats can do it in two hours when the water levels are high. These noisy, high-powered vessels now begin their journey at **Ban Don**, a small village on the Mekong some 10km (6 miles) north of Luang Prabang.

The trip north to Nong Khiaw passes through splendid mountainous scenery, with small villages clustered around every bend in the river. Soon after embarking at the confluence of the Ou and the Mekong, you reach the Pak Ou caves (see page 126). If you charter a boat, be sure to ask the boatman to make brief stops at one of the picturesque villages en route.

You will eventually arrive in **Nong Khiaw** ❾ a large village set amid glorious karst scenery, which seems to owe its existence to a bridge that crosses the river here. A further 10km (6 miles) upriver lies another attractive settlement, Muang Ngoi Neua – boats travel between the two, taking around one hour. Both places have basic accommodation available and, if you don't mind roughing it a bit, either town makes a wonderfully picturesque base in which to immerse yourself in the backwaters of Laos.

The aforementioned bridge is an important link in the Chinese-built

The Lao authorities do not tolerate opium smoking, especially among young backpackers who they believe may encourage local Lao youth to experiment with drugs. The sole exception is old hill-tribe men, who are discreetly tolerated. A British woman was sentenced to life imprisonment for trying to smuggle 680g of heroin out of Laos in 2009.

BELOW: limestone cliffs at the confluence of the Nam Ou and the Mekong near Luang Prabang.

TIP

Most slow boats have covered areas to protect passengers from the sun or, depending on the season, rain. Yet these areas are often packed with people, and many foreign visitors choose to travel, for much of the time, on the deck or even the roof. Be warned – serious sunburn is a real possibility: bring a hat, sun lotion, sunglasses and an umbrella, and avoid shorts and T-shirts.

BELOW: the cool mountain setting of Phongsali.

Route 1, which travels from Luang Nam Tha province in the west to Xieng Khuang province in the east, so if you choose not to travel further north on the Ou it is possible to secure public transport either towards Udomxai in the west (about three hours by bus) or to Sam Neua in the east, via Vieng Kham (7–8 hours in all), or through to Phonsavan in Xieng Khuang in the southeast (about 10–12 hours).

Travelling by boat up the Nam Ou is still an effective way to continue north from Nong Khiaw, at least when the waters are sufficiently deep – this can be an issue in the dry season between February and June. (If there are no boats, there are always daily buses from Luang Prabang, taking eight hours.) A wider variety of craft ply the river from here on up, catering to locals and making intermediate stops at villages totally unreachable by road. In addition to the ubiquitous speedboats, a slower variety of riverboat leaves Nong Khiaw for Muang Khua on a regular basis. What these craft forfeit in speed they gain in comfort. Unlike the speedboats, they

have covered cabins which give shelter from the sun.

The boat trip to Muang Khua takes anything between four and 12 hours depending on the season and, because of constant local demand for the service, prices are reasonable. The boat ride also offers a glimpse into the life of the people who have dwelt for centuries along the banks of the Ou. If you have chartered your own riverboat you should ask to stop in some of these villages. Although contact with the outside world is limited, the fertile land and river sustain the local inhabitants with abundant food and building supplies. The people, though not prosperous in a Western sense, are certainly contented. Visitors are welcomed.

Muang Khua to Phongsali

The village of **Muang Khua** ⑩ is, like Nong Khiaw, located next to a bridge that crosses the Ou. Road access is via Route 4, which runs from Udomxai in the west (3–4 hours) and goes east to the Vietnamese border at Sop Houn (Dien Bien Phu is just 35km/22 miles

further). It is possible to cross the border into Vietnam here, and this is fortunate as Dien Bien Phu is the site of the battle that doomed the French presence in Indochina. Muang Khua offers a wider choice of accommodation than Nong Khiaw or Muang Ngoi Neua, which is also fortunate, since if you are coming from Luang Prabang this will be about as much travel as can be comfortably accomplished in a day. Muang Khua itself is a tranquil and friendly town, with many people from the local ethnic minorities visiting the town for trade or transport.

Proceeding upriver from Muang Khua into the heart of Phongsali province, your next destination is **Hat Sa**. Again, in season, there is a choice between a powerful speedboat and a placid "slow boat", as the Lao name translates. The trip takes two hours by speedboat, six hours by slow boat. This section of the river is even more spectacular than the Nong Khiaw to Muang Khua sections, with thick primary forest cover and a never-ending parade of pristine villages. The mountains looming in the distance are of substantial elevations. The air is cool regardless of the time of year, and particularly pleasant after the often torrid plains. The village of Hat Sa is the northern terminus of river traffic on the Ou, although little but its remoteness and the variety of ethnic groups who visit it distinguish the place.

From here one can board a jeep or similar four-wheel-drive vehicle to travel the remaining 20km (12 miles) to Phongsali. The fact that this short passage requires up to two hours indicates the condition of the road.

Phongsali ❶ (population 25,000), capital of the province of the same name, is located along the lower slopes of Phu Fa (Sky Mountain). Its 1,400-metre (4,550ft) elevation guarantees a year-round temperate climate and cold winter nights. No doubt as a result of its strategic location,

sandwiched between China and Vietnam, the French took an interest in the area and established a garrison. A few traces of French architecture remain, but this is being quickly overshadowed by the utilitarian Chinese style of construction that characterises most towns near the frontier of Laos's immense neighbour. The French wrested Phongsali from Chinese control by a treaty in 1895. Prior to this time it was affiliated with the Tai Lü statelet of Sipsongpanna, and under Chinese suzerainty.

The province of Phongsali is ethnically one of the most diverse in Laos. In addition to the well-known Hmong, Akha and Yao there are several branches of Tai tribal groups, Vietnamese and Chinese, both long-term residents and recent immigrants. The Lao government, with its penchant for "unity in diversity", lists about 28 ethnic groups, although anthropologists would probably dispute this number. Phongsali's market is a good place to see the great variety of peoples who call the province home, although traditional costume

The ethnically diverse residents of Phongsali gather to watch a communal video screening.

BELOW: barber at Phongsali.

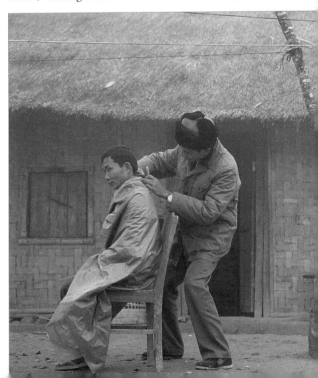

The Chinese People's Liberation Army built many of the roads in northwestern Laos during the Vietnam War, secure in the knowledge that the United States Air Force would not risk bombing them and bringing them directly into the war. Yet they did so not so much to help their purported Vietnamese Communist allies, as to keep the latter out of the area which they considered a traditional Chinese fiefdom.

BELOW: in full swing – the morning market at Luang Nam Tha.

is becoming far less visible these days. The oddly named Viphaphone Hotel offers reasonable accommodation.

South to Udomxai

From Phongsali, you have the option of journeying south on a relatively improved but still partially unpaved road towards Udomxai. After a steep descent, the road eventually joins Route 4 which runs from Udomxai to the Vietnamese border. Travel time is 6–7 hours, and the scenery is not as spectacular as that previously seen along the Nam Ou. In addition, the provincial capital of **Udomxai** ⑫ (also known as Muang Xay), although the key crossroads in the north, is not particularly attractive.

In the 1970s, Udomxai was the centre of Chinese support for the Pathet Lao forces in northern Laos. As payment for their road-building efforts, the Chinese were given carte blanche to log the Udomxai Valley, and the resultant deforestation makes for a somewhat dusty and bleak environment. The town still has a notably strong Chinese influence, but this is

now more commercial than political. In the centre, across the street from the bus station, a **Kaysone Monument** is located in the middle of a run-down park. As a backdrop the government has constructed a large stupa or *that* on a hilltop southeast of the town. Udomxai has a lively market, located in the centre of the town across from the tourist office.

Another, recently rediscovered, attraction, is the Chom Ong caves. The cave system is located 45km (28 miles) from the town near the village of Khmu Lu. The caves rank as the longest cave system in Northern Laos, spanning some 13.5km (8.5 miles) and containinh a variety of fossils. The Nam Kaang River flows through the lower stretches. The tourist office in town can help with trips to the cave system.

Luang Nam Tha

Winding its way northwest towards Luang Nam Tha, the Chinese-built Route 1 enters some spectacular mountain scenery, although some sections have been heavily deforested,

The Tai Lü

The Tai Lü are the original inhabitants of the former Tai principality of Sipsongpanna or "Twelve Thousand Rice Fields", most of which lies in southern China's Yunnan province (there known as Xishuangbanna). The French detached two of the 12 administrative districts, including Muang Sing, at the end of the 19th century and incorporated them within Laos. There are also substantial numbers of Tai Lü living across the Mekong in neighbouring Thailand and in northwestern Vietnam. A sophisticated and cultured people, they are generally very conscious of their shared roots. Their language, which is close to northern Thai, is spoken by some 700,000 people across the region, namely in China, Burma, Thailand, Laos and Vietnam.

both by logging and the slash-and-burn agricultural techniques used by local farmers. The area is home to sizeable populations of Akha, Hmong and Yao. At the village of **Na Toei**, about 90km (55 miles) from Udomxai, the road forks, with the right-hand route leading to **Boten**, a Lao village at the Chinese border. With a Chinese visa (obtainable in Vientiane) you can cross into China's Yunnan province from here.

If you bear left at Na Toei you will find yourself at the pleasant town of **Luang Nam Tha** ⑬ within the hour. During the Vietnam War, this area witnessed fierce fighting between the Pathet Lao forces and the CIA-backed tribal (largely Hmong) guerrillas, and after the war the devastated town was relocated about 7km (4 miles) north of its former site. It now boasts wide avenues (usually empty of traffic) and a pleasant location on the Nam Tha River. Wander down to the footbridge east of the town's main road at sunrise. The **morning market**, south of the "bus station" (in fact a large vacant field), is full of local products and people. Handicraft shops in this area offer interesting local Tai Lü and other textiles as well as woven bamboo artefacts. About 2km (1.2 miles) out of town on the road to Muang Sing, a European Union-funded project, the **Hat Yao Village Handicrafts Cooperative**, helps villagers get their handmade products to the market.

The former site of Luang Nam Tha, south of the "new town", is still home to a large market, a Buddhist temple, the airport and a boat landing. As the road south to the Thai border at Huay Xai is greatly improved (once an insecure track, now a safe but still slow 5–7 hours by bus), the boat traffic on the Nam Tha is diminishing. A good way to enjoy the scenery would be to negotiate a two-hour round-trip cruise. This is possible only after the summer monsoon rains have raised the waters to a navigable level.

Muang Sing

Continuing northwest on Route 3, a 60km (37-mile) two-hour trip leads through steep mountains and along raging rivers to the town of **Muang Sing** ⑭. Located on a fertile plain surrounded by mountains and irrigated by the waters of the Nam Yuan and Nam Ma, this town of 25,000 is a centre of Tai Lü culture and has a rich history. Muang Sing has existed as a small but important urban centre for hundreds of years as a result of its strategic location and agricultural wealth. At times it was under the rule of various northern Siamese principalities, but mainly of China. The British, and later the French, laid claim to it, the latter building a garrison which still exists today.

The predominant Lü people are a branch of the Tai ethno-linguistic family, who also inhabit the southern part of China's Yunnan province (the border lies just 10km (6 miles) from Muang Sing). They are arguably the most ethnically and culturally homogeneous of the many sub-groups of Tai outside their ancestral homeland (see panel).

Many of the roads in northwestern Laos are still dirt tracks, but with foreign investment paved roads are gradually taking their place.

BELOW: young monk at Wat Nam Kaew Luang.

A colourful minority shopper at Muang Sing's morning market.

BELOW: the northwestern region – Muang Sin in particular – may be historically linked to the poppy trade, but opium remains illegal in Laos.

Lü society is matrilineal: the women have strong influence in family decision-making, and are keen upholders of the group's traditions. A people known for their grace and physical beauty, they are Buddhists but also have a rich oral tradition of various mythical heroes and spirits. Among these tales is one that relates how they were taught to build their distinctive sloping roofed, stilted houses by a divine swan, and they still refer to their traditional style of dwellings as *heuan hong* ("swan houses").

A Tai Lü-style Buddhist temple, **Wat Luang Baan Xieng Jai** (free), located just west of the town's main street, near the river, shows the characteristic small windows and red lacquered pillars which typify Tai Lü temple architecture. In the centre of town, behind yet another Kaysone memorial, you can see the **former French garrison**, which is now a Lao army base, and a colourful market is located across the

main street from the memorial. If you go south for about 1km (0.6 miles), another Buddhist temple, **Wat Nam Kaew Luang** (free), is housed in an agreeable tree-filled compound. In addition to the Tai Lü, Muang Sing is also home to a large population of Yao, Akha and Lanten tribal peoples whose villages are located in the surrounding hills. Local guides can arrange trekking tours to these areas. At present the Lao government still "strongly discourages" visitors from staying overnight in tribal villages, more to protect the villagers from the visitors than the other way round.

Muang Sing is also noted for its **annual festival**, the Boun That Muang Sing. The festival's date varies according to the lunar calendar, but it is always towards the end of October or beginning of November, at the full moon. The festival occurs at a Buddhist stupa or *that* on a hill south of town. Since it is a Buddhist religious rite, the presentation of incense and candles at the stupa and the offering of alms to the monks who converge on the site for this event are

The Opium Trade

It would be remiss to discuss northwestern Laos without mentioning something that will certainly confront any visitor: the use of opium – even though it is notably less prevalent than it was just a few years ago. Muang Sing has historically been a centre of poppy production; during their period of rule the French sanctioned and monopolised the trade. Traditionally used as a medicine and by the elderly, opium is now discreetly proffered to foreign tourists on the streets of Muang Sing by emaciated local addicts, who use the profits from sales at inflated prices to finance their habits. Opium is *not* legal in Laos. The government does not appreciate Muang Sing's reputation, and unpleasant encounters between the police and foreigners using opium have been reported.

central to the festival, but it is also an important social and commercial gathering. The crowds dance to live bands in the evenings, with tasty snacks for the children and home-distilled spirits for the adults adding to the fun. Although not Buddhists, the local hill-tribe population would not dream of missing the fun, and attend in full regalia. Muang Sing is also an excellent venue for participating in the festivities associated with Lao New Year in April, or the rocket festivals that call for rain during the dry season – all festivals that are celebrated in neighbouring Thailand and Xishuangbanna in China.

Although the Chinese border is only a few kilometres northeast of Muang Sing, for the present only Lao and Chinese nationals are permitted to cross at this point.

From Muang Sing it is possible to double back to Luang Nam Tha and reach the Thai border at Huay Xai by road, but a much more interesting route is via **Xieng Kok**, a small village on the Mekong 75km (47 miles) west of Muang Sing. The road has been improved, and the trip takes two to three hours, passing through beautiful scenery along the Nam Ma. Across the Mekong from Xieng Kok is Burma, although only Lao and Burmese nationals are permitted to cross. With little to detain you in Xieng Kok (there is a guesthouse should necessity require), you can board a speedboat for the four-hour trip downriver to Huay Xai, river levels permitting. All boats stop at **Ban Muam**, which could be considered a centre of the Golden Triangle since the borders of Laos, Burma and Thailand converge here. Truck-buses leave Muang Sing for Xieng Kok early in the morning, so it's possible to reach Huay Xai the same day, although, as with all travel in Laos, be prepared for surprises.

Huay Xai and the Mekong River

Huay Xai ⑮, the Lao town across the Mekong from Chiang Khong in Thailand, is a popular entry point for visitors wishing to cross from Thailand. It is possible to get a 30-day Lao visa on arrival in Huay Xai.

TIP

The Tai Lü villages surrounding Muang Sing are interesting, and bicycles for hire in restaurants and guesthouses are an ideal way to explore. Just head north towards the village of Udomsin and take any side road that looks promising.

BELOW: snooker game by the river.

TIP

There is a certain amount of un-Laos-like hustle in Huay Xai. Travellers arriving from Thailand are likely to be accosted by vendors selling boat trips downriver to Luang Prabang or up to Luang Nam Tha. It's best to ignore them as tickets are likely to be cheaper when purchased directly from the boat operators at their respective jetties, or from agents in town.

Alternatively, you can apply for a visa from any Lao Embassy or Consulate abroad. Since becoming a legal port of entry, it has experienced a mini-boom, with new hotels, shops and even some palatial private homes in evidence. The long-proposed bridge (currently there is only a car ferry) has recently become closer to being realised. Once complete, and with the recently upgraded Huay Xai–Luang Nam Tha road, vehicular travel could proceed relatively easily between Bangkok and China and vice versa. Predictably the Thais and Chinese have been most enthusiastic.

Huay Xai itself is a pleasant little town ranged around the low hills that descend to the banks of the river. A Buddhist temple, **Wat Jom Khao Manilat** (free), can be reached by a long staircase with serpentine *naga* balustrades. Built in the late 19th century, the temple affords good views of the town and the river below. Nearby, **Fort Carnot**, built by the French, is visible from the outside, but is off limits to visitors since it is now a Lao military installation. Travel agents in town

offer trips to the nearby **sapphire mine** (the province's name, Bokeo, means "gem mine" in Lao), but the site is not particularly attractive, and the uninitiated who purchase the stones on offer will not be getting a bargain.

A three-hour ride northeast of Huay Xai, off Route 3, brings you to the **Gibbon Experience** (tel: 084-212 021; www.gibbonx.org), an exciting (but expensive) opportunity to see these long-limbed apes thanks to a system of zip-lines strategically hung below the jungle canopy. Two days are required. The Gibbon Experience has an office in Huay Xai.

Mekong transport

From Huay Xai there are several forms of river transport. The ubiquitous speedboats leave from about 2km (1.2 miles) south of town. These six-passenger craft can reach Luang Prabang in six to seven hours, or the town of Pakbeng in about half that time. Helmets and life jackets are supplied and obligatory by Lao law. Even so, not everyone enjoys the speedboat trip down the Mekong. The vast expanses of smooth water, unlike the Nam Ou that reaches north from Luang Prabang, allow the speedboat jockeys to propel their light but powerful craft at high speeds: exhilarating or nerve-racking, depending on your perspective, but certainly dangerous. Seven hours of this would rattle even the most steely nerved, so consider breaking the trip up with a night in Pakbeng. The fare per passenger to Luang Prabang is approximately US$50, and that to Pakbeng is about US$20. Hiring the whole boat will cost four to six times more than the individual fare.

A more placid alternative to the speedboats is the 40-person passenger ferries. Called *heua saa* (slow boats) by the Lao, they live up to their name. Reaching Luang Prabang requires spending one night en route at Pakbeng, arriving at Luang Prabang in the afternoon on the second day.

BELOW:
backpackers on the Mekong river boat between Pakbeng and Luang Prabang.

The boats leave in the early mornings from a terminal just north of the Lao immigration checkpoint in Huay Xai. Prices for the ferries are about US$40 from Huay Xai to Luang Prabang. Be sure to bring your own food, water, sunglasses and hat or umbrella.

A third travel alternative will appeal to those wishing to make this trip in style: if you have the budget, opt for Asian Oasis's (www.asian-oasis.com) comfortable cruise on a luxurious modern vessel, the *Luang Say*, which offers onboard refreshments and washrooms. The *Luang Say* leaves Huay Xai twice a week, stopping to visit scenic spots on the way to Pakbeng, where passengers spend the night at the Luangsay Lodge, located just outside the town. It then sets out the following morning to reach Luang Prabang in the afternoon. The price includes all meals, guides and accommodation (*see page* 321).

Some travellers choose a mixture of passenger ferry and speedboat travel by breaking the trip in Pakbeng. Obviously the slower boats give you a better chance of taking in the attractive scenery: mountains on both sides border this stretch of the Mekong, and the forest cover is often pristine. You may even see (domesticated) elephants bathing in the shallows.

Pakbeng to Luang Prabang

Pakbeng ⑯ is a pleasant small town at the confluence of the Mekong and Beng rivers. Built on steep slopes, it has several adequate guesthouses and restaurants, and many hill-tribe villagers visit its market. An interesting Buddhist temple, **Wat Sin Jong Jaeng** (free), just north of the town, has an exterior mural of the *sim* depicting earlier moustached Caucasian visitors. For those who do not wish to continue downriver to Luang Prabang, the improved road north from Pakbeng, Route 2, leads to Udomxai (150km/93 miles). The trip takes about 3–4 hours.

If you continue on to Luang Prabang by passenger ferry or the *Luang Say* you will arrive at the old city. Those travelling by speedboat will be deposited a few kilometres upstream at Ban Don, from where songthaews complete the journey.

BELOW: villagers watch as an elephant drags an old, expertly deactivated bomb across a tributary of the Mekong.

THE MEKONG VALLEY

Journey along the Mekong to visit the three pleasantly laid-back provincial capitals. This is the most developed part of the country, but still timeless, and temples and historic buildings abound.

For much of its length from a point west of Vientiane, the Mekong River marks the political divide between Laos and Thailand. From Vientiane all the way to Champasak, however, the two banks of the Mekong are closely related linguistically, culturally and ethnically – this rich, well-watered river valley is the very heartland of the lowland Lao, both in Laos and in Thailand's much larger, ethnically Lao northeast. Over the past two decades once-difficult relations between the two neighbours have improved beyond all recognition, and today new bridges are being built, both figuratively and literally, across the Mekong Valley.

The eastern bank of the Mekong is dominated by Laos's second- and third-largest urban centres after the capital, Vientiane. These are Tha Kaek (population 45,000) and Savannakhet (population 130,000). By no means large cities, they are both respectively linked and influenced by the neighbouring Thai towns, just across the Mekong, of Nakhon Phanom and Mukdahan.

Following the opening of the first Thai–Lao Friendship Bridge between Vientiane and Nong Khai in 1994, a second bridge was opened between Savannakhet and Mukdahan in 2007, and a third between Tha Kaek and Nakhon Phanom was opened in 2011. (A fourth Thai–Lao Friendship Bridge further to the north, between Huay Xai and Chiang Khong, is currently being developed.) The Savannakhet–Mukdahan bridge is part of an "East–West Corridor" linking Vietnam with Thailand via Laos. This greatly improved communications network represents both the increasing economic importance of the Mekong Valley and the strengthening cultural and political links between Laos and Thailand.

Main attractions
THA KAEK
LIMESTONE CAVES
SAVANNAKHET
HEUAN HIN KHMER TEMPLE

LEFT: fishing nets in the Mekong near Tha Kaek. **RIGHT:** Mekong Valley transport.

Southern Laos

Tha Kaek and environs

Located directly across the Mekong from Nakhon Phanom in Thailand, **Tha Kaek ❶** is Lao for "guest landing", a reference to its former function as a boat landing for foreign traders. This pleasant town, located 350km (220 miles) southeast of Vientiane via Route 13 (buses take around six hours), still greets its foreign visitors as its name suggests. Although shortly after the revolution it was renamed Muang Khammuan, the name Tha Kaek appearing to have sounded insufficiently nationalistic to the current regime, the only place one sees this appellation used is on government maps.

Historians have concluded that the area just to the south of the present-day city was settled by the Funan and Chen La Khmer kingdoms around the 5th century AD and was known as Sri Gotabura. The current site was chosen by the French, and building began in 1910. Little remains of Tha Kaek's distant past, but the French era is still evident, not only in architecture but in the central *place de la ville* and fountain.

The most atmospheric section of Tha Kaek is the pleasant tree-lined esplanade along the river, extending from the old fountain (at the end of the central city square) north to the ferry landing. Directly west of the fountain is the former colonial-era **customs house**, now housing the Tourist Police office. As you go north along riverside Setthathirat Road, a few tables shaded by large trees are good for a cold drink. On the right side of the street, after the large blue-painted four-storey **Mekong Khammuan Hotel** (tel: 51-250 777), lies **Wat Nabo** (daily; free), a tree-filled temple which also houses a school and a large banyan tree. Adjacent to Wat Nabo, the **Sooksomboon Hotel** (tel: 51-212 225) is worth a visit. This used to be a police station. It was built in the 1930s in an unusual blend of Art Deco and neo-rococo styles. Further north is the **passenger ferry landing** to Nakhon Phanom: ferries leave throughout the day. Back on the other (south) side of the fountain square, a boat restaurant called **Smile Barge Restaurant** (tel: 51-212 150), serving fresh fish dishes, is berthed on the Mekong.

To the east of town, across the road from the Lao Development Bank, the large **Km 2 Market** consists of two sections – the outer "dry" section, whose vendors sell every daily necessity you can think of, and the inner "wet" area, where a fascinating array of fresh produce is sold.

Wat Pha That Sikhotabong (daily 8am–6pm; charge) is an active Buddhist temple on the riverside about 6km (4 miles) south of Tha Kaek. The complex includes an impressive *stupa*, a worship hall and Buddha images. The *stupa* was built during the reign of King Setthathirat, the Lao monarch who ruled in the mid-16th century. The name of the temple is the Lao spelling of Sri Gotabura, the 5th-century Khmer

BELOW: many Lao women are pipe-smokers.

settlement, and local lore relates that the site has been sacred since antiquity.

Other side trips worth making from Tha Kaek are to the various **limestone caves** about 10–20km (6–12 miles) east of the town on the unpaved Route 12. They are all located down side roads without signposts, so engaging the services of a local jumbo (motorised trishaw) driver to serve as a guide is necessary. One popular cave, **Tham Nang Aen** (daily; charge) – *tham* is Lao for cave – unfortunately suffers from the presence of multicoloured fluorescent lights that have been installed to "enhance the atmosphere". As recently as 2004 a major new cave, **Tham Pha Pa** (daily 8am–noon and 1–4pm; charge), was discovered by a local man, featuring over 200 bronze Buddhas thought to be several hundred years old. An attractive cave closer to the town is **Tham Xiengliab**, through which a stream flows.

For more information, contact the Provincial Tourist Office (tel: 51-212 512), or call **Thakhek Travel Lodge** (tel: 030-530 0145). The lodge provides useful travel details and helps make arrangements for tour options in the area, including "The Loop", which is a popular three-day circuit by a combination of motorbike and boat through the remote areas of Khammuan and Bolikhamxai provinces, to explore caves and swimming spots and enjoy stunning views along the way.

Northeast of Tha Kaek, about 90km (55 miles) on Route 13 and another 130km (80 miles) east on Route 8, is the town of **Lak Sao ❷** (Lak Xao). The headquarters of the military-controlled Mountainous Areas Development Company (MADC), the town, which had a population of 24 in 1984, is now home to almost 30,000 people. The government is now promoting Lak Sao as a tourist destination, emphasising the attractive limestone karst formations, the forest cover and the tribal villages. The hype is justified – this is a wonderfully scenic area. Route 8 continues on to the Vietnam border 33km (21 miles) away, and border crossings are permitted in either direction.

BELOW: meander through an underground landscape at Tham Nang Aen.

Savannakhet

The 125km (78 miles) of main road between Tha Kaek and **Savannakhet** ❸, the second-largest urban centre in Laos, takes around 2.5–3 hours by bus (or around 8 hours direct from Vientiane). Also known (again, only officially) as Muang Khanthabuli and (unofficially) as "Savan", it is not without interest, and is one of the best places in Laos to catch a glimpse of the old French ambience (decaying old buildings along the Mekong, baguette vendors and coffee), but lacks the small-town charm of Tha Kaek. Located across the Mekong from the Thai city of Mukdahan, this growing city is a major transit point for trade between Thailand and Vietnam, even more so since the 2007 opening of a second Friendship Bridge across the Mekong just to the north of town. Route 9, one of the best roads in Laos, runs east to the Vietnamese border and has long been the main overland crossing point into Laos for travellers coming from Vietnam.

As in Tha Kaek, the most appealing part of Savannakhet is the street running parallel to the river, Tha He Road. Towards its northern end is **Wat Sainyaphum** (daily; free), an active temple complex housing a school building constructed in an interesting mixture of French colonial and Buddhist architectural styles, a *sim* (ordination hall) with fantastic stucco bas-reliefs of camels and rhinoceros on the exterior walls, and French tiled floors. The southern gate of the temple is an exceptionally well-executed example of Theravada Buddhist temple architecture. A drum tower and many trees add to the atmosphere of this temple, the oldest (founded 1896) and largest in Savannakhet.

Across the street on the river embankment, more arcane deities are worshipped at a **Chinese temple** called San Jao Suttano. A pantheon of varied spirits – derived from the *san jiao* or "three religions" of Mahayana Buddhism, Daoism and Confucianism – are venerated here, with Kuan Yin, the Goddess of Mercy, notable among them. The raised pavilion is small, but rich with incense smoke and mystical imagery.

The name Savannakhet is derived from the Lao Savanh Nakhon, which literally means "city of paradise".

BELOW: colonial relics in Savannakhet.

*Buddha images at the
That Ing Hang stupa.*

BELOW: supplies
being carried along
the Ho Chi Minh
Trail in 1969.

A range of stalls and small cafés next to Wat Sainyaphum offers a variety of Lao dishes as well as the ubiquitous Beer Lao, served at open-air tables. Housed in a colonial-era villa on the riverfront nearby, the Hotel Mekong offers live music in the adjacent nightclub, which caters mainly to visiting Vietnamese businessmen.

A few blocks away from the river on Sutthanu Road is a historically significant **statue of Than Kou Voravong** (1914–54), a hero in the resistance against the Japanese and Minister of Defence under the royalist regime. The elegant statue, depicting him clad in the upper-class *sompot* (men's collarless shirt), was cast after Voravong's assassination, but changing political winds did not allow this allegory of the vicissitudes of Lao politics to be erected until 1995.

A couple of blocks north from the statue, the **Dinosaur Museum** (Kanthabuli Road; daily 8am–noon and 1–4pm; charge) displays Jurassic-era bone samples that have been unearthed at five different sites in Savannakhet province.

Further south along the waterfront is the **passenger ferry terminal**, and around 300 metres/yds beyond that is the Savannakhet Provincial Museum (Mon–Fri 8–11.30am and 1–4pm; charge). Housed in an old colonial pile, it showcases war memorabilia and has a great deal of information on Kaysone Phomvihane, president until 1992.

Turning away from the river at the passenger ferry terminal onto Si Muang Road, you pass through the old commercial town centre, where the colonial ambience still prevails. A few hundred metres further in this direction, **St Teresa's Catholic Church** (daily) attends to the spiritual needs of Savannakhet's Christian community, most of whom are Vietnamese.

The Ho Chi Minh Trail

The Ho Chi Minh Trail was less an actual route than a frequently shifting and complex network of jungle trails, concealed from the air by heavy foliage, along which the Communist North Vietnamese sent men and supplies to their southern compatriots, the National Liberation Front, better known as the Viet Cong. Crossing the Vietnamese Cordillera south and west of the port of Vinh, the trail entered Laos in the vicinity of present-day Route 8 and followed the spiny, jungle-covered Truong Son, or "Long Mountains", south through Lao territory to Cambodia and southern Vietnam. Far removed from the Pathet Lao base areas further north (see page 136), the trail had little to do with Laos – except that, of course, it ran across Lao territory.

In their attempts to cut this vital communications artery, the US Air Force bombed the entire region between Bolikhamxai in the north and Attapeu in the south, a territorial violation that the Lao could do nothing about, and one which was kept secret from Congress. At the end of the war, in 1975, the local peoples and the newly installed Lao PDR government were left to pick up the pieces. This is a process which continues today, and may do so for decades to come, as the amount of ordnance dropped on Laos during the war made it the most bombed country, per capita, in the history of modern warfare.

About two blocks northeast of the church, **Wat Rattanalangsi** (daily; free) is a large but modern temple whose claims to fame are its glazed windows and a large reclining Buddha image.

To explore further in Savannakhet you'll need to hire a jumbo or taxi. Two kilometres (1.2 miles) east of the river, along Sisavangvong Road, is the **Talaat Savan Xay**, a large covered building with stores offering an eclectic mixture of jewellery, upmarket goods and basic commodities. The vendors and their customers can be as interesting as the goods on sale, with Lao, Thai, Vietnamese, Chinese and other ethnic-minority people all present. Outside the building, a motley crowd of makeshift stalls sells fresh produce and other daily necessities: come before noon if you wish to witness the hustle and bustle of a local market, as these stalls are all cleared out by lunchtime.

East and south from Savannakhet

Continuing a further 10km (6 miles) east on Route 13 and then 3km (2 miles) down a secondary road to the right, you come to **That Ing Hang** ❹ (daily 7am–6pm; charge); the Lao word *that* refers to any shrine said to contain a relic of the Lord Buddha. This is a site of great religious significance to the Lao. Both the site and the lower part of the structure itself date to later Khmer times (9th century AD), as indicated by the Hindu erotic art on the doorways. As with many Khmer religious sites in the region, That Ing Hang was restored and converted to a Buddhist place of worship during the time of the kingdom of Lan Xang – in this case, during the 16th century. The French, during their rule in Laos, again restored the *that*. In spite of this mixture of cultural influences, the 25-metre (80ft) -high stupa, which stands on top of a hollow chamber containing Buddha images (entry allowed only to men), retains an elegant and powerful presence.

For those with either a thirst for adventure or a profound interest in Khmer civilisation, a trip to **Heuan Hin** ❺ (literally, stone house) could be worthwhile. Located on the Mekong, 75km (47 miles) south of Savannakhet, this Khmer temple, which dates from the 6th century, is set in a small grove of plumeria trees. The ruins remain unrestored, and most of the bas-relief stone carvings which once decorated the site have been removed. Nonetheless, it's a pleasant three-hour cruise downriver from Savannakhet.

Some 160km (100 miles) east of Savannakhet via Route 9 – the main transport artery into Vietnam – lies Xepon (also spelled Sepon), one of the closest towns to what was once the Ho Chi Minh Trail (see panel). Old Xepon was destroyed during the war and rebuilt 5km (3 miles) to the west; the battle-scarred old town is littered with destroyed and damaged military detritus, half-covered by the jungle. The area is still rife with unexploded ordnance (UXO), so it is essential to keep to the marked paths.

It has been calculated that, between 1964 and 1973, Laos – and especially the area around the former Ho Chi Minh Trail – was struck by one B-52 bombload every eight minutes, 24 hours a day. Many of the explosives dropped were cluster bombs, releasing a total of around 260 million "bombie" anti-personnel mines. Experts in UXO clearance believe that around 80 million of these failed to explode.

BELOW: Wat Sainyaphum.

THE MEKONG RIVER

The world's 11th-longest river is a vital transport artery for both Laos and Cambodia, while its relatively unpolluted waters are an important source of fish.

The Mekong is truly a mighty river, rising on a distant Himalayan plateau in China and flowing south and east for 4,350km (2,700 miles); en route, it passes through Burma, Laos, Thailand, Cambodia and Vietnam before flowing into the South China Sea just south of Saigon. It is the seventh-longest river in Asia, and the 11th-longest in the world. By the time it reaches its nine-branched delta in Vietnam, its flow is so great that the silt it carries extends the surrounding shoreline out to sea by more than 1 metre (3ft) each year.

For much of its passage through Laos, the Mekong remains relatively narrow, surging between sharp rocky outcrops and limestone cliffs, through largely uninhabited forest, as well as past all the country's major towns, linking Huay Xai in the north with Luang Prabang, Vientiane, Tha Kaek, Savannakhet and Pakse. Still largely undeveloped, in its remote reaches it provides a refuge for wildlife of all kinds (see opposite page). In southernmost Laos it surges over the Khon Phapheng Falls, which, although only 21 metres (69ft) high, stretch for more than 10km (6 miles) and are quite impassable to navigation.

Surging southwards into Cambodia, the Mekong broadens to majestic proportions, so that at the Chatomuk near Phnom Penh, where it joins with the Sap and Bassac rivers, it is almost too broad to see across. In contrast to its rapid passage through Laos, in Cambodia the river flows languidly through flat and fertile lowlands, cutting a deep channel between rice paddies and rubber plantations, and providing the major source of water for the great Tonlé Sap lake, Cambodia's "riverine lung" and an all but inexhaustible source of fish.

ABOVE: building materials are ferried to Silk Island near Phnom Penh. The Mekong is a vital transport link throughout the region, although marked seasonal variations in flow and the presence of numerous rapids restrict river traffic to small vessels.
BELOW: a fisherman casts his net in the lower reaches of the Mekong around Si Phan Don. River fish include various species of catfish and carp, some of which grow extremely large.

LEFT: a storm brewing near Pakse.

ABOVE: a rural scene near Kratie.

A RICH HABITAT

Despite concerns over damming projects and other environmental woes (see pages 36 and 189), the Mekong is still relatively unpolluted and rich in wildlife. Some 1,250 species of fish have been discovered in its waters, with new species being identified on a regular basis and more large fish than any river on the planet. Many of the villages along the river banks in Laos and Cambodia depend on fishing for their livelihood, with fishermen landing various species of catfish and carp. In the lower reaches, especially, some of these can grow extremely large: the giant river carp can reach a length of 1.5 metres (5ft) and weigh up to 70kg (150lb), while the Mekong giant catfish is the world's largest freshwater fish at up to 3 metres (10ft) and 315kg (650lb).

Aquatic mammals include the Irrawaddy dolphin, also known as the Mekong dolphin, which was once widespread but is now increasingly rare, with fewer than 100 surviving individuals in total; there are small populations around the Si Phan Don islands of southern Laos and around Kratie in Cambodia. A few endangered Siamese crocodiles also survive but, sadly, their days appear to be numbered, while the river dugong is also in serious decline. Semi-aquatic mammals include the smooth-coated otter and fishing cat, and the Mekong Valley is also an important migration route for birds.

ABOVE: Khon Phapheng Falls close to the Laos–Cambodia border.

RIGHT: dolphin-viewing trip near Kratie. Small populations of Irrawaddy dolphins survive in southern Laos and Cambodia.

SOUTHERN LAOS

Ancient temples, idyllic waterfalls, ethnic villages and captivating landscapes are just some of the attractions of the southern Lao regions, reached by scenic boat trips along the Mekong.

Vientiane

outhern Laos offers a great diversity of attractions in close proximity. Travellers seeking insights into ancient history and culture will want to linger at the Khmer temple of **Wat Phu**, while the **Si Phan Don** (Four Thousand Islands) region in the far south will appeal to anyone who appreciates scenic beauty and tranquil rural life. Of the main urban centres, Pakse still has sufficient Vietnamese and Chinese residents to feel distinctly Indochinese, while Champasak still carries the unexpected air of a former tiny Lao royal principality. The temperate **Bolaven Plateau** is home to a number of Mon-Khmer minorities and offers superlative natural beauty, but still bears some scars from the Vietnam War. Attapeu is, literally, the end of the road in southern Laos – but this is precisely its appeal.

Pakse and environs

The town of **Pakse** (Pakxe) ➏, unlike Tha Kaek and Savannakhet, can lay no claim to having been home to ancient civilisations. The French founded it in 1905, possibly to offset the influence of nearby Champasak (Ban Wat Thong, the "settlement of the golden temple"), which traces its lineage back to pre-Khmer inhabitants. Pakse (literally meaning "river mouth") is located at the confluence of the Don

and Mekong rivers, some 200km (125 miles) southeast of Savannakhet; frequent buses take three or four hours.

The population of about 75,000 is notable for its diversity and vivacity – Pakse is home to many ethnic Chinese and Vietnamese, and one senses a less restrained ambience here. The town is constructed on a grid of intersecting roads, so orientation is not difficult and the principal sights can be covered on foot within a day.

A walking tour should begin at the confluence of the two rivers; have coffee at

Main attractions

PAKSE
CHAMPASAK HISTORICAL
   HERITAGE MUSEUM
CHAMPASAK
WAT PHU
UM MUANG
SI PHAN DON
KHON PHAPHENG WATERFALLS
BOLAVEN PLATEAU
ATTAPEU

LEFT: a back road in Champasak.
RIGHT: Wat Luang, Pakse.

A small wall-mounted figure in a Pakse wat.

one of the small **outdoor food stalls** just above the road leading down to the river ferry. Walking down the ferry road and bearing left, you will find small long-tail boats for hire. An interesting excursion is to cross the Don River and visit **San Jao Suk Se** (daily; free). Located on the northern bank of the Don where it meets the Mekong, this quiet and idyllic temple serves local devotees of the various deities of Mahayana Buddhism, Daoism and Confucianism. Statues of a wide variety of wise men and minor gods line the walls of the incense-clouded temple.

Various other shrines dot the grounds, and the view of the Mekong and of Pakse is excellent. The best time to visit is morning, when the mainly elderly devotees come with offerings of food and drink for the gods and linger to chat among themselves. Be sure to negotiate a round trip with your boatman; the boat service to the temple is irregular.

Returning to Pakse proper, walk along the bank of the Don and turn right at any of the main roads, all of which lead to the **Central Market**.

The covered building housing the vendors here is a new structure – the former was completely razed to the ground in a 1997 fire, and for a few years, vendors simply operated around the old site, even though a vast **New Market** was built near the Lao-Japanese Bridge after the blaze. Next to the central market building is the more upmarket **Champasak Plaza Shopping Centre**. Long-distance buses to Vientiane depart from here.

A fine example of French colonial architecture, just north of the cloth shops, now houses the **Pakse Chinese Association**. As you return towards the main road that parallels the Don River, the impressive compound of **Wat Luang** (daily; free) is hard to miss. Surrounded by large funerary urns, often shaped like *stupas*, this temple, which was built in 1935, contains the remains of many of the former Champasak royal family, including Katay Don Sasorith, a staunch anti-Communist and prime minister during the royalist period. The Communist regime removed his statue which once stood in front of

the temple, but wisely stopped short of disturbing his remains. The temple also houses a large school for monks, located in a beautiful wooden building behind the temple on the banks of the Don.

Champasak Palace Hotel

From Wat Luang, you could be forgiven for hailing a jumbo to the next point of interest, the **Champasak Palace Hotel** (see also page 322) about 500 metres/yds east on busy Route 13. Construction of this edifice began in 1968; it was to serve as the residence of the last Prince of Champasak, Chao Boun Oum na Champasak. Boun Oum is remembered as a voluble and corpulent oriental potentate, renowned more for his *joie de vivre* than his political prowess.

He served as prime minister of Laos from 1960 to 1962. As the tides of war turned against his faction he fled the country in 1974, dying in Paris a few years later and fated never to occupy his pleasure palace that commands lovely views of the Don River and the Bolaven Plateau. After the revolution the building was completed and served as a venue for Communist Party congresses and accommodation for visiting dignitaries. In 1995 a Thai company succeeded in its negotiations with the Lao government and, after renovating the palace, converted it into a hotel. Although the hotel is highly recommended as *the* place to stay in Pakse, it is worth a visit even if you are based elsewhere. The foyer uses gilt woodcarvings to set an oriental tone, but the meeting hall behind it, with its murals showing happily cooperating lowland Lao and hill tribes gathering the bountiful harvest, still recalls the building's days as a meeting place for the Party elite.

The atmosphere is relaxed, so it is not hard to wander to the upper floors – though it is better to ask – where you can experience the effect that the building's intended inhabitant had planned. Huge pavilions (now hotel suites) are surrounded by private balconies, beneath which spread tiled terraces. The two top floors contain increasingly intimate reception rooms which command panoramic views of

Ornate woodcarvings in a doorway at Wat Luang.

Champasak was the smallest and least influential of the three Lao kingdoms that emerged after the break-up of Lan Xang, always overshadowed by the larger and more prestigious kingdoms of Luang Prabang and Vientiane. Between 1713 and 1904 it was ruled by a succession of 11 kings, before becoming a reduced-status princedom under the French. The last royal prince, Boun Oum, renounced his rights in favour of King Sisavangvong of Luang Prabang in 1946.

the entire region. Note the area just beneath the eaves on the upper floors of the building: as the Communists completed the building they added bas-reliefs of the new national symbol of Laos, which included the obligatory hammer and sickle. Not content with merely painting over such images of the past, the new proprietors have placed bad luck-deflecting *feng shui* mirrors over the slogan that extols the virtues of socialism. Without ever intending to be so, the Champasak Palace Hotel is now a living historical museum.

Celebrating past and present

Directly east of the Champasak Palace Hotel lies **Wat Tham Fai** (daily; free), which, because of its sprawling grounds, is the site of many temple fairs. Should you be fortunate enough to be in Pakse when such an event is taking place (usually timed to coincide with major Buddhist holidays), be sure not to miss it; otherwise the temple has little to recommend it to the casual visitor.

Ancient Champasak

Champasak is, by any standards, a remote and tranquil rural retreat town, yet about 1,600 years ago it was an important Khmer centre called Shrestapura or Kuruksestra, which is thought to have been the northern capital of the ancient Chen La Kingdom which dominated Cambodia and southern Laos between the 6th and 8th centuries AD. Today Shrestapura – known locally as Muang Kao, or "Old Town" – is little more than a barely discernible rectangular twin earthen rampart on the right (west) bank of the Mekong about 40km (25 milles) south of modern Champasak town, astride the dirt road leading to Wat Phu. Except from the air, it's difficult to detect the outlines of the ancient city, which measure about 2,300 metres by 1,800 metres (1.5 by 1 mile) and are protected on the east by the Mekong River itself. The Chinese seem to have known of its existence, however, Tang annals naming two kings, Shrutavarman and Shreshtavarman, who ruled there before the Khmer capital was transferred to Sambor Prei Kuk, near Kompong Thom in Cambodia, during the 7th century.

Today ancient Shrestapura is best known, at least among archaeologists of Southeast Asia, as being the site where the region's oldest inscribed stone stele was found. The stele, dating from the 5th century AD, records the founding of Shrestapura by King Devanika.

Another 200 metres/yds east on Route 13, a small **Chinese temple** (daily; free) offers pleasant respite from the heat. Housed on two levels, it contains the garish images of the gods venerated by local Vietnamese and Chinese Mahayana Buddhists.

A further 400 metres/yds east on Route 13 (it may be easier to hail another jumbo rather than walk) lies the **Champasak Historical Heritage Museum** (daily 8–11.30am and 1.30–4pm; charge). Currently something of a cultural mishmash, the museum nevertheless has some beautiful pieces on the ground floor, including carved sandstone 7th-century Khmer lintels from Um Muang (*see page 170*) and some less interesting photographs of Communist Party officials greeting visiting dignitaries. Unfortunately many of the exhibits are labelled only in Lao or French, while the friendly guides speak limited English. The first floor is more interesting, focusing on the various ethnic minorities who inhabit the region, including their jewellery and textiles.

After this admittedly lengthy day trip around Pakse (which, if you have the time, could be divided into two forays), a return to the starting point to watch the sunset at the confluence of the Don and Mekong rivers will provide an excellent perspective to reflect (over a chilled Beer Lao) on this varied and vibrant southern terminus of the Mekong Valley.

Downriver from Pakse

Travelling south from Pakse, you leave a Laos bustling towards modernity and re-enter a more rural past. There are regular buses and songthaews heading south to **Champasak** on the western bank of the Mekong River, the starting point for a visit to Wat Phu and nearby sights of historical interest. Alternatively, you can take a boat: depending upon your budget – and your pain threshold – there is a variety of options available for the 30km (20-mile) cruise down the Mekong.

From the Pakse ferry terminal, located on the Se Don about 200 metres/yds upstream from its confluence with the Mekong, covered public boats leave throughout the morning. Each vessel carries around 50 passengers, plus cargo. Choice of seating is either under or on the roof, although both chivalry and Lao custom require that women do not ride on the roof. Boats take 2–3 hours to reach Champasak, crisscrossing the river to deposit or collect passengers at various riverside villages en route. The fare is minimal. A faster, more comfortable and obviously more expensive alternative is to charter a smaller craft either from the same terminal or on the Mekong, just south of the confluence of the two rivers. These vessels carry 10–20 passengers (avoid the smaller, uncovered long-tail boats) and take just over an hour to reach Champasak.

A final option is to travel in style on the *Vat Phou*, a steel-hulled, air-conditioned cruiser with private bathrooms and 12 state rooms. The company operating this vessel offers guided tours of the Wat Phu and Si Phan

Don regions lasting three days and two nights, with both Lao and French cuisine served on board. Bookings can be arranged through the many travel agencies in Pakse. Prices vary according to season, but are never cheap. Check www.vatphou.com for more information.

Champasak

Prior to the establishment of Pakse by the French in 1905, sleepy **Champasak** ❼ served as the administrative centre for the Champasak region, and the residence of Champasak's royal family when it was an independent kingdom. All that is left of this sumptuous past today are two former colonial-era royal residences, now both guesthouses, located just south of the fountain circle that marks the centre of town.

While in Champasak, stroll along the tree-lined lanes and visit **Wat Thong** (daily; free), also known as Wat Nyutthitham, located on the road directly west of the royal residences. Formerly the temple of the local royal family, it is now the final resting place of many of its members, and captures

Men and women of the southern minorities smoke long pipes.

BELOW: Wat Phu, Champasak.

the essence of this city which time has eclipsed.

Faded grandeur notwithstanding, Champasak has a very agreeable ambience. With comfortable accommodation available in the Sala Wat Phou, a restored colonial hotel, the town serves as an excellent base from which to explore ancient Wat Phu.

Wat Phu

Ancient and magnificent, the complex of **Wat Phu** ❽ (daily 8am–4.30pm; charge) – literally "Mountain Temple" – is located on a site which has been sacred to at least three cultures. The Chen La Kingdom venerated the site from the 6th to the 8th centuries AD (reportedly placating the spirits with human sacrifices), and was followed by a pre-Angkor Khmer civilisation which built most of the present edifices, beginning around the 9th century. Lastly, the Theravada Buddhist Kingdom of Lan Xang converted the Hindu temples into Buddhist shrines.

What appears to have attracted the attention of all of these civilisations is an unusually shaped mountain behind the temple, Phu Pasak. The summit juts skywards to a narrow precipice, which to the Hindu Khmers seemingly called to mind the holy Shiva *lingam*, or phallus. Locals still refer to the mountain, colloquially if somewhat irreverently, as Phu Kuay (Mount Penis). This geological formation also brings to mind a Buddhist *stupa*, which enhances its mystical significance. Adding to the symbolic power of the site, an underground spring flows from the mouth of a cave near the top of the temple complex. Although it lacks the grandeur of Angkor, Wat Phu nonetheless exudes a presence that even those not impressed by its architectural significance will find palpable.

Located 9km (5.5 miles) south of Champasak, Wat Phu begins at river level and rises three levels to reach the foot of the mountain. Outside the complex is a large reservoir which in times past was the site of boat races and ritual bathing. The bathing (and fishing) continue, somewhat less ritualistically.

BELOW: the extensive Wat Phu complex.

As you enter the complex you can see the remains of palaces built by Champasak royalty, towards the end of their dynasty, from which they viewed the annual festivities held on the full moon of the third lunar month. An east–west axial promenade passes between two rectangular *baray* or bathing ponds and leads to the base of the middle level. At the top of a flight of irregular stone stairs two large quadrangular pavilions flank the central promenade. Some have suggested, from the deities carved into the stone, that the right-hand pavilion was used by male worshippers and the left by women, though scholars tend to dismiss this as a local myth. Currently only the former is open to visitors. As you climb through the small access door you can see Hindu bas-reliefs on the lintels. Most of the free-standing statuary has been removed or damaged.

Returning to the central promenade, you will pass some pavilions whose function remains uncertain, owing to their state of disrepair. About 10 metres (30ft) to the right of the central passageway is a stone *yoni*, the stylised Hindu female fertility symbol. This artefact is constantly covered with offerings of flowers and incense, illustrating the continuing power of the ancient Hindu symbols among today's Buddhist Lao.

The third level of the temple, which contains the main sanctuary, is approached by a steep flight of stairs flanked by frangipani trees (*dok champa* in Lao, the national flower). Large trees and the remains of statues surround the sanctuary, which is in a good state of preservation, as are the bas-reliefs on the lintels. When this was a Hindu site of worship, a stone Shiva *lingam* occupied the central place of veneration, bathed by spring water piped in from the cave; now large Buddha images take pride of place.

The mountain spring is still venerated by the Lao: bottles of the water are collected, and heads are held beneath the pipe emitting the spring water for both physical and spiritual refreshment. In the small cave behind the spring, worshippers have collected a variety of Buddhist and Hindu religious statuary, including what appears

Laos, like Cambodia, is now definitively a Buddhist country, with the only Hindus a handful of South Asians in Vientiane. Yet the influence of the region's former Hindu rulers under the Khmer Empire remains apparent, and has marked local and regional Buddhism permanently. Many Lao Buddhists continue to profess respect for Hindu deities such as Shiva and Vishnu, while the elephant-headed god Ganesh, known locally as pi ganet, is enduringly popular.

BELOW: a Champasak classroom.

TIP

One of the more unusual attractions of remote Don Khong is an abandoned and rusting locomotive that survives there, dating from French colonial times. Check this relic out by all means, but be aware that it stands amid patches of a kind of local "poison ivy" which produces painful swelling and irritating itching among those liable to allergies.

BELOW: the third full moon heralds the Wat Phu Festival.
RIGHT: prayer flags at Wat Phuang Kaew.

to be a stone Shiva *lingam*. Behind and to the right of the sanctuary, a stone carving depicts the Hindu trinity of Shiva, Vishnu and Brahma. Also to the right is a wooden Buddhist temple. A winding path leading from behind the temple (a small fee will secure the services of any of the young guides) leads to two interesting carvings of a crocodile and an elephant, the former thought to date from the early Angkor period, the latter from the 18th or 19th century.

Wat Phu is famous for its *boun* (festival), which attracts visitors from throughout Laos and beyond. The precise dates vary according to the lunar calendar, but in most years it falls in February. During the three-day event Wat Phu is filled with pilgrims, who make offerings at various sites of the temple complex, particularly the sacred *yoni* and the elephant and crocodile carvings. On the final day of the festival monks accept alms from the pilgrims, and in the evening a candlelight procession circles the pavilions at the lower level of the complex. Far from being a purely solemn event, the festival is

also characterised by a myriad of more worldly diversions such as boat races, cock fighting and kick-boxing competitions. In the evenings popular music and drinking add to the revelry.

Um Muang

Across the river on the east bank from Wat Phu, located in a forest about 1km (0.6 miles) north of the nearest village, Ban Tomo, is another Khmer ruin, **Um Muang** (also known as Um Tomo; free). This is thought to have been built in the 10th century, and to have been dedicated to Parvati, also known as Uma, the consort of the god Shiva. This temple is in a much greater state of disrepair than Wat Phu, but what remains is still mysterious and evocative of Champasak's distant past. The most interesting relic is a stone pillar carved with faces of an as yet unidentified deity who may, perhaps, be Shiva. There are also a few lintels still *in situ*, though others have been removed to museums for safe keeping.

The easiest and most direct way to visit Um Muang is from Champasak by long-tail boat, a return journey of

about two hours, depending on the season. Make sure to hire the boat for the return trip, or you risk getting stranded at Ban Tomo, which is not regularly served by river traffic.

Si Phan Don and Don Khong

After the historical and cultural focus of Wat Phu, the islands of **Si Phan Don** are a natural attraction, offering scenic beauty and a glimpse into the life of Laos's more remote rural population. The Mekong River is at its widest in Laos here, close to the Cambodian border: during the rainy season it is up to 12km (7.5 miles) across, and when the waters recede many small islands emerge. It is from this phenomenon that the Si Phan Don region takes its name, meaning "Four Thousand Islands".

One of the larger and permanently inhabited islands – 6km (4 miles) at it widest, 12km (7.5 miles) north to south – is **Don Khong ❾**, located about 120km (75 miles) downstream from Wat Phu. Taking the public passenger ferry is for the hardy; depending on the passenger and cargo load,

as well as the number of intermediate stops, the trip from Champasak can take 6–8 hours, but services are irregular these days. Alternatively, charters can be arranged from either Pakse or Champasak. The journey can also be made by road, along Route 13 on the east bank of the Mekong; it takes about 2–3 hours in a public bus from Ban Muang across the river ("Lot 13") from Champasak. Direct buses from Pakse also reach Hat Xai Khun, a village east of Don Khong.

Don Khong offers no sites of historical significance, but compensates by giving the visitor a glimpse of southern Lao river life. Being the largest and most "developed" island, it has decent accommodation in restored French villas from the colonial era, in the main town, **Muang Khong**, and a small choice of bucolic restaurants accessible by motorcycle or bicycle. The island can be explored by either; a reasonable dirt road goes right round its circumference, and there are several interesting villages dotted along it. Since all overnight visitors will stay in Muang Khong, an exploration logically begins

TIP

Don Det, in Si Phan Don, is a very laid-back place. Yet it has also started to attract a rather drug-orientated clientele, as well as a reputation for indolence, indulgence and easy morality among its visitors. This is well known to the local Lao police.

BELOW: the islands of Si Phan Don are said to number 4,000.

Emerging Si Phan Don

Southern Laos's "Four Thousand Islands" have remained remote and undeveloped throughout history. In the past decade or so, however, they have emerged as an increasingly important tourist destination, initially for backpackers and budget travellers, but now attracting a more upmarket clientele as well. Despite its name and the plethora of small islands that are scattered across the Mekong at this point, only three main islands have developed, so far, as tourist centres. These are Don Det, Don Khon and Don Khong. The most developed islands are Don Khon, with the best accommodation and – if things are working properly – 24-hour electricity, and Don Khong, which has the only surfaced road. In southern Laos times are changing, however, and Si Phan Don looks sure to become an important tourist destination.

Cycling to school. Bikes are the standard form of transport for the young people of rural Laos.

here. **Wat Phuang Kaew** (daily; free), located behind the Auberge Sala Don Khong, greets visitors with a massive and gaudy stucco Buddha image.

Heading north, you will find the oldest temple on the island, **Wat Jawm Thong** (daily; free), which has recently undergone restoration work. Interesting village temples can also be found at the southern tip of the island in Ban Huay and Ban Hang Khong, where a small temple, **Wat Hang Khong** (daily; free), is especially peaceful and attractive. Apart from the temples, Muang Khong is best enjoyed for its pleasant atmosphere and as a staging post en route to the islands further south.

Li Phi and Khon Phapheng waterfalls

Located just 15km (9 miles) by river south of Muang Khong, a one-hour trip which passes through a maze of small islands, **Don Khon** is the site of the **Li Phi Falls ⑩** (daily; charge), also known as Taat Somphamit. Also to be visited here are the remains of a 12km (7.5-mile) railway built by the

French to allow cargo transfer without having to circumvent the rapids and waterfalls that abound on this section of the Mekong. During low-water-level periods larger boats can reach only to **Don Det**, the island north of Don Khon, and a smaller long-tail boat navigates the channel between Don Det and Don Khon. Only basic accommodation is available in this area, and there is no electricity, so it is best explored on a day trip from Don Khong. Any of the Don Khong lodges can arrange such trips.

Disembarking on Don Khon, you can pause for refreshment at one of the riverside restaurants. Across the road is a former French hospital. Turning right on the road in front of the hotel, you pass through the village of **Ban Khon**, where a few colonial villas are shaded by trees. If you bear right where the road forks in the village you will reach the remains of a railway bridge built by the French. Passing beneath the bridge and turning left, you come to the remains of an old steam locomotive which once plied the only railway ever

constructed in Laos, in the early part of the 20th century. The hospital, villas and defunct railway all combine to epitomise the audacity and futility of the grand ambitions of *la mission civilisatrice*.

About 1km (0.6 miles) further down what becomes more of a path than a road, the Li Phi Falls rage over ragged boulders. Although the drop is only a few metres, their volume and power are impressive. A second set of falls is located about 500 metres/yds further downstream. Fishermen use traps and nets in the pools at the base of the falls.

A unique attraction of Don Khon is the endangered **Irrawaddy dolphin**, which can be seen off the southern tip of the island. This mammal can survive in both fresh and salt water, but it is now mainly indigenous to the lower reaches of large Asian rivers, such as the Mekong and Irrawaddy. Boats can be chartered at Kong Ngay beach, about 3km (2 miles) from Ban Khon.

The **Khon Phapheng** (Phapheng Falls; daily; charge) are the largest series of waterfalls on the lower Mekong. What they lack in height they make up for in sheer volume. Several of the cascades are visible from the east bank of the Mekong, about 10km (6 miles) south of the village of Ban Nakasang. From Don Khon or Don Det you must travel by boat to Ban Nakasang, and proceed south by land. The falls are a very impressive sight, and are best viewed from a pavilion located above them – three separate cascades merge at this spot. Fishermen clamber precariously across the raging torrents on bamboo ladders to lay lines, while birds dive through the spray seeking smaller fry. Phapeng has its share of vendors of roasted chicken and other local delicacies, and plenty of cold beer: it's a lovely spot for a picnic and a great conclusion to this tiring but certainly rewarding journey through a unique part of southern Laos.

The Bolaven Plateau

The lush **Bolaven Plateau** is known for its temperate climate and Mon-Khmer minority peoples; indeed, the name Bolaven means "place of the Laven", once the predominant ethnic group in

The remote province of Sekong, established as recently as 1984, is probably the most ethnically diverse in Laos. A mere 3 percent of the population is ethnic Lao, with the remaining 97 percent being divided among 14 distinct ethnic groups, all Lao Theung or "mid-slope" Lao, including the Alak (21 percent), the Katu (20 percent), the Tarieng (19 percent) and the Krieng (11 percent). Unlike the Lao, who are Sinitic, these minorities belong to the Austro-asiatic linguistic group.

BELOW: quiet meditation at Khon Phapheng.

The French colonialists were the first to recognise the agricultural possibilities of the temperate Bolaven Plateau, introducing coffee, rubber and banana as cash crops in the early 20th century. The region also produces a wide variety of fruit, vegetables and spices, including cardamom – yet today coffee remains king, yielding a valuable harvest of 15,000 to 20,000 tonnes a year.

BELOW: the Sekong River at Attapeu.

the region. Other attractions include waterfalls, boat cruises and, for those so inclined, visits to the Ho Chi Minh Trail (see page 158). Hotels and travel agencies in Pakse offer a variety of guided tours to the region, ranging from day trips to three- to four-day itineraries.

The plateau spreads over Salavan, Sekong, Champasak and Attapeu provinces, and with an average altitude of 1,200 metres (4,000ft) the area is suitable for the cultivation of temperate crops. The French introduced the production of coffee, high-quality stock of both arabica and robusta strains; production declined during the Vietnam War but is now experiencing a major renaissance.

In addition to the Laven minority, other groups include the Katu, Alak, Tahoy and Suay. All of these peoples have animist beliefs. The Laven in particular are famed for their handwoven cloth, with patterns of beads woven into the fabric. Foot looms are used to produce this cloth which, while not as fine as the work found in the north, certainly has a distinct style, more Khmer- than Thai-influenced.

A good starting point for an exploration of the region is the **Taat Lo** (Lo Waterfall), 94km (58 miles) northeast of Pakse. The road is paved throughout, and the journey time is no more than two hours; Laven villages can be visited en route. The falls drop only a few metres, but are wide and surrounded by lush vegetation. Taat Lo Lodge (tel: 034-211 889) offers attractive chalets overlooking the falls. Alak, Katu and Suay villages can be found near the resort, which also arranges elephant day treks. Alternatively, contact **Tim's Guesthouse and Restaurant** (tel: 034-211 885) for information on Taat Lo and for trips in Salavan Province. Further south, Taat Fan (see page 175) to the east of Pakse in Champasak province is another popular base for travellers wishing to explore the Bolaven Plateau.

The town of **Salavan** is located 40km (25 miles) northeast of Taat Lo. Devastated during the Vietnam War, it has been rebuilt and its only charm lies in its splendid isolation. Those interested in investigating the customs of the local Mon-Khmer ethnic minorities might consider a visit.

A more interesting itinerary upon leaving the Taat Lo area would be to take the turn-off to **Sekong ⓫** (Route 16), just east of the Taat Lo road. This two-hour journey passes through verdant coffee plantations with views of the mountains rising above the plateau to the southwest. Sekong town, like Salavan, has been rebuilt since the war, and has a continuing military presence. **Sekong Souksamlane Hotel** across from the market has an adjacent restaurant, and a good selection of minority handicrafts on sale. Otherwise the main reason to visit Sekong is to arrange a boat trip down the scenic Kong River to Attapeu, which takes about 4–7 hours.

Attapeu and environs

Arriving in **Attapeu ⓬** (now officially known as Muang Samakhi Xai, a Communist-era designation meaning "Victorious Harmony" that has failed

to enter into local use), you see why the Lao call this their "garden city". All the houses seem to be surrounded by trees and shrubbery, both ornamental and agricultural. But, although strong on rural atmosphere, the town is without any specific attractions.

East of Attapeu, however, you can reach the **Ho Chi Minh Trail**. In the **Sansai** district you can see abandoned and damaged war equipment, and, near the village of **Pa'am**, a long-defunct Russian surface-to-air missile and launcher, looking sad and incongruous in this rural setting. Although villages have been rebuilt, you can still see the crumbling foundations of temples destroyed by the bombing, and the defoliants used have left mainly scrub forests. Overall, the experience is unsettling but worthwhile. Those undertaking this trip should be particularly careful not to leave marked paths, since the concentration of unexploded ordnance (UXO) here is among the highest in Laos.

Attapeu is literally the end of the line in terms of vehicular travel, so you must double back about 50km (30 miles) north towards Sekong in order to return to Pakse. Around halfway between Attapeu and Sekong, a road built to service a large hydroelectric project leads westwards back to the Bolaven Plateau. About 30km (19 miles) along it is **Nam Tok Katamtok** (Katamtok Waterfall). After you have become accustomed to the short but wide waterfalls of southern Laos, this cascade is spectacular in its 100-metre (320ft) drop. A small pavilion provides a good viewing point, but no trails to the base are discernible, and the route would be precipitous and also hazardous due to the possibility of UXO. About 2km (1.2 miles) beyond the waterfall the road crosses a bridge, and to the right another small waterfall makes a pleasant picnic stop.

As you leave the more mountainous regions and descend to the lower-lying Bolaven Plateau, you will come to prosperous-looking **Alak villages**. These settlements are accustomed to visitors, and offer handicrafts for sale. **Paksong** ⓭ serves as a major market town where the region's farmers sell their crops, notably coffee, to middlemen from Pakse. The morning market is quite animated and filled with interesting minority groups who have descended from their home villages.

Beyond Paksong, on the way to Pakse, another spectacular series of waterfalls, **Taat Fan**, tumbles 120 metres (390ft) – believed to be the highest waterfalls in Laos. The **Tad Fane Resort** (Ban Lak 38; tel: 020-553 1400), with its wooden bungalows overlooking the spectacular falls and the dense forests of the Dong Hua Sao NPA, is a good place to base yourself. The resort can arrange guided treks into the area, which take one through coffee plantations to the top of the Taat Fan waterfalls and to two other sets of waterfalls in the area (a small charge is payable at each waterfall). The trek will also take you through minority villages and across the temperate Dan Sin Xay plain.

Reminders of the war years are visible all over the region. These American bombs stand outside a house in Attapeu.

BELOW: men sip rice alcohol through straws to celebrate the Lao New Year.

CAMBODIA

After its brutal recent past, Cambodia is now emerging as a beguiling destination. The magnificent ruins of Angkor are without equal, while the buzzing capital city, coastal resorts and untrammelled backwoods complete the picture.

A visit to Cambodia is truly a unique experience. Once the greatest city in the world, with over 1 million inhabitants, Angkor dominates the country's past and present, and is now making an invaluable commercial contribution to its future. Even after several visits one struggles to come to terms with the immensity of its scale; it is as though all the treasures of the Valley of the Nile were assembled in a single place. There is nowhere else like it on the face of the earth.

Of course Cambodia is more than just Angkor. There is Phnom Penh, once an exquisite hybrid of Cambodian and French architecture and – despite the destruction of the war years and depopulation by the Khmer Rouge – destined to become so again. Like Laos, Cambodia has retained many of the beneficial aspects of French colonialism, and there can be few more romantic settings in which to sample French haute cuisine and sip a glass of wine than by the Chatomuk, or Quatre Bras, where the Mekong, Bassac and Sap rivers come together.

There are also many wonderful temples, hundreds of years old and still buried in the forests, waiting to be discovered. Some are not yet accessible, but each year clearance and restoration work is pressed forward, so that in the not-too-distant future Cambodia is destined to become one of the region's major tourist destinations.

Finally, there is the Cambodian coast, once the weekend retreat of French colonial officials and the Cambodian elite, but which suffered badly under the puritanical Khmer Rouge regime. Now the coastal resort of Kep is being rebuilt, while the beaches of Sihanoukville are being developed into a tourist playground. Offshore, the warm waters of the Gulf of Thailand are studded with some entrancingly beautiful tropical islands. Meanwhile, in the remote and inaccessible Cardamom Mountains and elsewhere, national parks are being established, so Cambodia also looks set to develop as a major wildlife destination in the years to come.

PRECEDING PAGES: Angkor Wat; cyclo ride on the streets of Phnom Penh; rural scene on the banks of the Mekong River, near Kompong Cham. **LEFT:** Khmer sculpture at Wat Nokor, Kompong Cham. **ABOVE, FROM LEFT:** monks test out the waters at Kep; part of the 7km (4-mile) stretch of Kep beach.

AN ENVIRONMENT UNDER THREAT

Dominated by the Mekong River and the great
lake of Tonlé Sap, Cambodia is finding it hard
to reconcile ecological and economic priorities.

In contrast to the rugged terrain of Laos, Cambodia is relatively flat, low-lying land. Situated at the heart of Indochina, it has a total area of slightly over 180,000 sq km (70,000 sq miles), and shares land borders with Laos to the northeast, Vietnam to the east and southeast, and Thailand to the north and west. In addition, Cambodia has a 443km (277-mile) coastline on the Gulf of Thailand in the southwest. The country is divided for administrative purposes into 20 provinces and three municipalities. The capital, Phnom Penh (population 2 million), is in the southeast.

The lay of the land

Two water features dominate the landscape: the Mekong River and the great lake of Tonlé Sap. The Mekong enters from Laos and flows for around 500km (300 miles) through Cambodia, up to 5km (3 miles) wide in places, before passing into Vietnam bound for the South China Sea. The river splits in two at Phnom Penh, the first major division of its large delta, where the broader, northern branch retains the name Mekong, while the southern branch is known as the Bassac. Tonlé Sap lake, vital to the Cambodian economy, dominates the centre of the country (see page 189).

Beyond the Mekong-Tonlé Sap Basin, low-lying plains extend across much of central and northern Cambodia. Towards the periphery of the country, however, are several mountain ranges; the northern border with Thailand is marked by the Dongrak Mountains, a 350km (220-mile) range of south-facing sheer

LEFT: traditional farming methods persist.
RIGHT: female workers planting rice.

sandstone cliffs rising 180–550 metres (585–1,800ft) above the plain. In the southwest, covering much of the region between the Tonlé Sap and the Gulf of Thailand, two separate ranges, the Kravanh (Cardamom Mountains) and the Damrei (Elephant Mountains), form a remote upland area. It is here that Cambodia's highest peak, Mount Aoral (1,813 metres/5,892ft), is found. Beyond these ranges, on the coast, is a narrow lowland strip, cut off from the central plains and sparsely populated. In the northeast of the country, occupying the remote provinces of Rattanakiri and Mondolkiri, rise the eastern highlands. This region of thickly forested hills and plateaux, which extends east across the border into Vietnam and north into Laos, is wild and remote, but is becoming deforested at an alarming rate.

Cambodia also has many islands off its southern coast in the Gulf of Thailand. Koh Kompong Som lie to the west of Sihanoukville within a half-day boat trip. The Koh Ream Archipelago is scattered to the east towards the fishing village of Phsar Ream. Koh Tang is further out to sea, between four and eight hours' journey from Sihanoukville by boat.

Most of Cambodia's 13.5 million inhabitants live in small villages in the Mekong-Tonlé Sap Basin and practise subsistence wet-rice cultivation or fishing. Phnom Penh, emptied by the

transitional plains are covered with savannah grasses and small bushes.

The various mountain ranges in the country support several different forest types. Large areas of the Cardamom and Elephant mountains in the southwest are covered in virgin rainforest, where the upper canopy often reaches 50 metres (160ft). Elsewhere in these mountains, at the highest elevations, are subtropical pine forests. The eastern mountain ranges bordering Vietnam and Laos are covered with deciduous forests and thick grasslands.

Among Cambodia's larger animals are small populations of tigers, leopards, rhinoceros and

Khmer Rouge regime between 1975 and 1979, is now bursting at the seams, and many poorer people are being driven out by speculation and high land prices. Set against this, the government is distributing free land to poor farmers in undeveloped areas, such as around Bang Melea in Siem Reap province.

Flora and fauna

Cambodia plays host to a diversity of natural environments. The central lowland plains are largely agricultural; but outside the cultivated fields of rice, maize and tobacco and, in some places, rubber plantations, they are thinly forested, with scrub-like areas of reeds and grasses covering large areas. Around the periphery, the

elephants. Present in somewhat greater numbers are various species of bear, deer and wild cattle. There are also numerous smaller mammals, including monkeys, squirrels, voles and rats. The country is rich in birdlife: notable species include those found in wetland and grassland ecosystems such as cranes, herons, pelicans, cormorants, ducks and grouse.

Much of the wildlife is threatened, notably the rare Irrawaddy dolphins in the Mekong near Kratie (see page 294); on the other hand, genuine efforts are being made to establish national parks and nature reserves such as the bird reserve at Prek Toal (see box), and as these begin to generate income from tourism, so local people are learning to appreciate their value. Cambodia's first national parks were established as recently as 1993. Today there are seven – Kirirom, Preah Monivong, Kep, Ream, Botum Sakor, Phnom Koulen and Virachey. There are also 10 designated wildlife sanctuaries across the country.

Prek Toal Biosphere on the northwestern shore of Tonlé Sap is sometimes billed as the premier birdwatching destination in all Southeast Asia. It is home to a plethora of rare species, and is easily accessible by boat from Siem Reap.

Climate

Cambodia's climate is governed by the annual monsoon cycle. From May to October the southwest monsoon carries heavy daily rainfall. The northwest monsoon, between November and March, brings slightly lower temperatures and less precipitation. In between are transi-

5,000mm (200 inches) a year, while the central plains generally average only 1,400mm (55 inches). Greater problems arise when the southwest monsoon fails. This can cause severe food shortages for the many Cambodians dependent on the Tonlé Sap and its surrounding fer-

tional periods, with changeable cloud cover and rainfall, but consistently high temperatures. The coolest months are between November and January, though even then temperatures rarely fall below 20°C (68°F): Cambodia is generally a few degrees hotter than Laos.

The driest months are January and February, when often there is no rainfall, and the wettest usually September and October. Rainfall varies quite considerably from year to year and region to region. The southwestern highlands, with their seaward-facing slopes, can exceed

ABOVE, FROM LEFT: a disabled child serves as a potent reminder of the misery wreaked by landmines; fields given over to wet-rice cultivation.

tile soils for their sustenance. Droughts are not uncommon, and, despite the fact that historical evidence suggests they have always been a problem in the region, many blame irresponsible loggers in the more northerly countries on the Mekong for exacerbating the situation.

Environmental issues

Over the past four decades large-scale logging has continued unabated throughout much of Cambodia; estimates put the reduction in forest cover at around one-third since 1970. While the Khmer Rouge started the exploitation of the forests, subsequent governments have helped to accelerate it. With international demand for timber high, and stricter controls on logging and the export of wood continually being imposed in surrounding countries, Cambodia has not hesitated to cash in on its forests. Logging concessions have been sold to foreign nations, particularly Malaysia and Indonesia, bringing much-needed cash to the ailing economy, but with little thought for the future. Several times the government in Phnom Penh has rescinded concessions, but so far greed has proved too powerful, and new concessions continue to be sold.

Loss of forest cover and encroachment on previously uninhabited forests, together with many years of war, also continue to pose a seri-

mountains and the Gulf of Thailand. The delicate ecology here is threatened by commercial shrimp farming, largely the province of Thai entrepreneurs. To raise the profitable tiger-shrimps, mangroves must be cleared to make ponds. Fertilisers are added, and waste water is pumped out, an extremely destructive process which makes a farm useless within four years. As elsewhere in the region, offshore coral reefs are at risk from dynamite fishing.

Inevitably, the economic possibilities of the Mekong River have not gone unnoticed. As in other countries on the Mekong, various proposals have been made, mainly revolving around the

ous threat to the country's wildlife. As in neighbouring Laos, animal conservation still remains at best a minor concern. Many people still hunt – though, happily, the country is no longer a major game-hunting destination – and there is little education regarding the importance of maintaining a balanced ecosystem. Quite simply, most people are concerned only with finding their next meal. On the other hand, large areas of the country are still only lightly populated, and little-visited by locals or foreigners, so – with the exception of logging – environmental pressures are reduced.

Another habitat at risk is the salt marshes and mangroves which make up the narrow strip of land on the coast between the southwestern

establishment of hydroelectric facilities. So far little has come of these proposals, but they have brought to light the serious risks posed by similar projects upstream in Laos and China. Because Cambodia is so dependent on the annual rise in the waters of the Mekong and the Tonlé Sap for the fertile deposits this brings, any change in the flow of the river could have disastrous effects on agriculture. The possibility of a decline in fish is a concern. Furthermore, future developments upriver could severely affect the performance of hydroelectric stations and dams within Cambodia.

ABOVE, FROM LEFT: mine warning at Preah Vihear, northern Cambodia; Khmer woman chopping firewood in Kratie.

Tonlé Sap

Cambodia's great lake, swelling and shrinking with the seasons, sustains the country with its fertile sediment and abundance of fish.

The vast freshwater lake known as Tonlé Sap is truly a remarkable phenomenon. The very heart of Cambodia's rich agricultural and fishing economies, it is the riverine "lung" on which much of the country's prosperity depends. During the annual monsoon rains it swells greatly in size, becoming a natural reservoir which then gradually releases its accumulated waters during the long, hot months of the dry season. It also provides the surrounding plains with a never-ending supply of rich silt for farming, and is an equally reliable source of nutrition in the form of fish, snails, snakes, frogs and all manner of aquatic wildlife.

The lake, which is surrounded by a fertile rice-growing plain, dominates Cambodia's central northwest. During the dry season, approximately between November and May, the lake is at its smallest, though it still covers 2,500–3,000 sq km (950–1,160 sq miles). The Sap River runs from its southeastern corner to join the Mekong and Bassac rivers at Phnom Penh, some 100km (60 miles) distant.

The reversal of the Sap River

The confluence of these rivers, known in Khmer as Chatomuk or "Four Faces", and in French as Quatre Bras or "Four Arms", is remarkable for a unique phenomenon, the reversal of the Sap River. From May to October, during the annual monsoon rains, the hugely increased volume of the Mekong forces the Sap River to back up, and finally reverse its course, flowing northwards to flood the Tonlé Sap with vast quantities of fresh water and rich sediment. During this period the Tonlé Sap almost trebles in size, from 3,000 sq km (1,160 sq miles) to as much as 8,000 sq km (3,100 sq miles). At its lowest level, most of the lake is less than 2 metres (6.5ft) deep and is like a marsh with crisscrossing navigable channels; at its fullest the lake is as much as 14 metres (45ft) deep, and it can gain 70km (44 miles) in width.

Then, in mid-October, as the cool, dry winds begin to blow from the north and the level of the Mekong

RIGHT: out on the waters of Tonlé Sap.

diminishes, the flow of the Sap is again reversed, carrying the surplus waters of the Tonlé Sap southwards to the Mekong and Bassac deltas. The annual flooding of the Tonlé Sap makes the lake an incredibly rich source of fish, while the farmland around it benefits from an annual deluge of rich sediment.

The Tonlé Sap is mainly fished by Muslim Chams and migrant communities of Vietnamese. These peoples are less concerned about taking life than the Theravada Buddhist Khmers who till the nearby fields – not that the latter show any concern at all about eating the fish once it has been caught and killed by someone else. There are few dinner tables anywhere in Cambodia that are without a supply of

prahok – fermented fish paste from the great lake – and fish is a national staple.

The time of the October reversal of the waters is celebrated as Bon Om Tuk, one of Cambodia's most important festivals. For three days an estimated 250,000 revellers join in the festivities, which include longboat races, music, dancing, fireworks and a great deal of eating and drinking. Teams compete in the traditional boat racing, which is said to celebrate an event in 1177, when Angkor was invaded and sacked by a fleet of Cham warships which sailed up the Sap River and across the Tonlé Sap. The Chams were then defeated by the country's most illustrious monarch, Jayavarman VII. Bas-reliefs in the Bayon at Angkor commemorate the great victory.

DECISIVE DATES

Earliest Times

100 BC–AD 500
Establishment of a flourishing trading state called Funan in the Mekong Delta.

500–700
A proto-Khmer state, known as Chen La, is established inland from Funan near the confluence of the Mekong and Sap rivers.

The Greatness of Angkor

802–50
Reign of Jayavarman II, who proclaims himself a god-king and begins the great work of moving the capital to Roluos near Angkor.

889–908
Yasovarman I moves the capital to Angkor.

1113–50
Surayavarman II begins the construction of Angkor Wat.

1177
The Chams sack Angkor.

1181–1220
Jayavarman VII constructs the Bayon at Angkor Thom.

1352–1430
The Siamese Kingdom of Ayutthaya sacks and pillages Angkor four times, taking away the court regalia and many prisoners.

Division and Decline

1432
King Ponhea Yat abandons Angkor. Subsequently Lovek, to the north of Phnom Penh, becomes the capital.

1618–1866
The capital is moved to Udong, north of Phnom Penh.

The French in Cambodia

1863
The French force King Norodom to sign a treaty making Cambodia a French protectorate.

1866
A new capital is established at Phnom Penh.

1904
King Norodom dies and is succeeded by King Sisowath, who reigns until 1927.

1941
Thailand invades northwestern Cambodia.

1942
Norodom Sihanouk becomes king.

Independence and the Indochina Wars

1945
King Sihanouk declares Cambodian independence from France, with Japanese support.

1953
Cambodia gains full independence from France under King Sihanouk.

1954
At the Geneva Conference, France formally confirms its withdrawal from Cambodia.

1955
Sihanouk abdicates but retains real power for himself.

1965
Vietnam War escalates; Communist forces begin to seek sanctuary in eastern Cambodia.

1967
Pol Pot's group of Cambodian Communists – dubbed "Khmer Rouge" by Sihanouk – launches an insurgency in the northwest.

1969
US B-52 bombardment of Vietnamese sanctuaries in Cambodia begins.

1970
A coup is launched by right-wing General Lon Nol. Sihanouk takes refuge in Beijing.

The Zero Years

1975
Khmer Rouge take
Phnom Penh on 17 April;
cities are immediately
evacuated, and the country
is cut off from the
outside world. Brutal
persecution of Buddhism and
other religions.

1976
Large-scale starvation occurs
in the northwest of the country
as hundreds of thousands of
urban-dwellers are deported
there.

1978
Refusal to negotiate with
Vietnam over burgeoning
border war.

1979
Vietnamese troops invade
and overthrow Pol Pot
regime. People's Republic
of Cambodia
established.

Cambodia Reborn

1979–88
Up to 100,000 Vietnamese
forces are stationed in
Cambodia to prevent a DK
resurgence.

1989
Vietnamese forces start to
withdraw.

1991
Prince Sihanouk returns to
Phnom Penh.

PRECEDING PAGES: the southern
gateway to Angkor Thom. **ABOVE,
FROM LEFT:** stone image, the
Bayon, Angkor Thom; a grim
reminder at the Khmer Rouge
prison, Tuol Sleng; welcoming
Norodom Sihanouk back to
Cambodia after years in exile.

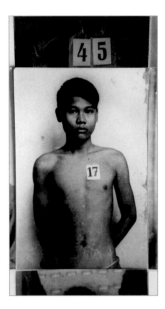

1993
General elections are held,
supervised by the United
Nations. Coalition government
of Prince Norodom
Ranariddh's FUNCINPEC Party
and Hun Sen's People's Party.

1996
Khmer Rouge forces split; Ieng
Sary defects to the
government in return for an
amnesty.

1998
Pol Pot dies in mysterious
circumstances and the Khmer
Rouge finally disintegrates.

1999
Cambodia joins ASEAN.

2003
Anti-Thai riots break out in
Phnom Penh.

2004
Hun Sen is re-elected by
parliament. King Sihanouk
abdicates on account of ill
health and Norodom Sihamoni
is elected to succeed him.

2005
A war-crimes tribunal to try
surviving Khmer Rouge
leaders receives UN approval.

2007
UN-backed genocide trials
begin.

2008
Hun Sen's ruling Cambodian
People's Party retains power in
elections.

2009
Former S21 commander Duch
is the first former Khmer
Rouge leader to stand trial;
tensions flare with Thailand
over the border dispute at
Preah Vihear.

2012
Duch is sentenced to life
imprisonment for genocide
and crimes against humanity;
trial of Ieng Sary, Nuon Chea
and Khieu Samphan
continues. Tensions over
border dispute with Thailand
remain high.

THE RISE AND FALL OF THE KHMER

Cambodia's history has been a story of rise and fall. The early days of Funan and Chen La were followed by the emergence of the powerful empire of Angkor, and in turn by a long period of decline ending in the loss of independence.

A s with the Lao, there is some controversy surrounding the origins of the Cambodian people. Some suggest that they originated from the south, in present-day Malaysia and Indonesia, while others point to the southwards territorial expansion from what is now mainland China, which would indicate a Tai or Sinitic link. What is clear is that at least 4,000 years ago the fertile flood plains of the lower Mekong and Bassac rivers, as well as the Tonlé Sap (Great Lake of Cambodia), were inhabited by a people of indeterminate origins, although logic dictates that they are at least partly ancestors of today's Cambodians.

Not a great deal is known about these early inhabitants, but they certainly baked earthenware pots to hold water and fermented toddy palm, or to store the fish in which the region has always abounded. It was a forested area which flooded frequently, so it should be no surprise that they lived in stilt houses, just as most rural Cambodians do today.

Conditions for settled agriculture were unusually rich. The waters teemed with fish, rice could be grown with little effort in the fertile soil around the Great Lake, and primitive boats were built to travel from stilt house to stilt house and from village to village. The region, moreover, was close to the South China Sea, within easy access of the developing trade routes between China, South Asia and the Middle East. All the prerequisites existed for the development of a potentially rich and advanced civilisation, which began to coalesce around the 1st century AD.

LEFT: carving at Sambor Prei Kuk. **RIGHT:** Ayutthaya; the Thai kingdom often influenced Cambodian affairs.

The first kingdom

The first civilisation to appear was the Kingdom of Funan (1st–6th centuries AD), almost nothing of which survives today beyond the ruins of the supposed capital, Oc Eo, deep in the south Vietnamese delta province of An Giang. Oc Eo was a trading port which is thought to have flourished between about AD 100 and 400, after which it became submerged; it was discovered in the 1940s. Excavations reveal evidence of trade links, however tenuous, with Southeast Asia, China, India, the Middle East and even as far as the Mediterranean and Rome. In other words, Funan made up part of the flourishing coastal trade network which girdled Asia at that time, from the region of Canton to the Red Sea.

The rise of the Khmer people

By 500 Funan appears to have been in decline, although the reason is unclear. Meanwhile, a new proto-Khmer state was developing further inland, near the confluence of the Mekong and Sap rivers, in the region of present-day Phnom Penh. The inhabitants of this state, known to the Chinese annals as Chen La, spoke a Mon-Khmer language and were strongly influenced by Indian religious traditions (see panel, page 198). They may be regarded as the progenitors of the first authentically Cambodian state.

The first dated Khmer-language inscription known to history dates from 611, while the earliest known Sanskrit inscription from the region dates from just two years later. The historian David Chandler employs these and other, later, inscriptions to deduce that early Cambodian society was divided, in general terms, into two classes – those who understood both Sanskrit and Khmer, and those who only knew and spoke the latter.

The division between the two classes was not merely linguistic; it was also between those who grew rice and those who did not. "It was everyone's ambition to be 'rescued from the mud', but very few succeeded," Chandler explains. It was the destiny of almost all Khmers

SANSKRIT AND KHMER

Sanskrit was the language of the gods and the priestly classes, and of matters of philosophic and esoteric concern. The records recount the genealogies of rulers, actions of the elite and meritorious deeds. They are all in highly polished verse. Khmer, by contrast, was the language of the *nak ta*, or "ancestor people", the indigenous, ordinary Cambodians. Inscriptions in Khmer are all in prose and record more mundane matters, such as temple administration, inventories of slaves, landholdings, tax and secular law. In this distinction between Sanskrit and Khmer lies much of the dichotomy which has distinguished Cambodian society to the present day.

to work the land and to plant and harvest rice. All else rested on this fundamental, immutable fact. When sufficient surplus had been accumulated the "greater ones" – those "rescued from the mud" – could be maintained, and in turn they could devote their energies to maintaining the complex administration which would be required to build Angkor (*see page* 199).

Life in Chen La

By around 800 the nascent Khmer state known to the Chinese as Chen La had developed into a fully-fledged kingdom, with its capital at Isanapura (modern-day Sambor Prei Kuk, near Kompong Thom). At the time Isanapura was, according to one contemporary commentator, "the most extensive complex of stone buildings in all Southeast Asia, built a century ahead of similar constructions in Java".

For several centuries, and certainly from the middle of the 3rd century AD, irregular tribute missions had been sent from the Lower Mekong Valley to China, and adventurous Chinese traders and other travellers had visited Funan and later Chen La. There is some confusion between descriptions of "Water Chen La", which may have been a Mekong Delta successor to Funan, with its capital at Vyadhapura (Angkor Borei, near Phnom Penh), and "Land Chen La", which lay further inland.

Around the middle of the 6th century, moreover, tribute missions seem to have stopped, perhaps at about the time that Funan was eclipsed by Chen La. Therefore very little is known of Chen La, or of why and how it developed.

The move inland

By the 7th century "Land Chen La" seems to have eclipsed "Water Chen La" in importance as the centre of the kingdom moved north-westwards, beyond Isanapura and towards the region which would eventually become Angkor. At the same time the state seems to have acquired a new cohesiveness, though precisely why remains uncertain. Chandler suggests that this may have resulted from increasing population density, improved wet-rice-farming techniques and victories in local, unrecorded wars, the last perhaps resulting in a protracted period of peace.

It is clear that by the 8th century "Land Chen La" was developing into an increasingly wealthy and centralised kingdom. Moreover, as the centre moved inland, away from the sea, it relied less on subsistence agriculture and trade, and more on organised manpower, irrigation technology and intensive rice production. In this way the foundations were gradually laid for the establishment of the Khmer Empire which would develop in the region of Angkor.

The empire of Angkor

The Angkorean period of Cambodian history is generally considered to have extended from AD 802 to 1431, although these dates should not be interpreted too literally – there were Khmers in the Angkor region before it became the capital, and Angkor was not completely deserted when the capital returned eastwards. Still, the six centuries between these two dates mark the peak of Cambodia's power and influence in Southeast Asia, as well as the pinnacle of Khmer artistic and cultural achievement.

The foundation of Angkor (meaning "city", from a Khmer variant of the Sanskrit *nagara*) is generally attributed to Jayavarman II. Little is known of him, but inscriptions dating from the 11th century – two centuries after the events in question – suggest that, as a young man, Jayavarman visited Java, returning in the late

8th century. He then travelled throughout the country from the Phnom Penh region, through the old capital at Sambor Prei Kuk, before settling in the region of Aninditapura, to the northeast of the Tonlé Sap.

Here he proclaimed himself a *devaraja*, or "god-king", creating a type of universal kingship clearly associating the ruler with the Hindu god Shiva. Although the records are few, it is clear that Jayavarman must have been a man of royal rank by birth and one who had already distinguished himself in various ways, not least in battle. Certainly his subsequent career involved numerous military campaigns, though the power he accrued also rested on a careful series of alliances, marriages and grants of land.

ABOVE, FROM LEFT: Khmer inscription at Lolei, Roluos; bust of Jayavarman VII, Royal Palace, Phnom Penh.

Jayavarman was undoubtedly successful: one inscription describes his realm as extending to "China, Champa, the ocean, and the land of cardamom and mangoes" (the last is probably central Thailand). An exaggeration, certainly – even at its height the Khmer Empire never reached as far north as China. Nonetheless, it is probable that Jayavarman's influence extended over all of present-day Cambodia as well as to neighbouring territories which today constitute parts of eastern and central Thailand, southern Laos and the Mekong Delta region of Vietnam.

As a consequence of his successes, Jayavarman II is remembered as the founder of the first

unified Cambodian state. He made his capital at Hariharalaya, an area today marked by the Roluos complex of monuments about 13km (8 miles) southeast of Siem Reap, the oldest temple group in the Angkor region.

Triad monarchs

Jayavarman was followed by a line of more than 30 monarchs who ruled from the Angkor region. Many of these incorporate the word *varman* (Sanskrit for "armour") in their titles. Not all are well known, nor did they all achieve greatness. Some, however, were clearly remarkable men, whose achievements, writ large in stone, retain the power to surprise and impress even today.

King Indravarman I (877–89) was one such, who during his rule established a "triadic" pattern that would be followed by

An inscription at Preah Ko tells of Indravarman as a monarch victorious in war: "In battle, which is like a difficult ocean to cross, he raised a pathway, made up of the heads of his arrogant enemies."

many subsequent monarchs. Firstly, he busied himself with major irrigation works to increase both the agricultural production of the state and his power. Next, he commissioned statues of his parents and other relatives and ancestors shown as various gods. Statues of Jayavarman II and his queen, for example, depict them as Shiva and his

---

INDIA'S PERVADING INFLUENCE

It is not clear when Indian traders first arrived in Southeast Asia, but commercial and cultural contacts are believed to extend back as far as 4,000 years. It is thought that these early Indian visitors sought wealth in the form of gold, tin, precious woods and spices, rather than conquest.

The region proved a rich source of valuable goods, as well as a fertile and receptive ground for the dissemination of Indian culture. So rich was Southeast Asia that the Indians named the region Suvarnabhumi, "Golden Land" in Sanskrit. In fact, Suvarnabhumi was more of a cultural and trading network than a single unitary state, encompassing the coastal

regions of Southeast Asia from Malaya and Sumatra, through Java and Bali to Cambodia and Champa. It is true that Chinese influence, too, was felt, particularly via Chen La in the Mekong Delta, but – with the exception of Vietnam – Indian influence remained dominant, with Tamil and other South Indians visiting, trading, settling, and converting the indigenous population to Hinduism. As a result, by the 5th century AD all of mainland Southeast Asia except Vietnam, as well as most of the neighbouring Malay region, was dominated by a number of closely related Hindu-Buddhist kingdoms ruled by semi-divine Maharajas or "Great Kings".

consort, and were made for the temple complex of Preah Ko, near Roluos.

The third stage of Indravarman's rule was characterised by the construction of a temple-mountain, made in the form of a stepped pyramid and dedicated to him. It was designed to serve as both his tomb and a lasting monument to the glory of his rule. Known as the Bakong, the temple-mountain was the first great Khmer religious edifice to be made from stone rather than brick, and it still survives at Roluos.

Indravarman was succeeded in 899 by his son, Yasovarman, who ruled until about 908

religion in the Khmer world at this time) and all still surviving. The largest, Phnom Kandal or "Central Mountain", lies near the heart of the Angkor complex.

Building Angkor

To construct Angkor, Yasovarman needed to be both a ruler of vision and a great builder. He ordered the construction of a vast reservoir, the Yasodharatataka, along the southern shore of which he erected temples to honour Shiva, Vishnu and the Buddha, for by this time Buddhism had already started to make a significant impact on Khmer customs and reli-

and was the monarch who began the move to Angkor, known as Yasodharapura in honour of its founder – the name Angkor did not come into general use until the 14th century.

Yasovarman's decision to move to Angkor was probably influenced by the presence in the region of a small hill on which he determined to build his own temple-mountain. In fact he built three, all symbolic representations of Mount Meru (the mythical Buddhist axis of the world; Buddhism was emerging as a new

ABOVE, FROM LEFT: Vishnu statue, Angkor Wat; a 19th-century engraving by Delaporte of the upper courtyard of Angkor Wat; Khmer warriors, the Bayon, Angkor Thom.

gious beliefs. He also ordered the construction of numerous temples on hills throughout his domains. The most noteworthy of these is the great Preah Vihear, set high on an all but inaccessible ridge of the Phnom Dangrek mountain range which separates Cambodia from northeastern Thailand.

Over the next century Angkor continued to expand, despite the construction of an elaborate rival city at Koh Ker, about 85km (53 miles) to the north, by a usurper king. By the time of Jayavarman V (968–1001), Angkor had grown considerably, and the ruler clearly commanded the loyalty of many thousands of field workers, stonemasons and soldiers. Jayavarman V was a Shivaist but was notably tolerant of Buddhism, which continued to exert an increasing influence at the royal court. One of the most beautiful temples at Angkor, Banteay Srei or "Citadel of Women", dates from this time.

Inevitably a great city like Angkor attracted trade and foreign businessmen, although it seems that most international commerce was in the hands of the Chams, Chinese and Vietnamese rather than the Khmers. Goods traded included porcelain, cloth and textiles, forest produce, rice, buffalo and slaves. Unfortunately, little information regarding such matters survives, but some can be gleaned from the complex and detailed bas-reliefs on the pediments of some Angkorean monuments, especially the Bayon.

Jayavarman V's patronage of Buddhism was continued by his successor, Surayavarman I (1002–50). However, Utyadityavarman II, who ruled between 1050 and 1086, was a devotee of Shiva, and he built a great temple-mountain, the famed Baphuon, to house the Shiva *lingam* (phallus) associated with his reign.

Military power and diplomacy

By the late 11th century the line of kings ruling at Angkor was in decline, with two or even

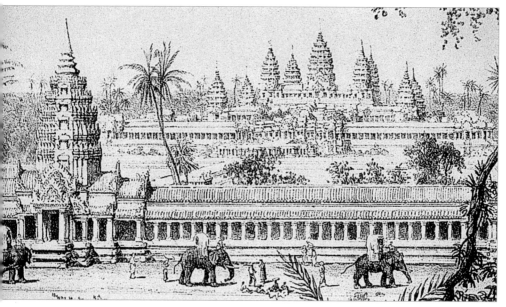

three rivals competing for the position of "universal monarch". At the beginning of the 12th century, however, a new dynasty was founded by Jayavarman VI (1080–1107), which was to rule the Khmer Empire for more than 100 years.

Little is known about the first two kings in this dynastic line, but the third, Surayavarman II (1112–52), was a powerful ruler who presided over a unified kingdom. As soon as he had ascended to the throne he began to act with vigour and speed to expand the territory and manpower under his control. His armies campaigned in the east, attacking both Vietnam and Champa. He employed mercenary troops drawn mainly from tributary regions in the west; it is likely that these included Siamese, who appear in the bas-reliefs at Angkor wearing grass skirts, carrying spears and marching out of step, in contrast to the serried ranks of Khmer soldiers.

Surayavarman II also established diplomatic relations with China – the first Angkorean monarch to do so, and possibly the first Khmer ruler since the days of "Water Chen La" to send missions to the Middle Kingdom. Unusually for a Khmer ruler, Surayavarman II was neither a partisan of Shiva nor a patron of Buddhism; rather, he was a devotee of the Hindu god Vishnu, and to the glory of this deity (and himself) he commissioned the

one inscription survives from this period – but the latter's assumption of power represents a high point in Angkorean history. By this time the population of Angkor's great city complex, Angkor Thom, is thought to have been over 1 million, making it the largest city in the world at the time.

As a young man Jayavarman VII (1181–1219) studied the doctrines of Mahayana Buddhism, the "Greater Vehicle" variant of the doctrine found in Vietnam, China and Northeast Asia, rather than Theravada Buddhism, "The Way of the Elders", more generally associated with Southeast Asia and Sri Lanka. This devotion to

largest and most magnificent of all the monuments at Angkor, the great temple complex of Angkor Wat (see page 280). Construction of this monumental building was begun early in his reign, and was not completed until after his death in about 1152.

Kingship and religion

There is little information about the three decades between Surayavarman II's death and the coronation of Jayavarman VII in 1181 – only

ABOVE, FROM LEFT: a 19th-century engraving of Angkor Wat; a stone carving in the South Gallery at Angkor Wat showing Surayavarman II surrounded by followers.

Mahayana Buddhism was to become a major feature of Jayavarman VII's reign, as he strove to associate traditional features of Khmer kingship – the *devaraja* concept of a universal god-king – with the teachings of Buddhism. This was at variance with the concept of divine Khmer kingship, which generally associated the ruler with Shiva or, less often, Vishnu, or, on occasion, with Hari-Hara, a composite of the two. The Khmer kings employed this association to emphasise their grandeur, while in the minds of their subjects it had much to do with rice production, irrigation and adequate rainfall.

The new *bodhisattva*-kingship instituted and promoted by Jayavarman VII differed from the forms which had gone before in that the king no longer sought to be represented as the devotee of a divinity, or as a *devaraja* drawn up to divinity in death. Rather, through a combination of meritorious acts, he sought to redeem both himself and his kingdom in the time-honoured Buddhist way.

Cham invasion

The French historians Paul Mus and Jean Boiselier identify the central event of Jayavarman VII's reign as the Cham invasion of 1177. The Chams (see page 221) had a powerful, marine-orientated kingdom in central and

and pillaged it. According to a Cambodian stele, the Cham King Jaya Indravarman IV "put the king to death, without listening to any proposal for peace".

Jayavarman, still three years away from his coronation, responded in kind. He defeated the Chams in a naval battle on the Tonlé Sap, while another Khmer prince killed the Cham king "with a hundred million arrows". From this point on, the Cham threat diminished – although this was largely due to Vietnamese expansion rather than the rise of Angkor.

On assuming his crown in 1181, Jayavarman

southern Indochina and controlled all of what is now central Vietnam between the 2nd and 12th centuries.

Jayavarman VII seems to have had some strong links with the Court of Champa and its capital at My Son, near present-day Da Nang in Vietnam. In the 1160s he seems to have spent some time there as either a guest or an exile, or perhaps leading a military campaign – as ever, the sources are sparse and imprecise. In 1177–8 the Chams invaded, first by water, and then by land. Their chief objectives seem to have been booty, prisoners of war and possibly revenge for earlier assaults against their own kingdom, especially by Surayavarman II. In 1178 they took the great city of Yasodharapura by surprise

VII found Angkor "plunged into a sea of misfortune and heavy with crimes". As a Buddhist – instead of a Hindu – monarch, he believed he owed little to his predecessors, and so over the next three decades he sought to stamp his authority on the Khmer Empire.

Once securely in power, Jayavarman VII put in place a major series of road-building and other public works programmes. He also built numerous public resthouses and reservoirs. He expanded the frontiers of his kingdom, bringing much of what is now central Thailand, southern Laos and southern Vietnam under his control. Jayavarman was also a temple builder *par excellence*. In 1186 he erected the Ta Prohm complex in honour of his parents; this was followed by Preah Khan ("Sacred Sword") in 1191, and finally the famous Bayon, with its hundreds of enigmatic faces, each representing a *bodhisattva*-like image of himself.

A new belief system

In many ways Jayavarman VII's reign can be seen as seminal for the development of Buddhism in Cambodia – not that he was anything but a syncretist: facilities and cells for Vishnuist and Shivaist devotees and for temple Brahmans were included in his major works. Nevertheless, it was from this time that Buddhism began to supersede Hinduism as the main belief system of the Cambodian people.

> Angkor Wat remains the largest religious monument ever built. Based on a model of the Hindu universe centred on Mount Meru, it required as much stone as the great pyramid in Egypt – yet is also exquisitely carved with bas-reliefs.

Yet the gradual conversion of the great majority of people to Theravada Buddhism during the 13th century is not solely attributable to Jayavarman's personal belief system – which was, in any case, Mahayanist. Equally important were his conquests to the west, where the south-moving Tai peoples and the long-established Mon population were already Theravada Buddhist. Wandering Sri Lankan monks may also have played a part in the conversion process.

The abandonment of Angkor

Following the reign of Indravarman III (1295–1308), the Kingdom of Angkor entered a period of slow but terminal decline of which we know relatively little. Few inscribed stelae survive – if, indeed, they were ever created, as the old Hindu-orientated elite gradually embraced Theravada Buddhism. Our knowledge of the period, such as it is, rests on Chinese records, one Cham inscription and a few Tai ones, the evidence of archaeology and the uncertain

ABOVE, FROM LEFT: bas-relief of Chams fighting Khmers at the Bayon; Hindu religious symbols, such as this *nandi* bull, declined with the 13th-century rise of Buddhism.

process of logical deduction. As a result, historians tend to disagree about the progress of events in Cambodia in the two centuries between about 1350 and 1550.

Return to the coast

What is clear is that the country's political and economic centre of gravity began a long but inexorable shift back from "Land Chen La" – that is, the Roluos-Angkor region at the head of the Tonlé Sap – to "Water Chen La" – the region around Phnom Penh, Lovek and Udong – in the mid-14th century.

Some historians argue that this striking rever-

sal of the Cambodian historical imperative was due to the rise of the Thai kingdoms (and especially that of the Kingdom of Ayutthaya) to the west and north of Angkor; others contend that the shift back to the southeast was more probably linked to the rapid expansion of maritime trade between China and Southeast Asia which took place during the late Mongol and early Ming dynasties in the 13th to 15th centuries. Proponents of the first school of thought tend to represent this as a period of Angkorean "decline", while those of the second, more recent, school, see it as a period of Cambodian "change". As is usual in such dialogues, there is doubtless an element of truth in both hypotheses.

The most reliable references we have, as well as the most numerous, are Chinese. According to the historian David Chandler, more than a dozen tributary missions were sent from the Khmer Empire to China between 1371 and 1419 – more than during the entire Angkorean period. The Chinese clearly valued these contacts which, as usual, were as much commercial as tributary missions, and afforded the visiting Cambodian delegates appropriate dignity and respect.

But what actually happened "on the ground"? Viewed from an Angkorean perspective, the great temple complexes dedicated to Hindu

Wars soon broke out, with the Siamese generally, though not always, gaining the upper hand. Angkor was captured and sacked on several occasions, most notably in 1431. In sparsely populated Southeast Asia the "spoils of war" usually meant seizing people rather than land (see page 53), and these Siamese victories would have meant the large-scale transfer of captured Cambodian prisoners to the west, which deprived Angkor of much of the massed labour necessary for the maintenance of its great irrigation systems, not to mention skilled stonemasons and other temple builders.

deities such as Shiva and Vishnu may have declined in significance as Buddhism became the predominant religion of the state.

The Siamese threat

Then there was the unsettling question of the Siamese. Once a tributary people who had served as mercenaries in the Angkorean armies, these relative newcomers to the region grew rapidly both in numbers and in strength, posing an increasing threat to the Kingdom of Angkor. This threat became palpable with the establishment, in 1350, of the Siamese Kingdom of Ayutthaya, centred on the Lower Chao Phraya River Basin, within easy striking distance of Angkor.

On a more mundane level, the first- and second-quality sandstone used in temple construction had begun to run out, and the builders were increasingly obliged to use poorer-quality laterite. The time had come to move elsewhere.

Maritime trade

Viewed, on the other hand, from a Phnom Penh perspective, the rich and expanding possibilities of maritime trade with China and elsewhere in Southeast Asia must have appeared tremendously attractive. As the Angkor region came under repeated Siamese attack, this commercial alternative to an apparently endless cycle of war, temple-building and intensive rice cultivation must have become appealing. Accordingly, historians suggest that while one portion of Angkor's population departed westwards in a slow haemorrhage of power as prisoners of the Siamese, another portion – perhaps a trickle, not a stream – migrated southeast, to the vicinity of Phnom Penh, in search of a more prosperous and more secure existence.

Significantly, this latter group of migrants would probably have included many of Angkor's richer and better-educated classes – clerks, merchants, overseas businessmen such as the influential Chinese community, and perhaps even private slave-owners and landholders.

Reasons for choosing the Phnom Penh region for a new capital were plentiful and logical. To begin with, there seems to have been the well-established tradition of royal rule from the Lower Mekong region dating back to "Water Chen La" and even Funan. In a way the Khmers were merely retracing their steps.

Beyond this there was the question of geographical location. Far from Ayutthaya and therefore (for some time, at least) safe from Siamese attack, the Phnom Penh region was strategically centred on the confluence of three rivers, the Mekong, Sap and Bassac, at a region known in Khmer as Chatomuk, or "Four Faces", subsequently known to the French as Quatre Bras, or "Four Arms" (see page 189).

15th–19th centuries: a shrinking nation

The final move from Angkor seems to have taken place sometime after 1432. Successive capitals were established, first at Lovek and then at Udong in the 15th and 17th centuries, both slightly to the north of Phnom Penh, and finally at Phnom Penh itself. Though smaller and less magnificent than Angkor, these new centres prospered, with international trade burgeoning, and distinct trading communities of Chinese, Malays, Portuguese, Spanish, Japanese and Arabs established in the area.

During these years the Khmer Empire frequently found itself at war with the Siamese court in Ayutthaya, sometimes emerging

victorious, but more often on the losing side. Meanwhile, Vietnamese migrants began to move into the still predominantly Khmer region of the Mekong Delta until, by the 18th century, the new arrivals outnumbered the original Khmers by as many as 10 times.

A direct result of Cambodia's gradual shrinkage, caught between the Vietnamese hammer and the Siamese anvil, was a commensurate growth in both Siamese and Viet interference in Cambodian affairs. Relations with the Siamese court were better than those with the Vietnamese; a shared Indic perception of the world and many other similar val-

ues made the courts of Ayutthaya and Phnom Penh at least mutually comprehensible to each other. There was little understanding for or sympathy with the Vietnamese court, however, particularly as the Nguyen rulers of central Vietnam began a sustained effort to "Vietnamise" Cambodian society, encouraging the wearing of Vietnamese clothes while also isolating Phnom Penh from direct contact with the outside world. The Cambodians were thought of contemptuously as the "little brothers" of the Vietnamese.

From this point onwards, anti-Vietnamese sentiment became established throughout Cambodian society – a theme that would continue into the present day.

ABOVE, FROM LEFT: Cham fisherman, Tonlé Sap, c.1890; 18th-century map of Siam (Thailand), Laos and the Khmer Empire (Cambodia); crude figures near a stupa in Udong.

FROM COLONIALISM TO THE KILLING FIELDS AND BEYOND

The modern history of Cambodia is one of tragedy: it is estimated that nearly a fifth of the population was killed in the brutal Khmer Rouge years.

By the mid-19th century the once-mighty Khmer Empire had been reduced to a weakened rump state, dominated in the east by Vietnam and in the west by Siam. This disastrous situation, which would almost certainly have resulted in the loss of Cambodian independence and the division of all remaining Cambodian territories between these powerful neighbours, was brought to an end in 1863 when King Norodom was persuaded to accept the establishment of a French protectorate over Cambodia. As a consequence Cambodia became a rather sleepy backwater under French protection – a colony, true, but still a definable nation.

French rule

Until 1941 all seemed to run smoothly in Cambodia. Most Cambodians accepted the French almost with relief as a welcome alternative to the expansionist Vietnamese, while the French helped transform the country into a regional rice bowl. Beyond this – starting with the adventurer Henri Mouhot (1826–61) – the colonials "rediscovered" the glories of Angkor, and contributed greatly to the establishment of two immensely significant truths which now form a central part of the Cambodian national psyche: firstly, that the Cambodians built Angkor; and, secondly, that French intervention saved most of Cambodia from division between Siam and Vietnam.

Not everyone agreed, of course. And in the vanguard of the anti-colonialist elements,

predictably, were the nationalists of the Indochinese Communist Party (ICP). Here, without descending too far into the racial maelstrom of Cambodian politics, a problem arose. Perhaps inevitably, the larger and more sophisticated Vietnamese element in the ICP dominated the lesser Lao and Cambodian contingents, leading to fears that "Big Brother" Vietnam might seek to replace the French as masters of a unified Indochina. Such, at least, were the fears of some Lao and, especially, a group of ultra-nationalist Cambodians for whom hostility towards and fear of Vietnam was second nature.

The events which followed resulted in a bitter civil war and, after Democratic Kampuchea's

LEFT: sobering exhibits at Phnom Penh's Tuol Sleng Genocide Museum include thousands of photos of prisoners, alive and dead. **RIGHT:** a royal prince c.1921.

seizure of power in 1975, the deaths of 2–3 million Cambodians – Khmers, Cham Muslims, ethnic Chinese, Thais, Vietnamese, Lao, Shan and various minority hill peoples.

How did this tragedy come about? Cambodian resistance to the French was of a very limited nature, but events elsewhere, in Europe and East Asia, were to intervene. In 1940 France fell to Nazi Germany. The colonial authorities in Indochina responded by supporting the pro-Nazi Vichy regime, and in 1941, with French backing, Norodom Sihanouk became King of Cambodia. On 9 March 1945 the Japanese armed forces moved to oust the

Vichy administration, and on 13 March, in response to a direct request from Japan, King Sihanouk proclaimed Cambodia independent and changed the official name from Cambodge to Kampuchea. Within a few short weeks, however, the French were back in an ultimately doomed attempt to restore their colonial presence in Indochina.

The Indochina Wars

What followed, tragically, were three consecutive Indochina Wars. The main protagonists were the Vietnamese Communists, who took on and defeated first the French, then the United States, and finally an unlikely alliance of fellow "Socialists" from China and Cambodia.

At first it appeared as though Cambodia might avoid serious involvement in Vietnam's long and vicious war with the French. Certainly most anti-colonialist fighting went on further to the north, culminating in the French debacle at Dien Bien Phu in 1954. Inevitably, however, as Ho Chi Minh's Hanoi-based government (The Democratic Republic of Vietnam) sought to take on and destabilise the Franco-American regime in Saigon (The Republic of Vietnam), Cambodia, together with neighbouring Laos, was drawn into the fray. Tentacles of the "Ho Chi Minh Trail" crossed and recrossed each other throughout Laos and into the remote northeastern Cambodian provinces of Rattanakiri and Mondolkiri.

In 1969, without Congressional approval, the USA began a series of massive air strikes against Viet Cong and NVA (North Vietnamese Army) bases in Cambodia. Huge areas of the eastern part of Cambodia were carpet-bombed by B-52 bombers flying out of Thailand and Guam, devastating much of the country and driving the surviving Khmer peasantry to despair. They responded in one of three ways – massacring ethnic Vietnamese by way of "revenge"; flooding into an already bursting Phnom Penh; or joining the nascent Khmer Communist insurgency, dubbed by Sihanouk the "Khmer Rouge" (KR). Indeed, had not Kissinger's "sideshow" in Cambodia taken place it is doubtful whether the few hundred Khmer Communists hiding in remote Mondolkiri could have ever seized power.

As it was, a tragedy was played out. In March 1970, while on a visit to Beijing, Sihanouk was overthrown in a coup d'état by the Cambodian military headed by General Lon Nol, who was anti-Communist and hostile to the Vietnamese, and the coup was tacitly supported by the USA. Lon Nol then sent two military columns northwards into Communist territory. However, though grandiosely named Chen La 1 and Chen La 2, they were comprised mainly of ill-trained and poorly armed boys, who were cut to pieces by the insurgents.

Meanwhile, as territories under the control of the Lon Nol regime shrank, Sihanouk took up residence in Beijing and allied himself with his erstwhile Communist enemies, the Khmer Rouge. Embittered by its casualties and the failure of its strategy, the USA withdrew most of its combat troops from Vietnam by 1973, leaving the Army of the Republic of Vietnam (ARVN) to fight the NVA with just US intelligence help and occasional air power.

The Khmer Rouge

Cambodia remained a sideshow – but word had spread amongst correspondents based in Phnom Penh that the Khmer Rouge were strangely different from the Viet Cong, the NVA and the Communist Pathet Lao. While they fought just as well, they were said to be quite merciless, and to be emptying small cities and towns of people as they fell under their control. Moreover, they were increasingly hostile to their supposed Vietnamese "mentors" –

often openly hostile child-soldiers swarmed into the city.

Almost the first order broadcast by the new regime, which called itself Democratic Kampuchea (DK), was the expulsion of the entire population of Phnom Penh on the pretext that a bombing raid

> *General Lon Nol was something of an enigma to the Americans. A senior military source once said "the only thing we know about Lon Nol is that if you spell his name backwards it is still Lon Nol".*

by no means the puppet army of Hanoi that had been imagined by the USA.

The true nature of Cambodian Communism as interpreted by the Khmer Rouge leadership began to become clear on 17 April 1975, when Phnom Penh fell to the KR fully two weeks before the NVA rolled into Saigon. Most residents of the Cambodian capital were openly delighted the war was at last over, and were prepared to give the victorious Communist guerrillas a courteous if careful welcome. Instead they watched with mounting dismay as groups of sullen-faced,

ABOVE, FROM LEFT: Lon Nol leaves Phnom Penh; Lon Nol's troops at the southern front.

ROYAL ALLIES CAST ASIDE

After the Khmer Rouge took power the former king, Sihanouk – the KR's erstwhile ally – was flown back to Phnom Penh from Beijing, where he was held under de facto house arrest in the Royal Palace. He was then forcibly retired; a statue was to be built in his honour, and he was to receive a pension of US$8,000 a year, but neither of these ever materialised. During the Zero Years around 20 of Sihanouk's family were murdered by the Khmer Rouge, and it is more than likely that he too would have become a victim had it not been for direct appeals on his behalf from such Communist luminaries as Mao Tse-tung, Chou En-lai and Kim Il-sung.

was to be launched by the USAF. In fact, KR policy was the complete ruralisation of Cambodian society – all cities, towns and major villages were to be emptied, and the population sent to work in the fields. This policy was implemented with extraordinary ruthlessness – even patients in operating theatres were turned out onto the street to fend for themselves. Those who could not do so or who argued were shot or beaten to death. Meanwhile, a search was instituted for all members of the former Lon Nol army, who were marked for execution. A similar fate awaited all "intellectuals", from university professors and doctors to anybody who spoke a foreign language.

Meanwhile, KR's shadowy elite, who would control the fate of DK, installed themselves in some considerable comfort in the administrative centre of Phnom Penh. The core group included, besides Pol Pot and Ieng Sary, the former schoolteacher Khieu Samphan, Thai-educated Nuon Chea – who would emerge as "Brother No. 2", and Vorn Vet. Also of considerable importance were two sisters, Khieu Ponnary and Khieu Thirith, the former married to Pol Pot, the latter to Ieng Sary.

Once in power, the new elite began building a "new society" through what they called a "Super Great Leap to Socialism" – clearly designed to surpass China's disastrous "Great Leap Forward". Society at all levels was divided and then subdivided into different groups. The "Old People" – those who had lived under KR rule before the fall of Phnom Penh – were most favoured, while the former city-dwellers, or "New People", were without any rights at all. In between were "Depositees": potential supporters of the revolution. A chilling but common threat made against New People in DK was "destroying you is no loss; keeping you is no gain". Tens of thousands were either bludgeoned to death, forced to labour on massive construction sites or sent to develop "new frontiers" in the malarial Elephant and Cardamom mountains.

Frontiers were sealed. All religion was banned, the Buddhist supreme patriarch murdered, temples were turned into rice barns and mosques into pigsties. Pol Pot announced that feeding monks was a crime punishable by death, but his associate Nuon Chea kept one temple with four monks open for his pious old mother. Pol Pot and his immediate henchmen saw traitors

HARD LABOUR AND ABSTINENCE

The barbarism of the Killing Fields apart, other nightmare Khmer Rouge policies made people miserable throughout the country, and the regime was increasingly despised. After the introduction of compulsory collectivised eating, in 1976, even the once-favoured "Old People" began to turn against the KR – though nobody questioned the regime directly and survived.

Orders were given to the effect that rice production should be increased threefold, and people laboured long into the night. They returned home to eat a thin gruel of rice chaff and morning glory vines, followed by long sessions of political propaganda, before being allowed a few hours' sleep. Marriage was permitted only with the permission of *Angkar* (the Organisation), and extra-marital sex was punishable by death. Women were obliged to cut their hair short and wear identical black clothing.

Medical treatment was basic in the extreme because most doctors had been killed, and those who had not were obliged to hide their identities to survive. KR "hospitals" were generally dirty shacks where illiterate teenagers administered injections of coconut juice.

Schools were closed, money was banned and any form of trading was made illegal. Even "foraging" for food such as lizards and insects after work was made a capital offence, so the entire population was kept in a state of perpetual hunger.

and Vietnamese agents everywhere they looked, and even as mad instructions were given for the country to be turned into a precise chequerboard of identically shaped rice fields, the dreaded *santebal* or secret police began a witch-hunt for opponents of the regime, real or imagined.

The Killing Fields

The interrogation and torture centre known as S21 or Tuol Sleng, a special prison under the direction of a high KR official known as Duch, became the nerve centre of this operation. During 1975 and the first part of 1976 the majority of the victims of KR brutality were ordinary control – and thereby that of their master, Pol Pot – across the entire country. Communist cadres and party members arrested and taken to Tuol Sleng were forced, under the most barbarous tortures, to confess to ridiculous conspiracies. Old revolutionaries like Hu Nim and even Vorn Vet were beaten and electrocuted until they signed statements that they worked for the CIA, Vietnam, the KGB or an unlikely combination of all three. Most were then taken to the nearby Killing Fields of Choeung Ek just south of Phnom Penh and executed with axe-handles or hoes "to avoid wasting bullets".

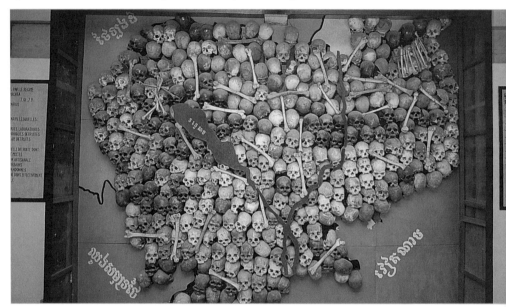

people, but as time passed so *Angkar* – the organisation – began to consume more and more of its own. Pol Pot particularly distrusted the khaki-clad troops of the Eastern Zone who had not been under his direct command during the civil war, denouncing them as "Khmer bodies with Vietnamese minds". In 1976–7 he unleashed his most loyal and most feared military commander, the one-legged General Ta Mok, against them.

Ta Mok and his dreaded *nirdei*, Southeast Zone soldiers, gradually extended their

ABOVE, FROM LEFT: King Sihanouk in Beijing; the "Map of Skulls" at Phnom Penh's Tuol Sleng Museum of Genocidal Crime was taken down in 2002 as it was deemed too disturbing

Attacks on Vietnam

It is now known that the DK regime systematically starved its population both as a method of political control and to raise rice exports to China and North Korea in exchange for armaments. But why did the KR need all this new weaponry? The war with Lon Nol and the USA was over and won, the people were incapable of rebellion, but by 1977 relations with Hanoi had reached an all-time low. Vietnam, the old enemy, was the new target.

Pol Pot openly announced his intention of recovering "Kampuchea Krom", or the Mekong Delta, from Vietnam (similar Khmer-speaking areas around Surin in northeastern Thailand would be recovered later). Vicious cross-border

Pol Pot

Born into a relatively prosperous family, the man who was to become one of the most reviled in history remains something of an enigma.

The Khmer Rouge leader Pol Pot, known to his followers as "Brother No. 1", was born in 1928 in the village of Prek Sbauv, near the provincial capital of Kompong Thom. He was the eighth of nine children of well-to-do farmers and was named Saloth

Sar. In common with most revolutionary Communist leaders, Saloth Sar was neither a peasant nor a proletarian; his family enjoyed close relations with the royal court in Phnom Penh.

In 1934 Saloth Sar was sent to live with his relatives at court. During this time he spent several months as a novice monk at Wat Bottum Vaddei, a monastery near the palace which was favoured by the royal family, and studied the Buddhist scriptures and Khmer language. Later he learnt French and studied at Russei Keo Technical College in Phnom Penh. Although not an outstanding student, he was chosen as one of a group sent for further education in Paris. Here he came into contact with Cambodian nationalists, including Ieng Sary, who would become one of his key associates.

In 1952, having returned to Cambodia without any qualifications but with a newly acquired and keen sense of nationalism, he joined the Indochinese Communist Party, which was dominated by the Vietnamese. Although secretly nurturing an intense hatred for all things Vietnamese, Saloth Sar rose steadily through the ranks and became General Secretary of the (still clandestine) Cambodian Communist Party in 1962.

Soon after that Saloth Sar and his close colleagues disappeared into the jungled hills of Rattanakiri province, where they began building the Communist guerrilla faction which King Sihanouk dubbed the "Khmer Rouge". During the subsequent years of civil war Saloth Sar used his increasingly powerful position to eliminate Hanoi-trained or pro-Vietnamese cadres – building, in essence, a movement which, though nominally internationalist, was deeply xenophobic, anti-urban and, above all, hostile to Vietnam.

In 1975 – Year Zero – the Khmer Rouge seized power and established the Democratic Kampuchea regime, but still Saloth Sar, now hiding behind the pseudonym "Pol Pot", remained out of the limelight. Between 1975 and his overthrow in 1979 he gradually eliminated all those whom he saw as a potential threat to his personal power – not to mention more than 2 million ordinary Cambodians who were murdered, worked to death or died of starvation.

Back to the jungle

Overthrown by the Vietnamese in 1979, Pol Pot and his followers took to the jungles where, for almost 20 years, their numbers dwindled through desertion, disease and military attrition. Pol Pot was eventually arrested by his few remaining comrades, and either died or was killed near Anlong Veng in 1998. In retrospect it is difficult to see what inner demons drove Saloth Sar to develop into the paranoid political monster Pol Pot. Certainly his elder brother, Loth Suong, who survived the Zero Years, was unable to explain it, commenting with obvious bewilderment that Pol Pot was "a lovely child".

Pol Pot never lived to face justice through the courts, nor did his chief military commander Ta Mok, who died in prison in Phnom Penh in 2006. However, a handful of the now-aged Khmer Rouge leadership, including Brother No. 2 Nuon Chea, Ieng Sary, Khieu Samphan and Duch, survived to go on trial before a UN-backed Genocide Tribunal which began proceedings in February 2009 and continues today.

LEFT: Pol Pot, a "lovely child" who was to become a monster.

attacks resulting in brutal rapes and massacres were launched around the Parrot's Beak area of Vietnam. Vietnam responded by launching warning counterattacks across the border, sometimes pushing 30km (20 miles) into Cambodia before withdrawing. The once-formidable KR soldiers offered weak opposition to the Vietnamese. Many of them were purged and demoralised, sick of killing their own people and far from loyal to the regime in Phnom Penh.

As the Vietnamese withdrew, so thousands of Khmers fled with them, taking refuge across the frontier in Vietnam. Among those who deserted at this time was a young Khmer Rouge commander called Hun Sen. Subsequently, in collaboration with the Vietnamese, he began to build a Cambodian liberation army with the aim of overthrowing Pol Pot and establishing a regime friendly to Vietnam in Phnom Penh.

The end of the Khmer Rouge

By the end of 1978 Khmer Rouge provocations had driven the Vietnamese to the brink of open warfare, and Hanoi took a decision to seize the eastern part of Cambodia as far as the Mekong River to create a *cordon sanitaire* (quarantine line) between its territory and the Democratic Kampuchea regime. This was not an easy decision to make, as Vietnam was war-weary and the leadership in Hanoi fully appreciated that such an attack would infuriate Cambodia's powerful ally China.

Vietnamese troops moved suddenly across the frontier on 25 December 1978. The Khmer Rouge put up little resistance, and the Vietnamese decided not just to occupy the eastern part of the country, but to seize Phnom Penh and overthrow the regime entirely. The discredited Khmer Rouge leadership fled in disarray to the Thai frontier, and a pro-Vietnamese administration, the People's Republic of Kampuchea, was set up in Phnom Penh on 8 January 1979.

Just one month later, on 17 February, China responded by invading Vietnam to "teach the Vietnamese a lesson". China's plan was to force Vietnam to withdraw its troops from Cambodia and send them instead to the Chinese frontier, but in the event this failed as the Vietnamese

held the Chinese in the north with locally based troops and militia, holding back their main force for defending Hanoi, and declining to withdraw any troops from Cambodia. The Chinese invasion of Vietnam was immensely costly and destructive to the Vietnamese, but China withdrew its forces in March 1979, without breaking Vietnam's will and without achieving any of its strategic targets.

There followed a decade of guerrilla warfare in Cambodia as Vietnam and its Cambodian allies in Phnom Penh fought a debilitating struggle against Khmer Rouge remnants – these guerrilla remnants backed by an unlikely col-

lection of international forces. This period is characterised by particularly cynical realpolitik in which Vietnam was condemned for occupying Cambodia even though just about everyone – China excluded – recognised that Vietnam had in fact done Cambodia a considerable service in overthrowing the Pol Pot regime.

Unfortunately for Vietnam, the continuing war in Cambodia was less about destroying the Khmer Rouge guerrillas than about bringing down the Soviet Union and ending the Cold War. A decision was taken by the UK and US governments of Mrs Thatcher and Ronald Reagan to bleed the Soviet regime economically by backing the Khmer Rouge. They were enthusiastically supported in this endeavour

RIGHT: Tuol Sleng torture cell, in what was formerly a high-school building.

both by China, at this time bitterly anti-Soviet, and by Thailand, which stood to profit from the resupplying of the Khmer Rouge guerrillas.

Despite the shocking evidence of Khmer Rouge brutality that was exposed by the Vietnamese invasion, "Democratic Kampuchea" retained its seat at the United Nations and was regularly supported by the United States, the United Kingdom and other Western governments, as well as by China. The Khmer Rouge fighting inside Cambodia were armed and financed by China, while – astonishingly – the British government went so far as to provide covert military training to Khmer Rouge forces.

faced with imminent bankruptcy, began to disintegrate. By 1991 the Soviet Union had ceased to exist, and Vietnam had lost its main ally and chief military and financial backer.

In fact, the writing had been on the wall since the death of Le Duan in 1986, and Vietnam had already begun to wind down its operations in Cambodia. Meanwhile the implosion of the Soviet Union and the approaching end of the Cold War meant that Western backing for the Khmer Rouge guerrillas was no longer politically necessary for the West, though China would continue to back its Khmer Rouge protégés well into the 1990s. After a decade of fight-

Cynical though this strategy was, it worked all too well. The Soviet Union, already fighting a losing battle in Afghanistan which it occupied between 1979 and 1989, was rapidly running out of money and could not afford to lavish unlimited military supplies on its Vietnamese allies. Meanwhile Vietnam, under the austere and doctrinaire government of Le Duan, was also on the verge of economic collapse and starvation.

By the late 1980s it was clear to Hanoi that it would have to reach a compromise over Cambodia and withdraw its troops. In 1986 Le Duan died and was replaced by the more flexible Nguyen Van Linh. In 1989 the USSR withdrew its last forces from Afghanistan and,

ing, it was now possible for a compromise to be reached in Cambodia, while Vietnam – now embarked on a series of economic reforms collectively known as *doi moi* or "renovation" – was desperately anxious to exit the Cambodian quagmire and avoid the fate of its erstwhile Soviet ally.

Crimes against humanity

In September 1989 Vietnam finally withdrew its forces from Cambodia, handing over control to the United Nations Transitional Authority in

ABOVE: Vietnamese troops arriving in Ho Chi Minh City, Vietnam, after withdrawal from Cambodia, 28 September 1989.

Cambodia (UNTAC). In May 1993, following UN-organised elections, Cambodia officially became a constitutional monarchy with King Sihanouk as head of state. The KR opted out of the elections, however, and this led to five more years of intermittent warfare during which the KR was gradually worn down. The KR leader, Pol Pot, died in 1998, while the last KR diehard, military leader Ta Mok, was captured near Anlong Veng in the north of Cambodia and taken to trial in Phnom Penh in early 1999. As a consequence, the power of the once greatly feared KR was broken for ever.

In 1999, Cambodia finally became a member

approval. Even so, political infighting and fear of just what such a trial might expose delayed the legal process until 2009, when Kaeng Kek Iew, better known as Duch, the former commandant of S21 interrogation centre, became the first KR leader to go on trial. He was convicted of genocide and crimes against humanity in 2011 and sentenced to life imprisonment. The trial of other senior KR leaders, all now in their dotage, continues. The most important defendants, former Brother No 2 Nuon Chea and Brother No 4 Ieng Sary, are quite likely to die of old age before a verdict can be reached. Meanwhile

of the Association of Southeast Asian Nations (ASEAN). Five years later, Sihanouk abdicated from the throne due to ill health. His second son, Norodom Sihamoni, was elected by a hastily assembled nine-member Throne Council to succeed him as king. Sihanouk retains the position of "King-Father" and spends much of his time in Beijing, returning to Cambodia for brief periods on an annual basis. Both he and his wife, Princess Monique, retain considerable affection in Cambodia, and their pictures are generally displayed with those of King Sihamoni in public buildings and many private houses across the country.

Then, in 2005, a war-crimes tribunal to try surviving KR leaders finally received UN

the only Cambodian woman indicted for Crimes Against Humanity, Ieng Thirith – the wife of Ieng Sary – has developed Alzheimer's Disease and is likely to be judged unfit to continue standing trial. Meanwhile Hun Sen remains in undisputed power, ruling with a very firm hand amid suggestions and accusations of corruption.

Nevertheless, in today's Cambodia personal freedoms are greater, the press is more independent and there is more evidence of increasing prosperity now than at any time in the past 50 years. After their experience of unparalleled suffering in the preceding quarter-century, most Cambodians remain relatively satisfied with the current order.

POPULATION, SOCIETY AND ECONOMY

Ethnic Khmers dominate, but Cambodia is also
home to a significant number of minority
groups. All have benefited from a strong
recovery of the economy.

Ethnic Khmer, Cambodia's predominant indigenous people, make up more than 90 percent of the country's 15 million population. The Khmers are a predominantly agricultural people, subsisting on a diet of rice and fish, and living in wooden stilted houses in villages of several hundred people.

Khmers tend to think of themselves as a single people, the dominant ethnic group of Cambodia, the founders of the Khmer Empire and builders of Angkor Wat. This is by and large correct, but it is also something of a simplification, constructed on a nationalist desire to emphasise Khmer unity in the face of external challenges, particularly from Vietnam. Certainly the Khmer can be considered a single entity, but they may also be further subdivided into Cambodian Khmer, the Khmer Krom or "Lower Khmer" of "Lower Cambodia" – that is, the Mekong Delta which now forms part of Vietnam, and the Khon Suay or Surin Khmers of Thailand, especially in

A citizen of Cambodia is generally referred to as a "Cambodian" regardless of ethnicity or linguistic background. This includes ethnic Vietnamese, Chinese or Thai immigrants. To be a Khmer, however, is something else again.

Sisaket, Surin and Buriram provinces, all former outliers of the Cambodian Empire which are now part of Thailand.

PRECEDING PAGES: children from a Vietnamese floating village near Phnom Penh head for school.
LEFT: Khmer man from a village near Kompong Cham.
RIGHT: woman wearing a *krama*.

The Khmers are among the longest-established of settled agricultural peoples in Southeast Asia, all speaking variants or dialects of the same Khmer language, which is a part of the larger Mon-Khmer linguistic group that includes Vietnamese and extends from the Kasi in eastern India, through the Nicobar Islands in the southern Bay of Bengal and the Mon in Burma, to the Senoi in Malaysia and the Bugan in China. It is one of the oldest language groups in Southeast Asia, linked by linguistic specialists with the larger Austroasiatic family, and it predates both Sino-Tai and Sino-Tibetan languages (such as Burmese) in the region.

Despite – indeed because of – the early migration of Khmer-speaking people into mainland Southeast Asia, little is known of the precise origins of the Khmers. It is thought that they arrived at least 3,000 years ago, probably from the north, at about the same time as ethnic Malays were migrating south from Taiwan to the Malay-Indonesian Archipelago. Why the Khmers migrated south remains unclear – it is possible that they may have been pushed south by expanding waves of Sino-Tibetan and Sino-Tai peoples, themselves under pressure from the expanding Han Chinese population to the north. The Khmer are related to the nearby Mon people of lower Burma and west-central Thailand who established the Mon Kingdom of Dvaravati which flourished between approximately AD 600 and 1100.

In recent decades, as elsewhere in the developing world, there has been a marked degree of urbanisation as Khmers move to cities such as Phnom Penh, Battambang, Sihanoukville (Kompong Som) and Kompong Cham. They remain the dominant political and cultural force of the Cambodian population, although their economic influence is far less, on a per capita basis, than that of the ethnic Chinese and Vietnamese. Most Khmers are Theravada Buddhists, although Christianity made a small number of converts during the 20th century.

THE KINGDOM OF CHAMPA

The earliest records of the Kingdom of Champa are Chinese, dating from AD 192. In these the Chams are described as having "dark skin, deep-set eyes, turned-up noses and frizzy hair", characteristics which are often still recognisable in the modern descendants of the Chams. The annals record that the Chams dressed, like the Malays, "in a single piece of cotton or silk wrapped about the body. They wear their hair in a bun on the top of their head, and they pierce their ears in order to wear small metal rings. They are very clean. They wash themselves several times each day, wear perfume, and rub their bodies with a lotion made of camphor and musk."

The Vietnamese

The largest national minority in Cambodia is the Viet Kieu or migrant Vietnamese, generally known in Cambodian as Youn. Because traditionally little love has been lost between Khmer and Viet, there is a tendency on the part of the Cambodian authorities to underestimate the number of Vietnamese in the country. According to figures published by the Cambodian government in 2003, there were just 100,000 Vietnamese residents, but independent estimates suggest there are now between 1.5 and 2.5 million. They tend to live in the big cities, where they work as restaurateurs or in other small businesses, or make a living as fishermen along the Mekong and Sap

Unusually, the Cambodian Chams are called to prayer by drum beats as well as the azaan – the call of the muezzin to the faithful – so familiar in Muslim lands.

rivers. Ethnic Vietnamese also make a disproportionately large contribution to Cambodia's sex industry.

Relations between Cambodia's dominant Khmer population and the Cambodian Vietnamese go back hundreds of years but have rarely been good. To compound the settlement

Cambodian nationals. Under the Lon Nol regime, between 1969 and 1975, anti-Vietnamese pogroms killed thousands and caused perhaps 150,000 to flee to the relative security of Vietnam. Under the Khmer Rouge all Vietnamese were seen as foreign agents and killed or expelled.

Today the ethnic Vietnamese remain the most vulnerable of Cambodia's ethnic minorities. Khmer hostility and suspicion remains visceral, and while Khmers will intermarry readily with Chinese, intermarriage with Viets remains rare. Cambodian state schools provide no instruction in Vietnamese, and current

and eventual seizure of former Cambodian territory in southern Vietnam – still called "Lower Cambodia" by the Khmers – the French imported large numbers of ethnic Vietnamese to work on the rubber plantations and to staff the Franco-Cambodian bureaucracy. This inevitably engendered jealousy and added to old antipathies.

After independence the unilateral military actions of both North Vietnam and South Vietnam compounded this issue. During the Sihanouk era the Cambodian Vietnamese were regarded as foreign residents and not

ABOVE, FROM LEFT: Street-food vendor, Phnom Penh; New Year celebrations.

Cambodian citizenship laws effectively deny rights of citizenship to ethnic Vietnamese. To make matters worse, ethnic Vietnamese are readily identifiable, especially in rural areas, by their trademark mollusc hats or non la. Even today they are at risk of violent attack, especially at election times. It remains difficult to see the situation improving in the foreseeable future.

The Cham

A second distinctive minority in Cambodian society is the Cham Muslims, one of the oldest, but nowadays least considered, peoples of Indochina. There are some 400,000–500,000 Chams in Cambodia, despite their having been particularly targeted for extermination by the Khmer Rouge in the 1970s. Gifted silversmiths, they also make a living by fishing and by butchering animals for their more fastidious Buddhist neighbours.

Chams are inheritors of a proud tradition that stretches back some 2,000 years: Champa was the first Indianised kingdom in Indochina, its founding predating both Chen La (6th century AD) and the first major expansion of the Vietnamese south from Tonkin (mid-10th century). At the peak of their power, about 12 centuries ago, the Chams controlled rich and fertile lands stretching from north of Hue, in central

Annam, to the Mekong Delta in Cochin China; yet today Vietnamese cities like Nha Trang and Da Nang dominate these regions. Only mysterious brick temples, known as "Cham towers", dot the skyline around Thap Cham and Po Nagar, while in Cambodia the name of an eastern province and its capital, Kompong Cham, remain as testimony to the lost kingdom.

The Chams are an Austronesian people, more closely linked, in ethnic terms, with the islands of the Malay-Indonesian world and the Philippines than with the mainland. We can only surmise that at some distant time they migrated from the Indonesian archipelago and settled in what is now southern Vietnam, and what we know of early Cham society seems to bear this out. Unlike their Viet and Khmer neighbours, whose society is based on intensive rice cultivation, the Chams had little time for agriculture. Their prosperity was based on maritime trade – and more than likely on a certain amount of piracy.

In 1471 the Chams suffered a terrible defeat at the hands of the Vietnamese. Champa was reduced to a thin sliver of territory in the region of Nha Trang, which survived until 1820, when the king and many subjects fled to Cambodia rather than submit to the Vietnamese. The Cham diaspora dates from this period, and the diverse Cham communities later established in Cambodia, Thailand and Laos trace their common origin to this event.

Most Chams moved up the Mekong, into territories that now constitute the Cambodian heartland. They settled along the banks of the great river north and east of Phnom Penh,

THE KRAMA, CAMBODIA'S TRADITIONAL CHEQUERED SCARF

Perhaps no garment is as distinctively Khmer as the Cambodian *krama*. Worn by men, women and children of just about every social class across the country, it is unique to Cambodia and to the sizeable ethnic Khmer communities in neighbouring northeast Thailand and southern Vietnam. It's not clear why the *krama* should be so uniquely Cambodian, though it has been speculated that it may be a link with the country's ancient Indic past, since turbans are more generally associated with South Asia than with Southeast Asia. Not that the *krama* is simply a turban – it has many more uses.

Generally chequered, and made of cotton or silk, *krama* are more than not brightly coloured in red and white, blue and white or black and white, though more expensive silk ones may be multicoloured and interwoven with gold thread. They are worn wrapped around the head to provide protection from wind, rains and especially Cambodia's blistering summer heat. They may also be wound around the shoulder or waist. Besides functioning as protection against the weather, they are used for carrying fruit, vegetables and even small children, as well as substituting for pillows, shopping bags and even sarongs. They make excellent towels for the face, and provide modesty when bathing in a stream or pond. And of course, for you the visitor, they make cheap, attractive and unusual souvenirs.

notably in the province and town of Kompong Cham, but also along the shores of the Tonlé Sap, Cambodia's great lake. Here they became well known and relatively prosperous through their skills as fishermen, settling into the ebb and flow of Cambodian life, and acquiring a widespread reputation for their abilities as practitioners of traditional medicine. During the 18th and 19th centuries Sunni Islam spread widely among the Cambodian Chams, while their fellows in Vietnam remained only partly Islamicised.

In 1975, when the Khmer Rouge seized power, nearly 400,000 Chams were living

rulers for centuries, were spared the worst of the Khmer Rouge excesses.

The one major exception to this policy was the Cham community, which was picked out for especially harsh treatment, probably because its members spoke a private community language unintelligible to the Khmer Rouge, read Arabic, wore distinctive clothing and followed an "alien" religion. Whatever the logic behind the decision, after the Khmer Rouge seizure of power in April 1975, anti-Cham policies were ruthlessly implemented.

During the ensuing three and a half years of terror, Cambodia's Chams were

peacefully along the Mekong north and east of Phnom Penh. They followed the faith of their fathers in over 100 mosques, caught fish, grew rice and tried to stay neutral in the war which was destroying Cambodia. Even before Pol Pot's seizure of power in 1975 the Khmer Rouge had begun implementing special policies towards Cambodia's various minority peoples. "Recent migrants" such as the ethnic Vietnamese, Chinese and Thai were marked for expulsion or death. By contrast, indigenous minorities, although mistreated by Cambodian

ABOVE, FROM LEFT: woman wearing a *krama* reproduced on an old 500 riel note; removing wheat husks.

AN INSPIRATIONAL PEOPLE

According to the historian David Chandler, after the Khmer Rouge victory of 17 April 1975 Pol Pot claimed to have derived revolutionary inspiration from the Khmer Loeu upland hill tribes – "people who had no private property, no markets and no money. Their way of life corresponded to the primitive communist phase of social evolution in Marxist thinking." In 1971, after eight years in the jungle, the KR ideologue Ieng Sary commented that the movement's tribal followers "may be naked, but they have never been colonised". At a lecture in Phnom Penh in 1976, he characterised the tribespeople as "faithful to the revolution... and possessing class hatred".

systematically victimised. All mosques – traditionally the spiritual and social centres of Cham community life – were either demolished or turned over to secular purposes for use as ammunition stores and Khmer Rouge barracks. Like their Khmer compatriots, only proportionately in much higher numbers, tens of thousands of Chams were murdered by the Khmer Rouge. By the time Vietnamese armed forces swept across the frontier in December 1978, between a half and two-thirds of the Cham community had been murdered, starved to death or driven out of the country.

The ethnic Chinese

Most of Cambodia's Hua Chiao, or Overseas Chinese, trace their origins to the southern coastal provinces of Hainan, Guangdong and Fujian. Authorities suggest that as many as 60 percent of Cambodia's ethnic Chinese belong to the Guangdong Teochiu group, followed by 20 percent "Cantonese" from Guangdong, 7 percent Hokkien, 4 percent Hakka from Fujian and 4 percent Hailam from Hainan Island. Estimates of their overall numbers vary from 500,000 to 1,200,000. In recent years a new wave of Chinese migration to Cambodia has got under way, and the presence of both Taiwanese and Malaysian Chinese in business circles is marked. The Chinese are almost exclusively urban, and, since they intermarry readily with urban Khmers, are not Muslim

> *The Khmer Krom or "Lower Khmer" are essentially the ethnic Khmer inhabitants of the Mekong Delta who were left residing in the area after the Vietnamese conquest in the 18th and 19th centuries.*

like the Chams, and are not disliked and feared like the Vietnamese, Chinese ethnicity is more readily subsumed within Khmer society. It is also interesting to note that fully 80 percent of the top Khmer Rouge leadership, including Pol Pot and Nuon Chea, were Sino-Khmers. Intermarriage between Khmers and Chinese is common and widespread, especially in urban areas. In this case, the Chinese

BORDER DISPUTES WITH THAILAND

Traditionally, Cambodians regard both their Vietnamese neighbours to the east and their Thai neighbours to the west with suspicion and even hostility. Despite their partially shared Mon-Khmer linguistic routes, the ethnic Khmer particularly distrust the Vietnamese, who they accuse of detaching and absorbing "Kampuchea Krom" – that is, "Lower Cambodia", or the area now comprising Saigon and the Mekong Delta. Relations with neighbouring Thailand are better than with Vietnam, but still far from good. As far as Khmer nationalists are concerned, Thailand occupies three northern Khmer provinces, identified with Sisaket, Surin and Buriram. More significantly, Cambodians as a whole dislike Thailand's

sometime claims to Angkor Wat, spiritual heart of the Cambodian nation, and remain mindful that the Thais occupied western Cambodia, including Angkor Wat, Siem Reap and Battambang, by force during World War II. Another bone of contention is the status of Preah Vihear (see page 300), the Khmer temple on the very fringes of Thailand's northeastern plateau. Awarded to Cambodia by the International Court of Justice in 1962, this decision was only grudgingly accepted by Thailand, and tensions in the area remain strong. The most recent flare-up came as recently as 2011, when several soldiers from either side were killed and the temple was closed for a while to general access.

often assimilate into Khmer society over two or three generations, though few if any forget their Chinese ancestry.

The Khmer Loeu

Other minorities include the Khmer Loeu or Upland Khmer – hill tribes of Mondolkiri and Rattanakiri, such as the Kuy, Mnong, Brao, Tapuon and Jarai, as well as th e Pear and Saoch of the southwest. Strangely, several of these groups fared comparatively well under the Khmer Rouge – ruthless in their treatment of "outsider" minorities – because they were seen as "pure", unpolluted by capitalism and an

KR's largely urban leadership for their knowledge of the jungle, survival skills and prowess as hunters. They were also "poor and blank": in Maoist terms, ideal vessels for indoctrination. Finally, they are said to have shown great obedience to authority.

Because of this belief in "the noble savage", and in sharp contrast to the KR treatment of national minorities such as the Vietnamese, who were systematically persecuted and subjected to policies amounting to genocide, the Khmer Loeu were generally well treated and absorbed, wherever possible, into the ranks of the revolution.

urban environment, even models of primitive communism (see panel). Collectively they probably number around 500,000.

In 1968, shortly after the Khmer Rouge took the decision to embark on an armed struggle, its leadership began operations in regions inhabited by non-Khmer upland minorities such as the Brao, the Tapuon and the Jarai. These people, traditionally looked down on by the Khmer and known by the derogatory term *phnong*, "savages", were of great interest to the

ABOVE, FROM LEFT: miniature banana-leaf boats sail on the Mekong River during the New Year celebrations; preparing fruit for sale in a Phnom Penh market.

Even before the KR seizure of power in 1975, many upland tribal people already served the KR leadership as special cadres, messengers and bodyguards.

Some indication of the position of trust attained by these tribal minorities – and of the culture shock caused to ordinary Khmers on seeing people they traditionally perceived as "savages" bearing AK47s in the midst of the victorious Communist forces – can be gleaned from contemporary accounts of the KR seizure of power. Peang Sophi, a factory worker in Battambang, recalls that the peasant soldiers who occupied his city were "real country people, from very far away. Many of them had never seen a city or printed words. They held Cambodian texts upside down, pretending to puzzle them out." Still more telling is an account by Dith Pran (who became widely known in the West through the film *The Killing Fields*), who comments on KR troops entering his village in Siem Reap: "They didn't even look like Cambodians; they seemed to be from the jungle, or a different world."

Other minorities

Three smaller groups who fared less well than the Khmer Loeu under the Khmer Rouge were the Thai, Lao and Shan. Faced with vicious discrimination in 1976–9, those Thais who

milk-producers. But they, too, fell foul of the Khmer Rouge – simply because of their ethnicity – and those not lucky enough to flee the country were killed en masse.

Economy and industry

The Cambodian economy was virtually destroyed twice in recent decades, first when the Khmer Rouge entered Phnom Penh in 1975, and again with the 1989 withdrawal of the Vietnamese and the collapse of the Soviet Union, a major source of aid. Today, with Phnom Penh's move away from Communist ideology to market economics, the situation

were not killed fled to neighbouring Thailand. Surviving Lao also fled in droves. The Shan – a few thousand were long-term residents of Pailin, where they worked as gem miners – were even less fortunate, and seem to have been wiped out entirely.

Finally, mention should be made of the South Asians, a few hundred of whom live in the larger cities like Phnom Penh and Battambang, working chiefly as small businessmen and traders. In the late 1960s several thousand South Asians, mainly identified as "Pakistanis" because of their Sindhi or Pathan origins, lived in the countryside around Battambang, Poipet and Siem Reap, where they specialised as cattle-breeders and

has improved, but the long-term development of the economy still remains a huge challenge, and prospects are not helped by the fact that corruption is so well entrenched. Cambodia became a member of ASEAN in 1999, and opened itself up to global markets in 2005 when it joined the WTO.

By far the largest sources of foreign revenue are wood exports and foreign aid, neither of which is sustainable in the long term. Another significant area of revenue, also of dubious long-term soundness, derives from the shipment of gold and cigarettes from other Asian countries to Vietnam, where tariffs are significantly higher. Other than timber and gemstones, also a source of income, Cambodia has few natural resources. Rubber used to be a major export, with the Soviet Union purchasing almost the entire annual production, but has become less important in recent years. The garment industry, however, is robust and continues to expand.

Various proposals have been made, mainly for the establishment of hydroelectric facilities. So far nothing has come of these proposals, but they have brought to light the serious risks to Cambodia posed by similar projects upstream in Laos and China. As Cambodia is so dependent on the annual rise in the waters of the Mekong and Tonlé Sap and the fertile deposits

For thirty years, Cambodia's brutal Khmer Rouge past was known to its younger citizens through word of mouth only. Pol Pot and Democratic Kampuchea were not included in the Cambodian school curriculum until 2009.

20 years or younger. Cambodia is attracting increased Foreign Direct Investment (FDI) – mainly Chinese, Taiwanese, Vietnamese, Thai and Malaysian – in the services sector. With the tourist industry growing stronger by the year (foreign arrivals rose from 2 million in

this brings, any change in the flow of the river could potentially have disastrous effects on agriculture. The possibility of a decline in numbers and species of fish in the lake and river is also of concern.

The Cambodian government continues to work with bilateral and multilateral donors, including the World Bank and IMF, to resolve the country's many pressing needs. The major challenge in the short to medium term is to adapt the economic environment to the country's demographic imbalance – more than 50 percent of the population is

ABOVE, FROM LEFT: en route to market; garment factory workers get a lift to work.

2007 to 3 million in 2011, and a targeted 5 million in 2015), there is potential for major expansion. This unprecedented growth has made tourism the nation's second-largest source of foreign exchange after textiles, and has transformed Siem Reap from a sleepy village 15 years ago to a fast-expanding tourism metropolis.

As in neighbouring Laos, new investment in education, basic infrastructure and telecommunications is making Cambodia increasingly attractive to foreign investors.

For the foreseeable future, tourism may be Cambodia's greatest chance of securing sustainable foreign exchange, with Angkor being one of the travel world's most marketable assets.

CULTURE, ART AND ARCHITECTURE

Despite attempts by the Khmer Rouge
regime to destroy many of the traditional
arts, Cambodian culture has managed
to survive in all its forms.

Defining the "cultural arts of Cambodia" is no simple matter. The main problem is deciding just where the "Cambodian" element starts and ends. To begin with, Khmer culture – together with that of the Mon and the Chams – is about the earliest known indigenous high culture in the region, yet even in the distant days of Chen La and early Angkor it drew heavily on Indian cultural, religious and artistic influences – so heavily, indeed, that Cambodian culture is generally defined as "Indic". The Khmers in turn went on to influence their neighbours, particularly the Lao and the Thais. Thai writing, for example, is derived from Khmer, as is much of Thai court language.

But who gave what to whom? Indicisation may have started with the Khmer Empire, but at times of Cambodian weakness and Siamese strength the flow was often reversed. An interesting if little-known example of this, through the unlikely medium of French colonialism, was the re-establishment of traditional court dance in the royal palace at Phnom Penh in the early 20th century. Standards had fallen so far in Phnom Penh that the French invited classical dance masters from the court of Bangkok to reinvigorate the tradition in Cambodia. Thus it is difficult to draw clear dividing lines between the Indic cultures of Southeast Asia. Much of what is Cambodian is also, with minor variations, Thai or Lao or, at one remove, Burmese or even Javanese.

The Ramayana

Perhaps the paramount example of this is the great Hindu epic, the *Ramayana*, which has

LEFT: dance school, Phnom Penh. RIGHT: Khmer sculpture, Wat Nokor, Kampong Cham.

influenced both Cambodian and Lao culture (music, dance, literature, painting) to a considerable extent. Known as *Reamker* in Khmer, it is a story as old as time and – at least in the Indian subcontinent and across much of Southeast Asia – of unparalleled popularity. More than 2,300 years ago, at about the same time as Alexander the Great invaded northwestern India, in another, less troubled part of that vast country the scholar-poet Valmiki sat down to write his definitive epic of love and war.

The poem Valmiki composed is in Sanskrit; its title means "Romance of Rama". The shorter of India's two great epic poems – the other being the *Mahabharata*, or "Great Epic of the Bharata Dynasty" – the *Ramayana* is, nevertheless, of considerable length. In its present form the Sanskrit version consists of some 24,000 couplets divided into seven books. It's astonishing, then, to think that people have memorised the entire work, and that since its initial composition it has enjoyed continual passionate recitation somewhere in Asia. Today it remains as vital as ever, though television, film and radio have brought it to a wider audience than Valmiki could ever have imagined – and its appeal continues to grow.

The story it tells, considered by scholars as more of a romance than an epic, begins with the birth of Prince Rama in the Kingdom of Ayodhya in northern India. Rama's youth is spent in the royal palace, under the tutelage of the sage Vishvamitra, from whom he learns patience, wisdom and insight, the qualities for a just and perfect king.

As a young man Rama wins the contest for the hand of Sita, the beautiful daughter of King Janaka. The couple marry, and for some time all is well – but then Rama falls victim to intrigue at the royal court, loses his position as heir, and withdraws to the forest for 14 years. Sita accompanies Rama into exile, as does his half-brother, the loyal Lakshmana.

Word of Rama's exile then reaches Ravana, demon-king of the island of Lanka. Ravana lusts after Sita and, having sent a magical golden deer

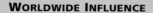

WORLDWIDE INFLUENCE

The *Ramayana* quickly became popular in India, where its recitation is considered an act of great merit. It was translated from the original Sanskrit into numerous vernacular versions, often works of great literary merit themselves, including the Tamil version *Kampan*, the Bengali *Krttibas* and the popular Hindi version, the *Ramcaritmanas* of Tulsidas. Other celebrations of the poem which continue to flourish in India today include the annual Ram-Lila pageant of northern India, and the Kathkali dance-drama of Kerala. So powerful was the *Ramayana* that it soon spread throughout the Hindu-Buddhist world, including Laos and Cambodia.

to lead Rama and Lakshmana off hunting, he seizes Sita and takes her to his palace in Lanka. Sita resists all his advances, while Rama and Lakshmana, realising they have been tricked, organise her rescue. Enlisting the help of the noble monkey-god Hanuman, among others, to invade Lanka and defeat Ravana and his devilish cohorts, Rama eventually manages to rescue Sita.

At this point in the story a darker side of Rama becomes apparent, as he accuses Sita of infidelity and requires her to undergo an ordeal by fire to prove her innocence. Rama seems satisfied, but on returning to Ayodhya he learns that the people still question Sita's virtue, and he banishes her to the forest. In exile, Sita meets the sage Valmiki and at his hermitage gives birth to Rama's two sons. The family is reunited when the sons come of age, but Sita, once again protesting her innocence, asks to be received by the earth, which swallows her up.

The impact of the *Ramayana* on Lao and Cambodian culture can scarcely be overstated. The love of Rama for Sita, the loyalty of Lakshmana and the heroism of Hanuman have left an indelible mark on many aspects of traditional drama, literature and dance.

The Phnom Penh murals

In 1831 King Rama III of Siam ordered master-painters to begin the great task of painting his inspiration directly from the Chakri royal complex in Bangkok.

Some 30 years later, following the completion of the Silver Pagoda at the Royal Palace in Phnom Penh, a decision was taken to tell the story of the *Ramayana* in murals along the

> A burgeoning contemporary art scene is now developing, especially in Phnom Penh and at Siem Reap. A number of younger artists have combined traditional Khmer art with Western modernism, creating an array of styles.

the *Ramayana* in murals at Wat Phra Kaew in Bangkok. Over several years the story of Rama, Sita, Ravana and Hanuman unfolded over hundreds of square metres of cloister wall, shaded from the sun by long roofs of orange tiles. At the time relations between the royal courts of Bangkok and Phnom Penh were close, and the *Ramayana* – in Thai, *Ramakien* – murals came to the notice of visiting Cambodian nobles. In 1866 Cambodia's King Norodom began building a new royal palace in Phnom Penh, using French and Cambodian architects but drawing much of

ABOVE, FROM LEFT: sections of a Ramayana mural in the Silver Pagoda, Phnom Penh.

inner face of the wall surrounding the complex. The resulting mural, which was not completed until the reign of King Sisowath, is protected by cloister-like arcades, and has been restored on a number of occasions.

King Norodom's decision to order the painting of the murals, together with the style and technique, was clearly influenced by the *Ramakien* murals at Bangkok, yet they have a charm and distinction which are their own, and in some sections are better preserved than their Bangkok counterparts.

Dance

The beauty and elegance of the Cambodian Royal Ballet has to be seen to be believed.

The writer Somerset Maugham was fortunate enough to witness a performance at Angkor in the 1920s, and enthused: "The beauty of these dances against the dark mystery of the temple made it the most beautiful and unearthly sight imaginable. It was certainly more than worthwhile to have travelled thousands of miles for this." The dancers had an even greater impact on Auguste Rodin, who exclaimed on seeing a performance in Paris in 1906: "These Cambodian women have given us everything antiquity could hold. It's impossible to see human nature reaching such perfection. There is only this and the Greeks."

As with other art forms, the ballet suffered badly in the terror of the Khmer Rouge period. Under Pol Pot – who had relatives in the Royal Ballet and spent some time with them in his youth – an attempt was made to destroy the ballet. Instruments were smashed, costumes and books burnt, while musicians and dancers were systematically killed.

Fortunately one or two dancers survived, among them Princess Bupphadevi, a favourite daughter of King Sihanouk, who was in exile in France. Today there are several *apsara* (celestial dancer) dance centres spreading the skills of Cambodian Royal Ballet, most notably at the Choreographic Arts Faculty at the Royal University of Fine Arts in Phnom Penh.

Performances are regularly given at other locations (see page 354).

Classical Khmer dance *(lamthon)* as performed by the Royal Ballet bears a striking resemblance to that of the Thai royal court, and indeed the two traditions influenced each other in turn and have now become practically a shared art form. Training takes many years, and elaborate costumes and headdresses are worn. It is a real spectacle that should not be missed. Cambodian masked theatre, known as *khaul*, is very similar to the Thai *khon*. Classical dances depicting incidents from the Buddha life-cycle stories, the *Jataka*, are often performed.

Music

Music has long flourished in Cambodia in both court and village settings, some kinds associated with specific functions, others with entertainment. In villages weddings are celebrated

> In the 1950s and 60s Cambodia was home to a lively local film scene. King Sihanouk was a rather self-indulgent movie fan and in the 1960s began making films which he wrote, directed and often starred in.

with *kar* music, communication with spirits is accompanied by *arakk* music, and entertainments include *ayai* repartee singing, *chrieng chapey* narrative, and *yike* and *basakk* theatres. At court, dance, masked and shadow plays and religious ceremonies are accompanied by *pinn peat* ensembles and entertainment by *mohori*

SHADOW PUPPETRY

In common with the inhabitants of the Malay world and southern Thailand, the Cambodians have a strong tradition of shadow puppetry, which they call *nang sbaek thom*, or "shadow plays". Generally performed during festivals, weddings and funerals, the plays are narrated by actors concealed beneath the puppet screen. A light behind the screen casts images of the puppets onto the screen for the audience to watch. The puppets are usually made of cow or buffalo hide, and can be very intricate in their design. Siem Reap in the northwest of the country (see page 272) is considered by many to be the original home of this art form.

ensembles. Temples often possess a *pinn peat* ensemble and a *korng skor* ensemble for funerals.

Traditional Cambodian music probably reached its zenith during the Angkor period. Carved on the walls of the great temples of Angkor and the vicinity are the *apsara* figures along with musical instruments: the *pinn* (angular harp), *korng vung* (circular frame gongs), *skor yol* (suspended barrel drum), *chhing* (small cymbals) and *sralai* (quadruple-reed flute). These are believed to have developed into the *pinn peat* ensemble.

Sometime around the year 1431 Angkor was looted by Siamese armies; the king and his

music and other art forms were revived and began to flourish again. During the French colonial period Cambodian classical dance and music were truly appreciated by a small circle of French intellectuals and academics, but on the whole Cambodian classical music made little impression on the average *colon*.

These days, foreign influences play a large part in Cambodian music. Cambodian and Thai musical tastes and traditions are close, and Thai ramwong (popular dance), luk-tung (peasant songs from the countryside) and popular music alike have swept Cambodia and are to be heard everywhere, from taxis to hotel foy-

musicians fled, and the city was abandoned and overrun by vegetation. Subsequently the capital was moved to Lovek, which itself was sacked by the Siamese in 1594. Khmer music and its functions were deeply affected by these events, and a new melancholic and emotional style is said to have emerged.

The period 1796–1859 represented a renaissance for the Khmer cultural arts. King Ang Duong, the greatest of the monarchs of this period, ascended the throne in 1841 in the then capital, Udong, and under his rule Cambodian

ABOVE, FROM LEFT: dancer from the Cambodian Royal Ballet; group of local musicians from Ta Prohm temple, Tonlé Bati.

ers. As with traditional ballet, there is a movement to re-establish traditional Cambodian music, and King Sihanouk's classically minded, ballet-dancing daughter Princess Bupha Devi has stated that "classical music is in the Khmer national soul". Even so, there are relatively few traditional orchestras to be heard except at religious shrines – notably at Tonlé Bati, as well as at Preah Khan and Neak Pean in Angkor.

There are two types of traditional orchestra in Cambodia, the all-male *pip hat* and the all-female *mohori*. Both comprise 11 traditional instruments, including flutes, gongs, xylophones and three-stringed guitars. Music is sometimes accompanied by song, either improvised ballads or court chants. At some festivals an orchestra known as *phleng pinpeat* will perform court music. Another type of orchestra is the *phleng khmer*, which performs at weddings. Popular music has been recently influenced by the Thais and Chinese.

Architecture

Cambodia is home to possibly the greatest and certainly the oldest high civilisation in mainland Southeast Asia, and the country is studded with outstandingly beautiful temple complexes, both Hindu and Buddhist, dating from the 6th to the 15th centuries. The early Khmer architectural tradition – dating from around AD 500 to around

1350 – is unsurpassed, and several structures, including Preah Khan (page 283), Ta Prohm (page 286), the matchless Bayon (page 278) and, of course, Angkor Wat (page 280), remain the chief cultural reason for visiting the country.

The temple architecture of ancient Khmer civilisation, both Hindu and Buddhist, is readily identifiable. Building materials include laterite surmounted by structures of sandstone and/or stucco-covered brick. Elaborately carved sandstone lintels feature scenes from the Hindu pantheon, commonly the churning of the primeval ocean of milk or Vishnu reclining on a lotus flower. Scenes from the *Ramayana* and, from around 1200 on, the Buddhist *Jataka*, illuminate bas-reliefs of extraordinary quality.

Angkor Wat has appeared on the flags of Cambodian regimes of all political persuasions, including the Khmer Rouge. The great temple complex is a potent image of national identity which has always transcended politics.

Everywhere, too, there are figures of *apsara* with jewellery and headdresses. (For more on the architectural styles of Angkor, see page 290.)

The glory of this Khmer architecture makes it all the more surprising that post-Angkorean temples, whether Udong or Phnom Penh period, are really quite undistinguished by comparison, and lack a distinctly Cambodian style other than the extensive use of unadorned cement and now, increasingly, reinforced concrete.

There are Rattanakosin-style Buddhist temples in Phnom Penh and Battambang, among other cities, reflecting former Thai colonial rule and continuing Thai cultural influence, and artistic merit is not always lacking. The influence of Siam is dominant, though few if any contemporary Cambodian temples can match up to their Thai counterparts. The Royal Palace is based on the court in Bangkok, and was constructed under the supervision of French architects (see page 255). Other buildings of note in the capital include the National Museum and a plethora of early 20th-century French colonial architecture. Similar architecture can be found in Siem Reap, Kompong Cham, Battambang and Kampot.

The presence of Cham Muslims in many towns means that mosques and minarets also form part of the Cambodian skyline. They are mostly unremarkable imitations of Middle Eastern Islamic architecture, but to the north of Phnom Penh some interesting mosques, painted in the Cham colour of pale blue in contrast to the traditional Islamic green, have been erected in the wake of Khmer Rouge persecution.

Between 1975 and 1979, the Khmer Rouge destroyed the Roman Catholic Cathedral at Phnom Penh, and temples and mosques were turned into storage barns or pigsties. Fortunately there were limits to this vandalism – Angkor and other wonders of ancient Khmer civilisation were either protected or ignored and left to the encroaching jungle.

LEFT: Ta Prohm temple, Angkor. **RIGHT:** Banteay Kdei, Angkor.

THE ROYAL BALLET OF CAMBODIA

The elegant and sophisticated tradition of the Cambodian Royal Ballet is thought to date back to the times of the kings of Angkor.

ABOVE: classical Khmer dance continues to be taught at the School of Fine Arts in Phnom Penh.

The tradition of royal dancing in Cambodia is at least 1,000 years old. Inscriptions indicate that the kings of Angkor maintained hundreds of dancers at their royal courts. The celebrated temple of Ta Prohm, endowed by Jayavarman VII in 1186, maintained no fewer than 615 dancers. The origins of Cambodian dance are not hard to discern – like so much in Khmer culture, they are rooted in Indic tradition, especially that of the *Ramayana*, though a great deal of cultural exchange has also taken place between the royal courts of Phnom Penh and Bangkok.

The Royal Ballet suffered particularly badly during the vicious years of Khmer Rouge rule, when Pol Pot – who had relatives who danced in the company – attempted to crush the tradition completely. Fortunately a handful of dancers survived, either in hiding in Cambodia or in exile in France, and today the ancient tradition is being carefully revived. There are currently around 50 teachers of classical dance and between 300 and 400 students at the School of Fine Arts in Phnom Penh, and another school has been established at Siem Reap near Angkor.

RIGHT: dancers depict scenes from the *Ramayana*. Great emphasis is placed on symbolic and graceful hand movements.
ABOVE: a performance at the Royal Palace, Phnom Penh, in the 1930s.

ABOVE: wall carvings depict *apsara* celestial dancers at the Chan Chaya Pavilion in Phnom Penh's Royal Palace.

CELESTIAL DANCERS

Cambodian mythology and, more particularly, Cambodian temples are both richly endowed with bas-reliefs and murals of *apsara* or celestial dancing girls. These nymphs are graceful, sensuous females who dance to please the gods and to keep the cosmos moving in an orderly fashion. In technical parlance, the term *apsara* refers to celestial females who dance or fly, while their sisters who merely stand, albeit with amazing grace, are called *devata* or "angels". Almost every temple has its quota of *apsara*, but it is generally agreed that the finest examples are to be found in the bas-reliefs at Angkor, and that the best *apsara* are in the "Churning of the Ocean of Milk" in Angkor Wat's East Gallery. In this epic scene from the *Bhagavad-Gita*, gods are encouraged in their creative endeavours by beautiful *apsara* flying above them.

RIGHT: a member of the Royal Ballet, performing the sacred dance of the *apsara* (celestial dancers).

ABOVE: a troupe of dancers from the Royal Ballet performing at the Chatomuk Theatre in Phnom Penh.

BELOW: most dancers in the Royal Ballet are women, but they may play male roles. Male and female roles are defined by elaborate costume.

CAMBODIAN FOOD

Like many things in the country in the aftermath of the Khmer Rouge period, Cambodian cuisine is experiencing a renaissance.

Khmer cuisine is often said to be like Thai food, but less spicy. This is partially true. Cambodian cuisine developed more than 1,000 years ago, before the local introduction of the chilli pepper by the Portuguese, or the founding of the first Thai kingdom in the 13th century. Unlike their neighbours to the west, the Khmer cooks kept chilli to the side, as a condiment rather than a central ingredient. Later Thai cooks derived many of their dishes from older Cambodian cuisine, adding chilli and other spices to create new national dishes. Of course other cultures have, in turn, strongly influenced Cambodia's food. Central in the nation's cuisine are soups and fish sauce from the Vietnamese and the Chams; Indian curries; stir-fries, fried rice and sweet and sour dishes from the Chinese; pastries, baguettes and coffee from the French; spices from the Far East, and fruit and vegetables from the Americas. Even so, Khmer cuisine has combined these elements

Traditionally the Cambodians ate with their hands. The Thais and French introduced forks and spoons, while the Chinese and Vietnamese lent chopsticks to the dinner table.

with a distinct set of flavours and ingredients to form a unique taste. Below is a list of the key ingredients found in every Khmer cook's palette:

Galangal is a light-coloured root that resembles ginger, although the flavour is much

LEFT: street vendor preparing food in Phnom Penh.
RIGHT: baguette seller by the banks of the Mekong at Kompong Cham.

milder. It is often ground into a paste before being added to a dish.

Kaffir lime is native to Indonesia and Malaysia. Its rind and leaves are ground and added to curries, soups and salads, lending a pungent, lemony flavour and deep green colour.

Lemon grass has a distinctive balmy, lemon flavour.

Palm sugar is reduced from palmyra or sugar palms. It has a richer, earthier flavour than cane sugar. It comes in solid, golden blocks or packed in jars, and can easily be crumbled or melted.

Prahok is a grey, fermented fish paste, with a pungent, salty flavour. It is used as a seasoning, condiment, or even primary ingredient.

Star anise is native to China and is used in

caramelised meats. It is also used medicinally as an aid to digestion.

Tamarind is a dark, sticky fruit native to tropical Africa. It hangs from the tree in long pods, with a thin layer of sour fruit surrounding a string of hard, black seeds. It was brought to Indochina by Indian traders long ago, and is commonly used to darken or sour soups and sauces.

Turmeric is a rhizome that is ground and added to curries to give a rich, orange colour. It has a faint, bitter flavour and a distinctive, mustard-like smell.

Finally, **kroeung**, or curry paste, forms the base of many Cambodian dishes, including the

> *Despite their Buddhist faith, the majority of Cambodians do not adhere to strict vegetarianism. "Vegetarian" dishes will often be cooked with fish sauce and incorporate animal fat or broth.*

less common sources of protein include locusts, water insects, various snakes and land crabs.

The national dish

Amok, a fish curry steamed in banana leaves, is Cambodia's best-known dish. *Amok chouk*

famous *amok*. It comes in green or red (*cham pour* seeds are added to give the red colour). The mix typically includes kaffir lime, galangal, turmeric, prahok shrimp paste, shallots and garlic.

The national diet

Cambodia's central staple is rice – indeed, the Khmer word for "to eat" is *nam bai*, directly translated as "eat rice". A meal without rice is merely a snack. Other important starches include manioc (also known as cassava), taro and sweet potatoes.

Fish and other seafood are the top protein on the menu, thanks to the abundance of life in the rivers, the Tonlé Sap lake and offshore. Beef, pork, chicken, duck and other poultry are widely available but more expensive than fish dishes. Other

is another version made with snails steamed in their shells. The curry sauce (*kroeung*) is steamed until solid, but smooth and moist. Less traditional variations may use chicken or seafood, and be served as a thinner, creamy soup contained in coconut husks.

Soups

Samlor, or traditional Cambodian soup, is served as an accompaniment to almost all main courses. Some of the better-known varieties include *samlor machou* (a tangy soup combining shrimp, tomatoes and fried garlic, garnished with fresh mint), *samlor machou banle* (sour fish soup), *samlor machou bangkang* (sour and spicy prawn soup, akin to Thai *tom yam* gung), *samlor chapek* (pork soup with ginger), *s'ngao moan* (shredded chicken breast simmered with lemon grass, holy basil, scallions and fresh lime), *b'baw moan* (a "hearty rice soup" with chicken, coriander, bean sprouts and fried garlic) and *kuy tieu* (rice-noodles cooked with sliced pork, bean sprouts, red onions and fish sauce). Additionally, *bobor* is rice porridge, and one of the cheapest meals you'll find, served with ginger and fish or poultry.

Salads

Cambodian salads are similar in form to Thai and Vietnamese salads, and thus very different from the concept of salads in the West. Typically sweet and tangy, they incorporate shredded meats and vegetables, mint and other herbs, banana flowers, and sour, shredded fruits like green mango and papaya. They are usually mixed with a fish-sauce dressing, not unlike Vietnam's *nuoc cham*. Salads are light and usually the first course or appetiser in a meal.

Eaten with rice

Well-known dishes eaten with rice include *saich moan chha khnhei* (stir-fried chicken with ginger), *an sam jruk* (sticky rice wrap with pork and mung beans), *nataing* (ground pork simmered in coconut milk, sliced garlic, peanuts and chilli peppers), *leah chah* (green mussels cooked with garlic, holy basil, red onions, chilli peppers and lime), *mee siem* (rice noodles sautéed with shredded chicken, soybeans, chives, red peppers, bean sprouts and fried egg), *cha'ung cha'ni jruk ang* (spare ribs marinated with mushrooms, soy sauce, garlic and black pepper, served with pickled cabbage), *trey aing k'nyei* (grilled catfish served with a sauce of ginger, salted soybeans and coconut milk), *moan dhomrei* (sliced chicken sautéed with holy basil, bamboo shoots, pineapple and kaffir lime leaves) and, finally, *chau haun* (mixed chicken, beef and shrimp cooked in a sauce of garlic, shallots, ginger, lemon grass and peanuts). Many of these dishes are available at restaurants in Phnom Penh and Siem Reap, but if you fancy trying one and it is not on the menu, just ask.

Desserts

A lot of great sweets are readily available in covered markets and on street corners. Puddings

and sweet soups (much like Vietnamese *che*) made with tapioca, coconut milk, beans, corn and fruit are a popular and inexpensive snack typically available in the evening. Sticky rice with coconut and mango, as well as a large range of custards, are also very popular.

Fruit

Cambodia has a large variety of tropical fruits that are common throughout Southeast Asia. Everyone will recognise the many varieties of *chek* (bananas), *svay* (mangoes), *l'howng* (papaya), *duong* (coconuts) and *menoa* (pineapples). More unusual fruits include the stinky

tourain (durian), enormous *khnau* (jackfruit), creamy *tiep* (milk fruit), hairy *sao mao* (rambutan) and purple *mongkut* (mangosteen). The last has been the focus of a recent health-food craze in the West, due to its high levels of antioxidants and other nutritional qualities. One tasty fruit to watch for is the *salacca*, or snake fruit, which is not normally available in neighbouring Laos or Vietnam. Its rough, red outer covering looks like snake skin, and the orange fruit inside looks dry but is surprisingly juicy and delicious, if a bit tangy.

Drinks

Chinese tea and Vietnamese coffee are the drinks of choice in Cambodia, although beer

ABOVE, FROM LEFT: street food, enticingly laid out; limes and chillies.

and local rice wines are a close second. Sugar palm wine is a strong but tasty home-made concoction sold from open bamboo containers, carried on the backs of motorbikes.

Teuk kalohk are fruit shakes, made with the fruit of your choice and ample amounts of sugar and condensed milk. Commonly sold at evening roadside stands, they are an enjoyable way to get your daily serving of fruit.

Vietnamese dishes

Vietnamese cuisine is widely available throughout the country. As in Cambodian restaurants, dishes are served all at the same time rather than by course, and are eaten with long-grain rice, *nuoc cham* (fish sauce) and a range of herbs and vegetables, generally with chopsticks.

Some of the more popular Vietnamese dishes include *cha gio*, small spring rolls of minced pork, prawn, crabmeat, mushrooms and vegetables wrapped in rice paper and then deep-fried. The spring rolls are frequently rolled in a lettuce leaf with fresh mint and other herbs and then dipped in a sweet fish sauce. Another dish eaten in a similar fashion is *cuon diep*: shrimp, noodles, coriander and pork wrapped in lettuce leaves.

Vietnamese soups are popular too. *Mien ga* is a noodle soup blending chicken, coriander, fish sauce and spring onions; *canh chua*, a sour soup served with fish, is a blend of tomato, pineapple, star fruit, bean sprouts, okra and coriander; and finally *pho*, often eaten for breakfast or as a late-night snack, is a broth of rice noodles topped with beef or chicken, fresh herbs and bean sprouts. Egg yolk is often added to *pho*, along with lime juice, chilli peppers and sweet bean sauce. *Pho* is generally served with *quay* – fried flour dough.

Other foreign foods

Chinese food (predominantly Cantonese) is widely available in the larger towns. In the west of the country, notably at Poipet, Sisophon, Battambang and Siem Reap, Thai cuisine is widespread. Siem Reap and Sihanoukville have a broad selection of foreign restaurants, while in Phnom Penh there are French, Mexican, Italian, Greek, Turkish, North Indian, South Indian, Sri Lankan, Malay and – increasingly – fast-food restaurants. The Sorya shopping centre is the best place in the country to find Western fast-food franchises.

Where to eat

The cheapest eats are found in street-side and market stalls, and the noodle shops where locals congregate. Markets are a great place to buy items for picnic lunches and snacks, although you may find that bargaining for individual components is overall more expensive than ordering meals-to-order at local eateries. It can be difficult for foreigners to haggle down to the low prices that locals pay, even when they know the price already.

UNUSUAL DELICACIES

Cambodians are adventurous eaters, perhaps even more so than their neighbours. In any village market you may find whole fried snake, barbecued field rat, grilled dog meat, fried baby frogs, frogs on skewers, fried giant water bugs and beetles – as well as more mundane offerings like marinated chicken feet, fried mole crickets and grasshoppers. *Pong tea kon* is a fertilised duck egg containing an embryo, and is a favourite roadside snack to accompany a beer. Certain towns are famous for particular items. The small town of Skuon, for example, on the main route between Phnom Penh and Kompong Cham, specialises in deep-fried tarantulas and "tarantula wine".

LEFT: collecting fruit from the top of the tree.
RIGHT: freshly fried snacks for sale.

CAMBODIA: PLACES

A detailed guide to the entire country,
with principal sites clearly cross-referenced
by number to the maps.

L ike Laos, Cambodia is often described as a small place. True, at 181,000 sq km (69,900 sq miles) it's not large – about the same size as Missouri and roughly three-quarters as large as Laos. However, it has more historic sites per square kilometre than almost anywhere else on earth. The Khmers were master-builders, and the product of more than a millennium of magnificent temple construction awaits the visitor.

Of course, the most important site in the country, if not in all of Southeast Asia, is the great temple-city of Angkor, which must not be missed. Other great temples, too, are now open to visitors – Ta Prohm and Phnom Chisor near Phnom Penh; the spectacular mountain-top sanctuary of Preah Vihear, though, is periodically out of bounds due to a long-running border dispute with Thailand.

Cambodia is geographically unique. Tonlé Sap, the great lake which dominates the west of the country, expands and shrinks with the rainy and dry seasons, providing a vast natural reservoir for the waters of the Mekong River. One way to visit Angkor is to take the boat from Phnom Penh, the country's shabbily elegant capital, across the Tonlé Sap to Siem Reap. En route it is possible to see something of the lifestyle of Cham and Vietnamese fisherfolk, many of whom spend all their lives on the water. The river port of Kompong Chang, located on the south side of the Sap River, is a quiet and attractive stopover for travellers to Tonlé Sap. Raised on astonishingly high stilts, the houses and shops at Kompong Chang are at water level during the rainy season, but stand many metres above the Sap River during the dry season, giving an indication of how the level of the Tonlé Sap rises and falls.

Finally, Cambodia has at least one thing that neighbouring Laos lacks – a coastline. Although dilapidated by years of neglect and deliberate destruction by the Khmer Rouge, Cambodia's "Riviera" is fast coming back into fashion. The port city of Sihanoukville offers beaches and some fine seafood, while the old resort town of Kep is being rebuilt and refurbished. Idyllic tropical islands such as Koh Kong, now developing resort facilities, complete the picture.

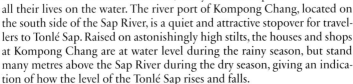

PRECEDING PAGES: North Gate, Angkor Thom; dragon-boat race on Tonlé Sap.
LEFT: Phnom Penh's riverside. **ABOVE:** fun in the water; stilt house at Tonlé Sap.

252

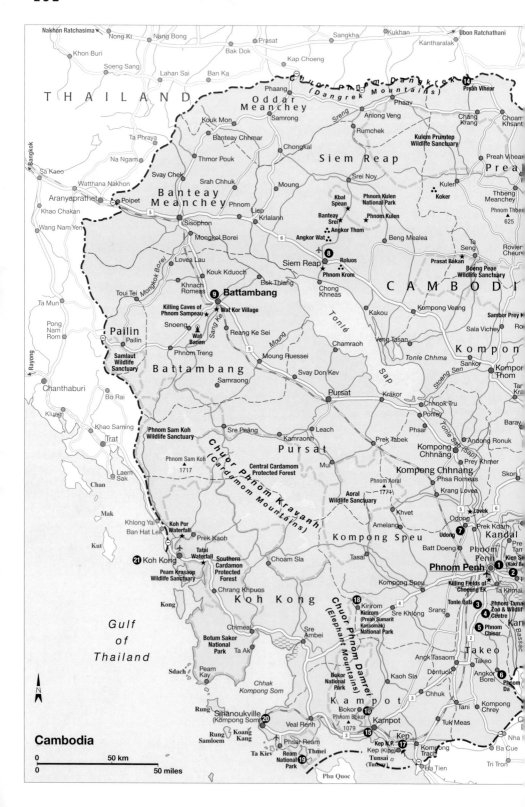

Cambodia

0   50 km
0   50 miles

PHNOM PENH

Phnom Penh's fortunes have risen and fallen with Cambodia's turbulent history, but the future looks bright as new skyscrapers, hotels, restaurants and shops move in with the booming economy.

Phnom Penh ❶, the Cambodian capital, is an attractive riverside city of broad boulevards and numerous sights to please the visitor. Until recently rather shabby and run-down owing to the long years of war and four years of Khmer Rouge abandonment, the future now looks bright, with new shopping centres, luxury residence complexes, enormous hotels, and fine-dining restaurants opening often. Most of the important attractions for the tourist are located beside or within walking distance of the Phnom Penh riverside, and this area also contains many of the best restaurants and cafés.

Once a Funan-era settlement, the city was re-founded in the 1430s, with the decline of Angkor and the shift of power eastwards (see page 203). The legend relates how a woman named Penh found four images of the Buddha on the shores of the Mekong River, and subsequently built a temple on the tallest hill in the area in which to keep them. The city that later grew up around the hill became known as Phnom Penh, or "Penh's Hill".

In 1772, now a major centre of commerce, Phnom Penh was completely destroyed by the Thais. The city was soon rebuilt but grew little until 1863, when the French took control.

A relatively prosperous period ensued. Growth continued until the Khmer Rouge arrived in 1975, forcing the urban dwellers into the countryside and leaving the city virtually abandoned.

The Royal Palace

A good place to start a tour of Phnom Penh, the extensive grounds of the **Royal Palace** ❹ (daily 8–11am and 2–4.30pm; charge) are off Sothearos Boulevard, immediately to the south of the National Museum. The palace was built in Khmer style with French

Main attractions
ROYAL PALACE AND SILVER PAGODA
NATIONAL MUSEUM
CENTRAL MARKET
WAT PHNOM
PSAR TUOL TOM PONG (RUSSIAN MARKET)
TUOL SLENG GENOCIDE MUSEUM (S21)

PRECEDING PAGES: the timeless charm of rural Cambodia. **LEFT:** Khmer fish seller. **RIGHT:** city street scene.

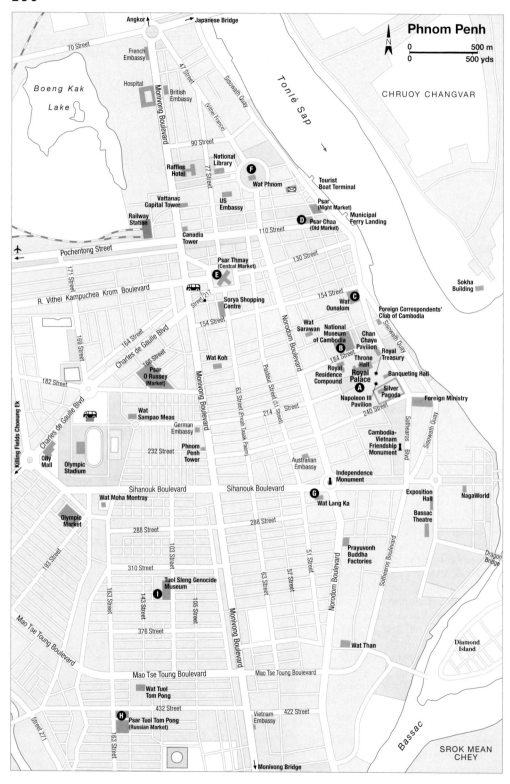

Phnom Penh

0 — 500 m
0 — 500 yds

Angkor ↑ ← → Japanese Bridge

70 Street

French Embassy

Hospital

British Embassy

Boeng Kak Lake

Monivong Boulevard

47 Street

(Vithei France)

Sisowath Quay

Tonlé Sap

CHRUOY CHANGVAR

90 Street

Raffles Hotel

National Library

77 Street

F Wat Phnom

Tourist Boat Terminal

Vattanac Capital Tower

US Embassy

Railway Station

Canadia Tower

Psar (Night Market)

Municipal Ferry Landing

D Psar Chaa (Old Market)

110 Street

Pochentong Street

130 Street

171 Street

R. Vithei Kampuchea Krom Boulevard

Street 217

Psar Thmay (Central Market) **E**

Sorya Shopping Centre

154 Street

C Wat Ounalom

Foreign Correspondents' Club of Cambodia

Sokha Building

184 Street

169 Street

164 Street

166 Street

Charles de Gaulle Blvd

154 Street

Wat Koh

Wat Sarawan

Norodom Boulevard

Pasteur Street (51 Street)

National Museum of Cambodia

B

Chan Chaya Pavilion

Throne Hall

Royal Treasury

182 Street

Psar O Russey (Market)

Monivong Boulevard

63 Street (Preah Trasak Paem)

214 Street

Royal Residence Compound

Royal Palace **A**

Banqueting Hall

Napoleon III Pavilion

Silver Pagoda

Foreign Ministry

240 Street

Sisowath Quay

Charles de Gaulle Blvd

Killing Fields Choeung Ek

Wat Sampao Meas

German Embassy

Phnom Penh Tower

232 Street

Australian Embassy

Cambodia-Vietnam Friendship Monument

Sothearos Blvd

City Mall

Olympic Stadium

Sihanouk Boulevard

Sihanouk Boulevard

Independence Monument

Exposition Hall

NagaWorld

Wat Moha Montray

288 Street

288 Street

G Wat Lang Ka

Bassac Theatre

193 Street

Olympic Market

103 Street

310 Street

51 Street

57 Street

Norodom Boulevard

Prayuvonh Buddha Factories

Sothearos Boulevard

Dragon Bridge

163 Street

143 Street

Tuol Sleng Genocide Museum **I**

105 Street

376 Street

63 Street

Monivong Boulevard

Wat Than

Diamond Island

Mao Tse Toung Boulevard

Mao Tse Toung Boulevard

Mao Tse Toung Boulevard

422 Street

Bassac

Wat Tuol Tom Pong

432 Street

Street 271

H Psar Tuol Tom Pong (Russian Market)

163 Street

Vietnam Embassy

SROK MEAN CHEY

↓ Monivong Bridge

assistance in 1866. It functioned as the official residence of King Norodom Sihanouk from the time of his return to the capital in 1991, followed by his son, King Norodom Sihamoni, who ascended to the throne in 2004.

The public entrance to the palace is opposite the now-closed, colonial-style Renakse Hotel, to the east of the palace grounds. Certain areas within the complex, including the king's residential quarters, are not open to the general public, but much of the rest of the site is accessible. Just beyond the entrance gate stands the **Chan Chaya Pavilion**, formerly used by Cambodian monarchs to review parades and for performances of classical Khmer dancing. Nowadays dance performances are regularly presented at the nearby Cambodiana Hotel.

Dominating the centre of the larger, northern section of the royal compound is the **Royal Throne Hall**. This was built as recently as 1917 in the Khmer style, the architect self-consciously borrowing extensively from the Bayon at Angkor. Inside the Throne Hall, the walls are painted with murals from the *Reamker*, the Khmer version of the *Ramayana*. As well as coronations, the Throne Hall is used for important constitutional events and, on occasion, for the acceptance of ambassadorial credentials.

To the right (northwest) of the Throne Hall stands the restricted **Royal Residence Compound** of the king, while to the left are several structures of interest. These include the **Royal Treasury**, the **Royal Banqueting Hall** and the **Napoleon III Pavilion**. The pavilion, which was renovated by French volunteers using French money, was originally given by Emperor Napoleon III to his wife, Empress Eugénie. In the 1870s, she had it dismantled and sent across the seas to Phnom Penh as a gift for King Norodom.

The Silver Pagoda

Leaving the main northern compound of the palace by a clearly marked gateway in the southeastern corner, proceed along a narrow southwesterly route that leads to the North Gate of the celebrated **Silver Pagoda** compound. Commissioned by King

Stained-glass window in the Napoleon III Pavilion of the Royal Palace, Phnom Penh.

LEFT: the Royal Palace gate.

To Give or Not To Give

The level of poverty in Cambodia is often shocking to first-time visitors. Conditions are much better than they once were, yet in many tourist areas you will encounter amputees, bedraggled women with malnourished babies, and stray-waif street children, all with their hands out, asking for money. It overwhelms some visitors, leading to the term "beggar burn-out".

Certainly Phnom Penh has a large share of impoverished people in genuine need of assistance. However, some of the people who flock to tourist areas to beg are choosing to do so in spite of other opportunities for assistance that are available to them. Scams abound (most commonly on the riverside) involving women who "borrow" or even rent babies and small children – some of whom they drug and physically abuse – to use them as props to gain sympathy while begging.

If you decide to give money to beggars, small amounts are best, but you should be aware that your gift may do more to placate your own sense of awkwardness than actually help the individual. For longer-lasting results, consider using your money to support one of the many charity shops, restaurants and schools around Phnom Penh, established to train and employ disadvantaged individuals – especially the city's youth.

TIP

The riverside serves as a home base for most visitors to Phnom Penh – especially backpackers. Here you'll find a surplus of great restaurants, bars, shops, affordable guesthouses and tuk-tuk drivers ready to take you to all the sights. Unfortunately the presence of tourists also attracts Cambodia's social evils – prostitutes, drug dealers, pickpockets and professional beggars are all very well represented here.

Norodom in 1892, and then extensively rebuilt by Sihanouk in 1962, the floor of the pagoda is lined with more than 5,000 silver tiles weighing more than 1kg each, or 5 tonnes in total. Rather disappointingly, almost the entire floor, except for a small area, is protected by a thick carpet, so the scale of the grandeur is not so obvious.

The pagoda is also known as **Wat Preah Keo**, or "Temple of the Emerald Buddha". It houses the sacred symbol of the nation, the Emerald Buddha, which dates from the 17th century and is made of crystal. There is also a much larger Buddha figure here, comprised of a total of 90kg (198lbs) of pure gold, encrusted with 9,584 diamonds, the largest of which is 25 carats. Photography within the building is forbidden.

National Museum of Cambodia

Continuing northwards from the Royal Palace on Sothearos Boulevard you will soon come to a public green, behind which is the **National Museum of Cambodia** ⓑ (227 Kbal Thnal, Preah Norodom Boulevard; tel: 023-217 643; www.cambodiamuseum.info; daily 8am–5pm; charge; no photography allowed, except in the courtyard). The museum, housed in a red pavilion opened in 1917, holds a wonderful collection of Khmer art, including some of the finest pieces in existence. As you enter, buy a copy of the museum guidebook, *Khmer Art in Stone*, which identifies and discusses the most important exhibits, including a 6th-century statue of Vishnu, a 9th-century statue of Shiva and the famous sculpted head of Jayavarman VII in meditative pose. Particularly impressive is a damaged bust of a reclining Vishnu which was once part of a massive bronze statue found at the Occidental Mebon Temple in Angkor.

Wat Ounalom

The headquarters of the Cambodian Buddhist *sangha* and Phnom Penh's most important temple, **Wat Ounalom** ⓒ stands northwest of the **Foreign Correspondents' Club of Cambodia** (FCCC) and the Royal Palace. Founded in 1443, this extensive temple suffered badly at the hands of the Khmer Rouge but is fast recovering. Unfortunately the

BELOW: National Museum of Cambodia.

once-extensive library of the Buddhist Institute, also housed here, will take many years to replace.

To the west of the main temple stands a *stupa* said to contain an eyebrow hair of the Buddha. Within the temple are several archaic Buddha figures, smashed to pieces by the Khmer Rouge but since reassembled. Also on display is a statue of Samdech Huot Tat, head of the *sangha* when Pol Pot came to power and subsequently killed. The statue was recovered from the nearby Mekong and reinstalled after the collapse of Democratic Kampuchea.

On leaving the temple, turn right (south) along Sisowath Quay, the road that runs along the Sap River. This is a delightful area of small riverside cafés and restaurants where it is possible to experience the international affluence of the new Cambodia. It is a good place to stop for Italian coffee and French pastries, or a burrito and gelato. Alternatively, the FCCC is a popular, if somewhat touristy, night spot and offers unsurpassed views across the Sap and Mekong rivers from its well-appointed second-floor restaurant.

North of Wat Ounalom

The *Psar Chaa*, or **Old Market ⓓ**, located near the riverfront at the junction of Streets 108 and 13, is a densely packed locale offering a wide selection of souvenirs, books, clothing, jewellery, dry goods, street food and fresh produce. Unlike some of the markets, it stays open late into the evening. A tidy, modern night market is held in the square across the street, facing the river, and is now a favourite spot for weekend souvenir shopping.

A short distance to the southwest, at the commercial heart of Phnom Penh, is the extraordinary *Psar Thmay*, literally "New Market", but generally known in English as **Central Market ⓔ**. Built in 1937 during the French colonial period, it is Art Deco in style and painted bright ochre. The design is cruciform, with four wings dominated by a central dome, and the overall effect has been likened to a Babylonian ziggurat. In and around the four wings almost anything you can think of is for sale, including electronic equipment, DVD, clothing, watches, bags and suitcases, and a wide variety of dried and fresh

Avoid touching people on the head. Cambodians believe that's where one's vital essence resides. Even a hairdresser will ask permission before touching.

BELOW: the Central Post Office.

TIP

The promenade around the Cambodia-Vietnam Monument, much like the area in front of the Royal Palace, comes alive every evening – especially at weekends. Families and couples lay out mats and recline or eat picnic dinners. Kids come to play games and buy street food from the many sidewalk vendors. The Royal Palace promenade also hosts popular free dance and aerobics classes.

BELOW: Wat Phnom.

foodstuffs. There are many gold and silver shops beneath the central dome which sell skilfully crafted jewellery as well as Khmer *krama* scarves, antiques, pseudo-antiques and other souvenirs. In 2009, Central Market was renovated. Now with new stalls, wider aisles and fresh paint, it is much cleaner, more orderly and safer than in the past. Within view of the Central Market is **Sorya**, Cambodia's premier shopping centre, and the best place in Cambodia for Western imported cloth, electronics and household items, as well as fast-food chains.

Built on a small mound in the north of the city not far from the banks of the Sap River, **Wat Phnom** Ⓕ (daily; charge) is perhaps the most important temple in Phnom Penh, and from it the capital takes its name. According to legend, around six centuries ago a Cambodian woman called Penh found some Buddha figures washed up on the bank of the Sap. Being both rich and pious, she had a temple constructed to house them on top of a nearby hill – in fact a mound just 27 metres (88ft) high, but still the highest

natural point in the vicinity – hence "Phnom Penh" ("the hill of Penh").

Wat Phnom, the temple built to house the figures, is entered from the east via a short stairway with *naga* balustrades. The main *vihara*, or temple sanctuary, has been rebuilt several times, most recently in 1926. There are some interesting murals from the *Reamker* – the Khmer version of the Indian *Ramayana* – and in a small pavilion to the south is a statue of Penh, the temple's founder.

Wat Phnom is eclectic, to say the least. Although dedicated to Theravada Buddhism, it also houses (to the north of the *vihara*) a shrine to Preah Chau, who is especially revered by the Vietnamese community, while on the table in front are representations of Confucius and two Chinese sages. Finally, to the left of the central altar is an eight-armed statue of the Hindu deity Vishnu. The large *stupa* to the west of the *vihara* contains the ashes of King Ponhea Yat (1405–67).

To the north and east of Wat Phnom, along Street 94 and Street 47 (also known as Vithei France), lie many dilapidated old colonial buildings, increasing numbers of which are being renovated. This is the old **French Quarter**. Should you wish to explore it, leave Wat Phnom by the main eastern stairway and walk due east to the Sap River, noting en route the colonial-style Post Office building, usually resplendent with large portraits of Cambodian royalty. At the river turn left onto Sisowath Quay and then take the next left turn down onto Street 47. Walk north along Street 47 to the roundabout, turn south down Monivong Boulevard, past the French Embassy (on the right) and the British Embassy (on the left), and then turn east by the railway station along Street 106. This route takes you past many examples of French colonial-style architecture.

South of the Royal Palace

As you walk south along Sotheros Boulevard from the palace you

will pass an extensive park, in the centre of which stands a statue in heroic Socialist-Realist style depicting two soldiers, one Vietnamese, the other Cambodian, protecting a Cambodian woman and child. This is the **Cambodia-Vietnam Monument**, dedicated to the supposedly unbreakable friendship that links the two peoples: of course the reality is somewhat different (see page 211).

At the southern end of the park, turning west along Sihanouk Boulevard, you will reach the pineapple-shaped **Independence Monument** – in fact, it represents a lotus – built to celebrate Cambodia's independence from France in 1953. Immediately southwest of this monolith is **Wat Lang Ka ⑥** (daily; free), the second Phnom Penh temple (after Wat Ounalom) to have been restored after the overthrow of the Khmer Rouge regime. Today it is a flourishing example of the revival of Buddhism in Cambodia. Saffron-robed monks abound, while newly painted murals from the *Jataka* (Buddha lifecycles) fairly gleam from the restored *vihara* walls.

While the Sisowath Quay offers views over the junction of the Sap and Mekong rivers, to understand the unique confluence of waters at Phnom Penh properly you should also see the Bassac River. This is best viewed from the Monivong Bridge, south of the city centre, which marks the start of Route 1 to Ho Chi Minh City. The confluence of the rivers, known in Khmer as **Chatomuk** or "Four Faces", is remarkable for a unique phenomenon: the reversal, from May to October, of the Sap River, which more than doubles the size of the Tonlé Sap. Then, in mid-October, as the level of the Mekong diminishes, the flow of the Sap is again reversed, carrying the surplus waters of the Tonlé Sap southwards to the Mekong and Bassac deltas. The time in October when the waters return to their normal course is celebrated as *Bon Om Tuk*, one of Cambodia's most important festivals (see page 356).

The Russian Market

The best market for souvenir bargains and discounted, locally manufactured

On national feast days, a ceremonial flame is usually lit on the pedestal of the Independence Monument.

BELOW: rough wooden shacks along the Bassac River.

A bureau de change at the Russian Market. Among the many souvenir items on sale here are Khmer Rouge banknotes – unique in that they were never actually issued.

BELOW: a reminder of the Khmer Rouge regime's brutality.

designer clothing is *Psar Tuol Tom Pong*, otherwise known as the **Russian Market** because of the many Russians who shopped here in the 1980s. It is located in the southern part of town, beyond Mao Tse Toung Boulevard (also known as Issarak Street) at the junction of Streets 163 and 432. Despite its unprepossessing appearance from the outside, this is a great place to shop for genuine and imitation antiquities, Buddha figures, silk clothing, silver jewellery and ornaments, gems and old banknotes from previous regimes.

Interestingly, the notes for sale include those of the Khmer Rouge, which had currency printed in China but then had a change of mind; in a radical frenzy, it outlawed money altogether, blew up the central bank and ultimately never issued any notes to the public. The Khmer Rouge money is readily recognised by both its pristine condition – it was never circulated – and the warlike themes on the notes: look for rocket-toting guerrillas, howitzers, machine-guns and fierce-faced Khmer Rouge girl-soldiers.

Head deeper inside to find the full selection and the best bargains. Outdoors, on the rear side, you can also find an ample selection of delicious street food. The market and S21 are often visited together.

S21: Tuol Sleng Genocide Museum

Not for the faint-hearted, just over 1km (0.6 miles) from Tuol Tom Pong Market, to the north of Mao Tse Toung Boulevard, stands the former Tuol Sleng Prison, now **Tuol Sleng Genocide Museum** ❶ (daily 7.30am–5.30pm; charge). Here, during Pol Pot's years in power, around 20,000 people were interrogated under torture and subsequently murdered, generally together with their families.

The former prison – once a school – is a chilling sight; the pictures of many of those killed stare out at the visitor in black and white from the museum walls, and primitive instruments of torture and execution are on display, as is a bust of Pol Pot. Many of the former classrooms were divided up in an incredibly

primitive fashion into tiny cells. Everywhere there are crude shackles and cuffs. Initially those executed here were people the Khmer Rouge perceived as "class enemies" and supporters of the former authorities, but soon the Communist regime began to consume itself in a frenzy of paranoia. By the time Tuol Sleng was liberated, in 1979, nearly all those suffering torture and execution were Khmer Rouge officials who had fallen from grace.

Kaing Guek Eav, better known as "Duch", was the Chief of Security and commanding officer at S21. In February 2009, Duch was the first high-ranking Khmer Rouge officer to be tried for his crimes in a hybrid Cambodian and United Nations Court under the "Extraordinary Chambers in the Courts of Cambodia". Duch, now an Evangelical Christian who voluntarily surrendered to authorities, is the only Khmer Rouge official not only to admit his crimes, but also to express remorse and agree to cooperate with the court proceedings (see panel).

The Killing Fields

Finally, for those with the stomach for the experience after visiting Tuol Sleng, about 12km (7.5 miles) southwest of the town are the infamous **Killing Fields of Choeung Ek** (www.killing-fieldsmuseum.com; daily 8am–5.30pm; charge). Here victims of the Khmer Rouge, including many from Tuol Sleng, were executed and buried in mass graves. Many of these graves have now been exhumed, and a *stupa*-shaped mausoleum has been erected in the victims' memory. It's a disturbing experience to view row upon row of skulls arranged in tiers in a tall plexi-glass case in the middle of the mausoleum.

In April 2006, Phnom Penh authorities made the very controversial decision to turn over management of the memorial to a private Japanese company, in order to develop the Killing Fields as a visitor attraction. The memorial has been upgraded with a new road and visitor centre, and a higher entrance charge to pay for them. The easiest way to get there is by taxi or tuk-tuk, although moto drivers will also readily make the journey.

"Land grabs" by developers in new districts around Phnom Penh began receiving international attention in 2008. Neighbourhoods that were once undesirable slums are now hot real estate as the city modernises. Poor families are often squatters with no legal deeds to their property, with little power to negotiate compensation for forced eviction. Some families who receive offers of compensation initially refuse, misguidedly holding out for a "better offer" that never comes.

BELOW: one of Tuol Sleng's many haunting faces.

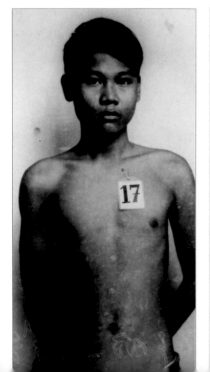

The Struggle to Bring the Khmer Rouge to Trial

Over three decades after the Khmer Rouge regime devastated the nation of Cambodia, a few of the senior cadres are finally being brought to trial. Despite overwhelming public desire for them to proceed, the trials have not been without controversy. The original US$60 million budget for three years was increased to $170 million for five years, but international funding was placed on hold when accusations of corruption within the court system surfaced. Since then there have been several resignations within the court, further complicating proceedings. Many have suggested that the high price would be better spent on social programmes in this impoverished country, while others argue that justice and closure for the victims is worth any cost.

Prosecutors would like to bring more than the initial five defendants to trial, but the government has restricted the scope for the time being. So many former Khmer Rouge officers run the present government – including Prime Minister Hun Sen himself – that the government fears a trial of larger scope would destabilise the country. Certainly, there are former Khmer Rouge officers, guilty of heinous crimes, freely going about their business at all levels of Cambodian society.

The proceedings of the Extraordinary Chambers in the Courts of Cambodia (www.eccc.gov.kh) are open to the public, though attendance has been low except for key court dates.

PHNOM PENH ENVIRONS

There are many interesting places within easy reach of Phnom Penh. Make a day-trip to see fine examples of classical Khmer temple architecture or gain an introduction to the Cambodian countryside.

Although the most important classical Khmer antiquities are either clustered at Angkor or scattered around the still relatively inaccessible fringes of the country, worthwhile historical sites within a short driving distance of Phnom Penh exist at Tonlé Bati and Angkor Borei to the south of the city, and at Udong, a former capital, to the north.

East to the Mekong

About 18km (11 miles) east of Phnom Penh, off National Highway 1, is **Koki Beach ❷** (Kien Svay). A low area of mudflats by the west bank of the Mekong, it is a popular picnic spot for locals from Phnom Penh at weekends and holidays. There are also numerous restaurants on stilts specialising in freshwater and seafood delicacies. The best way to get there is to hire a taxi or *moto* from Phnom Penh, as public boats are no longer available. For the truly impecunious, buses depart from Phnom Penh's Central Market.

Also accessible via National Highway 1 is the ferry town of **Neak Luong**, further down the Mekong. It was here that, in August 1973, a USAF B-52 accidentally dropped its entire load of bombs, levelling much of the town and killing or wounding more than 400 civilians – an incident which features prominently at the start of the movie *The Killing Fields*, and which was instrumental in bringing about a halt to the US bombing of Cambodia. Today there are no visible reminders of the tragedy in this busy little town.

South to Ta Prohm

Takeo province, due south of Phnom Penh and bordering Vietnam, is a very worthwhile destination where you can see some fine examples of classical Khmer temple architecture. Because the province is so close to Phnom Penh, it is relatively simple to visit some of these

Main attractions
KOKI BEACH (KIEN SVAY)
TONLÉ BATI
PHNOM TAMAO ZOO AND WILDLIFE CENTRE
PHNOM CHISOR
PHNOM DA
UDONG

LEFT: stupa in Udong. **RIGHT:** *apsara*, Ta Prohm temple, Tonlé Bati.

TIP

Cambodians are traditionally modest dressers. Even at the beach, girls will often swim fully clothed. Nude or even topless sunbathing is not acceptable in Cambodia.

temples on a day trip from the capital. Air-conditioned taxis are available in the vicinity of the Diamond Hotel on Monivong Boulevard in Phnom Penh.

Route 2 from Phnom Penh to **Takeo** is a good road, and the journey should only take 1–1.5 hours. This is a quiet, sleepy country town that makes a pleasant enough place to stop for a meal or – at a pinch – the night. Hotels are adequate, and Khmer, Vietnamese and Chinese food available. Looking around, you would scarcely guess that, during the Khmer Rouge period, Takeo was the headquarters of Ta Mok, the much-feared one-legged general who was arrested in 1999 and imprisoned in Phnom Penh. "Grandfather Mok" and his fanatical southwestern cadre made Takeo just about the most feared zone in the whole country. He died in a military prison in 2006.

You can take two days over this southward route, setting out from Phnom Penh early in the morning and heading directly to **Tonlé Bati ❸**, which is about 32km (20 miles) distant. The chief attraction around the lake is the laterite temple of **Ta Prohm** (daily; charge),

built by King Jayavarman VII on top of an earlier 6th-century Khmer shrine. The result is a well-preserved gem, not unduly large, but with some splendid decorative features. The main sanctuary has five chambers, in each of which is a statue or a Shiva *lingam*. Generally the shrine is favoured by fortune-tellers who will predict your future and read your palm for a few thousand *riel*. At almost any time a traditional orchestra will be playing outside the inner sanctum of the shrine, attracting offerings from pious visitors from Phnom Penh. Clouds of incense waft through the air, and the atmosphere is very much that of a living shrine.

An unusual feature of Ta Prohm may be found on the inner east wall of the sanctuary, about 3 metres (10ft) above the ground. This is a bas-relief which shows a woman carrying a box on her head while a man bows in supplication to another, larger woman. The scene purportedly represents a pregnant woman who gave birth to a child with the assistance of a midwife, but then failed to show the latter appropriate gratitude and respect. As a punishment, the midwife has condemned the woman to carry the afterbirth in a box on her head for the rest of her life. The crouching man is begging the midwife to forgive his wife.

Another small but unusual bas-relief on the inner north wall of the central sanctuary shows, in the upper part, a king sitting with his wife; in the lower part, because the wife was unfaithful, there is a representation of a servant putting her to death by trampling her under his horse's hooves.

Yeay Peau

A short distance from Ta Prohm – about five minutes' walk, on the north side of the approach road in the grounds of a modern temple – is the second of Tonlé Bati's attractions, the small temple of **Yeay Peau**. According to legend, during the early 12th century King Preah Ket Mealea was travelling in the Tonlé Bati area when he

BELOW: a Buddha in Udong.

met and fell in love with a young girl called Peau. Soon Peau became pregnant, and after a while gave birth to a boy, whom she named Prohm. The king, meanwhile, had returned to Angkor, leaving a ring and a sacred dagger so that the boy could travel to Angkor and identify himself to his father when he had come of age.

In time this came to pass, and Prohm visited Angkor where he lived with his father for several years. On his return to Tonlé Bati, Prohm failed to recognise his mother, seeing instead a woman so beautiful that he asked her to become his wife. Peau objected that she was his mother, but the young man stubbornly refused to believe this. Accordingly, it was decided that a contest should be held to see what should happen. If Prohm, assisted by the local men, could build a temple before Peau, assisted by the local women, could do so, then she would marry him. In the event the wily Peau released an artificial morning star using candles. The men, thinking that it was dawn and the women could not possibly beat them, went to sleep. The women went on to win the contest, and Prohm was obliged to acknowledge Peau as his mother.

That, at least, is the legend. Whatever the real events behind the building of the temples at Tonlé Bati, two classical Khmer temples exist, one named for Prohm and the other for his mother Peau. The latter is much smaller in size and less impressive than Ta Prohm; within it you can see a headless statue of Peau standing beside a seated Buddha.

Around 300 metres (yds) northwest of Ta Prohm is a lakeside picnic area, generally tranquil and free of crowds.

Phnom Tamao Zoo and Wildlife Centre

About 13km (8 miles) south of Tonlé Bati, turn left at the sign, and head another 6km (4 miles) to reach **Phnom Tamao Zoo and Wildlife Centre** ❹ (daily; charge). The centre, part zoo, part safari and part wildlife rehabilitation facility, is home to numerous wild animals confiscated from poachers, traffickers and people keeping them illegally as pets. Enclosures in the 80-hectare (198-acre)

The bear sanctuary at Phnom Tamao spreads over several acres and accommodates around 100 rescued sun bears and black bears.

BELOW: picking lotuses at Ta Prohm Temple, Tonlé Bati.

Window with elaborate shutters at Phnom Chisor.

site include a sizeable population of tigers, and the world's largest captive populations of Malayan sun bears and palliated gibbons. Leopards, Siamese crocodiles, macaques, Asian elephants, and the world's only captive hairy-nosed otter are also present. The centre operates a breeding facility for endangered species, and releases specimens into the wild when feasible. Both **Betelnut Jeep Tours** (tel: 012-619 924; www.betelnuttours.com) and **Free the Bears** (tel: 017-794 291; www.freethebears.org.au) organise enhanced tours of the centre, with special access to the wildlife for their guests.

Chisor Mountain

If zoos are not your thing, then after visiting Tonlé Bati you should continue south on Route 2 for around 23km (14 miles). The intersection for **Phnom Chisor** ❺ (Chisor Mountain) is located close by the two brick towers of **Prasat Neang Khmau** – the "Temple of the Black Virgin", once probably dedicated to the Hindu goddess Kali. A side road heads eastwards at this point, leading to the foot of Phnom Chisor which is about 4km (2.5 miles) distant. The climb to the top of the hill is 100 metres (330ft) up and involves tackling as many as 750 unevenly spaced concrete steps, but the effort is worth it because of the spectacular views from the top over the surrounding countryside. Snacks and cold drinks are available on the way up and at the top, but it is still a hot and exhausting climb in the heat of the day. Anyone less than superlatively fit should make at least two rest stops on the way up, as there is plenty of time to take in the sights.

The main temple at Phnom Chisor (daily; charge) stands on the eastern side of the hill. Constructed of brick and laterite, with lintels and doorways of sandstone, the complex dates from the 11th century, when it was known as Suryagiri. The isolation of the site, and the way the temple suddenly appears as you struggle over the crest of the hill, have led some writers to liken the temple's atmosphere to that of a Southeast Asian Stonehenge or Machu Picchu. Views from the far side of the temple, looking east, are spectacular.

The long, straight old road built by the original temple architects is clearly visible, and would make a far more appropriate access point if reclaimed from encroaching nature. Two lesser temples punctuate the progress of this road, and a large natural lake glistens in the distance.

When you have visited Phnom Chisor it is probably best to press on to Takeo for lunch, bypassing nearby Angkor Borei and Phnom Da, which can be visited during the afternoon to view the temples by the warm light of the descending sun.

Angkor Borei

To reach **Angkor Borei** from Takeo, head back northwards along Route 2 until you reach the turn east to Phnom Chisor. Follow this road beyond the hilltop temple, through the town of Sai Waa, until you reach the town of Prey Kabas. Just before you enter this settlement a side road leads away

BELOW: a new arrival at Phnom Tamao Zoo.

to the southwest and, about 5km (3 miles) along this road, the busy little market town that is your destination. It is believed that, almost 1,500 years ago, **Angkor Borei** was the site of Vyadhapura, the capital of "Water Chen La" before the centre of Khmer civilisation moved northwestwards to Angkor, but unfortunately there is little evidence of this to be seen at present. However, a new archaeological museum (tel: 012-201 638; daily 7–11am and 2–4pm; charge) opened in 2008 and displays a modest collection of artefacts from the Chenla and Funan kingdoms, including pottery, jewellery and statuary.

The temple of **Phnom Da** ❻ (daily; charge) can be reached by crossing the bridge to the south of Angkor Borei and driving – in the dry season – for around 5km (3 miles) to reach the site close to the Vietnamese border. The hilltop temple, which may date from as far back as the 7th or 8th centuries, is of brick and sandstone. Although one of the oldest stone structures in Cambodia, it is in a surprisingly good state of preservation. Nearby on another hilly outcrop is a smaller sandstone temple, thought to have been built about a century after Phnom Da, called **Asram Taa Asey**. This structure was probably dedicated to Hari-Hara, a distinctively Khmer god combining manifestations of Vishnu and Shiva in the same deity.

A word of caution about the whole Phnom Da region: during the hot and dry season it is easy to drive or be driven around, but during the rains the whole area from around Takeo to the Vietnam frontier is flooded, and it is necessary to hire a small boat in Angkor Borei and be taken to the temple sites by water.

North to Udong

Udong, a former capital of Cambodia, can be visited with ease from Phnom Penh on a day trip. Should you have the time and the inclination, however, a more rewarding and informative trip can be made by continuing by road northeastwards to stay overnight

in the large Mekong River city-port of Kompong Cham, returning to Phnom Penh the next day. In this way a small tour can be completed, encompassing royal tombs, rubber plantations and an archaic Hindu temple.

The city of Udong is located on low hills about 35km (22 miles) north of Phnom Penh. The road to follow is Route 5, which continues to Kompong Chhnang (not to be confused with the aforementoined Kompong Cham, which is accessed via Route 7), an important port on the Sap River 60km (37 miles) north of Udong. Route 5 winds north out of Phnom Penh on the west bank of the Sap River.

As you drive north, you will notice the **Chruoy Changvar** Peninsula between the Sap and Mekong rivers to the east. If you look closely, small minarets indicate the presence of two or three mosques in the rural villages of the peninsula, so near to and yet so far from Phnom Penh. In fact, the name "Changvar" is said to be derived from the island of Java in Indonesia, and the peninsula is home to one of Cambodia's fascinating but sadly decimated Cham

EAT

There is a saying that Cambodians will eat everything with four legs but a table. Visit any country market and you'll see that this is not far from the truth. A variety of bizarre animals is often for sale. For this reason, as well as habitat destruction, Cambodia's wildlife is in danger. Please don't buy wildlife products or eat wild animal delicacies.

BELOW: preparing street food in Takeo.

The Khmers and the Kingdom of Siam (now Thailand) have either been at war or engaged in territorial disputes for hundreds of years. The recent, ongoing skirmishes over Preah Vihear are merely the latest in an endless series of territorial fights.

Muslim communities – the Cham people suffered particularly badly under the Khmer Rouge regime.

Chruoy Changvar is reached by the **Japanese Bridge** (so named because in 1993 it was rebuilt with Japanese aid) and makes an interesting two-hour side trip from Phnom Penh, being particularly popular with city residents for its dozens of fine riverside restaurants. For Udong, however, ignore the bridge and continue north; you will pass through several prosperous Cham villages with newly restored mosques and silversmiths' workshops. The local Muslims are friendly, and it is quite acceptable to visit the mosques and take photographs of the turbaned Cham men, though – as with Buddhist temples throughout the country and mosques everywhere – shoes should be removed before entering a place of worship, and women should cover their heads. It's polite, too, to stay outside during prayers.

A ruined capital

Udong ❼ – the name means "victorious" – was the capital of Cambodia on

several occasions between 1618 and 1866. Today little remains of the former capital's days of glory, but the site (daily; free) is still certainly worth a visit. Two low ridges rise from the surrounding plains; unfortunately both bear the marks of extensive bombing during the years of the Second and Third Indochina Wars, and several of the *stupas* have been destroyed or are in ruins.

The larger of the two hills is called **Phnom Reach Throap**, or "Hill of the Royal Treasury". Here one can see the remains of an enormous Buddha figure – blown up by the Khmer Rouge. The site is also known as **Vihear Preah Ath Roes**. At the northwestern corner of the hill sit four stupas. The first is the tomb of King Monivong (r. 1927–41). The second is said to be the tomb of King Ang Duog (r. 1845–59), though an alternative to this disputed site is next to the Silver Pagoda in Phnom Penh. The third is the tomb of King Soriyopor (r. prior to 1618). The fourth stupa is said to contain a relic of the Buddha.

The smaller ridge has a few stupas and larger structures, including **Ta**

Tea Money

Law enforcement officers in Cambodia, much like those in neighbouring countries, have a notorious reputation for corruption. Most of the time foreigners need not interact with police or other government officials, but occasionally tourists find themselves solicited for bribes, often referred to as "tea money" by expats. The most common instances are when foreign drivers are stopped by police, or when tourists have to deal with customs officers and border guards.

Whether someone has committed a legitimate offence and the officer is providing an easy way out, or whether the officer has simply concocted a fake fine out of thin air, paying bribes is still obviously unethical. On the other hand, for some, it can save a lot of unnecessary frustration.

San Mosque. To the south sits **Phnom Vihear Leu**, which is crowned with a shrine, pagoda and a former Khmer Rouge prison.

A short distance northeast of Udong, but only accessible by boat from Prek Kdam, is the former royal city of **Lovek**. Situated on the west bank of the Sap River, Lovek was an interim Cambodian capital, between the times of Angkor and Udong, which flourished in the 16th century. In 1594 it was captured and looted by the burgeoning Kingdom of Ayutthaya, or Siam.

According to legend, the Siamese besieged Lovek in 1593 but were beaten back. Before leaving, however, they used cannons to fire silver shot into the bamboo fortifications surrounding the city. After the Siamese withdrawal the Cambodians tore down these barricades to get at the silver and, as a consequence, when the Siamese returned a year later, they took the city with ease. This legend may not be true, but it is closely associated with the years of Cambodian decay which followed the abandonment of Angkor, and when you look at Lovek today – or what can be seen from the banks of the Sap River – the former city seems symbolic of that period of decay.

After visiting Udong, retrace your drive down Route 5 for 4km (2.5 miles) to the small town of **Prek Kdam** on the banks of the Sap River. From here it's a short ferry ride across to the east bank of the river, followed by a 42km (26-mile) drive along Route 6 to the junction town of **Skon** (pronounced Skoon), famous for its residents' love of tasty fried tarantulas. The countryside is fertile and verdant (especially during the rainy season), with bright green rice paddies and thousands of spindly sugar palms stretching in every direction.

From Skon follow Route 7 for 47km (30 miles) to Cambodia's fourth-largest city, Kompong Cham (see page 294). The journey, along an excellent road, takes you through countryside rich in rubber plantations. Just outside the town – about 2km (1.2 miles) to the northwest – is the **Wat Nokor Bayon** (see page 294) temple complex, a modern temple set amid ancient ruins, which is best visited at sunset.

A naga balustrade at Udong: the hooded serpent represents Muchalinda, who sheltered the Buddha from a rainstorm.

BELOW: some of Udong's stupas silhouetted against the evening sky.

SIEM REAP AND BATTAMBANG

Ancient temples, some of the country's finest French colonial buildings, and memorials of genocide characterise Cambodia's principal western cities.

The west-central towns of Siem Reap and Battambang are very different from each other, but both have a lot to offer. Until a decade ago a dusty wild-west town, Siem Reap's proximity to Angkor has seen it undergo extensive development, with new luxury hotels, bars, restaurants and boutiques catering to the lucrative tourist trade. In contrast, Battambang remains a quiet backwater, noted for its fine French colonial architecture, sparsely visited Angkor-era temples and memorial to Khmer Rouge atrocities. It is possible to travel between the two towns by boat across Tonlé Sap lake in rainy season.

Siem Reap

Siem Reap **❽**, the base town for people visiting the nearby temples of Angkor (just 5km/3 miles away), is a relaxing and pleasant place located by the shady banks of the eponymous river. The town itself has few sights, though with Angkor so close at hand this is perhaps a good thing – the visitor will certainly feel the need to relax after a long day's sightseeing. From Phnom Penh Siem Reap can be reached by bus (around six hours) or express boat (5–6 hours), as well as by plane.

At the northern end of town is the celebrated Victoria Angkor Resort, and next door the **Raffles Grand Hotel d'Angkor ❹**, which has been sensitively restored by the Singapore-based Raffles Group. Over the years many well-known visitors to Angkor have stayed here, including such luminaries as W. Somerset Maugham, Noël Coward, Charlie Chaplin, Jacqueline Kennedy Onassis and Angelina Jolie. Directly opposite and south of the Grand Hotel are the **Royal Independence Gardens** (home to a horde of flying foxes) and the Amansara Resort, a former villa of King Sihanouk.

Southwards, along the bank of the river, lies the delightful old **French**

LEFT: Siem Reap waitress.

Quarter, which could as well be in Djibouti or Algiers were it not for the Khmer sights and sounds which pervade the area. Just south of the French Quarter is the **Old Market ❸**, or *Psar Chaa*, a popular traditional market with a very wide selection of souvenirs that is open until early evening. Look out for wonderful "temple-rubbings" on rice paper, which are reasonably priced and very attractive when framed. The south side of the market near the river is lined with vendors selling silk *krama* scarves and *sampots* (sarongs), woodcarvings, silverware, T-shirts, traditional toys and other souvenirs, while the northern half is mostly fruit, vegetable, meat, clothing and appliance stalls.

Souvenirs that are superior in quality, such as carved sandstone replicas of Angkor pieces, leather puppets and woodcarvings, can be found at the many shops, boutiques and galleries in the area around the market – especially **Pithnou Street ❸**. Most of these places have fixed prices for their offerings that are several times higher than those at the market.

In the evenings, the tourist crowd congregates on the street that has been nicknamed **Pub Street ❹** for its exhilarating variety of restaurants, pubs and cafés. Other hot spots include "**The Passage**" (a parallel alley to the south) and Pithnou Street. Another good early evening option is to stroll southwards along the river bank into the southern suburbs of the town.

Not to be missed are the two sites run by **Le Chantiers Écoles** (tel: 063-963 330; www.artisansdangkor.com; daily 7am–5pm), schools devoted to teaching fine silk weaving, stone and woodcarving techniques to disadvantaged youth. **Artisans d'Angkor ❺** is located a few hundred metres west off of Sivatha Street, and offers free tours of the carving workshop, where Angkor reproductions, furniture and small souvenirs are made. The **silk farm** also offers free tours where visitors can see every part of farming, harvesting and production of silk, and purchase some of the finest silk products in the country. A free shuttle service at 9.30am and 1.30pm makes the 16km (10-mile) trip from Siem Reap daily.

BELOW: street in the French Quarter, Siem Reap.

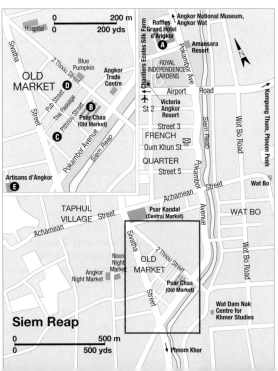

emerald green rice fields in the countryside outside Battambang.

BELOW: fish and winkles caught at Siem Reap.

Tonlé Sap

A particularly worthwhile excursion from Siem Reap lies south on the nearby **Tonlé Sap**, Cambodia's Great Lake. The road from the town leads towards **Phnom Krom**, the only hill in an otherwise completely flat landscape. Phnom Krom – which is gradually being quarried away – is surmounted by a 10th-century sandstone temple of the same name which may be reached by a long flight of steps. The climb, while tiring, is well worth it for the view over the nearby lake and north towards Angkor. The scenery varies greatly from season to season, as during the rains the Tonlé Sap expands considerably (see page 189).

During the wet season, Tonlé Sap laps at the base of Phnom Krom, and you can practically walk out to one of the **floating villages**, which move right up by the hill. Many of the houses are built on tall stilts, especially those nearer to the shore. In the dry season, you will have to travel about 5km (3 miles) further on, to **Chong Khneas**, where the "port" for Battambang and Phnom Penh is located. From here you can hire a boat with a driver to get out to the lake. Choose a boat with a good roof as a sun shield.

The "village" consists of a fairly wide main thoroughfare, with narrow passages between houseboats, stilt houses and extensive fish traps. The water isn't deep – in the dry season it would be possible to stand in some places – but it is immensely rich in silt and sediment, so the propellers of the boats look almost as though they are churning warm chocolate. The people are not rich, but there are all kinds of unexpected amenities in their unusual community: floating petrol stations, a police station, fish farms, floating restaurants and even pigsties. Men fish, repair vessels or work on their houses, women cook in kitchens at the stern of the boats, and children play on the wooden decks and landings, or swim in the muddy waters of the lake.

Also moving with the seasonal rise and fall of the lake is the **Greater Environment Chong Khneas Office**, popularly known as the Gecko Environment Centre (tel: 063-963 525; daily 8.30am–5pm; free). This centre's focus is to promote environmental awareness among the local community,

Education through Art

Phare Ponleu Selpak (The Brightness of Art) originated in the refugee camps along the Thai border in 1986, its central idea being to use artistic expression to help refugee children overcome the trauma of war. These child refugees then brought the concept back to Battambang, formally founding PPS in 1994. Thirty children live on site, supported entirely by PPS; while altogether PPS provides 1,250 disadvantaged students with a formal education, in conjunction with enrolment in either their music school, awareness theatre group, visual arts school or **circus school**. Check the show schedule at www.phareps.org. To visit, head almost 1km (0.5 miles) west from the Vishnu roundabout on NH5, then turn right, continuing for about half a kilometre (0.3 miles).

and is worth visiting for its displays on the flora and fauna found in the area.

Battambang

Battambang ❾, Cambodia's second-largest city, is located 5–6 hours southwest of Siem Reap by bus, or 4–9 hours by boat (the trip is faster in the rainy season). The town has some of the country's finest examples of colonial architecture, especially around the riverfront and market, where old merchant shops exhibit the typical blue wooden shutters, rounded archways, second-floor balconies and triangular roof braces in the French style.

The **Provincial Museum** (Street 1; Mon–Fri 8–11am and 2–5pm; charge) is a pleasant little museum along the river between the **Old Iron** and **Old Stone** bridges. Within the single showroom are statuary and a few ceramics from the Angkor period, as well as a sizeable Buddha collection and some examples of metalwork from archaeological finds. If you visit Wat Banan or Wat Ek Phnom, this visit rounds out the experience by showing you the sorts of items housed in the temples when they were in use.

Further south along the river, Battambang's nightlife epicentre is in front of the **central post office**. A **night market** with food stalls is set up here every evening, along with live entertainment on the busy weekends.

Around Battambang

Battambang's most interesting sights are located outside the city. Heading out 2km (1.2 miles), stop at **Wat Kor Village** to see the **21 Khmer heritage houses**. Two of these old wooden stilt-houses are open to visitors, of which **Khor Sang** (daylight hours; donation) is the more popular. The owner proudly gives a guided tour of the "new house", built in 1907, and the original home connected at the back, built in 1890.

Heading 28km (17 miles) south along Stung Sangker through the countryside, **Banan Mountain** rises 71 metres (233ft) out of rice paddies and coconut groves. After climbing 358 steps, you will come

to **Wat Banan** (daylight hours; charge), its five crumbling towers reminiscent of a miniature Angkor Wat. It was built by Udayadityavarman II in the 11th century, but was badly damaged in fighting between the Vietnamese and Khmer Rouge. Ladies at the bottom will offer to carry your things up the mountain, show you around, and massage you at the halfway rest stop, all for a meagre US$5.

Looping back to Phnom Penh, about 12km (8 miles) from the city, the **Killing Caves of Phnom Sampeau** (daylight hours; charge) tunnel into the peak of the mountain, accessible by a steep road from the parking area below. Here the Khmer Rouge pushed people through the roof of the caverns to their death on the rocks below. A stairway leads down into the main cavern where a new glass monument holds the skulls and bones of victims next to a large reclining Buddha. Visitors will constantly be solicited for donations to build one of several wats under construction on the mountain's summit. A steep staircase leads down the mountain from the wats on the highest peak – this is best left to descents.

Battambang's so-called "bamboo train" is a small platform on wheels powered by a petrol engine. It runs from O Dambong, a few kilometres south of the Old Stone Bridge, to O Sra Lav, about 30 minutes southeast of the city. The makeshift train cars, called norry, are designed to be quickly dismantled whenever they meet a larger train headed in the opposite direction. They've become a primary tourist attraction now, although they can still carry a dozen Cambodians and up to 3 tonnes of cargo.

BELOW: stilt house on Tonlé Sap.

ANGKOR

This ancient capital of the Khmer kingdom is the cultural and spiritual heart of Cambodia. Although monumental in scale, it offers intimate glimpses into lives lived in a distant past.

Angkor is one of the wonders of the world. Perhaps nowhere else on earth, except in the Valley of the Nile in Egypt, are the relics of antiquity found in such overwhelming grandeur. Dating from the golden years of the Khmer civilisation between around AD 800 and 1300, Angkor is a unique repository of incredible craftsmanship on a staggering scale. The sense of a mysterious "lost world" is heightened by the jungle setting, with some of the temples (notably Ta Prohm and Preah Khan) surrounded by writhing roots, lianas and giant forest trees.

When the French first opened this remarkable site to tourism it was usual to distinguish between the "Small Circuit" comprising the central temples of the complex, and the "Great Circuit", taking in the outer temples. Today, when air-conditioned taxis have replaced elephants and horses as the most popular means of transportation here, it still makes a great deal of sense to follow – at least approximately – these designated routes. Therefore in this chapter the two circuits are described in turn; the Small Circuit starts on page 278, the Great Circuit on page 283 and descriptions of sites beyond the circuits on page 287.

Angkor Wat itself refers to just one part of the rambling complex. Angkor Thom, to the north of Angkor Wat, encompasses many fine temples and palaces, including the Bayon, Preah Khan and Ta Prohm. At Roluos, to the southeast of both Angkor Wat and Angkor Thom, are the earliest surviving Khmer relics in the entire Angkor area, predating Angkor Wat by about 200 years. Most visitors generally take either two or three days to explore the site, but one could easily spend longer.

The entrance to the site is just 5km (3 miles) north of Siem Reap. The road to Angkor leads past the

LEFT: Ta Prohm covered with the roots of a banyan tree. **RIGHT:** gate at Angkor Wat.

Angkor National Museum (see margin tip, page 284), to a tollbooth. Buy your visitor's pass or have your pass inspected here before you proceed on your tour. The pass is sold in one-day (US$20), three-day (US$40) and seven-day (US$60) blocks (see also margin tip on the Angkor complex). It cannot be extended and the days must run consecutively.

About 1km (0.6 miles) beyond the tollbooth the road reaches the south side of Angkor Wat, and you will catch your first sight of the famous monument. For the moment, however, it is probably better to drive past Angkor Wat by the west road and visit the city of Angkor Thom, as the former should be visited in the later afternoon when the complex is best illuminated by the sun.

THE SMALL CIRCUIT
Angkor Thom

Angkor Thom 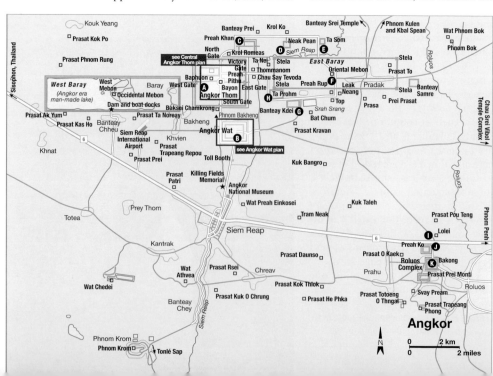, or "Great City", encompasses a huge, square area of land enclosed within an 8-metre (26ft) -high defensive wall and outer moats approximately 100 metres (330ft) wide.

Each side of the wall is about 3km (2 miles) long, and it has been suggested that, at the height of its wealth and power, the city may have supported as many as 1 million people. The founder and architect was the Buddhist King Jayavarman VII (1181–1220), probably the most prolific builder the Khmer Empire ever produced.

There are five gateways into Angkor Thom, each approached by a causeway built across the moat. As you approach from the south the view of the fortifications is impressive. The causeway is flanked by 108 large stone figures, 54 gods on the left and an equivalent number of demons on the right. In the distance, at the far end of the causeway, the southern gateway bears four huge enigmatic faces facing in the cardinal directions.

The Bayon

Passing through this prodigious gateway, the road continues northwards for around 1.5km (1 mile) to reach the **Bayon** ❶, at the centre of Angkor Thom. This temple, which should be entered from the east, was built in the

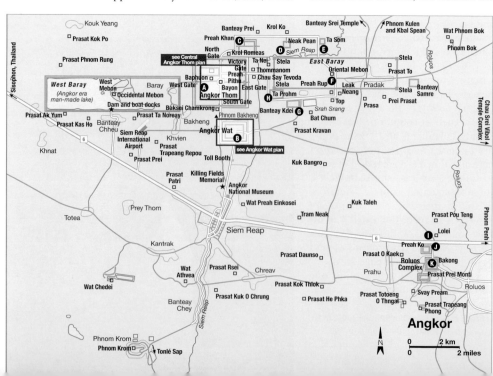

Angkor

0 — 2 km
0 — 2 miles

late 12th century by Jayavarman VII. Always a favourite with visitors, the Bayon is possibly the most celebrated structure at Angkor after Angkor Wat itself, and justly so.

It is thought to represent a symbolic temple-mountain and rises on three levels, the first of which bears eight cruciform gateways. These are linked by galleries that contain some of the most remarkable bas-reliefs at Angkor; they combine numerous domestic and everyday scenes with historical details of battles won and lost by the Khmers. The domestic scenes, many of which are in smaller bas-reliefs below the main war scenes, show details of fishermen, market scenes, festivals, cockfights, removing lice, hunting, women giving birth, and so on. It is unusual to find such graphic depictions of everyday, mundane life at Angkor, as most bas-reliefs are of a religious nature. There are also everyday scenes from the royal court, including nobles, wrestlers, sword fighters and dancing girls.

To view the bas-reliefs, which are well worth an hour or two of your time, it is best to start near the east entrance to the Bayon and proceed clockwise, via the south wall, keeping the carvings to your right. The **East Gallery**, which is in an excellent state of preservation, features a military procession of Khmer troops, elephants, ox-carts, horsemen and musicians. Parasols shield the commanders of the troops, who include Jayavarman VII. The **South Gallery** is spectacular and contains some of the finest bas-reliefs of all. The early panels depict the great naval battle that took place on the Tonlé Sap in 1177. The Khmers have no head coverings and short hair, while the Cham invaders wear strange hats which resemble long hair. The fighting is intense, with bodies falling from the boats and sometimes being taken by crocodiles. The **North Gallery** depicts entertainers such as acrobats, jugglers and wrestlers, as well as local wildlife.

After viewing the galleries, spend some time at the third level examining the vast, mysterious faces with their sublime smiles. The central shrine, which is circular, is also at the third

Stone carving on the Bayon depicting daily life.

BELOW: sunlight catching pillars at Angkor Wat.

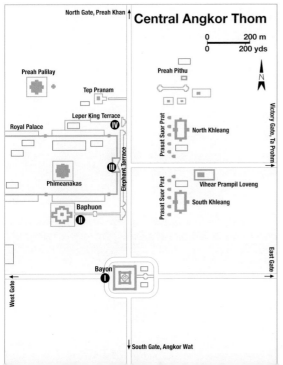

Central Angkor Thom

North Gate, Preah Khan

0 — 200 m
0 — 200 yds

Preah Palilay

Tep Pranam

Preah Pithu

Royal Palace

Leper King Terrace

Prasat Suor Prat

North Khleang

Elephant Terrace

Phimeanakas

Prasat Suor Prat

Vihear Prampil Loveng

South Khleang

Baphuon

Victory Gate, Ta Prohm

East Gate

West Gate

Bayon

South Gate, Angkor Wat

A security guard at Angkor Wat with pet lizard for company. Visitors should stay on the well-used paths as there may be mines on some outlying paths.

BELOW: the Elephant Terrace at Angkor Thom.

level, and features the faces of the *bodhisattva* Avalokitesvara.

Kings' terraces

Next is the mighty **Baphuon** ⑪ – now open to the public after years of restoration (see panel) – and the former royal palace of Phimeanakas, where you reach the celebrated **Elephant Terrace** ⑫. Also built by Jayavarman VII, this structure is over 300 metres (970ft) long, and has three main platforms and two lesser ones. The terrace was probably used by the king, the royal family, ministers and generals to review their forces, and perhaps to watch other entertainments. The whole terrace is elaborately decorated not only with the sandstone elephants which give it its name, but also with detailed tigers, lions, geese and lotus flowers.

Immediately to the north stands the **Leper King Terrace** ⑭. Like the Elephant Terrace, this much smaller structure dates from the late 12th century and is chiefly remarkable for its many bas-reliefs. After seeing this, you should head southwards back to the Bayon and leave Angkor

Thom by the South Gate. A few hundred metres beyond the South Gate, to the west side of the road, the hill of **Phnom Bakheng** rises 67 metres (218ft) above the surrounding plains. This is an ideal spot from which to view the distant spires of Angkor Wat at sunset (although it does get horribly crowded), but it is worth climbing at any time of the day. On the east side a steep and treacherous stairway (currently closed for improvements) provides a swift but difficult means of ascent. Alternatively, and much more easily, a winding path leads to the summit via the south side of the hill.

ANGKOR WAT

From Phnom Bakheng hill continue south to **Angkor Wat** ⑬. By any standards this must be the highlight of any visit to the Angkor region – the great temple is simply unsurpassed by any other monument. Construction of this masterpiece is thought to have begun during the reign of Surayavarman II (1112–52), and to have been completed sometime after his death. Authorities claim that

the amount of stone used in creating this massive edifice is about the same as that used in building the Great Pyramid of Cheops in Egypt, though Angkor Wat has many more exposed surfaces, nearly all of which are elaborately carved to a remarkable standard.

Angkor Wat was established as a Hindu temple dedicated to the god Shiva, but it is also thought to have been envisaged as a mausoleum for Surayavarman II. Its orientation is different from that of most temples at Angkor, as the main entrance is from the west rather than the east: this is thought to be related to the association between the setting sun and death. The bas-reliefs – one of the most important elements of the temple – are intended to be viewed from left to right, conforming to Hindu practice.

The sheer scale of Angkor Wat is difficult to grasp in a single visit. The area of land covered by the complex is around 210 hectares (500 acres) and it is surrounded by a moat which is 200 metres (650ft) wide. Just walking to the central shrine across the moat and along the main causeway is a humbling experience. At the end, the main towers of the temple rise to an astonishing 65 metres (210ft) through three separate levels. At the third level there are five great towers – one at each corner, and the great central spire. These towers are conical, tapering to a lotus-shaped point.

Yet, despite these overwhelming statistics, Angkor is a very human place. Vendors of all kinds of goods, from cold drinks and snacks to the ubiquitous sarongs and *krama* (Khmer scarves), are everywhere. Cattle wander across the main temple enclosure, while buffalo laze and flick their tails in the broad moats surrounding the complex.

Angkor Wat: first level

Proceeding along the central causeway, you should enter the central sanctuary at the first level and turn right to walk round the entire gallery of bas-reliefs – no small feat, as there is much to see. Near the entrance to the first gallery there is a huge stone standing figure with eight arms bearing symbols which indicate that the statue was of Vishnu. In recent times,

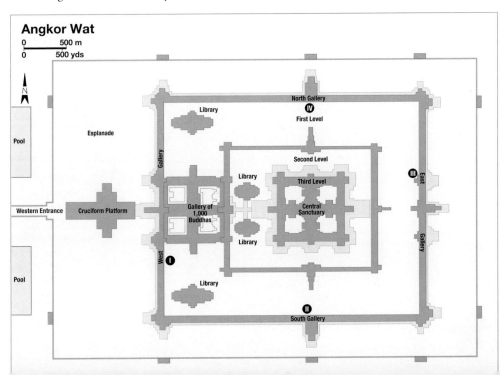

Angkor Wat

0 ———— 500 m
0 ———— 500 yds

N

Pool

Esplanade

Library

North Gallery

IV

First Level

Gallery

Second Level

Library

Third Level

East

III

Western Entrance

Cruciform Platform

Gallery of 1,000 Buddhas

West

I

Library

Central Sanctuary

Gallery

Pool

Library

Library

South Gallery

II

Exploring Angkor Wat can be thirsty work, but there are plenty of vendors around with a supply of cool drinks.

however, a Buddha head has replaced that of Vishnu, and the statue is now much venerated by local Buddhists.

The bas-reliefs of Angkor's first-level galleries are all truly remarkable, but even so some stand out. Look for the following highlights:

In the West Gallery ❶
The Battle of Kurukshetra: The southern part of the west gallery depicts a scene from the great Hindu epic, the *Mahabharata*, in which the opposing Kauravas and Pandavas clash with each other.

The Battle of Lanka: This panel depicts a well-known scene from the *Ramayana* and must be considered one of the finest bas-reliefs at Angkor Wat. It depicts a long struggle between Rama and the demon-king of the island of Lanka, Ravana.

In the South Gallery ❶
The Army of King Surayavarman II: This splendid panel shows the victorious army in triumphal march. Surayavarman rides a great war elephant and carries a battleaxe. He is shaded by 15 umbrellas and fanned by numerous servants. The main ranks of

Khmer soldiers march in close order. To the west is one of the earliest representations of Thais, at this time fighting as mercenary troops for the Khmer Empire. Contrasting with the serried ranks of the Khmers, the Thais march out of step and wear long, dress-like sarongs.

The Scenes of Heaven and Hell: The scenes on this panel, depicting the various rewards and punishments of heaven and hell, are truly terrifying. Those who have done well and accumulated merit in this life seem to be fine – they approach Yama, the judge of the dead, apparently confident of passage to heaven – but, beneath them, sinners are being dragged to hell by hideous devils wielding heavy clubs.

In the East Gallery ❶
The Churning of the Ocean of Milk: This is probably the best executed and most spectacular of all the bas-reliefs at Angkor. In one huge, brilliantly carved panel, 88 *asura* (devils) on the left (south side) and 92 *deva* (gods) on the right (north side) churn the ocean of milk with a giant serpent for 1,000 years. Their purpose is to extract

the elixir of immortality, which both covet. Overhead finely carved *apsara* sing and dance to encourage the gods and devils in their endeavour.

The Victory of Vishnu over the Demons: Vishnu, riding on a *garuda*, is engaged in mortal combat with legions of devils. Perhaps predictably, the powerful god takes on all comers and, despite the odds, emerges victorious.

In the North Gallery
The Victory of Krishna over Bana: In this panel Vishnu, as Krishna, rides a *garuda*. A burning walled city is the residence of Bana, the demon-king. The *garuda* puts out the fire and captures Bana; then, in a spirit of mercy, Krishna kneels before Shiva and asks that the life of the demon-king be spared.

The Battle between the Gods and the Demons: This finely carved panel features yet another battle scene. Here gods of the Brahmanic pantheon struggle with various devils. The gods are distinguishable by their traditional mounts and aspects: Shiva, for example, rides a sacred goose, while Vishnu has four arms and is seated on a *garuda*.

Angkor Wat: upper levels

After examining the galleries of bas-reliefs, you should enter the central complex and climb up to the second level by the usual steep flights of steps. The exterior of this level is rather plain, but within more than 1,500 *apsara* – celestial dancers – grace the walls.

In times past, only the king and the high priest were allowed on the top (third) gallery of Angkor Wat. The central sanctuary rises 42 metres (137ft) above the top level, bringing the overall height of the central tower to the same height as that of the cathedral of Notre-Dame in Paris.

The central sanctuary and the third level of Angkor Wat are ideal places to visit at sunset. Superb views are available across the entire temple, and – perhaps for the first time – it is possible to grasp clearly the stupendous size of the entire complex. As the

sun sinks, warm, golden or red rays of sunshine pierce the elaborately carved sandstone window buttresses, illuminating the very finest and best-preserved *apsara* to be found anywhere at Angkor. It is truly an unforgettable experience. The uppermost level is once again open to visitors, with the installation of safer wooden stairways. This follows the death of a Japanese tourist who slipped and fell down the treacherous, narrow stone steps.

THE GREAT CIRCUIT
Preah Khan

From Siem Reap head north past Angkor Wat, through Angkor Thom, to the North Gate. Next, turning due east, stop opposite the row of cold-drink stalls directly in front of the west entrance to **Preah Khan** , the temple of the "Sacred Sword", also founded by the Buddhist King Jayavarman VII. Built in the style of the Bayon and dedicated to Buddhism, the temple served as both a monastery and the centre of the former royal city. There is a magical quality which comes from the feeling of proximity to

Angkor Wat means literally "The City which is a Temple". Surrounded by a broad moat, the five-towered temple stands in the midst of 210 hectares (500 acres) of land, now mainly forested but once an extensive city with royal palaces, administrative buildings and dwellings for the ordinary people.

BELOW: stone carving showing sinners being taken to hell at the South Gallery, Angkor Wat.

TIP

The **Angkor National Museum** (daily 8.30am–6.30pm; www.angkornationalmuseum.com; charge), formerly known as the Angkor Conservatory, is situated on the road between Siem Reap and the main entrance. The well-equipped galleries provide an excellent introduction to Angkor and the civilisation that built it. Many visitors, however, give it a miss – being either impatient to see the real thing in situ, or baulking at the relatively expensive entrance fee.

BELOW: the temple of Neak Pean.

nature; this is because the temple still awaits full restoration, and great trees with smothering roots still cling to the sandstone and laterite walls.

An inscribed stone stele, found at Preah Khan in 1939 and removed for safekeeping to the Angkor National Museum, indicates that the temple was once the heart of the ancient city of Nagarajayacri. The central sanctuary was dedicated in 1191, during Jayavarman VII's reign. However, Jayavarman was followed by a series of Hindu-oriented kings who did their best to Hinduise the great Buddhist sanctuary. Accordingly, images of the Buddha were chipped out of their niches, and elsewhere in the interior of the shrines Buddha images were transformed into *rishi*, or ascetics, by the simple addition of beards.

The central sanctuary of Preah Khan is cruciform, with four entrances. Look for the "Hall of Dancers", with its finely carved rows of *apsara* which decorate the walls. If you are agile enough to clamber over (and sometimes under) the great piles of fallen stone in the northeastern section of the main sanctuary, you can visit the "Shrine of the White Lady" – an elegant figure, supposedly not an *apsara* but the wife of Jayavarman VII, tucked away in a hidden room. The shrine is still venerated, and supplicants light incense and leave offerings of money. You will need a guide to find this out-of-the-way spot, but the effort is worth it.

Neak Pean

After leaving Preah Khan, head eastwards along the road leading to the East Baray. About 2.5km (1.5 miles) from Preah Khan a track leads southwards for around 300 metres (975ft) to the temple of **Neak Pean** , or "The Coiled Serpents". This structure, which dates from the second half of the 12th century, was built by Jayavarman VII and dedicated to Buddhism. Located in the midst of the Jayatataka on the North Baray, Neak Pean now remains dry for most of the year, but it was once an island, and its whole purpose is closely connected with water.

The temple, which is quite small by Angkorean standards, is set in an artificial pond 70 metres (230ft) square.

This central pool is surrounded at the cardinal points by four smaller square pools set somewhat more deeply into the earth. In the centre of the main pool is a circular island bearing a stepped laterite shrine dedicated to the *bodhisattva* Avalokitesvara. Two intertwined serpents circle the base of the island and give the complex its name. The central pool is said to represent the Himalayan Lake Anavatapta, located at the summit of the universe, which was believed to give birth to the four great rivers of the world. These four rivers are represented at Neak Pean by four gargoyle-like heads which, when opened, would permit water to flow from the main pool to the four smaller pools. In times past, pilgrims to Neak Pean would consult with resident priests and then repair to the appropriate pool, where servants of the shrine would release a plug and allow the magical waters of the central pool to pour out over the supplicant.

About 2km (1.2 miles) east of Neak Pean stands the tranquil and charming temple of **Ta Som** Ⓔ. Built in the late 12th century by the indefatigable Jayavarman VII, and inevitably dedicated by him to Buddhism, the Bayon-style temple was also built to honour Jayavarman's father. Ta Som is not one of the "great" temples of Angkor in that it is not monumental in size. What makes it special, however, is its setting on the northeastern limits of the great Angkorean complex. It is off the beaten track, sees relatively few visitors, and as a consequence is filled with birdsong and the sound of cicadas.

In the East Baray

Located in the midst of the East Baray, the 10th-century **Oriental Mebon** is another example of an artificial temple-mountain representing Mount Meru – one of the enduring themes of classical Khmer architecture. Surrounded by three laterite enclosure walls, the "mountain" rises through three levels before culminating in a central platform bearing four smaller outer towers and one larger central tower. The stairways at the foot of the artificial mound are flanked by carved sandstone lions, while elephants stand

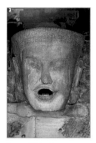

One of the four stone gargoyles at Neak Pean, used to divert water from the main pool into smaller pools below.

BELOW: the ruins of the temple of Ta Som.

A naga (river serpent) statue looks out from the landing stage over Srah Srang (Royal Bath).

BELOW: monks passing through the gate into Phimeanakas Temple, the Baphuon.

astride the corners of the second and third levels.

Close by is **Preah Rup** , a Hindu temple dedicated to the god Shiva, which also dates from the 10th century. Visitors to Preah Rup should climb to the top of the monument for excellent views north across the East Baray, as well as southwest, where the distant spires of Angkor Wat can be distinguished in clear weather.

As you leave Preah Rup heading west, the road passes the great reservoir of **Srah Srang**, or "Royal Bath". This large body of water, 300 metres (970ft) by 700 metres (2,270ft), was built on the orders of Jayavarman VII and, especially in the late afternoon and evening, makes a delightful sight as buffaloes bathe in its tranquil waters. At the western side of the lake is a sandstone landing stage flanked by

lions and bearing a large *garuda* on the back of a three-headed serpent.

Immediately west of the landing stage a gateway in a high laterite wall gives access to **Banteay Kdei** , the "Citadel of the Cells". The temple was used as a Buddhist monastic complex until the mid-20th century. As a consequence it is less overgrown than some of the other outer temples, and very pleasant to stroll through. Visitors are advised to follow the central corridor through the "Hall of the Dancing Girls" – so called from a bas-relief of dancers cut into the wall – and on to the central sanctuary, which contains a recent Buddha image, still much venerated by the local people.

Ta Prohm

Finally, and ideally towards the end of the day, the route leads past Banteay Kdei for a distance of about 1km (0.6 miles) to reach the spectacular temple of **Ta Prohm** , or "Ancestor of Brahma". This very large complex was, yet again, the work of Jayavarman VII and dedicated to Buddhism. A stone stele, now

Restoring Baphuon

Baphuon is a massive three-tiered temple-mountain built in the 11th century by King Udayadityavarman II (1050–66). It represents Mount Meru, and was dedicated to the Hindu god Shiva. A central tower with four entrances once stood at the summit. In its days of glory it would have been 50 metres (164ft) high, and it certainly made an impression on the Chinese visitor Chou Ta-kuan (see page 289), who described it in 1297 as "a tower of bronze... a truly astonishing spectacle, with more than ten chambers at its base". It is sufficiently important to have given its name to an 11th-century style of Khmer architecture. In the 15th century Baphuon was rededicated to Buddhism, and a 9 metre by 70 metre (30 by 230ft) reclining Buddha was added to the temple's second level on the west side. Baphuon had long since collapsed, probably because the massive central tower rested on sandy ground. The École Française d'Extrême-Orient began the process of carrying out restoration as long ago as 1960, but had to abandon the work when the Second Indochina War spilt over into Cambodia and made the war effort too risky. Restoration started again in 1995, again under the guidance of French archaeologists, and until recently, visitor access was restricted. It is now possible to visit Baphuon and climb to the very top for views of much of Angkor Thom.

removed to the Angkor National Museum, tells us quite a lot about it: for example, in its prime the temple owned 3,140 villages and was maintained by some 79,365 people, including 18 high priests, 2,740 officials, 2,202 assistants and 615 dancers.

Ta Prohm is a long, low complex of buildings all on the same level, with a series of concentric galleries connected by passages that provide shade in the heat of the day. The entire complex is surrounded by a rectangular laterite wall of around 700 metres (2,270ft) in width by 1,000 metres (3,300ft) in length. What makes Ta Prohm so special is that, following an unusual archaeological decision, the jungle has been only partly cut back, so that the buildings are covered with the roots of huge banyan and kapok trees which rise high above the temple. In an otherworldly scene, spectacular writhing limbs bind lintels and crack vaulted passageways, while parrots fly in the upper canopy and break the stillness with their sharp cries. Rather breaking the spell, local children often follow tourists around this part of Angkor, which can be somewhat trying – best advice is to politely appeal to them to leave you in peace.

Ta Prohm was used in the filming of *Tomb Raider* in 2000. The central courtyard features in the scene where Angelina Jolie picks a jasmine flower and is promptly dropped into a deep vault.

BEYOND THE CIRCUITS
The Roluos complex

Some 11 centuries ago King Jayavarman II (802–50), remembered as the founder of the first unified Khmer state, made his capital at Hariharalaya ("The Dwelling Place of Hari-Hara", a deity combining the attributes of both Vishnu and Shiva). Today the Roluos complex of temples, which are the oldest in Angkor, marks the site of this first Angkorean capital.

Roluos is located to the southeast of the other temples.

Founded by King Yasovarman I (889–908), **Lolei ❶** was dedicated to the Hindu deity Shiva. Most people come here to see the magnificent carvings and well-preserved stone inscriptions, though the four central brick towers are somewhat tumbledown and covered with shrubbery. Just to the south stands **Preah Ko ❷**, the "Sacred Bull". Built by King Indravarman I (877–89), it is set amid attractive rural scenery and, being somewhat off the beaten track, is usually tranquil and rarely visited. The main sanctuary consists of six brick towers set on a low laterite platform. A short distance beyond Preah Ko rises the solid mass of **Bakong ❸**, a late 9th-century Hindu temple dedicated to Shiva. A thousand years ago Bakong was the central feature of Hariharalaya. It is built as a temple-mountain on an artificial mound surrounded by a moat and outer enclosure walls. Bakong, which is easily the largest monument of the Roluos group, is best entered from the east by a processional way

Since the final collapse of the Khmer Rouge in the late 1990s, Angkor has gradually reopened to the world. Miraculously, in a country so devastated by war, the great temple complexes survived remarkably unscathed, and today, after painstaking clearance of unexploded ordnance and dense vegetation, restoration and conservation are once again well under way.

BELOW: the roots of banyan and kapok trees, Ta Prohm temple.

decorated with seven-headed *naga* serpents.

Banteay Srei

The justly famed temple of **Banteay Srei** lies about 30km (20 miles) northeast of Siem Reap. While Angkor Wat, Angkor Thom and the Bayon impress by their sheer size, Banteay Srei inspires through meticulous detail. It is, indeed, a scrupulously executed miniature temple complex carved in fine pink sandstone – and in the quality of the stone and the soft, almost mellifluous charm of the colour lies much of the temple's appeal. Founded in the second half of the 10th century, Banteay Srei is of rectangular design, enclosed by three walls and the remains of a moat. The central complex consists of a number of structures including, most importantly, shrines dedicated to Shiva (the central and southern buildings) and to Vishnu (the northern building). The main themes represented in the

At Kbal Spean, images of Hindu deities are carved onto the river-bed.

BELOW: library buildings at Banteay Srei.

many elaborately carved lintels and frontons are derived from the Hindu epic, the *Ramayana*. Also worthy of note are the finely carved figures of male and female divinities set in recessed niches of the central towers.

Mountain pilgrimage sites

Phnom Kulen is considered sacred by the Khmers and has been a pilgrimage site for many centuries. Legend has it that it was here King Jayavarman II proclaimed himself as god-king in AD 802, giving rise to an independent Cambodian state. Although it has been open to tourism for several years now, reaching the mountain is still a fairly arduous undertaking. Phnom Kulen is about 40km (25 miles) northeast of Siem Reap and about 15km (9 miles) beyond Banteay Srei in the direction of the former Khmer Rouge stronghold of Anglong Veng. It's a strenuous 90-minute climb to the top of the mountain, where there is a small pagoda called **Wat Chuop**. There are fine views from the summit at 487 metres (1,598ft) across the surrounding forested uplands, and a walk of a further 30 or so minutes will bring you to a small river – leading ultimately to the Tonlé Sap – in which numerous *linga* have been carved to sanctify the holy water as it makes its way down to the plains.

Much quieter and more isolated is **Kbal Spean**, established as a hill retreat by Khmers in the mid-11th century. Located about 10km (6 miles) beyond Banteay Srei on the same rough dirt road, it's quite a climb up to the densely forested hill, and in places you have to pull yourself up fairly steep paths with jungle vines. It's well worth the effort, though – the river flows under a natural sandstone bridge and over dozens of carvings of *linga*, as well as representations of Rama, Lakshmi, Hanuman and Vishnu. In recent years some of the carvings have been hacked from the rock by art thieves, but there is still enough here to make Kbal Spean impressive indeed.

A Portrait of Angkor

A unique 13th-century Chinese manuscript sheds light on the workings of the great city of Angkor, and its Indic traditions.

A Chinese envoy, Chou Ta-kuan, visited Angkor during the reign of Indravarman III (1296–1308) and left a detailed manuscript describing his experiences. This unique document provides a window on all aspects of 13th-century Angkorean life – as it is unconstrained by the Indic tradition of excluding ordinary people from literature.

Chou Ta-kuan tells us that the Khmer Empire, known to its inhabitants as Kan-po-chih (Cambodia), began at present-day Vung Tau (Vietnam); all of the southern Mekong region lay within its boundaries. Chou recognised three religious traditions established at Angkor: Brahmanism, Buddhism and Shivaism. Most familiar, both to him and to the present-day visitor, were the Theravadan Buddhists, known by a Tai term, Chao Ku. The Shivaists were already a declining influence at this time; Chou found their temples poorer than those of the Buddhists, housing a Shiva *lingam*.

Chou records: "The walled city of Angkor was some five miles in circumference. It had five gates, with five portals. Outside the wall stretched a great moat across which massive causeways gave access to the city. The Palace stands to the north of the Golden Tower and the Bridge of Gold; starting from the gate its circumference is nearly one-and-a-half miles. The tiles of the central dwelling are of lead; other parts of the palace are covered with pottery tiles, yellow in colour... Out of the Palace rises a golden tower, to the top of which the ruler ascends nightly to sleep. By contrast, the houses of the ordinary folk were thatched with straw, for 'no one would venture to vie with the nobility'."

Class system

In fact, as Chou makes clear, late 13th-century Khmer society was rigidly stratified by class. At the base of the pyramid were slaves, many of whom were reportedly captured "mountain tribes". They were set apart from free people by various prohibitions: they could not sleep in houses; on entering a house they had to prostrate themselves before

beginning work; they had no civil rights; their marriages were not recognised by the state; and they were obliged to call their owners "father" and "mother". Slaves often tried to run away, and when caught would be tattooed, mutilated and shackled.

Above the slaves were a number of classes who were free but not part of the nobility. These included slave-owners, landholders, resident and visiting traders and, most probably, market traders, who according to Chou were mainly women. The position of other "free" people outside the elite is a matter for speculation, but it is clear that a considerable number of ethnic Chinese had already settled in the city by this early date. Chou, naturally enough, remarks on this, explaining that his compatriots liked Angkor as it was so warm that there was no need to spend much money on clothes, while food was plentiful and women "easily persuaded".

The king and his immediate entourage, the high elite, topped the pyramid. Chou was perplexed by the king's relative accessibility, which was so unlike the Emperor of China's court. In fact, his approach to royal audiences seems closer to the Sukhothai system of Siam than to the Chinese (or Viet).

Chou may not have known it but, by the end of the 13th century, the Khmers, influenced by both the rising power of their Thai neighbours and the growing strength of Theravada Buddhism, were reaffirming their Indic identity even as they paid tribute to China.

RIGHT: the Leper King Terrace, Angkor Thom.

ANGKOR ARCHITECTURAL STYLES

Cambodia's top tourist attraction is one of the greatest architectural ensembles on earth, with a sumptuous range of exquisite styles and details.

Angkor Period architecture is generally dated from Jayavarman II's establishment of Hariharalaya as Khmer capital near the site of present-day Roluos at the beginning of the 9th century. From this time until the eventual 15th-century abandonment of Angkor, art historians identify 10 distinct architectural styles, each named after its most famous example:

875–90 Preah Ko: this style is characterised by the use of brick towers and stone lintels. Sculptured figures are larger and heavier than in pre-Angkorean traditions.

890–925 Bakheng: the use of Mount Meru as a model for temple-mountains evolved, often with five towers arranged in a quincunx (one at each corner of a rectangle with the fifth in the middle).

921–41 Koh Ker: this short-lived style was developed during the reign of Jayavarman IV. The finest surviving examples are Sugriva and Valin, two monkey-headed brothers from the Ramayana, at the National Museum in Phnom Penh.

945–65 Pre Rup: this style, developed during the reign of Rajendravarman, expands on the Bakheng style with five towers arranged in a quincunx, but higher, steeper and with more tiers.

967–1000 Banteay Srei: characterised by exquisitely ornate carvings and distinctly sensuous *apsara* and *devata* female figures.

965–1025 Khleang: marked by the increasing use of massive stone blocks and limited decoration, cruciform *gopura* gateways and long galleries.

1025–1080 Baphuon: Khmer architecture close to its majestic apogee. Vast proportions and long, vaulted galleries. Sculpture combines increasing realism and narrative sequence in bas-reliefs.

1080–1175 Angkor Wat: the apex of Khmer architectural and sculptural genius.

1180–1240 Bayon: considered a synthesis of previous styles.

1240–1432 Post-Bayon: distinguished by the use of raised causeway terraces. The chief example is the Terrace of the Leper King at Angkor Thom.

ABOVE: detail from the Elephant Terrace, dating from the Bayon period (1180–1240). This time is characterised by a noticeable decline in quality of materials (laterite rather than sandstone), and increasing use of Buddhist – as opposed to Hindu – imagery.
BELOW: one of the five towers at Angkor Wat, the greatest of all Khmer temple-mountains. Construction began in the early 1100s. It has the finest bas-relief narratives, and the art of lintel carving, too, reached its zenith during this period (1080–1175).

CLASSICAL KHMER TEMPLE LAYOUT AND IMAGERY

The central feature of the classical Khmer temple is a stylised representation of Mount Meru of Hindu mythology, with the mountain symbolised by the tiered base and central tower. The concept was extended through the Bakheng period (see page 290) with the addition of more towers and a causeway leading across the surrounding moat. Angkor Wat marks the final, spectacular, evolution of the style.

Main entranceways – with a few exceptions, notably at Angkor Wat itself – are from the east, marked by decorated gateways or *gopura*. The central temple complex, generally set within several concentric enclosure walls, is usually characterised by the presence of *linga* (male phalli) and their counterpart, the female *yoni*. In times past, lustral water was poured over *linga* and *yoni*, often conjoined, before being used as a source of blessing and purification.

Statues of the major Hindu deities Shiva, Vishnu and Brahma are often present, often joined by other figures from Hinduism including Nandi, the bull mount of Shiva, *naga* serpents, and the *garuda*, the half-bird, half-human mount of Vishnu.

As Buddhism gradually replaced Hinduism from around the 11th century onwards, images of the Buddha and scenes from the *Ramayana* were used in temple consecration and decoration.

ABOVE AND ABOVE RIGHT: Angkor is still venerated by Cambodian Buddhists today, with some of the ancient temples functioning as shrines.

RIGHT: images of *apsaras*, heavenly dancers, adorn many of the temple walls around Angkor. The most sensuous examples of this Hindu style date from the Banteay Srei period (967–1000).

CENTRAL AND NORTHEAST CAMBODIA

The Mekong River is essential to life in Cambodia. This chapter explores the riverine towns and countryside upstream from Phnom Penh, and the remote northeastern provinces – Ratanakiri and Mondulkiri.

It is difficult to overstate the importance of the Mekong to Cambodia. Rising in Tibet, it flows for more than 4,000km (2,500 miles) through six different countries before reaching the sea, but it is in Cambodia that the river is at its most complex. After passing through the Si Phan Don or "Four Thousand Islands" region of southernmost Laos and roaring over the Khon Phapheng Falls, the Mekong enters Cambodia and flows south through Stung Treng, Kratie and Kompong Cham provinces. Up to this point it is still just a large river. When the waters reach Phnom Penh, however, they are joined by the Sap River from the northwest, while the Bassac River breaks away towards the southeast.

Around 1,500 years ago, when an independent kingdom centred on the Phnom Penh region first emerged, it was dubbed "Water Chen La" by the Chinese annalists because of its dependence on the Mekong. Over the intervening centuries little has occurred to change the Cambodian people's reliance on the Mekong for their fundamental existence. If it has aptly been said that "Egypt is the gift of the Nile", then the Mekong – together with its related rivers the Sap and the Bassac – remains Cambodia's lifeline.

North to Kompong Cham

The easiest and most convenient way to explore the Cambodian Mekong used to be to set out by boat from Phnom Penh. Unfortunately, public boats leaving from Phnom Penh or Kompong Cham have stopped running now that road improvements have led to cheaper and quicker bus rides. These days the only way to get to Kompong Cham and Kratie from the capital is by road. National Highway 7 has been improved though remains under frequent construction, making

Main attractions

WAT NOKOR BAYON
KRATIE
DOLPHIN-SPOTTING AT SAMBOR
STUNG TRENG
LUMPHAT WILDLIFE SANCTUARY AND
    VIRACHEY NATIONAL PARK

LEFT: girl at Wat Nokor Bayon.
RIGHT: Mekong river traffic.

BELOW: meet the locals – Khmer family from a village near Kompong Cham.

the journey to Kompong Cham under four hours. There are regular connections to the towns by taxi and bus. The latter leave from Psar Thmay (Central Market) in Phnom Penh.

The 120km (75-mile) journey from the capital northeast to **Kompong Cham** , Cambodia's fourth-largest city, is straightforward, on good roads. There are no major attractions in the prosperous city itself, though there are some attractive old buildings, and the Mekong Hotel, located right on the waterfront, provides a pleasant location to have a drink or something to eat while watching life on the great river which sweeps by endlessly. Small boats with one or two fishermen cast their nets and drift slowly downstream. Occasional ferryboats still ply the river, and large cargo ships push their way upstream against the muddy waters, to take on or offload goods, especially rubber from the extensive plantations in the region. If you have time only for lunch, a couple of good restaurants near the junction of Monivong

Boulevard and Vithei Pasteur Road serve Khmer and Chinese food.

The entrancing ruins of **Wat Nokor Bayon**, an 11th-century sandstone and laterite temple, are located some 2km (1.2 miles) to the northwest of the town. The complex is a fascinating blend of the contemporary and the archaic. It was originally dedicated to Mahayana Buddhism, but at some point, probably during the 15th century, the temple was rededicated to Theravada Buddhism, and a modern temple set amid the ancient ruins still functions as a Buddhist centre today. There are numerous niches and hidden shrines, and a large reclining Buddha within.

Kratie

Leave Kompong Cham by way of the Japanese-built bridge across the Mekong, which opened in 2002 and provides direct road access between Phnom Penh and Ho Chi Minh City. From here, it is approximately another 2.5–3 hours to **Kratie** ⑪, pronounced "kra-chey" (and sometimes spelt "Krâcheh").

There is an unexpected charm to this isolated riverside port, which still retains some fine, if inevitably decaying, examples of French colonial architecture. One reason for Kratie's relatively good state of preservation is that it fell under Khmer Rouge control at an early stage in the civil war, and was not subjected to either fierce fighting or subsequent bombing. There are three or four hotels along the waterfront by the boat dock, and several restaurants serving variations on Cambodian, Chinese and Vietnamese cuisine. The waterfront also has several small establishments selling beer and soft drinks which make an excellent place to sit and watch the sunset over the Mekong. The administrative section of the town lies to the south of the dock beyond the hotels, while a large market beside the dilapidated road leading east to Phumi Samraong and Snuol, towards the Vietnamese frontier, serves most of Kratie province.

The Mekong dolphin

It's possible to charter a boat or take a taxi to travel the 30km (20 miles) north of Kratie to the peaceful riverside village of **Sambor** ⑫, with its attractive **temple**. If you travel on the river there is a chance of seeing the rare Mekong dolphin, an endangered species which is making something of a comeback in the waters near Kratie, and which has become a major attraction. More correctly known as the Irrawaddy dolphin, this is a delightful and sociable mammal which has been driven to the verge of extinction by fishermen using explosives and nets, collisions with rafts of teak logs, and fatal encounters with the sharp propellers of speeding long-tail boats.

In Cambodia nowadays it is common to blame the Khmer Rouge for all manner of ills, from the looting of ancient temples to the destruction of the country's natural habitat. In line with this, Cambodian fisheries experts assert that Mekong dolphins were slaughtered wholesale by the Khmer Rouge for their meat and oil, claiming that "five dolphins a day were killed in the Tonlé

Sap alone". It was recently estimated that there are no more than 150 of these rare creatures surviving in the waters of the Middle Mekong, about half in Laos and the remainder in the Cambodian provinces of Kratie and Stung Treng.

Fortunately tourism may provide an economic stimulus for the protection and preservation of this unique species; certainly the Cambodian Ministry of Tourism is conscious of the potential attraction of dolphin-watching, and announced its intention of promoting the natural environment of the Middle Mekong as "an alternative destination to Angkor". The boatmen of Kratie know where the dolphins are to be found and will take visitors to see them for a small fee.

One such destination is the village of **Kampi**, about 17km (11 miles) north of Kratie, where a group of around 25 dolphins is said to be found. Visitors report that it is generally possible to see several of these large mammals, which grow to 2–3 metres (6–10ft) in length, hunting and playing offshore. The dry season, when water levels are lower, is the best time for spotting them. It is also easier to find them early

Guardian at the entrance of Wat Nokor Bayon.

LEFT: there are still some wild elephants in the northeastern forests.
BELOW: detail at Wat Nokor Bayon.

Just to the south of Kompong Cham, the river island of Koh Pbain is a popular picnic spot. In the dry season it is reached by a rickety bamboo bridge that is taken down and reassembled on an annual basis as the waters rise. The inhabitants are mainly Cham Muslims, whose men fish the river while the women weave cotton karma (see page 222) on looms set up in the shade beneath their houses.

BELOW: dolphin-spotting on the Mekong near Kampi.

in the morning or during the late afternoon when they are feeding.

Beyond Kratie, the Mekong continues due north for 140km (88 miles) to the riverside town of Stung Treng. The improved road from Kratie to Stung Treng runs inland, well away from the river, while the latter attains widths of several kilometres in these remote reaches. It takes between three and four hours to reach Stung Treng by express boat from Kratie, and services are far from regular. Until around 2002 there was a risk of banditry along this stretch of river, but these days the journey is considered perfectly safe.

Stung Treng

The town of **Stung Treng** (Stoĕng Trêng) ⑬ nestles on the banks of the Tonlé Sekong lake a short distance from the east bank of the Mekong. It is a small place, surprisingly clean, with a well-maintained park beside the waterfront. Passable accommodation is available, and the usual selection of Khmer and Chinese dishes is served in a couple of small restaurants located to the west of the covered market – the latter has

a dubious reputation as an important centre for trading in endangered species, including tiger and bear parts. There's nothing much to do or see in this sleepy backwater (less sleepy than it was, however, due to a new Chinese-built road to the Lao border), but Stung Treng does make a suitable base for trips upriver. It is now possible to charter a boat for a day trip to the Lao frontier about 50km (30 miles) north of the town.

The Cambodian border post at the hamlet of Phumi Kompong Sralau is marked by a small border station flying the Cambodian flag, while a little upstream at the Lao settlement of Thai Boei another building flying the Lao flag marks the frontier of the Lao province of Champasak (see page 167). Foreigners can now cross into Laos at this point, provided they have a valid Lao visa (obtained in Phnom Penh), and vice versa from Laos to Cambodia. It is now also possible to proceed upriver to the Lao town of Hat Xai Khun and thence to Pakse and Champasak. Make enquiries in Stung Treng before setting out.

It is also possible to cross the Mekong by boat from Stung Treng to

the small settlement of Thalabarivat, where the ruins of a pre-Angkorean temple may be seen. Similarly, a weekly boat runs from Stung Treng up the Tonlé Kong to Siempang.

The Northeast: Ratanakiri and Mondulkiri provinces

To the east of Stung Treng and away from the river lies the beautiful and undeveloped upland province of **Rattanakiri**, home to some of Cambodia's least-known tribal peoples. It is possible to reach Ban Lung, the provincial capital, by road from Stung Treng, but the journey is arduous and takes at least 10 hours – far longer in the rainy season, when the road becomes impassable. There is an airport in Ban Lung, but it is only open to private and chartered flights. The Ministry of Tourism is keen to promote both Rattanakiri and the adjoining province of **Mondolkiri** as destinations for ecotourism and trekking, but this project remains in its infancy.

As a part of this drive, and to protect threatened wildlife, almost half of Rattanakiri has been designated a protected area, including **Lumphat Wildlife Sanctuary** and **Virachey National Park**. Lying along the southern frontier of Laos and the western frontier of Vietnam, Virachey is very remote. Fauna which may be seen includes the slow loris, pig-tailed macaque, gibbon and douc langur, as well as wild elephant, gaur, bintang and sometimes even tiger. The area is also home to some of Cambodia's smallest and least assimilated minorities, including the Kavet, Brao, Kreung, Krachok and Jarai peoples. Despite its remoteness, Virachey is among Cambodia's best-administered national parks, offering organised tours from the park headquarters at Ban Lung. Roads within the province, as in neighbouring Mondolkiri, remain poor – though they are constantly being upgraded – but access by air (when it becomes available again) between Phnom Penh and Ban Lung is easy, and most of both provinces are readily accessible by four-wheel-drive vehicle except during the rainy season, approximately between June and October.

Irrawaddy (a.k.a. Mekong) dolphins can be seen in the river north and south of Kratie.

BELOW: cheerful face at Wat Roka Kandal.

Minorities

Ethnic Khmer are in a minority in remote Mondulkiri, where 80 percent of the population is made up of 10 tribal groups, the ethnic Phnong being the largest. The remaining 20 percent are Khmer, Chinese, Vietnamese and Cham. The population lives mainly by agriculture, planting rice, fruit trees and vegetables. Others grow strawberries, coffee, rubber and cashew nuts. Although most new houses are built in Khmer style, traditional Phnong houses can still be visited. Jars and gongs are considered the most important possessions of the Phnong and other indigenous minority peoples, valued in the traditional and spiritual spheres as well as in purely material terms. It was these tribal groups that were fêted by the Khmer Rouge for their "uncorrupt" and unmodernised way of life (see page 225).

LAO AND CAMBODIAN FESTIVALS

Visiting either of the two countries when they are energised by one of their exuberant festivals makes a special trip even more memorable.

The vast majority of festivals in Laos and Cambodia are derived from Buddhism and are tied to the lunar calendar. Buddhist festivals celebrated in both countries include the **Magha Puja** or "Day of the Four Auspicious Occasions" (January/February); the **New Year Festival** (April); **Vesak** or "Buddha's Birthday" (May or June); and **Boun Haw Khao Padap Dinh** (Laos, August) or **Bon Pchum Ben** (Cambodia, September/October), both of which worship deceased friends and family members.

Travellers often confuse the Khmer Water Festival, known as **Bon Om Tuk**, with Khmer New Year, due to the spirited nature of both celebrations, and the fact that Cambodians throw water in the New Year. However, Bon Om Tuk, which occurs in October or November, commemorates the victory of King Jayavarman VII over the Chams at Angkor in 1177. It also marks the time each year when the current of the Tonlé Sap River reverses its course. The three-day event, which rivals the Khmer New Year in its riotous exuberance, is celebrated in both Phnom Penh and Angkor with highly competitive boat races. The longboats are colourfully decorated and rowed by up to forty participants. It's a very busy time, so book accommodation well in advance. A month later, a similar festival, known as **Boun Awk Phansa**, is celebrated in Laos.

Other notable events include an ancient fertility festival in Laos known as the **Boun Bang Fai** or "Rocket Festival", and **Bon Choat Preah Nengkal** ("Ploughing of the Holy Furrow") in Cambodia. Both usually occur in May.

ABOVE: Cambodia's Bon Om Tuk festival takes place in October or November to mark the reversal of the current of the Tonlé Sap River. Also known as the Khmer Water Festival, it is celebrated with boat races and a great deal of water-based high jinks.

BELOW: the Buddhist Magha Puja festival is marked at Wat Phu near Champasak. In Laos it is usually called the Boun Makha Busa.

RIGHT: at the Bon Pchum Ben festival in September or October, the villagers of Vihear Sour village, 50km (30 miles) northeast of Phnom Penh, organise buffalo-racing and Khmer wrestling during the 15-day event, held in memory of the spirits of the dead.

THE NEW YEAR

Both Cambodia and Laos celebrate the New Year with festivities during the same week in April. The Khmer New Year is celebrated on 14–16 April and known as Chol Chnam Thmey. The Laos New Year, likely derived from the former, is celebrated on 13–15 April, and known as Boun Pi Mai. New Year's Eve is marked by fireworks at the stroke of midnight (apparently 1.36am in Cambodian reckoning). The eve and morning of the first day are times when families worship their ancestors at special holiday altars, and then visit the local pagoda to make prayers and offerings to Buddha. In temples people erect sand mounds representing Culamuni Catiya, the stupa at Tavatimsa, where Buddha's hair and diadem are said to be buried. Afternoon activities for young people during the holiday focus on traditional games – which include dousing each other with water and smearing talcum powder on each other's faces. The second day of the festival is a time to donate to charity and do symbolic works of merit. On the third day people visit local temples to bathe Buddha statues and receive baptisms from monks.

ABOVE: a New Year parade at Luang Prabang. The former royal capital of Laos is the best place to experience this joyful occasion, with various events lasting for a full three weeks.

ABOVE: water-splashing at the New Year. Foreigners are not exempt, so take care of valuables.

TOP AND RIGHT: New Year festivities in Laos often involve parades of masked characters.

PREAH VIHEAR

The temple of Preah Vihear is one of the most impressive Khmer historical sites. Closed by war for more than 20 years and in a sensitive border area, it is only intermittently accessible.

S et high on a cliff on the edge of the Dangrek Mountains overlooking Cambodia, **Preah Vihear** (known to the Thais as Khao Phra Viharn) is remarkable both for its interesting Khmer architecture and for its stunning location. Long claimed by both Thailand and Cambodia, the temple complex was finally awarded to the latter by the World Court in 1963, though the question of ownership still rankles with many Thais. This has led to periodic military skirmishes, resulting in the occasional temporary closure of the site to visitors. At the time of going to press, the dispute has cooled down and the site is once again open to the public (from the Cambodian side) with free admission to encourage Cambodia-based tourism there.

When it is open to tourists, the best access is via the province of Si Saket, in eastern Thailand. Possible bases are the Thai cities of Surin, Si Saket and Ubon Ratchathani, or the small Thai town of Kantharalak, which is just 30km (20 miles) away. The temple is best visited as a day trip. Leave very early in the day if you want enough time to explore properly: the site is large and closes early.

When approaching from the Thai side is possible, visitors must pay 100 *baht* entrance charge and deposit their passports with the Thai border police. The road to the temple stops abruptly at the Thai frontier, and visitors must proceed on foot across a rocky plateau, down a steep embankment, and then up a long slope to the initial – steep and tricky – temple steps. Thais often complain bitterly about the damage to the site, insisting that things would be very different if the temple was still in Thai hands.

Currently, however, access is from the Cambodian side via Anlong Veng. The road has been upgraded, but is dangerously steep at the top and unpaved along the bottom half. Visitors are required to purchase a ticket and use local transport (jeep or motorbike).

LEFT: overlooking the cliff face at Preah Vihear.

They are not allowed to walk or use their own transportation.

Temple on a peak

Preah Vihear is an extraordinary place, possibly the most impressive Khmer historical site after Angkor. Although in need of extensive restoration, the temple is quite magnificent, and one is left wondering how the original builders transported such massive blocks of stone to the peak of the Dangrek escarpment – a height of 550 metres (1,800ft). In fact, Preah Vihear took around 200 years to build, starting during the reign of Rajendravarman II in the mid-10th century and only reaching completion in the early 12th century during the reign of Surayavarman II. It was the latter monarch, a visionary builder, who also began the construction of Angkor Wat. It is thought that the Khmers held the locality in reverence for at least 500 years before the building of the temple.

Constructed in the Baphuon and early Angkor styles, Preah Vihear was originally Hindu and dedicated to Shiva. Of the four main *gopura*, or elaborately decorated gateways, the first two are in serious disrepair, though fine examples of carving – *apsara* and divinities – are still visible. The third and fourth *gopura* are comparatively well preserved, with a finely carved lintel depicting Shiva and his consort Uma sitting on Nandi, the bull.

The temple comprises five separate stages, with the massive bulk of the fourth, main sanctuary perched high on the clifftop. Here the great *prasat* or central spire has been thrown to the ground, and mighty blocks of carved stone lie in a tumbled heap. Everywhere there are army bunkers along the temple, ready to return fire, should Thailand decide to provoke yet another fight.

The temple is now firmly under the control of the Cambodian army, and young soldiers watch silently as a regular stream of visitors explores the ancient site. Once through the main temple complex, head for the clifftop behind for breathtaking views across the plains below.

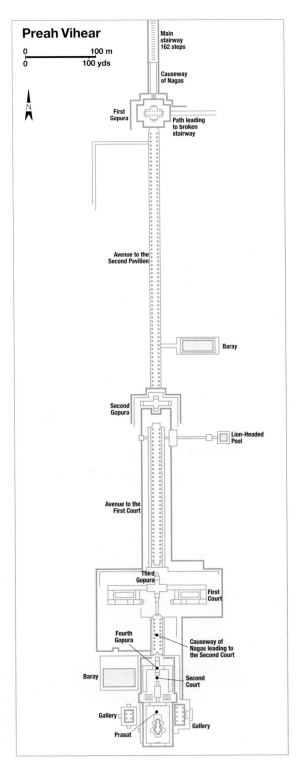

Preah Vihear

0 ———— 100 m
0 ———— 100 yds

N

Main stairway 162 steps

Causeway of Nagas

First Gopura

Path leading to broken stairway

Avenue to the Second Pavilion

Baray

Second Gopura

Lion-Headed Pool

Avenue to the First Court

Third Gopura

First Court

Fourth Gopura

Causeway of Nagas leading to the Second Court

Baray

Second Court

Gallery

Gallery

Prasat

THE CAMBODIAN COAST

Old French beach resorts are reawakening as foreign tourists and Phnom Penh's wealthiest head back to sand and surf. All the while, the country's greatest ecological treasures are only just being discovered.

In times past, before the war years, the Cambodian coast enjoyed an idyllic reputation among middle-class Cambodians, French colonialists and wealthy foreign visitors alike. Perhaps because of this historical association with domestic and foreign elites, the palm-fringed southern coast – a region studded with the elaborate villas of the wealthy, including that of King Sihanouk at Kep – fared particularly badly under the harsh rule of the obsessively anti-urban Khmer Rouge. Kep, in particular, was systematically razed to the ground, while ordinary people (except fishermen) were moved away from the coast to prevent the possibility of flight from the DK "people's paradise" by way of the sea. Even the movements of those permitted to fish were tightly monitored by Khmer Rouge cadres, while traffic through the port of Kompong Som was limited to the occasional exchange of Cambodian raw materials for Chinese and North Korean armaments and other aid.

Today all this has changed, and relatively fast. The coast is being developed as a tourist destination, and foreign investors have joined local businessmen in developing hotels, resorts and better-quality restaurants. To be sure, there is some way to go – but for the people of Phnom Penh and for foreign travellers, trips to the coast and long hours of swimming and sunbathing by the Gulf of Thailand are back in vogue.

There are two main routes south from Phnom Penh to the coast: National Highway 3 via Angk Tasaom to Kampot, and National Highway 4 via Kompong Speu to Sihanoukville. The 148km (95-mile) drive from Phnom Penh to Kampot takes 2.5–3 hours by taxi, while the well-surfaced road from the capital to Sihanoukville is 230km (143 miles) long and takes approximately 3–3.5 hours to cover. The

LEFT: mermaid statue on Kep Beach.
RIGHT: girl in a coastal fishing village.

Bamboo pipes are used for carrying palm toddy (made from the juice of coconut palms). Toddy is widely collected in Cambodia and used for making sugar or alcoholic drinks.

BELOW: a backstreet in Kampot city.

railway service south was discontinued; however, a new renovation is under way to revive Cambodia's rail lines.

Kampot

Kampot ⑮, the capital of the eponymous province, is a small, relaxed town of around 39,000 people. Just 5km (3 miles) inland, by the banks of the Sanke River, there is a coastal feel to the place which adds to its rather languid appeal. "Downtown" Kampot centres on a large roundabout space about 400 metres (1,300ft) east of the river. This area is the main commercial hub and also the location of the two best hotels. The road north from the roundabout leads out past a large covered market – a favourite with visitors from Phnom Penh, who stop off here to buy the fresh seafood for which Kampot is renowned. Of more interest to the foreign visitor, however, is the series of narrow, colonnaded streets leading west from the roundabout to the riverfront. Although in need of restoration, there are some fine examples of French architecture to be seen in this warren, as well as the best of Kampot's restaurants.

Travellers staying overnight in Kampot should check into one of the hotels at the roundabout, head east towards the river for a bite to eat, then walk the length of the delightful riverfront which, shaded by casuarina trees, offers views of the nearby Chuor Phnom Damrei (Elephant Mountains). There are some particularly handsome colonial buildings in this area, notably the **Governor's Residence** and the main post office at the southern end of the riverfront. Fishing boats cluster on the far side of the Sanke River.

There are just a few popular sites to see outside Kampot itself. One is Phnom Chhnork, a Funan-era cave temple about halfway between Kampot and Kep, reachable by tuk-tuk and located behind an unmarked wat.

Bokor National Park

Kampot shelters in the lee of the Chuor Phnom Damrei, a wild region of wildlife-rich forests and sheer rock

outcrops. About 37km (23 miles) northwest of town and located within **Bokor National Park** is the 1,079-metre (3,506ft) -high former hill station of **Bokor** ⓰. Often shrouded in mist, the hill resort was built by the French in the early 1920s, but later fell on hard times under the Communist guerrillas and the Khmer Rouge. The hillsides still harbour the danger of landmines, so visitors should keep to the tracks.

The ruins of the old hill station include the **Black Palace** complex, King Sihanouk's former retreat, the old **Bokor Palace Hotel** (now under renovation) and a small, abandoned church. The area went under extensive redevelopment by a Korean investor for several years, and was closed to the public. A new resort, casino and cable car are now open. Thankfully too, the national park road leading up the mountain has re-opened and visitors can once again explore the area. Undoubtedly, however, the casino will affect the previously peaceful atmosphere.

The journey up to Bokor Mountain requires a long and winding ride along a new road with hairpin turns. Visitors will be rewarded for their efforts, with absolutely spectacular views of the coast and cool (sometimes distinctly chilly) mountain air. If you wish to spend a night at the hill station, hostel-style accommodation is available, but do bring your own food, as there are no shops or restaurants (apart from the casino) at the top. Enquire at the ranger station (tel: 015-832 517).

Kep

Another old, celebrated resort town is **Kep** (Kipe) ⓱, known to the French as Kep-sur-Mer. The 30km (20-mile) drive from Kampot can be covered by *moto*. In prewar times the 7km (4-mile) stretch of palm-fringed beach was lined with the villas of rich Cambodians and French settlers, but then the Khmer Rouge arrived and destroyed virtually every building in town.

Today Kep is back on the tourist circuit, though much rebuilding remains to be done. Ruined villas and mansions, purchased (speculatively) by Cambodia's powerful elite for a pittance in the 1990s, dot the countryside. Some are currently occupied by squatters, but will eventually be redeveloped. For now the ruins add to the atmosphere. Although there are good hotels and restaurants here, many visitors choose to stay in Kampot, driving out to Kep for a day of sunbathing, fishing, swimming and indulging in the excellent local seafood – particularly crab.

Kep has two beaches: **Coconut Beach** is just south of a giant crab statue, and **Kep Beach** is overlooked by a statue of a nude fisherman's wife. Despite their popularity, however, the beaches are not the country's finest, and white sand has been trucked in from Sihanoukville to rejuvenate them in the past.

A short distance off the Kep shore lies **Koh Tunsai**, also known as "Rabbit Island", which can easily be reached by boat and makes a popular

Some of the final scenes of City of Ghosts (2002), starring Matt Damon, James Caan and Gérard Depardieu, were filmed in Bokor National Park, at the ruins of the Bokor Palace Hotel.

BELOW: the beachfront at Kep.

TIP

Within Ream National Park, ranger-led boat trips on the Prek Tuk River last about 6 hours. Trips to the nearby islands of Koh Ses and Koh Thmei can last all day. Stops can include beaches, fishing villages and snorkelling (bring your own equipment). Freshwater dolphins, dugongs and spot-billed pelicans are among the wildlife that can be seen in the estuary.

BELOW: the Indochinese tiger or Corbett's tiger (panthera tigris corbetti).

excursion. The island has four small but beautiful beaches with good swimming and snorkelling. The large island clearly visible to the south is Phu Quoc and belongs to Vietnam, as does the smaller Hai Tac Archipelago scattered to the southeast. The sea frontier in this region is still in dispute between Cambodia and Vietnam, and ownership of Phu Quoc in particular remains a serious bone of contention between the two countries. As a consequence, visitors sailing in the vicinity of Kep should remember to keep well inshore and to the west to avoid possible confrontations with Vietnamese patrol boats. The land frontier with Vietnam is only about 50km (30 miles) east of Kep, and the border crossing to the Mekong Delta town of Ha Tien is now open to international travellers.

Kirirom and Ream national parks

It is possible to travel directly from Kampot to Sihanoukville using National Highway 3, paralleling the run-down railway line, but most people will prefer to use National Highway 4 from Phnom Penh. This 230km (144-mile) journey takes between two and three hours by bus or taxi. Sihanoukville International Airport is 18km (12 miles) east of town. Flights were suspended in 2007 when a flight went down near Bokor hill station but have resumed from Siem Reap on a limited basis.

The road passes through the small provincial capital of Kompong Speu before rising over a forested spur of the Chuor Phnom Damrei. Just before the small settlement of Sre Khlong, a dusty road rising into the mountains leads to the former hill station of **Kirirom** ⓰ – a sign to the right of the road announces Preah Sumarit Kossomak National Park in Roman script. Once the hot-season retreat of wealthy Phnom Penh residents, Kirirom was – like Kep – deliberately blown up by the Khmer Rouge. At present it is still seldom visited, but as the site of Cambodia's first officially designated national park it is beginning to flourish again.

Cambodia's National Parks

Nearly 25 percent of Cambodia (43,000 sq km/16,602 sq miles) has been designated as wildlife sanctuaries, national parks or some other form of protected land reserve. Unfortunately, though, the government lacks the resources, and, in some cases, the desire to protect the parks adequately. As such, illegal logging and poaching are serious problems. Even with the help of several prominent NGOs, it's a battle that won't be won in the near future.

Protected areas of interest to travellers include Peam Krasaop Wildlife Sanctuary, the Southern and Central Cardamoms Protected Forests, and the national parks of Botum Sakor, Ream, Bokor, Kep and Kirirom. Most of these areas have had little encroachment by development and are a treasure trove of endangered species. Undoubtedly they also hide many "new" species, unknown to science. Tigers, elephants, gaur, leopards and langurs are found in the jungles, while aquatic species include the Irrawaddy dolphin, humpback dolphin, dugong and sea turtles.

Park rangers are paid precious little for their jobs, and confront many dangers in their work – including poachers armed with assault rifles. Please consider tipping generously when taking a guided tour. It not only encourages their conservation efforts but also discourages them from joining in illegal activities themselves.

After crossing the Chuor Phnom Damrei, Route 4 forks as it drops down to the coast; the southern fork leads to **Ream National Park ⑲** (tel: 016-767 686; daily 9am–5pm; charge), while the western route continues to Sihanoukville. Just 18km (12 miles) from town near the airport, Ream includes 210 sq km (81 sq miles) of coastal forests, including the Prek Tuk Sap estuary, mangrove forests, isolated beaches and two islands, as well as coral reefs. English-speaking rangers lead guided hikes and boat trips around the park, though the resident macaques, pangolins, sun bears and muntjac (mouse deer) are most likely to be seen after dark when the park is closed.

Sihanoukville

For the foreseeable future, Sihanoukville ⑳, also known as Kompong Som, will remain the heart of Cambodia's "Riviera". Like Kep, this town was once a holiday haven for the rich, and fortunately the Khmer Rouge wrought less thorough destruction here, probably because the deep-water port and railway terminus provided a key communications link with Phnom Penh. Nowadays, the resort town is packed at weekends with visitors from the capital. As the country's third-most-visited tourist destination, Sihanoukville is seeing a steadily increasing number of foreign visitors, and can be crowded during the dry season. There are numerous hotels and guesthouses of all classes, with many run by expat Westerners. Sihanoukville's restaurants offer a wide choice of cuisines, and seafood is fresh and plentiful. The city also has a healthy nightlife, with countless beach bars, several discos and nightclubs, numerous examples of the increasingly common karaoke bar, and even a casino.

The main activities are, as one might expect, sunbathing and swimming. There's also good snorkelling and fishing, while diving trips are available with experienced dive instructors. In all, Sihanoukville has about 10km (6 miles) of beachfront, divided into four main beaches.

Starting in the north, the first stretch of sand is **Victory Beach Ⓐ**, between the harbour and Koh Pos Island – really

Occheuteal Beach, Sihanoukville.

BELOW: a vendor tucks into one of her cooked tarantulas, with a live one going spare.

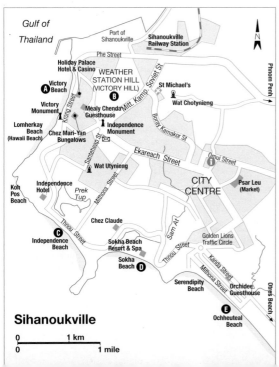

Sihanoukville

0   1 km
0   1 mile

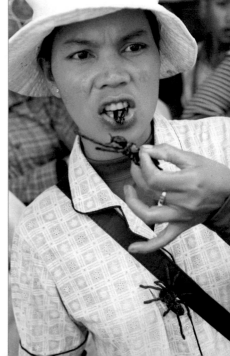

two beaches divided by a rocky point and a small hillock – about 2km (1.2 miles) long. The north end is more developed, with several restaurants and budget-priced bungalows. Right above the beach here is **Weather Station Hill** (also known as Victory Hill), once the main backpackers' area, comprising a plethora of guesthouses, restaurants and bars, travel agencies, CD shops and internet cafés. Lately it's become known as one of Sihanoukville's red-light districts, though some of the legitimate venues here adamantly oppose the trend. The southern stretch of Victory Beach is popular among Cambodians. Also known as Lomherkay Beach, it is lined with beach shelters and shack-style stalls.

Further south is a tiny stretch known as Koh Pos Beach, where the waves are rougher. **Independence Beach** , between the renovated Independence Hotel and the south-western peninsula, is popular with weekenders from the capital but is often deserted midweek. It has few facilities. **Sokha Beach** , between the peninsula and a Cambodian army base, offers a beautiful stretch of white sand, shady palm trees and adequate facilities. It is dominated by the lovely Sokha Beach Resort and Spa, but access to the beach is available to non-guests, including use of the resort pool, for a small fee.

Finally, **Ochheuteal Beach** , stretching away to the south of the town, is around 4km (2.5 miles) long, and relatively tranquil. Of all the beaches, this is by far the most popular, with numerous bars, restaurants and hotels recently opened or under development. It offers the widest variety of food and accommodation. The area at its extreme northern end is nicknamed Serendipity Beach, and here you will find bungalows, guest-houses and restaurants situated right on the sand. The far southern end of the beach is known as Otres Beach, though much of this section is being developed, and includes an enormous mansion owned by Prime Minister Hun Sen.

Visitors should note that Sihanoukville is a surprisingly spread-out place. The rather shabby and

Sex Tourism

Human trafficking, particularly in the form of sex tourism, is an epidemic in Cambodia. Most of the effort in combating the problem has been directed toward Western paedophiles seeking child prostitutes – much of which is happening in Sihanoukville. Unfortunately half of the perpetrators – Asian and, particularly, Cambodian paedophiles – are largely overlooked. Visitors should be aware that all forms of prostitution are illegal in Cambodia. Thankfully a number of Western countries, including Australia, the USA and the UK, have adopted strict new laws allowing prosecution of its citizens for under-aged sex abroad. Report suspicious behaviour to the Cambodian Hotline (tel: 023-720 555) or ChildSafe Hotline (tel: 012-296 609; www.child-safe-cambodia.org).

characterless town centre, with its busy markets and torn-up asphalt-and-rubble streets, is about 2km (1.2 miles) away from the port and railway station. Most visitors prefer to stay out at one of the beaches.

Diving off the Gulf islands

There are a number of offshore islands which can be visited by arrangement with one of several companies offering boat charters. Locals divide these islands into three groups: the **Kompong Som Islands**, lying close to the west of the port within an easy half-day's trip; the **Ream Islands**, which are scattered to the east towards the fishing village of Phsar Ream; and, finally and more distantly, the **Koh Tang Islands**, which lie further out to sea, between four and eight hours' journey from Sihanoukville.

Local diving companies recommend the Kompong Som group, and more especially Koh Koang Kang together with Koh Rung Samloem, for swimming and snorkelling when the prevailing winds are from the southwest (March to October). Koh Rong is home to the new, ultra-exclusive Song Saa Resort. The Ream group, more protected by the bulk of the mainland, is reportedly a better bet during the cool season (November to February), when the winds blow from the north. For snorkelling, the waters around Koh Chraloh, Koh Ta Kiev and Koh Khteah are highly recommended, though the proximity of the mainland and related high levels of silt can reduce visibility, especially in choppy weather. Finally, Koh Tang, Koh Prins and the nearby islands are recommended for more serious divers who may wish to spend a night or two away from Sihanoukville, either moored in the lee of one of the islands or camping on shore. This whole area is rich in a diverse marine life, with large fish, excellent visibility and sunken wrecks that can be explored with appropriate supervision. The most experienced and knowledgeable diving operator in

Sihanoukville is **Chez Claude** (hilltop near Sokha Resort; tel: 012-824 870; www.claudecambodge.com), which has been managing a diving resort since 1992.

The coastal "Wild West"

The coast to the west of Sihanoukville is almost completely undeveloped. There are no roads hugging the coastline around Kompong Som Gulf, and a journey overland to the isolated but beautiful province of Koh Kong requires a long drive on the newly developed National Highway 48. There is also an alternative route by sea, but at the time of writing it was suspended. **Tunlop Rolork**, a small fishing port about 2km (1.2 miles) north of Sihanoukville's main harbour, maintains a small fleet of fast boats which provide a passenger service to Koh Kong. These vessels are really intended to serve as river ferries and are ill-suited to rough weather in open seas, so are certainly best avoided during the southwest monsoons which blow between June and October. During the cool season,

Portable street vendor's wagon selling baguettes and snacks.

BELOW: the harbour at Krong Koh Kong.

TIP

Koh Kong was once a popular spot for Thailand's expats to make "visa-runs", until new Thai laws made this less practical. Like all border crossings in Cambodia, both sides of the line inspire complaints about corruption and questionable fees.

however, they provide a fast and convenient way of travelling along the coast to Thailand. The journey from Sihanoukville to Koh Kong takes between three and four hours, with boats leaving daily at noon. Check with local tour companies for the status, well in advance.

The alternative is to travel back up Route 4 toward Phnom Penh, as far as the small junction village of Kaong – a distance of about 60km (37 miles) – and then turn left for 15km (9 miles) to reach the small port of **Sre Ambei**. This is really the start of the Cambodian coast's "Wild West". It soon becomes apparent from the wide range of Thai goods available in town that Sre Ambei, although notionally a fishing port, is a smugglers' haven which flourishes on illicit trade with nearby Trat and Koh Kong. Goods are brought in by sea from Thailand and discreetly despatched to Phnom Penh and all points north via Route 4, thereby avoiding the docks and customs officials of Sihanoukville.

BELOW: maybe one to avoid…

There are a couple of dubious guesthouses, but Sre Ambei really is not a nice place to stay overnight. It does, however, provide a good base to visit **Stung Phong Roul Waterfall**, one of the most scenic in the country. The falls are 20km (12 miles) northeast of town, halfway to Kirirom National Park, via a rather treacherous road. Sre Ambei also has an attractive Buddhist temple, located on the hill behind the main market. Shared taxis from Sihanoukville do the journey in around 1.5 hours.

Koh Kong

The route that the fast boats take to Koh Kong cuts west across Kompong Som Gulf before turning into the open waters of the Gulf of Thailand and heading north along the coast. Most boats take the opportunity to stop briefly at Koh Sdach, the most important of the tiny and remote **Samit Islands**, where the really adventurous traveller may choose to stop overnight and take another boat in the morning. There is basic accommodation (try Mean Chey Guesthouse; tel: 011-788 852), as well as a number of fishermen's restaurants – though, as with Sre Ambei, smuggling is clearly a lucrative pastime in these waters and Koh Sdach is, by any standards, a smugglers' den. There is not a great deal to do or to see here other than snorkelling, though, and most travellers will prefer to head straight on towards Koh Kong.

About two hours' drive from Koh Sdech, **Koh Kong** ㉑ – confusingly the name of the province, the provincial capital *and* an offshore island – is a fast-developing coastal resort designed especially to appeal to visitors from neighbouring Thailand (particularly those renewing visas). It is also a convenient point for entering or leaving Cambodia by land. When Thailand shortened the length of visas available at land borders a few years ago this stunted the growth of Koh Kong as a visa-run destination.

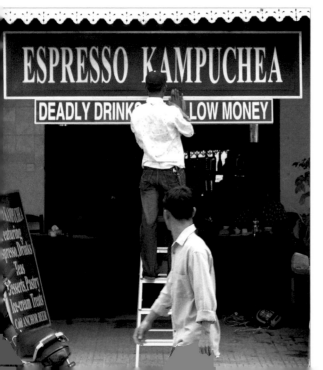

Nonetheless, the place has something of a Thai feel to it, being a clearing point for imported Thai goods, both legal and illegal, where the Thai *baht* is as welcome as the Cambodian *riel*. Before the "Zero Years" of the Khmer Rouge, Koh Kong was largely settled by ethnic Thais who had lived there for generations. After the Khmer Rouge victory most of them fled across the nearby border to Thailand. In the years since the Khmer Rouge were toppled from power, local Thais have moved back to Koh Kong in significant numbers, and Thai is widely spoken and understood here.

Koh Kong's most exciting development, however, is as a base for ecotourism. The nearby **Koh Kong Conservation Corridor** encompasses the **Cardamom Mountains**, **Peam Krasaop Wildlife Sanctuary**, **Koh Por** and **Tatai waterfalls**, **Koh Kong Island**, **Southern and Central Cardamoms Protected Forests**, and a portion of **Botum Sakor National Park**. All of these sights present endless outdoor activities and opportunities to see endangered species.

Koh Kong is just 10km (6 miles) by taxi from the border post of Ban Hat Lek, and the presence of Cambodia's larger neighbour is everywhere to be felt. Nearly all the consumer goods on sale in town are brought in by road or ferried in from Thailand. A casino on Cambodian territory just opposite Ban Hat Lek attracts many Thais keen to enjoy the gambling denied them by law at home. Should you decide to leave Cambodia here, take a taxi to the border post of Ban Hat Lek on the Thai side; from there, minibuses leave at regular intervals throughout the day for Trat, whereupon you can transfer to a fast, air-conditioned bus to Bangkok. Depending on the traffic and the time of day, it will take around five hours to reach Bangkok's eastern bus terminal at Ekamai from Trat.

Thanks to the newly engineered Highway 48 that passes through wetlands, forests and the Chuor Phnom Kravanh (Cardamom Mountains), Koh Kong is now more firmly connected to Phnom Penh and the rest of Cambodia. There is also an airport, with direct flights to and from Phnom Penh several times a week.

Cambodia's forests harbour an immense quantity and variety of insect life, including numerous colourful butterfly species.

BELOW: Serendipity Beach, Sihanoukville, next along from Ochheuteal Beach.

INSIGHT GUIDES TRAVEL TIPS
LAOS & CAMBODIA

TRANSPORT

GETTING THERE
AND GETTING AROUND

By Air

There are three international airports in Laos: **Wattay International Airport** in Vientiane, **Luang Prabang International Airport** in the old capital, and **Pakse International Airport** in Champasak province. Vientiane is served by international flights from Thailand (Bangkok and Chiang Mai), Vietnam (Ho Chi Minh City and Hanoi), Cambodia (Phnom Penh and Siem Reap), China (Kunming), Malaysia (Kuala Lumpur) and South Korea (Seoul). Most visitors travel via Bangkok, from which there are daily connections to Vientiane as well as to Luang Prabang. It is also possible to fly to Luang Prabang from Chiang Mai.

To save money on flying into Laos, one option is to fly from Bangkok to the northeastern Thai town of Udon Thani (for onward travel by road to Vientiane) or to Ubon Ratchathani (for onward travel by road to Pakse in southern Laos). From Udon Thani, the **Thai-Lao International Bus** takes visitors across the Friendship Bridge to Talaat Sao in Vientiane six times daily (8am, 10.30am, 11.30am, 2pm, 4pm, 6pm); from Nong Khai, the bus leaves six times daily (7.30am, 9.30am, 12.40pm, 2.30pm, 3.30pm, 6pm); alternatively, public buses (No. 14), tuk-tuks, songthaew (trucks converted into passenger vehicles) and taxis are also available. From Ubon Ratchathani, the Thai-Lao International Bus takes visitors to Pakse 4 times daily (7.30am, 9.30am,

BELOW: bicycling at dawn, Luang Nam Tha.

ABOVE: a tuk-tuk speeds through Vientiane.

2.30pm, 3.30pm) and takes 3 hours.

Lao Airlines (tel: 021-212 051/54; www.laoairlines.com) is the national carrier and provides regular services between Vientiane and the following regional destinations: Bangkok, Chiang Mai, Hanoi, Ho Chi Minh City, Phnom Penh, Siem Reap, Singapore and Kunming. There are also connections between Luang Prabang, Bangkok, Chiang Mai, Udon Thani, Hanoi and Siem Reap. There are flights between Pakse and Bangkok, Ho Chi Minh City and Siem Reap.

Bangkok Airways (www.bangkokair. com), Thai (www.thaiairways.com), Vietnam Airlines (www.vietnamairlines. com.vn), China Eastern (www.flychina eastern.com) and Jin Air (www.jinair. com) provide regular flight services to Laos. Check with the individual airlines for flight schedules and fares. Budget carrier Air Asia (www. airasia.com) offers cheap flights from Bangkok to Udon Thani as well as to Ubon Ratchathani, and has a direct flight between Kuala Lumpur and Vientiane.

Departure tax is included in ticket prices.

By Land

There are at present 17 international border checkpoints. You can obtain a 30-day tourist visa-on-arrival (VOA) at these checkpoints, unless otherwise indicated (see list below). As visa regulations may change without notice, check with a Lao Embassy or Consulate before travelling.

From China, you can enter via the Mengla-Boten checkpoint in Luang Nam Tha province. From Thailand, enter via one of eight checkpoints at: Chiang Khong/Huay Xai in Bokeo province; Huay Kon/Muang Ngeun and Nakasing/Nam Hong, both in Sainyabuli province; Beung Kan/ Paksan in Bolikhamsai province (no VOA); Nakhon Phanom/Tha Kaek in Khammuan province; Mukdahan/ Savannakhet in Savannakhet province; Chong Mek/Vang Tao in Champasak province (near Pakse); or Nong Khai/Vientiane via the Lao–Thai Friendship Bridge. The last checkpoint is the most popular among foreign visitors. If you are entering Laos at Huay Xai (Bokeo), Tha Kaek (Khammuan) or Savannakhet, there is a short ferry crossing across the Mekong River.

From Vietnam, you can cross at: Sop Houn/Tay Trang in Phongsali province; Nam Xoi/Na Maew in Hua Phan province; Nam Can/Nam Khan in Xieng Khuang province; Cau Treo/ Nam Phao in Bolikhamsai province; Na Phao/Chalo in Khammuan province; Lao Bao/Dansavanh in Savannakhet province; and Bo Y/ Ngoc Hoi in Attapeu province.

From Cambodia, you can enter by the Voen Kham/Si Phan Don crossing.

On Arrival

From Vientiane's Wattay International Airport the journey into the centre of town (about 4km/2.5 miles) is a painless 15-minute drive by taxi or tuk-tuk. Large hotels often provide limousine service from the airport if arranged prior to check-in. There is no airport bus service or public transport.

From the Luang Prabang International Airport the journey into the centre of the city (about 4km/2.5 miles) takes about 15 minutes by taxi, tuk-tuk or minitruck. Again, large hotels often provide limousine service from the airport if arranged prior to check-in. No public transport is available.

The journey by public bus or the Thai-Lao International Bus from the Lao–Thai Friendship Bridge to Talaat Sao (Morning Market) in the centre of Vientiane takes about 30 minutes. The journey can also be made by tuk-tuk, taxi or private car. The larger hotels can provide limousine pick-up service from the bridge if the arrangement is made prior to arrival at the border.

By Air

Lao Airlines (tel: 021-212 051; www.laoairlines.com) flies to several domestic destinations, and its service has improved in recent years, though

Bangkok Airways
57/6 Srisawangwong Road, Luang Prabang
Tel: 071-253 334
www.bangkokair.com
China Eastern
Souphanouvong Road, Vientiane
Tel: 021-213 300
www.flychinaeastern.com
Lao Airlines
2 Pangkham Road, Vientiane
Tel: 021-212 051/4
www.laoairlines.com
Thai Airways
70/101–103 Luang Prabang Road, Vientiane
Tel: 021-222 527/8
www.thaiairways.com
Vietnam Airlines
2nd Floor, Lao Plaza Hotel, 63 Samsenthai Road, Vientiane
Tel: 021-217 562/618
www.vietnamairlines.com

ABOVE: loading provisions onto a Nam Ou riverboat.

schedules still tend to be irregular and dependent on demand and on the weather. It is not uncommon for flights to be cancelled or delayed. Visitors are advised to confirm their flight reservation prior to travelling even if they have a confirmed ticket, and to arrive at the airport early, especially during peak seasons and around holidays.

The main routes are Vientiane–Luang Prabang, Vientiane–Pakse and Vientiane–Xieng Khuang. Less frequent domestic destinations include Udomxai, Huay Xai, Luang Nam Tha and Savannakhet.

There is an airport departure tax of 10,000 kip (about US$1.20) per passenger flying a domestic route.

If you have the budget, it is possible to charter a helicopter with a foreign pilot through **Westcoast Helicopter** in Vientiane. **Lao Air** (www.lao-air.com) also provides charter services on its helicopters and fixed-wing planes. A number of regional airlines also have offices in Vientiane (see box).

Lao Air Company
Wattay International Airport, Vientiane
Tel: 021-513 022
www.lao-air.com
Lao Westcoast Helicopter
Wattay Airport, Vientiane
Tel: 021-512 023
Email: enquiries@laowestcoast.com
www.laowestcoast.com

By Road

The road system in Laos has improved tremendously. An array of foreign governments and international aid organisations is currently funding road-improvement projects. However, many roads remain in poor condition. Inter-provincial transport by bus and truck is widely available, which makes it possible to visit at least part of every province in Laos.

Regular buses, many air-conditioned, supply the main national highways. There are also an increasing number of minivan operations springing up to take passengers in more comfort and slightly quicker than the regular buses. For more remote routes, large flat-bed trucks fitted with wooden seats, pick-ups, or trucks converted into passenger vehicles by the addition of two long wooden benches in the back (all of which are known as songthaew) are the most common forms of road transport.

Tuk-tuks, Jumbos and Taxis

For short trips in the centres of town, stick to tuk-tuks and jumbos (a larger version of the tuk-tuk); the pedicab (samlo) has virtually disappeared with the increase in motorcycle and car traffic. In Vientiane the city bus system is of little use to tourists, as it only runs between the centre of the city and outlying villages. Car taxis in Vientiane can be found in front of major hotels, the morning market and the airport – always negotiate the price before you set out.

By Boat

Not so long ago the 7,400km (4,600 miles) of navigable waterways in Laos constituted the country's only transport network. Today, they remain, by and large, a great way to get around the country. Services grind to a halt on some of the shallower stretches of water during the dry season.

The main long-distance river trip for tourists runs from Huay Xai in the northwest down to Luang Prabang. Boats take two days to reach Luang Prabang, overnighting in the riverside village of Pakbeng; alternatively, there are speedboats, which reach Luang Prabang in 6 to 8 hours. These vessels use a powerful engine mounted on a wooden boat and reach speeds of 80km (50 miles) per hour. Safety is a concern (also, bring earplugs). The beautiful Nam Ou River, which flows into the Mekong near Luang Prabang, is navigable most of the year as far north as Hat Sa near Phongsali and is considered one of the best river cruises in Laos.

These days, the route from

LAOS ◆ **317**

TRANSPORT

ACCOMMODATION

EATING OUT

ACTIVITIES

A – Z

LANGUAGE

Vientiane to Pakse in the south is mainly used for cargo traffic, but smaller passenger ferries from Pakse to Champasak and Don Khong still run.

A luxury alternative for river enthusiasts is now available on two routes. In the north, the vessel *Luang Say* travels from Huay Xai to Luang Prabang with an overnight stop at an attractive lodge near Pakbeng. The boat carries 40 passengers in comfort, and makes stops at points of interest along the way. In Southern Laos, the *Vat Phou*, a steel-hulled vessel with 10 staterooms, makes a four-day round-trip cruise from Pakse to the Si Phan Don area, visiting the famous Khmer temple site of Wat Phou as well.

Throughout the country, river taxis are available for short trips to sites such as temples and caves that are inaccessible by road.
Asian Oasis
Vientiane, tel: 030-525 8436
Luang Prabang, tel: 071-252 553
Bangkok, tel: 66 2-655 6246
Chiang Mai, tel: 66 53-278 338
www.asian-oasis.com

Bicycle and Vehicle Hire

Perhaps the best way to get around any town in Laos is to hire a bicycle, or, for more ambitious day trips, a motorcycle. Bicycles can be hired for the day from restaurants and guesthouses in towns throughout Laos, and small motorcycles can be hired from dealers in Vientiane, Luang Prabang and Savannakhet. Cars, pick-ups and 4WD vehicles are available for hire from private operators in Vientiane.
Asia Vehicle Rental (Europcar)
354 Samsenthai Road, Vientiane
Tel: 021-217 493
www.europcarlaos.com

Cycle Touring

Increasingly Laos is becoming a destination for long-distance cycle touring. Most cyclists bring their own bicycles with them; however, there are bicycle shops in the main tourist hotspots that sell bikes that may be used for touring. There are currently no hire options for long-distance cycling in Laos.

There are a few practical steps to enhance the cycle touring experience in Laos, the major one being what to take. The most important fact is that Laos, even in the rainy and cool seasons, is a hot place. It is important to pack light. With this in mind, cycling with backpacks, or camel packs for water, is not recommended.

Accommodation is plentiful and, therefore, there is no need to camp or take camping equipment. Likewise, most guesthouses will supply a towel and toiletries, even in the more remote areas of the country.

Another major piece of advice is spares – take spares for your bike. Whilst most towns and villages will have a local bike mechanic, there are always sections between that may need spares to be utilised. Take a spare inner tube, a puncture repair kit and a pump as a minimum. However, it is also prudent to take a spare spoke and a multi-tool to allow roadside repairs.

Maps and directional equipment are not essential, mainly due to the small number of roads and the reasonable signage in the country.

Finally, sunscreen, hats and sunglasses are all vital pieces of equipment. The average cyclist will spend 8–10 hours a day cycling in the sun. The choice of clothing needs to fit the conditions: usually loose-fitting tops and sportswear bottoms, with sandals or specific cycling shoes on the feet. Comfort in the warm, humid environment is crucial.

BELOW: Mekong riverboats.

ACCOMMODATION

HOTELS, GUESTHOUSES AND YOUTH HOSTELS

Choosing Accommodation

Hotel and guesthouse standards in Laos, especially in the larger towns, have improved tremendously in recent years, though there are still relatively few luxury hotels, and these are mainly located in Vientiane and, increasingly, Luang Prabang. There are smaller, "boutique" hotels and spas in many locations, especially in Luang Prabang, where the old town's UNESCO-protected status prohibits the building of multistorey structures that would change the former royal capital's character. Some of the most interesting places to stay include former royal palaces or villas, such as Villa Santi in Luang Prabang and the Champasak Palace Hotel in Pakse. Elsewhere, in the Mekong Valley towns like Savannakhet and Tha Khaek, as well as in Luang Prabang and Vientiane, former French colonial buildings are being similarly restored to function as boutique hotels or superior-quality guesthouses. Hotels are springing up at a pace in locations with tourist attractions – Phonsavan is one such place. The Laos tourist industry is driving a hotel-building frenzy in places previously reserved for backpacker-style guesthouses.

Away from the few main tourist areas, however, it's a different matter. Most accommodation is adequate – and improving – but aimed at a backpacker clientele, since wealthy businesspeople have little need to visit or stay in places like Attapeu, Luang Namtha or Udomxai. Therefore accommodation tends to be very reasonably priced, whether at mid-range or cheaper budget establishments.

Except in large, first-class hotels in Vientiane and at a few other locations, service can be slow, but is almost always friendly. Booking ahead by internet is easier than by telephone if you don't speak Lao (or Thai). Cable television has become increasingly common in recent years, with unlimited access to international news programmes – the Lao authorities, despite being at least notionally Communist, make no attempt to restrict access to services such as the BBC, CNN or Al-Jazeera. Most quality hotels have gone wireless over the past five years, and even if there is no internet access in your room, the chances are that you can get online in the hotel lobby. Upcountry or in backpacker guesthouses it's still rare to find wireless internet access, but the chances are there will be an internet café just around the corner.

There are no truly outstanding websites for accommodation in Laos, and those that do exist are often out of date. Perhaps the best are www.laos-hotel-link.com and www.asiawebdirect.com/laos.

VIENTIANE

Anou Paradise Hotel
3 Heng Boun Road
Tel: 021-213 630
www.anouparadise.com
Located in the heart of Chinatown, this clean, modern two-storey hotel has attractively furnished rooms with beautiful hardwood floors, air conditioning and satellite TV. It is a good option for those on a budget who also want a taste of the good life. Adjoining cabaret nightclub. **$$**

Ansara Hotel
Off Fa Ngum Road, between Wat Chan and Wat Ong Teu
Tel: 021-213 514
www.ansarahotel.com
With just 12 rooms and 2 suites this exquisite hotel, located in a quiet lane close to the river, is the perfect place to relax in Vientiane. All rooms are a mix of traditional Lao and contemporary Asian design with an attention to detail rarely found in many Lao hotels. One of the best views in Vientiane. **$$$**.

Avalon Hotel
70 Phnom Penh Road
Tel: 021-263 597
www.avalonbooking.com
Located some distance back from the river on a quiet residential side street, but well placed for most of Vientiane's sites, the Avalon has 32 air-conditioned, spacious rooms all with cable TV. **$$**

Best Western Vientiane Hotel
2–12 François Nginn Road
Tel: 021-216 906
www.bestwestern.com
A pleasant, well-situated hotel just around the corner from the Mekong. The rooms come with beautiful wooden floors, individual balconies overlooking the street below, breakfast and airport pick-up. **$$**

Chanthapanya Hotel
138 Nokeo Khumman Road
Tel: 021-244 284
www.chanthapanya.com
A friendly, family-run establishment with 31 air-conditioned rooms, a swimming

pool, spa and gym. It is close to the river and also an easy walk to the town's bustling night market. **$$**

Day Inn Hotel
59/3 Pangkham Road
Tel: 021-223 847/8
www.day-inn-hotel.com
Refurbished colonial structure with a refreshingly light and airy interior, large rooms and an excellent downtown location. Good coffee shop and friendly staff. Renovations have added outbuildings which are better value than the main building. **$$**

Don Chan Palace
6 Ban Piawat, off Fa Ngum Road
Tel: 021-244 288
www.donchanpalacelaopdr.com
Located 10 minutes from the airport, this 14-storey five-star hotel was built for the 2004 ASEAN summit and commands good views over the Mekong and Vientiane. All rooms have internet access, cable tv and all the usual amenities. **$$$**

Douang Deuane Hotel
Nokeo Khumman Road
Tel: 021-222 301
Email: dd_hotel@hotmail.com
This five-storey hotel is centrally located and the 55 good-value rooms come with parquet flooring and satellite TV. Rate includes breakfast and free airport transfer. They also run a guesthouse, the Douang Deuane 2, situated right across the road. **$**

Green Park Hotel
12 Khu Vieng Road
Tel: 021-264 097/8
www.greenparkvientiane.com
A local Vientiane family have developed this beautifully designed boutique hotel. Exquisite two-storey buildings surround a central courtyard and swimming pool. Lao-style rooms and fittings, plus the Champa Lao Spa and Sala Nong Chan Restaurant make this an excellent choice. **$$$**

Hotel Beau Rivage Mekong
Fa Ngum Road
Tel: 021-243 350
www.hbrm.com
Overlooking the Mekong

River, but a little to the west of downtown Vientiane, this boutique hotel offers peace and quiet in its well-furnished rooms, which include free wireless internet access, cable TV and IDD phone. The hotel's riverside bar and restaurant, The Spirit House, serves an international menu. **$$**

Inter City Boutique Hotel
24–25 Fa Ngum Road
Tel: 021-263 788
www.intercity-lao.com
A great view of the Mekong from all the riverside rooms plus a restaurant with a good variety of Western and Lao dishes. Huge rooms offer cable TV and are finely decorated with some superb Asian arts. **$$**

Lane Xang Hotel
Fa Ngum Road
Tel: 021-214 102
www.lane-xang.com
Situated on the banks of the Mekong, the Lane Xang has well-equipped rooms and good service at very reasonable rates. The restaurant has an international menu as well as traditional Lao dance performances every night. **$$**

Lani Guest House
281 Setthathirat Road
Tel: 021-215 639/216 103
www.laniguesthouse.com
A charming converted residence set back from a main road in the heart of Vientiane's central district, the Lani offers 12 spacious rooms, each with phone and hot shower, and a nice outdoor terrace. Big trees and an adjacent temple lend atmosphere. **$$**

Lao Orchid Hotel
Chao Anou Road, near Wat Chan
Tel: 021-264 134/6
www.lao-orchid.com
Slightly set back from the river and within walking distance of some of Vientiane's more interesting temples, the Lao Orchid provides large, comfortable rooms, all air-conditioned, with satellite TV. **$$**

Lao Plaza Hotel
63 Samsenthai Road
Tel: 021-218 800
www.laoplazahotel.com
This hotel is located right in

the centre of the city and dominates everything in the central quarter. It comes complete with all the services you would expect from an international-standard luxury hotel, including a pool, a fitness centre and a nightclub, email access and a piano bar where you can enjoy free drinks and listen to a lounge singer. Credit cards accepted. **$$$**

Mali Namphu Guesthouse
114 Pangkham Road
Tel: 021-215 093
www.malinamphu.com
In the heart of Vientiane near the Namphu Fountain, the well-appointed rooms come with hot showers, air conditioning and cable TV for a modest price. Breakfast is included. Very good value. **$**

Mercure Vientiane
10 Samsenthai Road
Tel: 021-213 570
www.accorhotels.com
Located just out of town towards the airport, the 172 room Mercure is a comfortable business hotel known for its beautiful swimming pool, tennis court and fitness centre. **$$**

New Lao Paris Hotel
100 Samsenthai Road
Tel: 021-222 229
www.laoparishotel.com
Good location in the heart of downtown Vientiane, this comfortable mid-range hotel offers internet facilities and a restaurant with Lao, Thai, Vietnamese and Western food. **$$**

Ramayana Gallery Hotel
Lane Xang Avenue
Tel: 021-214 455
www.ramayana-laos.com
Situated near the morning market on Vientiane's main avenue, the Ramayana (formerly the Royal Dokmaideng Hotel) offers a Chinese restaurant, swimming pool, fitness centre and internet facilities. Rooms are beautifully decorated with traditional Lao furnishings. **$$$**

Sala Inpeng
63/6 Inpeng Road, Ban Wat Chan
Tel: 021-242 021
www.salalao.com
Comfortable bungalows in a

lovely garden setting close to the river and with the option of breakfast served on your own private balcony, the Sala Inpeng affords good value. **$**

Settha Palace Hotel
6 Pangkham Road
Tel: 021-217 581
www.setthapalace.com
Once known as one of the grandest hotels in Indochina, the Settha Palace was originally built by the French in the early part of the last century. Magnificently restored, it is probably the most elegant place to stay in town, offering spacious guest rooms and suites with private terraces in a graceful colonial-era building. It also features period furniture, a first-class restaurant, a beautiful swimming pool and a sidewalk café. **$$$**

Vansana Phonthan Hotel
7 Phon Than Road
Tel: 021-413 895
www.vansanahotel-group.com
Quite a way out of town but quiet as a result, the Vansana offers a swimming pool and sauna, massage service, restaurant and a nightclub famous for traditional ballroom dancing. **$$**

Vannasinh Guest House
51 Phnom Penh Road
Tel: 021-218 707
Clean, quiet and well run, the Vannasinh is located on the outskirts of Chinatown and serves pretty good breakfasts. **$**

Vayakorn Guesthouse
91 Nokeo Khumman Road
Tel: 021-241 911
www.vayakorn.com
Centrally located with clean, well-furnished rooms and a coffee shop, on a quiet street near good restaurants and shopping. Four storeys tall, with some pleasant views. **$**

Viengthong Guesthouse
8 Fa Ngum Road

PRICE CATEGORIES

Price categories are for a double room in high season:

$ = under US$30
$$ = US$30–80
$$$ = more than US$80

Tel: 021-212 095
www.viengthong-gh.laopdr.com
Friendly, comfortable guesthouse located near the river. All rooms

are air-conditioned with hot-water bathrooms attached. **$**
Villa Sisavad
117/12 Ban Sisavad Neua

Tel: 021-212 719
www.villasisavad.com
This family-run guesthouse is located some distance from the downtown area,

not far from the Patuxai, but does have its own swimming pool and delightful tropical garden. Good value considering the price. **$**

VIENTIANE ENVIRONS

Ban Hom

Dreamtime Eco Retreat
Tel: 020-7789 5721
www.dreamtime-laos.com
Located in the forest some 25km (15 miles) to the west of Vientiane along the Mekong River, this is the place to experience nature in Laos. The retreat has seven bungalows, some by the river and others in the forest. **$**

Ban Pako

Ban Pako Eco Lodge
Tel: 030-988 4611
www.banpako.com
Located along the Nam Ngum River about 50km (30 miles) northeast of

Vientiane, this spot is popular with expats taking a weekend break. Beautiful scenery and superb swimming, boating and whitewater rafting. The best way to reach Ban Pako is to drive or take the public bus as far as Som Sa Mai village, then a short local boat trip downstream. **$$**

Vang Vieng

Elephant Crossing Hotel
Ban Viengkeo
Tel: 023-511 232
www.theelephantcrossinghotel.com
Wonderfully situated on the Nam Song River with views of the surrounding karst peaks. All 31 rooms boast

private balcony and air-conditioning. **$$**
Thavonsouk Resort
Riverfront
Tel: 023-511 096
www.thavonsouk.com
Originally opened in 1999 following the first influx of foreign visitors to Vang Vieng. Since then major renovations have turned this laid-back resort into one of the town's top picks. Accommodation is a mix of riverfront bungalows, Lao-style house and garden apartments. An excellent choice for travellers wanting a touch of luxury in a backpacker-dominated market. **$$**

Vansana Vang Vieng Hotel
Ban Sisavang
Tel: 023-511 598
www.vansanahotel-group.com
Part of a small Lao hotel chain, the Vansana's main attraction is its riverside swimming pool. The gym and business facilities set it apart from other Vang Vieng accommodation. **$$**
Villa Nam Song
North end of town by the river
Tel: 023-511 637
www.villanamsong.com
Sixteen beautifully designed rooms all with great views across the river, a beautifully landscaped garden, plus a first-class restaurant. **$$$**

LUANG PRABANG

3 Nagas
Sakkarine Road
Tel: 071-253 888
www.3-nagas.com
This boutique hotel housed in a huge restored villa has what could well be the loveliest rooms in town. All suites have four-poster beds, large bathtubs and private verandas. The restaurant-café serves excellent French and Lao food. **$$$**
Ancient Luang Prabang Hotel
Sisavangvong Road
Tel: 071-212 264
www.ancientluangprabang.com
Well situated in the middle of town near Wat Mai and the Royal Palace Museum, this boutique hotel has 12 of the finest rooms in town, each beautifully designed with satellite TV and Wi-fi. **$$**
The Apsara
Kingkitsarath Road
Tel: 071-254 670
www.theapsara.com
A charming seven-room

boutique property decorated with furniture and artefacts from Indochina. Rooms are spacious and comfortable. The restaurant is known for its fine Western food given a Lao twist. **$$$**
The Apsara Rive Droite
Ban Phanluang
Tel: 071-254 670
www.apsara.com
Situated opposite its sister property, on the far bank of the Khan River, the Apsara Rive Droit has rapidly gained a reputation for excellence since it opened in 2010. The hotel has its own boat to regularly ferry guests to and from the old city. **$$$**
Auberge Le Calao
Rim Khong Road
Tel: 071-212 100
www.calaohotel.com
Beautifully restored colonial mansion near Wat Xieng Thong, with great views of the Mekong from each room's private balcony. **$$**
Chitchareune Mouang Luang Hotel
Bunkhong Road

Tel: 071-212 791
One of the largest hotels in Luang Prabang, built in a mixture of traditional and modern styles. Attractive open-air restaurant. **$$**
The Grand Luang Prabang
Xiengkeo Palace
Tel: 071-253 851
www.grandluangprabang.com
This resort hotel is located 5km (3 miles) down the Mekong from Luang Prabang on a scenic bend in the river, and built in a mixture of French Art Deco and Luang Prabang architectural styles. The restaurants and all 76 of the luxuriously appointed guest rooms have views of the river. **$$$**
La Résidence Phou Vao
Phou Vao Road
Tel: 071-212 530
www.residencephouvao.com
On a hilltop overlooking Luang Prabang, this hotel has stunning views over the surrounding mountains. Neither in town nor too far away, the hotel has an

attractive ambience and a swimming pool with a view. **$$$**
Maison Souvannaphoum
Rue Chao Fa Ngum, Ban That Luang
Tel: 071-254 609
www.angsana.com
Originally Prince Souvanna Phouma's official residence, this place has rooms with terraces, and a garden. You might even be able to sleep in the prince's old room (book in advance). **$$$**
Phousi Hotel
Setthathirat Road
Tel: 071-212 192
www.phousihotel.laopdr.com
Well located for trips up Phu Si Hill, this hotel has a very pleasant garden. Popular with group tours. **$$**
Satri House
57 Pothisarat Road
Tel: 071-253 491
www.satrihouse.com
A former colonial residence with a lovely garden and swimming pool on a quiet street near the fountain. It

has 25 rooms and suites, decorated with style. **$$$**

Sayo Guest House
Kounxoau Road
Tel: 071 252 614
www.sayoguesthouse.com
Tucked away on a quiet street in the heart of the tourist district, this charismatic guesthouse has 20 rooms. All rooms are tastefully decorated with nice Loa cultural touches. The staff are friendly and attentive. **$**

Sokxai Guest House
Keely Village, Sakkarine Road
Tel: 071-254 309
www.sokxaiguesthouse.com
A beautifully renovated old house with 7 comfortable, air-conditioned rooms and within easy walking distance of some of Luang Prabang's most attractive temples. **$$**

Souk Lan Xang Guest House
20/2 Xieng Thong, near Wat Nong
Tel: 071-260 477
www.souklanxang.weebly.com
In an excellent location

down a lane near the Mekong River, this traditional old wooden house is a family-run place with large, well-furnished rooms. Considering Souk Lan Xang's situation in the heart of old Luang Prabang it offers very good value. **$**

The Villa Santi Resort
Tel: 071-252 157
www.villasantihotel.com
This resort 4km (2.5 miles) south of the town offers 55 beautifully decorated rooms in a rural setting with

mountain views. Set amid rolling hills, there is also a swimming pool. **$$$**

Villa Chitdara 2
18/2 Ounkham Road, Ban Wat Nong
Tel: 071-212 886
www.villachitdara2.com
A lovely, family-run guesthouse located in a renovated old colonial-style house overlooking the Mekong River. The owner, Mr. Vong, is a mine of useful local knowledge and an excellent host. **$**

NORTHEASTERN LAOS

Phonsavan

Auberge de la Plaine des Jarres
1km (0.6 miles) southeast of the town centre
Tel: 061-312 044
Email: info@plainedesjarres.com
Known locally as the Phu Pha Daeng Hotel, this pleasant establishment stands on a hillside overlooking the town. A series of cabins with attractive fireplaces, very

welcome on chilly evenings, are situated amid a beautiful garden. **$$**

Maly Hotel
1km (0.6 miles) southwest of the bus terminal
Tel: 061-312 031
www.malyht.laotel.com
Caters to all budgets; more expensive suites have TV and air conditioning. The helpful owner runs excellent tours to the jar sites. **$–$$**

Vansana Plain of Jars Hotel
1km (0.6 miles) northwest of the town centre
Tel: 061-213 170
www.vansanahotel-group.com
The Vansana has more amenities than anywhere else in Phonsavan. The hotel is on a hill, so make sure you ask for a room with a view of the valley: it's a superb vista and infinitely

better than looking at the drab town. **$$**

Sam Neua

Khaem Xam Guest House
Phati Road
Tel: 064-312 111
Close to the river, this four-storey establishment with its wide range of rooms is the best value in Sam Neua. **$**

NORTHWESTERN LAOS

Huay Xai

Thaveesinh Hotel
Sekhong Road
Tel: 084-211 502
Close to the ferry landing point, this rather soulless concrete building has more amenities than anywhere else in town and a wider range of rooms. **$**

Luang Nam Tha

The Boat Landing Guest House and Restaurant
Ban Kone
Tel: 086-312 398
www.theboatlanding.com

Located near the old town, 6km (4 miles) south of the new, this lodge offers wooden bungalows near the Nam Tha River. Activities offered include boat trips, tubing, mountain biking and trekking. The restaurant is the best place in the area to try local specialities as well as the usual standbys. **$$**

Zuela Guesthouse
Luang Nam Tha opposite the night market
Tel: 086 312 183
www.zuela-guesthouse.com

A lovely wooden house with a good restaurant and garden, the family-run Zuela also rents good bicycles and motorbikes. **$**

Pakbeng

Luang Say Lodge
Tel: 071-252 553 (Luang Prabang office)
www.luangsay.com
Sitting above the Mekong, the Luang Say comprises 17 beautiful, traditional Lao-style teak bungalows giving great views of the river and neighbourhood. **$$**

Phongsali

Viphaphone Hotel
Tel: 088-210 111
With large, comfortable rooms in the heart of the town, the Viphaphone is the best hotel in Phongsali. Good restaurant. **$**

Udomxai

Surinphone Hotel
Tel: 081-212 789
Great value for air-conditioned rooms with satellite TV and hot water. **$**

MEKONG VALLEY

Savannakhet

Daosavanh Resort and Spa Hotel
Ban Thahea
Tel: 041-252 188
www.daosavanhhtl.com
A clean, comfortable

modern resort with a fitness centre, swimming pool and superb views of the Mekong River, slightly to the south of the town centre. **$$**

Hoongtip Hotel
79 Phetsarath Road
Tel: 041-212 262
One of the better hotels in town, but still nothing special. Four storeys tall but no lift. Has a disco and a restaurant. **$$**

PRICE CATEGORIES

Price categories are for a double room in high season:
$ = under US$30
$$ = US$30–80
$$$ = more than US$80

Hotel Mekong
Tha He Road
Tel: 041-212 249
Old colonial building on the river front. Rooms in the old building have good views of the Mekong. **$**

Nanhai Hotel
Santisouk Road
Tel: 041-212 371
The largest and possibly the most luxurious place in Savannakhet, this Chinese-style hotel has a good restaurant attached. Quite a long way out of town. **$$**

Phonepaseuth Hotel
Santisouk Road
Tel: 041-212 158
A little way away from the river, but nevertheless a very comfortable, clean hotel. Across the road there is a swimming pool with free access for guests. **$$**

Phonevilay Hotel
137 Phetsalat Road
Tel: 041-212 284
Also known as the Riverside Resort, this quiet hotel has a large garden with bungalows on the river 1km (0.6 miles) south of town. **$**

Tha Kaek

Khammouane Hotel
Setthathirat Road
Tel: 051-250 777
Large hotel with air-conditioned rooms and a restaurant. Faces the river in the centre of town. The hotel can help arrange tours to the outlying areas and also to Vietnam. **$**

Riveria Hotel
Setthathirat Road
Tel: 051-250 000
www.hotelriveriathakhek.com
Large, tastefully decorated

rooms with great Mekong views make this modern, business hotel the best deal in town. **$$**

Sooksomboon Hotel
Setthathirat Road
Tel: 051-212 225
Fascinating, quirky interior decoration in this former French colonial police station. Perfectly situated on the Mekong with great views of Thailand. Air-conditioned rooms in the main building are good value, with hot water and satellite TV. **$**

Southida Guest House
Chao Anou Road
Tel: 051-212 568
Just a stone's throw from the Mekong, this family-run guesthouse provides comfortable and well-maintained rooms that come with air conditioning, hot

shower and TV. Some rooms have a balcony. The restaurant serves a variety of well-prepared local food. **$**

Thakhek Travel Lodge
Ban Vienvilay Moung, Route 13 between Km2 and Km3
Tel: 030-530 0145
Email: travell@laotel.com
A cosy backpackers' lodge with a variety of room types. The restaurant serves some of the best food in town, especially Western. The guesthouse can also provide very useful tips on trips to the various outlying areas of interest, including the increasingly popular three-day circuit known as "The Loop", through remote areas of Khammuan and Bolikhamsai provinces to explore caves and stunning scenery. **$**

SOUTHERN LAOS

Attapeu

Attapeu Palace
Ban Wat Luang
Tel: 031-211 204
This enormous hotel, just opposite the post office, seems somewhat out of place in Attapeu with its limited number of visitors, but it is being slowly upgraded, and facilities are certainly the best in town. **$**

Bolaven Plateau

Taat Lo Lodge
Taat Lo Waterfall
Tel: 034-211 889
www.tadlolodge.com
This lodge offers attractive chalets overlooking the Taat Lo falls; bookings can be made through travel agents. The open-air restaurant is a travellers' meeting place. **$$**

Tad Fane Resort
Ban Lak 38
Tel: 020-553 1400
www.tadfane.com
Set on the edge of the Dong Hua Sao National Protected Area and located about 12km (8 miles) from Paksong, the coffee capital, this resort consists of seven bungalows, some of which have splendid views across the valley of the Taat Fan

waterfalls. Guided treks into the village can be arranged. **$$**

Champasak

Sala Wat Phu
Main Street
Tel: 031-212 213
Pleasant rooms and a good attached restaurant in a French-era building which has been well restored. Some of the rooms have balconies, and there's an attractive garden. **$$**

Don Khone

Khonephapheng Resort and Golf Club
13 South Road, Ban Napeng
Tel: 030-516 0444
www.khonephaphengresort.com
Situated just 2km (1.2 miles) from the famous Khon Phapheng Falls, all 40 of the resort's beautiful wooden bungalows have private balconies facing the Mekong. Considering the resort's excellent facilities, room rates are something of a bargain. **$$**

Don Khong

Villa Muong Khong Hotel
Khemkhong Road, Ban Kang Khong

Tel: 031-213 011
www.laonatural-vlmkhotel.laopdr.com/
With a great view of the mighty Mekong, the Villa Muong Khong offers a variety of air-conditioned rooms, a fine restaurant serving both Lao and international food, and a pretty garden. **$$**

Pakse

Champasak Grand Hotel
Lao Nippon Bridge, Mekong Riverside Road
Tel: 031-255 111
www.champasakgrand.com
To the east of the main town, this large business hotel overlooks the bridge to Thailand. All rooms are air-conditioned with internet access, satellite TV and minibar. Other facilities include a number of good restaurants and lounges, swimming pool and fitness centre. **$$–$$$**

Champasak Palace Hotel
No. 13 South Road
Tel: 031-212 263
www.champasakpalacehotel.com
This huge hotel, overlooking the town of Pakse and the Sekong River, is the

former residence of the last Prince of Champasak, Boun Oum. Facilities include a fitness club and a bar. **$$**

Pakse Hotel
No. 5 Road, Ban Wat Luang
Tel: 031-212 131
www.hotelpakse.com
Conveniently located in the centre of town across from the Champasak Shopping Centre, this hotel offers rooms with en-suite bathroom, refrigerator and TV. In-house restaurant. **$$**

Salachampa Hotel
No. 10 Road
Tel: 031-212 273
www.salachampahotel.com
With lots of old-world charm, this centrally located French colonial villa provides large wooden-floored rooms, en-suite bathrooms and some of the most tasteful antique furniture in southern Laos. **$**

EATING OUT

RECOMMENDED RESTAURANTS, CAFES & BARS

What to Eat

Lao food is quite simple, making use of the country's abundant fresh vegetables, freshwater fish, chicken, duck, pork and beef. The staple of the Lao diet is sticky rice, which is used as a tool to eat most food by hand. Chopsticks are used only for Chinese and Vietnamese dishes. Spices used in Lao cuisine include lemon grass, hot chillies, peanuts, coconut milk, ginger and the unique *paa daek*, or fermented fish paste. One of the most common Lao dishes is *laap*, a "salad" made from minced meat, chicken or fish, mixed with lime juice, mint leaves and other spices. *Laap* is served with a pile of fresh leaves and eaten with sticky rice. Papaya salad *(tam mak hong)*, another favourite, is a mix of green (unripe) papaya, lime, hot chillies and fish paste, to which can be added ingredients like peanuts and tomatoes.

Thai, Chinese and Vietnamese food are common in Laos, a testimony to the political and cultural influences of the three surrounding powers. Vietnamese rice-noodle soup *(foe)* is often eaten for breakfast, lunch or a snack, and is served with a variety of fresh vegetables and condiments. Vietnamese spring rolls *(yaw)* are very popular, and are usually served with fresh leaves, cold rice-noodles and assorted dipping sauces. The French left their mark with baguettes *(khao jii)*, which are widely available and usually served as sandwiches with pâté, sliced meats and vegetables. Bakeries also now form a major slice of the culinary trade in Laos: all major tourist towns will have several bakeries selling an assortment of breads and baked cakes.

Lao sweets often involve a mixture of sticky rice and/or coconut, and

ABOVE: Luang Prabang's daily market.

are sold at markets in little packages made from banana leaves.

Where to Eat

Both Vientiane and Luang Prabang have a good selection of Lao and French restaurants, with the occasional Thai, Chinese and Vietnamese place thrown in. There are also a few good Indian restaurants, as well as places serving Lao food that has been sanitised (or at least toned down) for foreigners. Backpacker destinations such as Vang Vieng and Si Phan Don are well attuned to the tastes of their particular clientele, and it's easy enough to get Thai-Lao food or Western backpacker fare. Elsewhere in Laos it's another matter altogether, and dining choices are generally limited to noodle stalls, small rice-and-curry restaurants, and the occasional large Chinese establishment. One good thing about truck stops is that they tend to remain open quite late at

night, indeed until their clientele has shut down for the night. Restaurants away from the major towns and backpacker areas close early – it may be difficult to get anything to eat after about 9pm. Even in Luang Prabang things close quite early, and most restaurants and eateries will be closed by 10.30pm, with a few bars lingering on to nearer midnight.

Drinking Notes

Certainly the most popular beverage in Laos is the domestically produced Beer Lao, a mild and refreshing beer served in glass bottles and cans. Draught or "fresh" beer *(bia sot)* is also served in pitchers at simple bars and beer gardens in Vientiane. Lao men like to drink, and you can find them at these establishments every night of the week, and even during the day at weekends. *Lao-lao* is an incredibly strong rice whisky served at parties and important occasions such as weddings. *Khao kham* is a deliciously sweet wine, red in colour and made from sticky rice; it makes a pleasant after-dinner liqueur.

Coffee is grown on the fertile Bolaven Plateau in the south, and is some of the best in the world. It is usually served in a glass, not a cup or mug, mixed with both sugar and sweetened condensed milk. As this mixture results in a very strong, very sweet taste, Lao coffee is often served with a glass of weak tea or hot water as a chaser. Iced milk coffee *(café nom yen)* is popular as well, served with sweetened condensed milk over ice.

Fresh fruit juice – lemon, orange, coconut and sugar cane, among others – is served in outdoor stalls throughout Vientiane and other cities, while fruit shakes are also widely available.

VIENTIANE

In addition to being the political and economic centre of Laos, Vientiane is a culinary capital as well, where an enormous variety of excellent food can be found at reasonable prices. In particular, the French restaurants are some of the finest in Asia. Thanks to both its wide choice and its great value, Vientiane is arguably the best place to dine in Southeast Asia.

Lao

Bunmala
Khu Vieng Road
Tel: 021-313 249
Famous among Lao and expats alike for its excellent grilled chicken, duck and fish, papaya salad, sticky rice and fresh beer. Always crowded with Lao men passing the time for hours on end on weekend afternoons or weekday evenings. **$$**

Kua Lao
111 Samsenthai Road
Tel: 021-215 777
www.kualao.laopdr.com
An upmarket Lao restaurant which offers good-quality Lao and Thai food in a beautiful French colonial mansion. Nightly traditional Lao music and dance performances. **$$**

Makphet
Setthathirat Road, near Wat Ong Teu
Tel: 021-260 587
Spicy Lao food, cooked to perfection. The restaurant provides training to disadvantaged youngsters enabling them to eventually enter the food and beverage business themselves. **$$**

Nang Kham Bang
97/2 Khun Bulom Road
Tel: 021-217 198
This place offers some of the best Lao food in town, including specialities such as stuffed frogs, roasted quail, grilled chicken and fish. Always crowded with a mix of expats, government officials and Thai businessmen. **$**

Soukvimarn Restaurant
Bartolomie Road, near That

Dam
Tel: 021-214 441
www.laofoods.com
A small but highly regarded restaurant just around the corner from That Dam stupa, Soukvimarn serves good Lao meat, fish and soup dishes. **$$**

Tamnak Lao Restaurant
100 That Luang Road
Tel: 021-413 562
Well regarded by locals and foreigners alike, this restaurant serves very good Thai and Lao dishes. **$$$**

Bakeries

Le Banneton
46 Nokeo Khumman Road
Tel: 021-217 321
Breakfast bagels, baguettes and French pastries and perhaps the best selection of coffees in town coupled with some excellent choices for lunch make the Banneton a welcome addition to Vientiane's café scene. **$**

Joma Bakery Café
Setthathirat Road
(opposite Kop Chai Deu)
Tel: 021-254 333
www.joma.biz
The first of a chain of excellent bakeries to be found in Laos and Vietnam, this Canadian-owned café serves yoghurt, granola, salads, quiches, soups and sandwiches; in addition there are wonderful baked goods. **$$**

Le Croissant d'Or
96 Nokeo Khumman Road
Tel: 021-223 741
www.croissant-dor.com
The best croissants and French pastries in Vientiane, and a nice outdoor seating area just across from Wat Mixai. **$$**

Liang Xiang Bakery
111 Chao Anou Road
Tel: 021-212 284
On the main street in Chinatown, this small shop sells pastries of an entirely different quality, but the prices are cheaper and the ice-cream sundaes excellent. **$**

Maison du Café
70 Pangkham Road

Tel: 021-214 781
Also known as Life Coffee Break, this cosy little café serves a range of coffees, sandwiches and snacks, and can also arrange tourist visas, visa extensions and bus, train and air tickets. **$**

Paradice Ice Cream
Lane Xang Road
Tel: 021-312 836
www.ice-cream-laos.com
A French-owned ice-cream parlour serving delicious fresh-fruit sorbets in homemade cones. Coffees, sandwiches and light meals can also be enjoyed here. **$$**

Scandinavian Bakery
74/1 Pangkham Road
(near Namphu Fountain)
Tel: 021-215 199
www.scandinavianbakerylaos.com
Run by a Swede, the bakery serves fresh bread, pastries, sandwiches, cakes and good European-style coffee (with free refills). Outdoor seating on the fountain circle is available, CNN is always on the satellite TV, and the message board will give you a taste of expat life in Vientiane. **$$**

Chinese

Beijing Restaurant
Mekong Hotel,
Luang Prabang Road
Tel: 021-212 938
Known for its crispy duck, this clean restaurant offers a variety of Chinese dishes. **$$–$$$**

Chinese Liaoning Dumpling Restaurant
Chao Anou Road
Tel: 021-240 811
A favourite with the expat community, mainly due to its excellent selection of dumplings and fine vegetarian dishes. **$**

Guangdong Restaurant
91–93 Chao Anou Road
Tel: 021-217 364
Located in the heart of Chinatown, this place offers dim sum and other Cantonese specialities. **$$**

Hong Kong Restaurant
82/9 Samsenthai Road
Tel: 021-216 062
Authentic Cantonese flavours and also a small

selection of dim sum. If you are with a group it might be worth sampling the whole roast suckling pig. **$$**

May Yuan
Lao Plaza Hotel,
63 Samsenthai Road
Tel: 021-218 800
www.laoplazahotel.com
Elegant dining room specialises in dim sum and offers lunch specials in addition to the à la carte menu. **$$$**

French

Bistro 22
22 Samsenthai Road
Tel: 021-214 129
Close to the Sacred Heart Catholic Church, Bistro 22 has quietly built a reputation for its excellent French dishes; the set three-course lunch is good value. **$$$**

Chokdee Café
Fa Ngum Road, Ban Xieng Nyeun
Tel: 021-263 847
www.chokdeecafe.com
Actually a Belgian bar and restaurant, the Chokdee serves some of the very best French/Belgian food in town. A wide choice of soups, salads and desserts plus a superb choice of Belgian beers. **$$**

La Belle Epoque
Settha Palace Hotel,
6 Pangkham Road
Tel: 021-217 581
www.setthapalace.com
One of Vientiane's most exclusive and long-standing restaurants, the Belle Epoque maintains its charm and presents the visitor with an elegant dining experience. **$$$**

La Terrasse
55/4 Nokeo Khumman Road
Tel: 021-218 550
Busy almost every night of the week, La Terrasse is one of the best deals in town, serving hamburgers, pizzas, large salads, grilled brochettes, Tex-Mex fare like burritos, and an array of mixed drinks (including Margaritas). **$$**

Le Côte d'Azur
63 Fa Ngum Road
Tel: 021-217 252
One of the hottest spots in

Vientiane, this French restaurant offers a bright, spacious and comfortable dining room and an extensive menu featuring excellent Provençal fare – fresh seafood, creative salads and some of the best pizza around. **$$$**

Le Provençal
Nam Phu Circle,
73/1 Pangkham Road
Tel: 021-216 248
Located on Vientiane's central circle, this place offers French and Mediterranean cuisine, including pizzas, pastas, seafood, grilled steaks, salade Niçoise and a good wine selection. **$$$**

Le Silapa
17/1 Sihom Road
Tel: 021-219 689
Considered by resident expats as the best place for Western food in Vientiane, Le Silapa serves high-standard French food from an often-changing menu. The restaurant has an unusual programme to help Lao children: for every bottle of wine opened, a donation is made to treat children's health problems. **$$$**

Namphu
Nam Phu Circle
Tel: 021-216 248
One of the oldest upmarket establishments, the Namphu has a good bar and serves excellent French and German food, including pâtés and some impressive desserts. Expats rave about the blue-cheese hamburgers. **$$$**

Restaurant Le Vendôme
Wat Inpeng Road
Tel: 021-216 402
A less expensive French option, this cosy little restaurant is hidden on a back road just opposite Wat Inpeng and offers traditional French dishes; the candlelit outdoor terrace is a very nice touch. **$$**

Santisouk Restaurant
Nokeo Khumman Road
Tel: 021-215 303
This place has been around since before the revolution, and was once known as Café La Pagode. It is known for its sizzling steak and *filet mignon* platters, good breakfasts and retro

ABOVE: tasty fare at Km 52 Market, near Vientiane.

atmosphere. Also serves Lao food. **$**

Indian

Nazim Restaurant
39 Fa Ngum Road
Tel: 021-223 480
Extremely popular with tourists and expats alike, the halal menu has a southern Indian feel. Though the interior is plain, the food is tasty, especially the vegetarian dishes. **$$**

Taj Mahal
Setthathirat Road
Tel: 020-561 1003
Tasty and reasonably priced dishes, with vegetarian options also available. **$**

International

Khop Chai Deu Restaurant-Bar
54 Setthathirat Road, next to the Namphu Fountain
Tel: 021-251 564
www.khopchaideu.com
A lovely outdoor food garden in the grounds of an illuminated (and pleasantly dilapidated) two-storey French mansion, this place serves a wide range of food, including barbecue dishes, soups and salads, an international menu, ice creams and desserts, as well as an economical lunch buffet. A live band plays most evenings after 9pm. **$$**

Sticky Fingers
10/3 François Nginn Road (opposite Tai Pan Hotel)
Tel: 021-215 972
Open until late, this popular restaurant and bar with a lively atmosphere serves

Lao and international dishes. Breakfast, great cocktails and deliveries are available. **$$**

Xayoh Grill House
Samsenthai Road (next to the National Cultural Hall)
Tel: 021-261 777
A well-decorated and airy place, good for burgers, pizza and drinks. A travellers' meeting place. **$$**

Italian

Aria Mixai
8 François Nginn Road
Tel: 021-222 589
www.ariaorg.com
Wood-fire oven pizzas and home-made pasta, excellent lunchtime buffet and a strong wine list make this one of Vientiane's very best restaurants. **$$$**

L'Opera
Namphu Circle
Tel: 021-215 099
One of the most upmarket restaurants in Vientiane, L'Opera offers excellent Italian food in a romantic setting. The Italian owner ensures service is impeccable and that opera music is always playing. Frequented by the diplomatic and business communities, the restaurant's takeaway *gelati* bar is a highlight. **$$$**

Japanese

Fujiwara
Luang Prabang Road
Tel: 021-222 210
A mid-price Japanese restaurant offering an extensive menu. The sashimi is

very good, and local expat Japanese rate this place very highly. **$$**

NOS Sushi
Hang Boun Road
Tel: 021-265 000
A long list of Japanese favourites, but it's the sushi that really catches the attention, all prepared in front of you. **$$**

Sakura Japanese Restaurant
Km 2, Luang Prabang Road
Tel: 021-212 274
Sakura is perennially popular among Japanese expats for its high-quality (and highly priced) sushi sets and traditional Japanese ambience. **$$$**

Spanish

I-Beam
Setthathirat Road, opposite Wat Ong Teu
Tel: 021-254 528
Vientiane's very own tapas bar. It's definitely worth trying the tasting menu, and they also have a good selection of wines. **$$**

Thai

Just for Fun
Pangkham Road
Tel: 021-213 642
www.justforfun.laopdr.com
This funky little shop serves

PRICE CATEGORIES

Price categories are per person for a meal without drinks:

$ = under US$5
$$ = US$5–15
$$$ = more than US$15

TRANSPORT

ACCOMMODATION

EATING OUT

ACTIVITIES

A – Z

LANGUAGE

a good variety of Thai and Lao dishes (all available in vegetarian varieties), herbal teas, great coffee and the best chocolate cake in town. You can also buy traditional Lao handicrafts here. **$**

Linda Sathaporn Restaurant
Dongpalan Road
Tel: 021-416 214
A bit far out of town, the

well-known Sathaporn serves all sorts of Thai curry and noodle dishes in its spacious dining room, or for takeaway. **$**

Vegetarian

Khouadin Vegetarian
Nong Bon Road
Tel: 021-215 615
The daily buffet is a great collection of Lao and Thai vegetarian dishes. **$**

Vietnamese

PVO
Fa Ngum Road
Tel: 021-214 444
This old Vientiane favourite, now on the river front, dishes up a good range of Vietnamese food. Spring rolls served with vegetables, cold rice noodles and peanut dipping sauce are the speciality of the house, as are the superb baguettes

stuffed with pâté. **$**
Viengsavanh
43/3 Heng Boun Road
Tel: 021-213 990
A small, popular restaurant in Chinatown known for two dishes: barbecued pork meatball sets served with a peanut sauce, and raw beef strips that diners cook in pots of coconut water and eat with various sauces. **$**

VIENTIANE ENVIRONS

ABOVE: the French connection – baguettes in Vientiane.

Vang Vieng

Luang Prabang Bakery
Near Wat Kang
Tel: 023-511 145
Highly popular travellers' café with some excellent

coffee and cakes, as well as good breakfasts. **$**
Organic Mulberry Farm Café
Ban Sisavang
Tel: 023-511 174

Connected to the Organic Mulberry Farm located a few kilometres north of Vang Vieng, the café serves delicious shakes made mostly from home-grown produce.

The mulberry shakes are particularly good. **$**
Peeping Som's Bar and Restaurant
Main street, near Wat Kang
A great mix of Western and Lao food. The people who run the place are happy to share their local knowledge and the place has a selection of board games such as backgammon. **$**
Xayoh Riverside
Sisavang Road
Tel: 023-511 088
www.xayohgroup.com
With a picturesque riverside location, the Xayoh, part of the Ban Sabai Bungalows, does a range of good international food, including steaks and pizzas. They also serve a few interesting Lao dishes. **$**

LUANG PRABANG

The Apsara
Kingkitsarath Road
Tel: 071-254 670
www.theapsara.com
An excellent fusion menu of Lao and Thai dishes is served here. The open-air bar and dining area, which overlooks the Khan River, is a good place to lounge at. **$$$**
Blue Lagoon
Ban Choumkong, beside the Royal Palace Museum
Tel: 071-253 698
www.blue-lagoon-restaurant.com
Elegant Swiss-German establishment with an extensive and sophisticated menu as well as a long wine list. Set in a tranquil garden

courtyard. **$$$**
Joma Bakery Café
Chao Fa Ngum Road (next to the post office)
Tel: 071-252 292
www.joma.biz
A well-known and well-regarded bakery and café selling a splendid variety of pastries and breads. **$**
Le Café Ban Vat Sene
Sakkarine Road
Tel: 071-252 482
www.elephant-restau.com
Run by the same owner as the famous L'Eléphant restaurant, this quiet and lovely café features pastries, sandwiches and salads. Order a Lao coffee to wash it all down. **$$**

Dyen Sabai
Ban Phan Luang, near Wat Phan Luang
Tel: 020-510 4817
www.dyensabai.com
An excellent Lao restaurant located on the other side of the Khan River opposite the old city. Specialises in a Lao-style fondue cum barbecue, and, in season, the mango and sweet sticky rice is excellent. **$**
L'Eléphant Restaurant
Ban Wat Nong
Tel: 071-252 482
www.elephant-restau.com
An elegant French brasserie situated on a corner in the most picturesque part of the old city. A daytime tea salon

and a variety of daily specials including vegetarian meals make this many visitors' favourite restaurant in Luang Prabang. **$$$**
Lao Lao Garden
Phu Si Road
Tel: 020-7777 0446
Serve-yourself Lao barbecues are the standard here, but they also do some good laap dishes, including an unusual vegetarian one. There's a long list of cocktails to choose from. **$**
Luang Prabang Bakery
17/1 Choumkong Village, Sisavangvong Road
Tel: 071-252 499
www.luangprabang-bakery.com
Café-style establishment

serving excellent salads, quiches, sandwiches and tasty pastries. **$**

Tamarind
Next to The Apsara Hotel
Tel: 071-213 128
www.tamarindlaos.com
One of Luang Prabang's truly exceptional dining experiences, the Tamarind offers a wonderful selection of

traditional and modern Lao cuisine. The fruit and vegetable juices are particularly refreshing on a hot day. **$$**

Tamnak Lao Restaurant
Sakkarine Road, Ban Wat Saen
Tel: 071 252 525
www.tamnaklao.net
Sister restaurant of the successful Tamnak Lao in Vientiane. The restaurant

prides itself on the freshness of Its dishes, nothing is pre-prepared and the food is all the better for it. They also run a respected cooking school opposite Villa Santi in a nearby lane. **$$**

Tum Tum Cheng Restaurant and Cooking School
Sakkarine Road

Tel: 071-253 187
Tastefully decorated, this third TTC branch to open in Luang Prabang serves Lao and Lao-European food. Cooking classes are also held here; Chef Chandra will show you how to prepare Lao meals and select ingredients. **$$**

MEKONG VALLEY

Savannakhet

Au Rendez-Vous Restaurant
179 Ratsavongseuk Road
Tel: 041-213 181
A short walk from the Xayamoungkhoun Guesthouse, this restaurant serves a good selection of reasonably priced Chinese and Khmer dishes and a few Western ones. **$**

Cafe Anakot
Ratsavongseuk Road
Tel: 020-7774 8154
www.cafeanakot.blogspot.com
Run by a friendly Japanese woman, this is a good choice for a healthy breakfast, although it's open all day serving a wide selection of dishes including chicken pesto and cheddar cheese sandwiches. **$**

Hoongtip Garden Restaurant
79 Phetsarath Road
Tel: 041-212 262
An extensive choice of Lao, Thai and Chinese dishes makes this probably the best place in town. It's attached to the hotel of the same name in an attractive old wooden building. **$**

Lao Paris
Si Muang Road
Tel: 041-212 792
Offering a small variety of Lao, Vietnamese and French food, this simple place even serves French wine by the glass. The service tends to be polite rather than friendly. **$$**

PK Cuisine
Si Muang Road
Tel: 041-212 022
This small eatery serves

good-value Thai food. Open for lunch and dinner. **$**

Tha Kaek

Kaysone Restaurant
Just off Chao Anou Road, centre of town
Tel: 051-212 563
The Kaysone is known as much for its fine selection of ice cream as its Lao specialties and Korean barbecue. **$**

Noodle shops
Riverside, Setthathirat Road
Large shady trees cover a few tables by the banks of the Mekong; a good place to sit and have a cold drink or order noodles from across the road. **$**

Phavilai Restaurant
Fountain Square
A good place for basic Lao cuisine and Chinese noodle dishes. Located on a city

square that exudes colonial atmosphere. **$**

Smile Barge Restaurant
Tel: 051-212 150
A floating restaurant on the river with good Lao dishes and drinks. Stay the evening if you are inclined to partake of the karaoke sessions. **$**

Southida Guesthouse
Chao Anou Road
Tel: 051-212 568
Located near the Mekong, Southida has a restaurant that serves good local food. **$**

Thakhek Travel Lodge
Ban Vienvilay Moung,
Route 13 between Km 2 and Km 3
Tel: 030-530 0145
Although a little far from the centre of town, this is the place to go if you are hankering for Western food. **$**

SOUTHERN LAOS

Champasak

Saythong Restaurant
Just south of the roundabout on the main street
Tel: 031-920 092
Superbly located, overlooking the Mekong, and renowned for its large portions, the Saythong serves Lao dishes and a smattering of travellers' favourites. **$**

Don Khong

Pon's
Pon's River Guest House,
Ban Kang Khong
Tel: 031-214 037
www.ponnsriverguesthouse-donkhong.com
Plenty of fresh fish straight out of the Mekong, the fish soups are particularly good.

The menu is extensive, mainly Lao and Thai, but there are a few Western standards to fall back on, too. **$**

Pakse

Bolaven Cafe
No. 13 Road South
Tel: 031-214 791
Great place for excellent fair-trade coffee and a hearty breakfast. Plenty of cakes and desserts and some good noodle dishes served all day by the friendly Mama Tan. **$**

Jasmine Restaurant
No. 13 Road
Tel: 031-251 002
The Jasmine now has some stiff rivalry from the Nazim

Indian Restaurant, but still comes out on top. A small selection of Malay dishes accompanies a reasonable variety of Indian dishes; the Rogan Josh is recommended. **$**

Ketmany Restaurant
No. 13 Road, Ban Phabath
Tel: 031-212 615
Situated next to @d@m's Internet Café, this air-conditioned restaurant (with outdoor seats) serves Chinese, Lao and Western dishes, as well as ice cream and drinks. **$**

Na Dao
Near the Japanese Bridge
Tel: 020-5550 4884
The only really fine dining experience to be found in Pakse. The chef owner built

his reputation in Vientiane and then relocated to Pakse serving a mix of French and Lao specialities. **$$$**

Attapeu

Thi Thi Restaurant
Near Wat Luang Muang Mai
Tel: 036-211 303
Serves good Vietnamese food and also some seafood dishes. Tickets for the buses to Vietnam are sold here. **$**

PRICE CATEGORIES

Price categories are per person for a meal without drinks:

$ = under US$5
$$ = US$5–15
$$$ = more than US$15

ACTIVITIES

THE ARTS, NIGHTLIFE, FESTIVALS, SHOPPING AND SPORT

THE ARTS

Cultural Performances

Lao classical music and dance began to re-emerge in the 1990s after years of suppression by the Communist regime which considered them to be a link with the non-Socialist past. Folk dances and music fared rather better because they were considered indigenously Lao, rather than the foreign-influenced classical traditions. Performances of the dance drama known as *Phra Lak Phra Ram*, based on the Indian epic *Ramayana*, are regularly staged, accompanied by classical music that is rather similar to the Thai classical music tradition.

Since Luang Prabang is the former capital of royal Laos, it is not surprising that the traditions are best kept there. Cultural performances are held within the **Royal Palace** (National Museum) compound at the Royal Ballet Theatre on Mondays, Wednesdays, Fridays and Saturdays at 6pm. The performance includes Lao classical and folk dances and music, as well as traditional ballet enactments of episodes from *Phra Lak Phra Ram*. For information tel: 071-253 705 or 020-5597 1400.

In Vientiane, you can catch these performances at major hotels and the **Lao National Theatre** on Manthatulat Road. The latter has a nightly traditional dance and music performance, tel: 021-242 978. Lane Xang Hotel features a nightly traditional dance show at its restaurant, while Dok Champa Restaurant at the Lao Plaza Hotel offers Lao classical music and dance performances at dinner time from Monday to Friday.

NIGHTLIFE

Laos is not known for its wild nightlife. In fact, outside of Vientiane and Luang Prabang (and to some extent Vang Vieng), it is virtually non-existent. The government has played a role in this, seeing such venues as bars and nightclubs to be corrupt Western influences. The authorities have little tolerance for prostitution, and sexual relationships between a Lao citizen and a foreigner who are not married to each other are still prohibited by law.

Of cultural interest is the mis-named Lao "disco" which in fact has live music and a variety of dance styles including *lam wong*, a traditional Lao group folk dance, as well as ballroom dancing. Hotels in Vientiane have Western-style discos with high-volume Thai and Western favourites and are frequented by the young elite and some foreigners. A less frenetic option for an evening on the town is the pub scene. These pubs cater to foreigners with well-stocked bars, relaxing music and atmosphere.

In Vientiane, Khop Chai Deu and Sticky Fingers, in addition to being good restaurants, are also excellent places to hang out in the evenings (see pages 325 and 325).

Vientiane

Bars

Blue Note Pub
Lao Plaza Hotel
63 Samsenthai Road
Tel: 021-218 800

In the basement of the Lao Plaza Hotel, the Blue Note has a modern sound system and private karaoke rooms. Upstairs, at the Lobby Lounge, an acoustic band plays live between 8.30 and 10.30pm from Monday to Saturday.
Déjà Vu
Namphu Circle
Tel: 020-561 0735
This small, upmarket bar serves a wide range of cocktails that are highly recommended. Open until midnight.
Jazzy Brick
43/1 Setthathirat Road
Tel: 020-771 1138
Another upmarket pub that features good wines, low light and soft jazz music. It usually opens until quite late.
Kong View
183 Souphanouvong Road
Tel: 021-520 522
www.view-goodview.com
A great place to sit and watch the sun go down over the mighty Mekong with an iced pitcher of Beer Lao and a variety of snacks.
La Cave des Châteaux
Namphu Circle
Tel: 021-212 192
A French-style wine merchant offering imported French wines, cheeses and meats for tasting and takeaway.
Mekong Deck
Fa Ngum Road
Tel: 021-263 226
Overlooking the Mekong, the swanky Deck is a multi-level dining and drinking experience. A good selection of cocktails and excellent for sunset views over the river.
Samlo Pub
101 Setthathirat Road
Tel: 021-222 308
An old-fashioned pub catering shamelessly to older male expats, complete with darts, snack food and other entertainment.

Sala Khounta (Sunset Bar)
Fa Ngum Road
A simple wooden structure in a row of similar establishments overlooking the Mekong, this bar is a popular place for Vientiane residents to meet after work, drink beer and watch the sun hit the horizon.

Spirit House
9/93 Fa Ngum Road
Tel: 021-243 795
www.thespirithouselaos.com
This stylish riverfront establishment serves an array of cocktails, beers and wines. It's also possible to get a breakfast here, as they open at 7am. Yet another place to catch one of Vientiane's spectacular sunsets.

Wind West
Luang Prabang Road
Tel: 021-217 275
Very popular American-style bar and restaurant. It has good food, live music most evenings, and sees some wild (by Vientiane standards) nights.

Nightclubs

Don Chan Palace
6 Ban Piawat, off Fa Ngum Road
Tel: 021-244 288
A popular place for young Lao. It tends to stay open later than the other clubs.

D'Tech Disco
Mercure, 10 Samsenthai Road
Tel: 021-213 570
Standard nightclub and disco serving up expensive drinks and high-energy dance music.

Future
Luang Prabang Road
Tel: 021-235 969
A popular spot for young singles, Lao and expat alike, this disco offers mainly bland Thai pop.

Marina Nightclub
Km 3, Luang Prabang Road
Tel: 021-216 978
Popular with the Vientiane high-school and college set; the DJ at Marina plays Thai and Western pop hits accompanied by bright flashing lights and TV screens in a classy interior.

Pakluk
Sakkarine Road
Tel: 021-214 592
A trendy nightclub with a timber dance floor. Located behind the Mahosot Hospital.

Phatoke Laoderm
Senglao Hotel, Chao Anou Road
Tel: 021-263 981
A dinner theatre with Lao musicians accompanying your meal followed by an elaborate traditional dance performance.

Luang Prabang

Restaurant l'Eléphant
Ban Wat Nong
Tel: 071-252 482
This classy restaurant in the heart of the old city has a pleasant bar and good hors d'œuvres. It's all very restrained – there is no music, and it's not open past 11pm.

Hive Bar
Opposite Wat Aphai, Ban Aphai
Tel: 071-212 880
Luang Prabang's liveliest bar with regular fashion shows and hip-hop dance demonstrations from local Lao youths, all great fun.

Martin's Pub
Phommathay Road, near Wat Aphai
Martin's has a wide range of cocktails, beers and whiskeys and does some good bar snacks.

Maylek Pub
Setthathilat Road
Tel: 071-252 560
Travellers meet here to listen to low-volume Western music and swap tales of the road. Well-stocked bar.

FESTIVALS

January

International New Year's Day (1 Jan)
A public holiday celebrated with private basi ceremonies and, these days, large and boisterous parties.

Pathet Lao Day (6 Jan)
A public holiday.

Boun Pha Wet (Movable)
During this festival, the birth story, or Jataka, of Prince Vessantara, the Buddha's penultimate existence, is told. It is regarded as an auspicious time for Lao males to be ordained into the monkhood. Temples in villages throughout Laos celebrate the three-day festival with sermons, fortune-telling, processions, and dance and drama performances.

February

Boun Makha Busa (Magha Puja) (Movable)
This festival (which in some years falls in January) commemorates a central speech given by the Buddha to a group of enlightened monks in which he is said to have set out the first series of monastic regulations and predicted his own death. It is celebrated with chanting, offerings and candlelit processions at temples throughout the country.

Boun Makha Busa is celebrated with particular aplomb at the ruins of Wat Phu outside Champasak, where it includes elephant races, water buffalo and cockfighting, and traditional music and dance performances.

Vietnamese Tet/Chinese New Year (Movable)
The Chinese and Vietnamese communities in Vientiane, Pakse and Savannakhet celebrate the New Year with private parties, firecrackers, parades and visits to temples. In Vientiane, Chinese opera is often performed near the waterfront.

March

Lao Women's Day (8 Mar)
Lao Women's Day is an official public holiday for women only, but as the absence from the office of nearly half the workforce makes getting anything

BELOW: festivities at the Lao New Year, Vientiane.

done even harder than it already is, it has become a popular day for men to take off too.

People's Party Day (22 Mar)
A public holiday.

April

Boun Pi Mai (Lao New Year)
In Laos, *Pi Mai*, or New Year, is the most fervently celebrated event of the year. It is a time when the entire country stops working and begins to party – only three days are official public holidays, but most Lao take the whole week off. Citizens remove Buddha images from the temples in order to clean them with scented water, and then take to the streets to douse one another – an act of cleansing and purification in anticipation of the end of the dry season. Foreigners are a particular target. Offerings are made at temples, and small mounds of sand or stone are built in temple courtyards and (in Luang Prabang) on the banks of the Mekong River to request health and happiness in the New Year.

In Luang Prabang the celebration is especially beautiful, and includes a large, colourful parade filled with a variety of traditional Lao costumes, music and dance, the procession of the sacred Prabang Buddha image, a Miss New Year beauty contest, and a handicraft fair.

May/June

International Labour Day (1 May)
A public holiday occasionally marked by trade fairs and parades in the capital.
Boun Visakha Busa (Movable)
Starting on the 15th day of the sixth lunar month, the Boun Visakha Busa festival celebrates the Buddha's birth, enlightenment and passing away, and is marked at temples by ancestor worship, chanting and preaching, and candlelit processions in the evening.
Boun Bang Fai (Movable)
The *bang fai*, or rocket, festival is a pre-Buddhist ceremony in which villages compete to produce the highest-flying home-made bamboo rockets, fired into the sky in order to celebrate fertility and call for the rains. The festival is filled with traditional music, dance, folk-theatre performances, processions and lots of sexual imagery. Men and women alike will cross-dress and display oversized wooden phalli and small statues depicting sexual acts. Participants perform crude acts, it is said, in order to anger the gods, who retaliate by sending thunderstorms

down on the fields.
The Lao take this ceremony very seriously: when it was banned by the Communists in 1976 the Party was blamed for that year's poor harvest – and the festival was reinstated the following year.

July

Boun Khao Phansa/Khao Watsa (Movable)
This festival marks the beginning of the three-month Buddhist "rains retreat", during which time monks are forbidden to wander outside their temples and must spend their time in prayer and meditation. It is the traditional time of year for Lao men to enter monkhood temporarily. The *tak baat*, or alms-giving ritual, can be seen at temples around the country.

August/September

Boun Haw Khao Padap Dinh (Movable)
The living pay respect to the dead, usually by making an offering at the local temple so that the monks will chant on behalf of the deceased.

October/November

Boun Awk Phansa/Awk Watsa (Movable)
Awk Phansa marks the end of the monks' three-month fast and retreat during the rainy season. In Vientiane this religious festival is

quite spectacular; on the first day at dawn, donations and offerings are made at temples around the city; in the evening, candlelit processions are held around the temples, and hundreds of colourful floats decorated with flowers, incense and candles are set adrift down the Mekong River in thanksgiving to the river spirits; the next day an exciting longboat-racing competition is held on the Mekong.

November

Boun Pha That Luang (Movable)
This three-day religious festival is held in and around That Luang stupa, the national symbol of Laos, where hundreds of monks gather to accept alms and floral offerings from Lao and Thai worshippers alike. The festival includes a candlelit procession circling That Luang, a grand fireworks display, and an international trade fair near the temple that lasts for one week.

December

Lao National Day (2 Dec)
This public holiday commemorating the 1975 Communist victory in Laos is marked by military parades and official speeches, and is probably the only time in Laos that you will ever see the hammer and sickle displayed in public.
Hmong New Year (Movable)
Hmong New Year celebrations occur throughout the month on different

BELOW: the Makha Busa festival is a major event at Wat Phu, Champasak.

dates in different villages, and include colourful displays of traditional costumes made from silk and silver jewellery. Performances of musical instruments like the *teun* flute and Hmong-style *khene* pipe are common. The Hmong also enjoy activities such as the *mak khon* cotton-ball-throwing ceremony, ox fighting, spinning-top races and crossbow demonstrations.

SHOPPING

Vientiane

A number of shops featuring Lao textiles, woodcarvings, jewellery and traditional handicrafts have sprung up on the streets of downtown Vientiane. Upmarket boutiques selling home furnishings and interior designs cater to tourists and expats alike. The Morning Market (Talaat Sao) on Lan Xang Avenue is certainly the best place to check for any of these items; it is open all day, and sells almost anything you could possibly want. Vientiane's main shopping streets are Samsenthai and Setthathirat roads where a mixture of handicrafts, jewellery, silk and hill-tribe products can be purchased.

Textiles

Laos has a rich and now thriving textile tradition. Textile production has traditionally been performed exclusively by women, and the art is now being encouraged by the UN and other development agencies as a means of income for Lao women. Lao textile weavers use silk and cotton fabrics, and natural dyes of five main colours: black, orange, red, yellow and blue. Central motifs include animals such as the river serpent, dragon, deer and lion, and geometric symbols

Jewellery

Bari Jewellers
366–8 Samsenthai Road, Vientiane
Tel: 021-212 680
This Indian-owned shop sells traditional Lao jewellery in addition to gold and silver pieces and precious stones.
Saigon Bijoux
367–369 Samsenthai Road, Vientiane
Tel: 021-214 783
A well-established boutique with an extensive selection of gold and silver; the jeweller can make new pieces as well.

like triangles and spirals.
Main products include women's wraparound skirts, shoulder bags, shawls, shoulder sashes for men and women, and blankets. At specialised shops you can also find antique textiles, wall hangings and furniture coverings. Weaving styles and techniques, including even loom design, vary widely by region and ethnic group. In general southern Laos is known for its *ikat*, or tie-dye, designs and foot-loom weaving technique, while in the north weavers use frame looms and the weft brocade style.

Camacrafts
Nokeo Khumman Road, Vientiane
Tel: 021-241 217
www.camacrafts.org
Camacrafts is a non-profit store that markets Hmong and Lao handicrafts made by village women. The attractive range includes products for the bedroom, such as duvets and pillowcases, items for the kitchen, such as oven mitts and potholders, as well as smaller items like bags and purses. Well worth a visit.

Carol Cassidy Lao Textiles
84–86 Nokeo Khumman Road, Vientiane
Tel: 021-212 123
www.laotextiles.com
The most famous textile shop in the country, Lao Textiles sells beautiful silk fabrics using a mixture of tapestry, brocade and *ikat* techniques, all hand-dyed with natural dyes. Housed in a French colonial mansion, it is run by an American woman, Carol Cassidy, who uses Lao textile patterns combined with her own contemporary designs. The pieces, including scarves, home accessories and wall hangings, are very expensive, as many end up in museums and private galleries overseas. The dyeing, spinning and weaving process can be seen at the workshop behind the shop.

Lao Cotton Company
Ban Khounta Thong, Souphanouvong Road, Vientiane
Tel: 021-215 840
www.laocotton.com
A state enterprise formed in 1996, Lao Cotton offers lightweight, good-quality shirts and other casual wear, linens and decorative fabrics, and cotton-leather products such as purses and handbags.

Mulberries
Nokeo Khumman Road, Vientiane
Tel: 021-263 371
www.mulberries.org
Sharing the same shop space as Camacrafts, this not-for-profit boutique specialises in the handmade

production of naturally dyed traditional Lao silk. The shop also offers a collection of silk clothing, scarves, shawls and other products for sale. Mulberry food products, as well as mulberry green and red tea, are also available at the store. The company does its own silk farming, weaving and silk dyeing in Phonsavan in Xieng Khuang province. To arrange a visit to the silk farm (Mon–Sat 7.30am–4.30pm; located 30 metres/yds past the bus station on Route 7 outside Phonsavanh), email info@mulberries.org. Mulberries also has a branch in Luang Prabang, above the Joma Bakery Café.

Nikone Handicraft Centre
Dong Mieng Road, Vientiane
Tel: 021-212 191
Email: nikone@laotel.com
Popular among the Vientiane expat community, this large shop near the Russian Circus sells textiles and other Lao handicrafts.

Furnishings and Gifts

Carterie du Laos
118/2 Setthathirat Road, Vientiane
Tel: 021-241 401
A wide selection of postcards, handmade cards and original photography from French photographer Michel Huteau.
Couleur d'Asie
61/8 Nam Phu Circle, Vientiane
Tel: 021-223 008
www.couleurdasie.net
This chic boutique sells beautiful home furnishings and interior design accessories with a Lao accent. Coffee, tea and snacks are served in the tea corner.
Mandalay
26 François Nginn Street, Vientiane
Tel: 021-218 736
www.mandalao.com
A French-owned boutique featuring Southeast Asian styles of rosewood, teak and ebony furniture.
Monument Books
124/1 Nokeo Khumman Road, Vientiane
Tel: 021-243 708
www.monument-books.com
With branches in Luang Prabang and Pakse this is the best foreign-language bookshop in Laos. They carry a range of popular fiction, non-fiction and travel books in a number of languages.
Phai Exclusive Crafts
3/1 Thongtoum Road, off Thong Khankham Road, Vientiane
Tel: 021-214 804
An upmarket shop featuring expensive furniture, home accessories, jewellery and bamboo crafts.
Satri Lao
79/4 Setthathirat Road, Ban

Mixay, Vientiane
Tel: 021-219 295
www.satrilao.laopdr.com
A shop offering antique textiles,
traditional Lao jewellery, antique
coins and silverware, contemporary
furniture and reams of beautiful silk.

Galleries
Kanchana
102 Samsenthai Road
That Dam Square
Tel: 021-213 467
Kanchana sells a wide range of high-
quality silk fabrics and products. The
store can also arrange visits to its Lao
Textile Museum, which showcases
traditional silk fabrics from the
various ethnic groups in Laos.
Treasures of Asia
105 Setthathirat Road, Vientiane
Tel: 021-222 236
Features Lao painting, sculpture,
handicrafts and design from local
artists and students from the National
Faculty of Fine Arts.
T'Shop Lai Gallery
Wat Inpeng Street, Vientiane
Tel: 021-223 178
A French-owned gallery showing
traditional and contemporary prints
and paintings, stylish Lao-accented
furniture and a few interesting antique
maps of the region.

Luang Prabang

Luang Prabang is justly famous for
its extensive night market, held daily
between about 4 in the afternooon
and 10 at night along Sisavangvong
Road between the traffic circle at
the Phousi Hotel and the National
Museum. While the market is open,
Sisavangvong Road is closed to motor
traffic, and covered stalls are set up
right across the road with just narrow
passageways to walk down. It's a great
place to buy souvenirs, as there is
remarkably little in the way of tat, and
most of the items on sale are both
well made and artistically designed.
Look here for clothing and fabrics,
paintings, paper lanterns, chopsticks,
cutlery, duvets, cushions, chess sets
– the range of choice is considerable,
and includes Items imported from
Vietnam, as well as local Lao products.
The atmosphere is laid-back and
pleasant, the market vendors polite,
softly spoken and helpful. Of course,
it's a market – so expect to bargain.
But the vendors are not overly
grasping, prices are good, and quality
is surprisingly high. Also worth visiting
is the early morning fresh market
along a narrow street to the west of
the National Museum. Goods on sale

include every kind of fresh fruit and
vegetable, all tastefully displayed,
as well as meat, poultry and bush
food. Even if you're not interested in
buying, this is a wonderful place to
take photographs, while the locals are
welcoming and helpful.

Textiles
Camacrafts
Ounkham Road, Luang Prabang
Tel: 071-254 594
www.camacrafts.org
A similar operation to the one found
in Vientiane selling a range of Lao and
Hmong handicrafts on a non-profit basis.

Haute Couture and Clothing
Couleur d'Asie
Ounkham Road, Luang Prabang
Tel: 020-787 5424
www.couleurdasie.net
Famed international designer
Viviane Inthavong has now opened
her second store. The boutique
specialises in some remarkable
men's and women's fashions.

SPORT

Badminton

One of the most popular recreational
activities in Laos, badminton is
played on courts throughout the
country's larger towns – there are
courts in people's backyards, hotel
and guesthouse grounds, or just in
the street.

Bowling

Ten-pin bowling is another popular
sport in Laos. In Vientiane, try either
the **Lao Bowling Centre** at Khun
Bulom Road, tel: 021-218 661, or
the **Vientiane Bowling Centre** at
Thadeua Road, tel: 021-313 823.

Cycle Touring

Many companies offer cycling tours
around Laos, an increasingly popular
cycle destination. Additionally many
companies offer cross-border tours
in Southeast Asia. These tours vary
in duration and areas/sights visited.
The tours are mostly inclusive of
hotel, guide and drinks/snacks.
Many charge extra for bicycle rental
and single participants. Tours can
be tailored to individual needs.
These tours can be excellent value
for people with limited time or those
who want to travel as part of a group.
The companies generally will offer

tours to the tourist highlights in Laos,
including Luang Prabang, the Plain of
Jars/Phonsavan and Vientiane.
Spice Roads Cycle Tours
14/1 B Soi Promsi 2, Sukhumvit 39,
Bangkok, Thailand
Tel: +662-712 5305
www.spiceroads.com
This Thai-based cycle tour company
has been offering tours across the
region for many years. The guides
are all local and the tours are fully
supported.
Tiger Trail Outdoor Adventures Laos
Ban Muang Nga Village, Route 13,
Luang Prabang, Laos
Tel: 071-252 655
www.laos-adventures.com
Specifically offering guided cycle tours
in Laos, this company enjoys a solid
reputation for conscientious travel
and local support.
**Red Spokes Cycling Adventure
Holidays**
29 Northfield Road, Stamford Hill, London
Tel: +44-207 502 7252
www.redspokes.co.uk
This UK-based company offers cycle
tours worldwide and is probably the
largest tour company operating in Laos.

Football

Increasingly popular as a national
sport, football (soccer) matches
can be seen every weekend at the
National Stadium in Vientiane.
Government offices, high schools,
local companies, villages and even
expat groups organise teams to
compete. Inter-province matches are
played on fields and stadiums in the
provincial capitals.

Golf

Like in other Southeast Asian
countries golf is becoming more and
more popular and new golf courses
are slowly appearing. Vientiane has a
few golf courses catering to the local
business community, but owing to the
limited facilities many expats head
for a newer resort complex over the
border in Nong Khai at weekends.
Dansavanh Golf and Country Club
Ban Phonkham, Toulakhom District
Tel: 030-520 0666
www.dansavanh.com
A beautiful 18-hole course located
to the north of Vientiane next to
Nam Ngum Lake, green fees are
reasonable and the club has a free
shuttle service operating from town.
Lao Country Club
Km 14, 555 Thadeua Road, Vientiane
Tel: 021-812 071
An 18-hole course with a clubhouse

that serves European food.

Vientiane Golf Club
Km 6, Route 13 South, Vientiane
Tel: 021-250 681
Email: berttitus@hotmail.com
An 18-hole course with a small
pro shop that sells and hires
supplies, and a clubhouse
offering refreshments and a social
atmosphere.

Kattor

Kattor is a traditional Lao sport in
which a woven rattan (or, increasingly
these days, plastic) ball is kicked
around a circle. The objective is to
keep the ball in play, and players
earn points for the style and level
of difficulty of their kicks. These
days, *kattor* is often played with a
volleyball net, using the same rules
as volleyball, except that only the foot
and head can be used to direct the
ball. The skills of some incredibly agile
players can be witnessed in public
places in the late weekday afternoons
in cities and towns throughout Laos.

Outdoor Adventure

A number of outdoor adventure
activities have sprung up recently in
Laos, including white-water rafting,
tubing, kayaking and trekking, a lot
of it rather disorganised. All these
pastimes come together in one place,
Vang Vieng. Unfortunately the town
has also picked up a poor reputation
for lax safety precautions and a
number of people have been killed on
the river over the last few years.

Fitness Centres and Swimming

A number of hotels in Vientiane
operate swimming pools and fitness
centres that are open for public use
for a small fee, usually between
US$5 and $10 per day.
   The Australian Embassy
Recreation Club is private, and you
need to be a guest of a member in
order to use the pool.

**Australian Embassy Recreation
Club**
Km 3, Thadeua Road, Vientiane
Tel: 021-314 921

Lane Xang Hotel
Fa Ngum Road, Vientiane
Tel: 021-214 102
www.lane-xang.com

Running

The Hash House Harriers is an
international expat organisation
founded by British civil service officers
in Kuala Lumpur just after World War
II, named after the restaurant where
they would meet after work to drink
and organise a run. The chapter in
Vientiane holds a run each Monday at
5pm. The course, different every week,
may take you through forests and rice
fields in addition to dusty roads. Check
the notice boards at the Scandinavian
Bakery (see page 324), Phimphone
Market, or Asia Vehicle Rental (see
page 317) for the week's location. The
run is followed by dinner and drinking.
   The Vientiane Hash House Harriers
also meet every Saturday afternoon
at Nam Phu Circle before heading

Lao Plaza Hotel
63 Samsenthai Road, Vientiane
Tel: 021-218 800
www.laoplazahotel.com

Mercure
10 Samsenthai Road, Vientiane
Tel: 021-213 570
www.accorhotels.com

Ramayana Gallery Hotel
Lane Xang Avenue, Vientiane
Tel: 021-214 455
www.ramayana-laos.com

Best Western Vientiane Hotel
2–12 François Nginn Street,
Vientiane
Tel: 021-216 906
www.bestwestern.com

off to a challenging running course
outside the city. For more complete
information on all Hash House runs
and other events check their website
at www.hashlaos.com.

Squash and Tennis

The Australian Embassy Recreation
Club operates a squash court available
to members and their guests. A
number of hotels in Vientiane have
tennis courts that are open to the
public for a fee (see Fitness Centres
and Swimming box). A cheaper option
would be one of the city's private
tennis clubs, though they have none of
the amenities of a hotel facility.

Mercure
Samsenthai Road, Vientiane
Tel: 021-213 570

Vientiane Plaza Hotel
Sailom Road (north of That Dam),
Vientiane
Tel: 0212-265 365
www.vientianeplazalao.com

Vientiane Tennis Club
Next to the National Stadium
(a.k.a. Chao Anouvong Stadium),
Nokeokoummane Road, Vientiane

Thai Kickboxing

Thai kickboxing, or *muay thai*, has
become quite popular among Lao,
where it has risen above the rank of
an amateur activity with the recent
success of Lao boxers in international
competitions. In the game any part
of the body except the head can be
struck or used to strike the opponent.
Spectators often wonder at the
remarkably high kicks to the neck,
but the emphasis in *muay thai* boxing
is on neither kicking nor punching –
blows by the elbow and knee are the
most effective way to win.

BELOW: taking time off for a game of volleyball in a village near Kratie.

A – Z

A HANDY SUMMARY OF PRACTICAL INFORMATION, ARRANGED ALPHABETICALLY

A

Admission Charges

Admission charges remain something of an inexact science in Laos. As a basic rule, the further away from Vientiane and Luang Prabang, the less likelihood there is of having to pay admission charges. National museums and some of the more celebrated temples in Luang Prabang and Vientiane now impose a small charge, usually of US$1–2.

B

Budgeting for Your Trip

Laos remains a relatively inexpensive country, though of course it is possible to spend more if you stay in the most expensive hotels and dine in the most expensive restaurants. Essentially, budget travellers should allow US$30 a day, but even less than that away from Vientiane and the other main towns. Mid-range costs are around US$40–80 a day, while top end, including a self-drive car, will cost in the region of US$100–200 per day.

C

Children

The family is the centre of Lao life and locals will take great pleasure in seeing a travelling family. Companionship and assistance will be abundant. Parents, however, should prepare their children for all the minor inconveniences and delays common when travelling in a developing country and, of course, take extra care with hygiene matters.

Children should never approach dogs, monkeys or other small animals anywhere without proper adult supervision; the risk of rabies is much higher here than at home.

For children from more temperate climes the tropical sun can be fierce, so high SPF sun-block lotion and hats are important.

Climate

Laos, like most of mainland Southeast Asia, has three main seasons. The rainy season, marked by the arrival of the monsoon between May and July, can last until as late as November. During this season, the weather is as hot and sticky as a bowl of sticky rice and – as one would expect – often wet; temperatures during the day average around 30°C (86°F) in the lowlands and 25°C (77°F) in the mountain valleys.

The monsoon is followed by a dry, cool season, from November until mid-February, which is overall the best time to visit. Days are still warm to hot, but overnight temperatures in the Mekong River Valley can drop as low as 14°C (57°F). It is notably colder in the north during these months: Luang Prabang averages around 28°C (82°F) in the day but just 13°C (55°F) at night in December and January, and often lower than that.

The third season, dry, increasingly hot and dusty, begins in late February and lasts until May; temperatures in the Mekong River Valley reach 38°C (100°F) in March and April. Again the

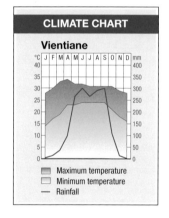

temperatures are somewhat lower in the northern hills, particularly at night.

What to Wear

In general, the Lao seem quite happy with the recent influx of tourists to their country. One aspect of this trend they tend to dislike, however, is the way many travellers dress while in Laos. The Lao are very conservative when it comes to dress, and expect foreign visitors to respect this custom.

Women should avoid clothing that bares the thighs, shoulders or breasts; long trousers, walking shorts and skirts are acceptable, while tank tops, short skirts and running shorts are not. Both men and women should dress conservatively, especially when making a visit to a temple or government office.

Sandals or shoes that can be taken off and on easily are a sensible idea, as shoes must always be removed before entering a Lao house or temple. See also Etiquette.

Whatever the season, bring lightweight cotton clothing and a light jacket or pullover for those rare, welcome, cool nights during December and January.

Crime and Safety

Petty crime as far as the visitor is concerned is almost non-existent in Laos, although over the last few years the number of tourists reporting thefts has certainly risen. By following a few simple rules most crimes are easily avoided. It is best not to flaunt your money and other valuables and always keep a lock on your packs and suitcases. The usual rules apply when travelling on buses and boats: keep a watch on your belongings and don't carry too much money in trouser pockets. Drugging and robbing tourists on long-distance buses and in restaurants has occurred recently, so the rule must always be to politely refuse food or drink from strangers and never leave food or drink unattended. When riding on buses try to get a seat near the middle of the vehicle. One danger is that presented by unexploded ordnance (UXO): the golden rule is to avoid straying off paths in remote areas, particularly in the east of the country, Be aware that though drugs such as marijuana are readily available in Laos, they are illegal and police will come down hard on offenders. It is not unusual for a local to sell to a foreigner and then turn them into the police later.

Customs

There is little security at Laos's border checkpoints. Restrictions on drugs, weapons and pornography apply, but there is no limit on the amount of Lao and foreign currency you can bring into the country.

The duty-free allowance for each visitor is 1 litre of spirits, 2 litres of wine and 200 cigarettes, 50 cigars or 250g of tobacco, and a reasonable amount of perfume. One regulation worth keeping in mind is the restriction on Buddha images and antiquities; travellers have been stopped on

Electricity

The electric system in Laos runs on a 220V AC circuit, and most outlets use two-prong flat or round sockets. Even in Vientiane, blackouts do happen, most often when the rains are heaviest in July and August. Some rural areas receive electricity only at certain times, while many villages manage to survive without any power at all.

ABOVE: prayer flags at Wat Phuang Kaew, Don Khong.

exit and detained while authorities examine a purchase to ensure that it is not a national treasure.

See also the Laos Customs website www.laocustoms.laopdr.net.

D

Disabled Travellers

Facilities for disabled travellers scarcely exist in Laos, and this is a difficult country for the disabled to travel in – at least beyond Vientiane and Luang Prabang. Relatively few hotels or guesthouses have elevators, and there are no special ramps for wheelchairs.

E

Embassies and Consulates

Lao Embassies and Consulates Overseas

Note that there is no diplomatic representation in the UK
Australia
1 Dalman Crescent, O'Malley, Canberra, ACT 2606
Tel: 61 2-6286 4595/6933
www.laoembassy.net
Cambodia
15–17 Mao Tse Tung Boulevard, Box 19, Phnom Penh
Tel: 855 23-426 441/424 781
Email: laoembpp@canintel.com
China (Beijing)
11 Dongsi Jie, Sanlitun, Beijing 100600
Tel: 86 1-532 1224
Email: laoemcn@public.east.cn.net
China (Kunming; Consulate)

Room 3226 Camellia Hotel, 154 East Dong Feng Road, 650041 Kunming
Tel: 86 871-317 6623/6624
Email: laokun02@public.km.yn.cn
France
74 Avenue Raymond Poincaré, 75116 Paris
Tel: 33 1-4553 0298/4554 7047
www.laoparis.com
Germany
Bismarckallee 2A, 14193 Berlin
Tel: 49 30-8906 0647
Email: hong@laos-botschaft.de
India
A 104/7, Parrmanand Estate, Maharani Bagh, New Delhi 110065
Tel: 91 11-4132 7352
Email: amblaodl@ndb.vsnl.net
Indonesia
Jalan Kintamani Raya C15 No. 33, Kuningan Timur, Jakarta 12950
Tel: 62 21-522 9602
Email: laoemjkt@cabi.net.id
Japan
3-3-22 Nishi Azabu, Minato-Ku, Tokyo 106
Tel: 81 3-5411 2291/2
Malaysia
25 Jalan Damai, 55000 Kuala Lumpur
Tel: 60 3-2148 7059
Philippines
34 Lapu-Lapu Street, Magallanes Village, Makati, Manila
Tel: 63 2-852 5759
Russia
Ul. Katchalov 18, 121069 Moscow
Tel: 7 495-203 1454/291 7218
Singapore
101 Thomson Road, 05-03A United Square
Tel: 65-6250 6044/6741
Email: laoembsg@singnet.com.sg
Sweden
Badstrandvagen 11, Box 34050, 112-65 Stockholm
Tel: 46 8-618 2010

TRANSPORT

ACCOMMODATION

EATING OUT

ACTIVITIES

A – Z

LANGUAGE

ABOVE: a monsoon storm closes in.

Email: laoembassy@telia.com
Thailand (Bangkok)
520, 502/1-3 Soi Sahakarnpramoon,
Pracha-Utit Road, Bangkok 10310
Tel: 66-2539 6667
Email: embalao@bkklaoembassy.com
Thailand (Khon Kaen; Consulate)
171/102-103 Prachasamosorn
Road, Khon Kaen
Tel: 66-4324 2856
Email: embalao@bkklaoembassy.com
United States
2222 S Street NW,
Washington DC 20008
Tel: 1 202-332 6416/7
www.laoembassy.com
Vietnam (Hanoi)
22 Rue Tran Binh Trong, Hanoi
Tel: 84 4-942 4576/9746
Vietnam (Ho Chi Minh City; Consulate)
93 Pasteur Street, District 1,
Ho Chi Minh City
Tel: 84 8-829 9275/7667
Vietnam (Danang; Consulate)
12 Tran Quy Cap
Tel: 84 51-821 208/824 101

Foreign Embassies in Vientiane
Australia
Km 4, Thadeua Road, Ban Wat Nak
Tel: 021-353 800
www.laos.embassy.gov.au
Cambodia
Thadeua Road, Ban Thatkhao
Tel: 021-314 952
Email: camemb.lao@mfa.gov.kh
China
Wat Nak Road, Ban Wat Nak Noi
Tel: 021-315 100/3
Email: embassyprc@laonet.net
France
Setthathirat Road, Ban Sisakhet
Tel: 021-267 400
www.ambafrance-laos.org
Germany
26 Sokpaluang Road,
Ban Sokpaluang
Tel: 021-312 110/1

Email: info@vien.diplo.de
India
2 Thadeua Road, Ban Wat Nak
Tel: 021-352 301/4
Email: indiaemb@laotel.com
Indonesia
Phonkheng Road, Ban Pholsaat
Tel: 021-413 909/910
Email: kbrivte@laotel.com
Japan
Sisangvone Road, Ban Sisangvone
Tel: 021-414 400/3
www.la.emb-japan.go.jp/en/embassy/
embassy.htm
Malaysia
23 Singha Road, Ban Phonsay
Tel: 021-414 205/6
www.kln.gov.my/perwakilan/vientiane
Philippines
Ban Saphanthong Kang
Tel: 021-452 490
Email: pelaopdr@laotel.com
Russia
Km 4, Thadeua Road,
Ban Thaphalanxay
Tel: 021-312 219
Email: rusemb@laotel.com
Singapore
Km 3, Thadeua Road, Ban Wat Nak
Tel: 021-353 939
www.mfa.gov.sg/vientiane
Sweden
Sokpaluang Road, Ban Wat Nak
Tel: 021-315 003
Email: ambassaden.vientiane@foreign.
ministry.se
Thailand
Avenue Kaysone Phomvihane
Tel: 021-214 581/2
www.thaiembassy.org/vientiane
United States
19 Rue Bartholomie, That Dam Road
Tel: 021-267 000
www.usembassy.gov
Vietnam
85, rue 23 Singha, Ban Phonsay
Tel: 021-413 409
www.mofa.gov.vn/en

Etiquette

The best thing any visitor to Laos
can do is smile, smile and smile
again. As in other Buddhist countries,
remember to dress neatly (see
also What to Wear), and always
remove your shoes when entering a
private house or a temple. Women
should avoid touching monks – to
give a monk anything, first pass
it to a male to hand to the monk.
Keeping calm in tense situations
is most important; the Lao do not
take kindly to someone losing
their temper. The only thing anger
achieves is more frustration. Beware
of touching someone on the head: it
is believed that one's vital essence

Emergencies

Police Tel: 191
Fire Tel: 190
Ambulance Tel: 195

resides in the head and therefore
even a hairdresser will always ask
permission before touching.

G

Gay and Lesbian Travellers

As with the attitude towards women,
there exists in Laos a dichotomy
between the political (Communist)
and social (Buddhist) perceptions of
gays. While the traditional attitudes
towards homosexuality are relaxed, the
government takes a dim view. While
travelling gay couples are not affected
by this, the law prohibits "cohabitation"
between Laos and foreigners,
regardless of their sexual orientation.

H

Health and Medical Care

Laos is still a developing country, and
it is a good idea to take the necessary
health precautions before arriving.
The following immunisations, some
of which require multiple injections,
are recommended: hepatitis A,
typhoid, diptheria, tetanus, hepatitis
B, polio and tuberculosis. Optional
vaccinations include rabies and
Japanese B encephalitis, a mosquito-
borne disease that is very rare.
Medicine to combat malaria –
common in Laos outside Vientiane
– is available, but consult a doctor
before beginning any medication.
   While in the country, be
particularly careful of water and ice;
only consume water that comes
from carefully sealed containers or
has been boiled thoroughly. Heat
exhaustion and prickly heat can result
from dehydration and salt deficiency,
so drink lots of fluids, avoid intense
activity when the sun is strongest,
and rest frequently during the day.
Travellers' diarrhoea is quite common,
though usually not serious; be sure
to avoid dehydration problems by
replacing the fluids your body will lose.

Medical Services
Medical services in Laos are limited;
the most extensive are in Vientiane,

where even the two state hospitals, **Mahosot** and **Clinique Setthathirat**, are not up to international standards. Even the **International Clinic** at Mahosot is best reserved for only minor injuries. The **Friendship Hospital** is a specialised medical centre for trauma and orthopaedics. Most foreign residents requiring minor medical attention choose to visit the **Australian Embassy's** clinic, but pay US$50 per consultation. All numbers are for Vientiane.

Australian Clinic
Australian Embassy, Thadeua Road
Tel: 021-353 840
Setthathirat Hospital
Nong Bone Road, Ban That Luang
Tel: 021-413 720
Friendship Hospital
Phontong Road, Ban Phonsavang
Tel: 021-413 302/3
International Clinic, Mahosot Hospital
Setthathirat Road
Tel: 021-214 022
Many Vientiane residents and expats opt for facilities just across the river in Thailand.
AEK Udon International Hospital
555/5 Posri Road, Udon Thani, Thailand
Tel: 66 42-342 555
www.aekudon.com
Nong Khai Wattana Hospital
1159/4 Moo 2, Prachak Road, Nong Khai, Thailand
Tel: 66 42-465 201/8
www.wattanahospital.net

I

Internet

Internet cafés are found all over town in Vientiane, Luang Prabang and Vang Vieng, which receive the highest numbers of travellers, and connections are very good. Costs are also low in these major towns because of stiff competition, and can be as cheap as 100 kip per minute (about US$0.10). In many of the other provinces, internet facilities are becoming increasingly available and reliable, but costs are higher in places in which only one or two shops offer internet-based services. Visual internet telephony and PC-to-phone services are also well supported. In addition, stored-value pay-as-you-use internet cards, for use with land lines, can be purchased from Lao Telecom branches and at some internet cafés and retail outlets.
City Internet Centre
Khun Bulom Road

Lao Massage

In addition to the services of major hotels, good massage parlours can be found in major cities around the country. Traditional Lao massage can be quite rigorous, so be prepared to have every part of the body worked.

Vientiane
Wellness Massage Centre
Setthathirat Road, opposite Wat Inpeng
Tel: 020-7744 1516
Traditional massage parlour with

Tel: 021-250 111
Planet Online
6th Fl, ANZV Commercial Bank Building, 33 Lan Xang Road, Vientiane
Tel: 021-218 972
www.planet.laopdr.com

M

Media

Newspapers and Magazines
The Lao government produces two newspapers for the expat community in Vientiane: the English-language *Vientiane Times* (www.vientianetimes.org.la) and the French-language *Le Rénovateur* (www.lerenovateur.org.la). The latter has a far snappier design, and also tends to be more up-to-date on current events in town, so go for that one if you can read French. The state-run *kpl News* (www.kpl.net.la) puts out a daily news bulletin in English. The *Bangkok Post* and *The Nation*, the two main English-language dailies from Bangkok, are available in hotels, shops and restaurants in Vientiane. *Sayo Magazine* is a monthly business and lifestyle publication and has interesting travel articles. It is also widely available in shops and hotels in the capital.
Vientiane Book Centre sells current issues of *Time* and *Newsweek*, as well as a reasonable selection of new and used fiction, travel guides and non-controversial books on Laos. The nearby Kosila Bookshop specialises in second-hand books. In addition, a good selection of English-language coffee-table books and other trade titles, maps and postcards are found at Monument Books, which also stocks French titles.
Kosila Bookshop
Nokeo Khumman Road
Tel: 021-241 352

a number of different packages to choose from.
Sokpaluang Temple
Sokpaluang Road
Traditional massage, herbal saunas, herbal tea.

Luang Prabang
Lao Red Cross
Wisunalat Road
Housed in a beautifully restored Lao-French building, the Red Cross offers traditional herbal saunas and a combination Swedish-Lao massage.

Monument Books
124/1 Nokeo Khumman Road
Tel: 021-243 708
Vientiane Book Centre
54/1 Pangkham Road
Tel: 021-212 031

Television and Radio
The Lao government broadcasts on one radio station – Lao National Radio – throughout the country, but most Lao rely on Thai radio for entertainment. Expats often use shortwave to pick up programmes from the BBC, VOA and Australia Broadcasting Corporation.
Lao National Television now has two channels but, again, almost all Lao prefer Thai television; as you make your way around the country, you will probably find most televisions tuned to one of the popular Thai soap operas. Satellite TV is now widely available in Vientiane and Luang Prabang, offering channels like CNN, MTV and BBC World Service.

Money

The unit of currency is the kip, and notes are now issued in the following denominations: 500, 1,000, 2,000, 5,000, 10,000, 20,000, 50,000 and 100,000. There are no coins, and notes smaller than 500 have been rendered obsolete. While stores and services in Laos are officially forbidden to use any other currency, virtually any merchant will (gladly) accept US dollars or Thai baht in lieu of the shaky kip. Nonetheless, one should keep a supply of the local currency on hand for making small purchases.
You can buy kip at foreign exchange banks and other exchange offices. At time of press, US$1 was roughly equivalent to 7,900 kip. The kip is not a convertible currency outside Laos and should therefore be used

up before departure. It is possible to change kip into US$ at Vientiane airport, sometimes at Luang Prabang airport, and possibly at a private money changer (for a lousy rate). Otherwise it's virtually impossible.

Most major international currencies, as well as travellers' cheques in US dollars, pounds sterling, and often euros, can be exchanged at banks and money changers in major towns. The Lao almost always use cash, but credit cards are accepted at more and more hotels, restaurants and shops in Vientiane and Luang Prabang, where a 5 percent service charge is sometimes added to the bill. Cash advances can also be obtained on a visa/MasterCard in Vientiane. There are some ATMs in Vientiane now, though they may not always be reliable. Banks are usually open Monday to Friday 8.30am–4pm.

Vientiane

ANZ Vientiane Commercial Bank
33 Lane Xang Avenue
Tel: 021-222 700
Banque pour le Commerce Extérieur Lao
1 Pangkham Street
Tel: 021-213 200
www.bcellaos.com
Indochina Bank
Capital Tower, 116, 23 Singha Road
Tel: 021-455 000-2
www.indochinabank.com
Joint Development Bank
82 Lane Xang Avenue
Tel: 021-213 532-6
www.jdbbank.com
Lao Development Bank
13 Souphanouvong Road
Tel: 021-213 300-4
www.ldb.org.la
Siam Commercial Bank
117 Lane Xang Avenue
Tel: 021-213 500-1
www.scb.co.th

Western Union
Krungsri Ayuthaya Bank, 84/1 Lane Xang Avenue
Tel: 021-214 575-7
www.krungsri.com

Luang Prabang
Lao Development Bank
Wisunalat Road
Tel: 071-212 185
www.ldb.org.la

Savannakhet
Lao Development Bank
30 Oudomsin Road
Tel: 041-212 226
www.ldb.org.la

Pakse
Lao Development Bank
No. 13 Road South
Tel: 031-212 173
www.ldb.org.la

Huay Xai
Lao Development Bank
Ban Konekeo
Tel: 084-211 492
www.ldb.org.la

Tipping
Tipping is not expected in Laos, except at a few upmarket restaurants in Vientiane and Luang Prabang, where you might leave 10–15 percent if a service charge has not already been added to your bill. Taxi and tuk-tuk drivers also do not expect to be tipped, unless the trip was unusually difficult or much longer than originally expected.

O

Opening Hours

Government offices are officially open 8am–noon and 1–4.30pm, Monday to Friday. But don't expect to

get anything done after 11.30am or before 2pm, during which time most employees are enjoying lunch and a midday rest at home.

Most shops close for an hour during lunch, and are open for a half-day on Saturday. Almost all businesses are closed on Sunday.

P

Photography

Internet cafés and photographic shops are attuned to the needs of the travelling digital photographer, and can transfer images stored on a digital camera memory card to a CD ROM. Shops in the major towns will carry memory cards and batteries.

On the whole Lao people do not object to having their pictures taken, but it is still polite to ask permission before doing so as some will actively dislike having their pictures taken. Always show restraint when photographing people at prayer, and monks. Avoid photographing anything to do with the military.

Postal Services

The Lao postal service offers reliable service at reasonable prices. There are post offices in every provincial capital, painted in the same colour scheme of mustard yellow. For sending packages abroad, most expats use the **Express Mail Service (EMS)**.

Receiving incoming mail at the main post office in Vientiane is possible, although remember that all packages must be opened and their contents displayed for inspection. Residents check their boxes at the post office daily, as there is no home-delivery service.

A number of international courier agencies offer their services in Vientiane:
DHL Laos
#031 Group 03,
Ban Wattaynoy Thong,
Nongno Street
Tel: 021-214 868
www.dhl.com.la
Express Mail Service (EMS)
Vientiane Post Office
Tel: 021-216 425
FedEx
Behind Vientiane Post Office
Tel: 021-223 278
www.fedex.com/la/
Lao Freight Forwarder
Km 3, Thadeua Road
Tel: 021-313 321

BELOW: banknotes of the Lao currency, the kip.

www.laoff.laopdr.com
Overseas Courier Service Laos
8 Luang Prabang Road,
Ban Khountathong
Tel: 021-263 378
www.ocs.co.th/Laos/
TNT Express Laos
Luang Prabang Road, 3rd floor, Thai
Airways International Office
Tel: 021-261 918
www.tnt.com

Public Toilets

These scarcely exist, and most
people will be obliged to use hotel or
restaurant toilets in the towns, or the
great outdoors when upcountry. The
upside is that toilets are generally
clean. Bring your own paper, or learn to
use water to wash with like the locals.

R

Religious Services

A number of religious communities in
Vientiane offer services to the public:

Christian
Catholic Centre
35/269 Samsenthai Road
Tel: 021-216 219
Church of the Holy Spirit
ARDA Centre
93 Luang Prabang Road
Tel: 021-217 162
www.the-chs.org
Church of the Sacred Heart
193 Samsenthai Road
Tel: 021-216 219
Lao Evangelical Church
Luang Prabang Road, Ban Nakham
Tel: 021-216 052, 216 222
Seventh Day Adventist
Nong Bone Road
Tel: 021-412 270, 412 701

Baha'i
Baha'i Faith Centre
Luang Prabang Road
Tel: 021-216 996

Muslim
Jamia Masjid
Ban Xengyen, near Namphu Circle
Tel: 020-5561 3302

T

Telephones

Until 1990, Laos was connected
with the world, except Thailand

Public Holidays

The following days are observed
as official public holidays. The
public holidays associated with
the beginning and the end of
the Buddhist fasting period are
movable lunar dates:
1 January New Year's Day
6 January Pathet Lao Day
20 January Army Day
14 February Chinese and
Vietnamese New Year
8 March International Women's Day
22 March People's Party Day
13, 14, 15 April *Pi Mai Lao* (Lao
New Year)
28 April Vesak Day (Buddha Day)
1 May Labour Day
1 June Children's Day
June/July Khao Pansa (Buddhist
fasting period begins)
13 August *Lao Issara* (Free Laos
Day)
September/October Bouk Ok
Pansa (End of Buddhist fasting
period)
12 October Liberation Day
2 December Lao National Day

and the USSR, by only one phone
line – only one incoming or outgoing
international call could be placed
at a time. Things have changed a
lot since then, with all major towns
linked by phone and International
Direct Dialling (IDD) widely available,
providing a reliable service to more
than 150 destinations worldwide.
International calls can be made
from Lao Telecom offices (usually
operator-assisted), at post offices, or
from public phones with IDD facility.
For the last you will need to purchase
a phone card, which is available at
post and telecommunication offices
as well as many shops throughout
the country. Fax services are also
available at most Lao Telecom
offices and many post offices. Many
other places, such as hotels and
guesthouses, also have phone, fax
and email facilities.
To call long distance within
the country, dial 0 first, then the
provincial area code and number. For
international calls, dial 00, the country
code, then the area code and number.
Mobile phone numbers in Laos
normally begin with the prefix 020.

Mobile Telephones
Mobile phone coverage is surprisingly
good throughout the country. In
addition to Lao Telecom (Laotel; Call
Centre tel: 101), a handful of other
local service providers also offer

mobile phone services, including
Enterprise of Telecommunications
Lao (ETL). Visitors with GSM-enabled
mobile phones can buy a starter kit
from ETL (www.etllao.com) for US$5,
which consists of a SIM card with
a local phone number and about
20,000 kip (about US$2) worth of
stored value, from which international
and local calls and text messages can
be made. The credit can be topped up
at any outlet bearing the "Tango" sign.

Tourist Information

**Lao National Tourism
Administration**
Lane Xang Avenue, Ban Hatsady
Tel: 021-212 248/251
www.tourismlaos.org
This government-run tourism office
can provide some good information
about tours in the country. It is also
cooperating with local tour operators
in providing ecotourism tours. See
also www.ecotourismlaos.com for more
internet resources.

Websites
Ecotourism Laos: Set up by the Lao
National Tourism Administration, this
site offers information on Lao travel
facts and practicalities; advice on
the dos and don'ts in the country;
suggestions on travel-related
activities. There are also online maps
and a photo gallery, and listings for
accommodation and tour operators.
www.ecotourismlaos.com
Lao Embassy in the US: A good
place to check for current information
on visa regulations, this site
includes helpful links to government
departments and affiliated
organisations. www.laoembassy.com
Vientiane Times: The website of the
Ministry of Information and Culture's
English-language newspaper, offering

Telephone Area Codes

Champasak	031
Huay Xai	084
Luang Nam Tha	086
Luang Prabang	071
Pakse	031
Paksan	054
Phongsali	088
Sainyabuli	074
Sam Neua	064
Savannakhet	041
Sekong	038
Tha Kaek	051
Udomxai	081
Vang Vieng	023
Vientiane	021
Xieng Khuang	061

TRANSPORT
ACCOMMODATION
EATING OUT
ACTIVITIES
A – Z
LANGUAGE

Time Zone

Laos is 7 hours ahead of
Greenwich Mean Time (GMT).

archived articles and good links to
other news sources about Laos. www.
vientianetimes.org.la
Mekong Express: Although this
business-oriented site has not been
updated for a few years it still hosts
some of the most detailed maps
of the country with particularly
detailed Vientiane road plans. It
also offers helpful information
on some of the other states of
the Greater Mekong Subregion:
Thailand, Vietnam and Cambodia.
www.mekongexpress.com
Travel Lao PDR: A comprehensive
and regularly updated site offering
detailed travel information
and contacts for hotels and
transportation. www.travel.laopdr.com
Greater Mekong Subregion: Official
tourism website for this region,
covering Laos, Cambodia, Myanmar,
Thailand, Vietnam and Yunnan
province (China). www.visit-mekong.com
Visit Laos: This informative website
has general information on Lao
language, history and culture, and on
each province. www.visit-laos.com
Travelfish: This contains well-written
and up-to-date write-ups on Laos and
its 18 provinces. Included are travel
information, hotel and restaurant
reviews, suggested activities, a
travellers' forum and an FAQ section.
www.travelfish.org
Tripadvisor: A treasure trove of advice
and reviews, (good and bad) from
fellow travellers, covering restaurants,
accommodation, nightlife and much,
much more. www.tripadvisor.com

Travel Agencies

Vientiane
Diethelm Travel Laos, Ltd.
Namphu Circle
Tel: 021-213 833
Email: nataly.w@la.diethelmtravel.com
www.diethelmtravel.com
Exotissimo Travel
44 Pangkham Street
Tel: 021-241 861
www.exotissimo.com
Green Discovery Laos
Hang Boun Road
Tel: 021-264 528
www.greendiscoverylaos.com
Inter-Lao Tourism
111 Ban Mixay, Setthathirat Road
Tel: 021-214 669
www.interlao.com

ABOVE: Lao postage stamps.

Lane Xang Travel
Pangkham Street
Tel: 021-212 469
www.lanexangtravellaos.com

Luang Prabang
Diethelm Travel Laos, Ltd
Ban Visoun, No. 94
Tel: 071-261 011-3
Email: ditralpt@etllao.com
www.diethelmtravel.com
Exotissimo
44/3 Ban Wat Nong,
Khem Khong Road
Tel: 071-252 879
Email: go.laos@exotissimo.com
www.exotissimo.com
Lane Xang Travel
Wisunalat Road
Tel: 071-212 793
www.lanexangtravellaos.com
Tiger Trail
Ban Muang Nga
Tel: 071-252 655
Email: info@laos-adventures.com
www.laos-adventures.com

Pakse
Diethelm Travel Laos, Ltd.
Ban Thakang
Tel: 031-212 596
Email: dtlpkz@etllao.com
www.diethelmtravel.com

V

Visas and Passports

To enter Laos you must have a valid
passport. Citizens of all countries are also
required to apply for an entry tourist visa,
except as follows: Brunei Darussalam,
Cambodia, Malaysia, Philippines,
Singapore, Thailand and Vietnam. Thirty-
day single-entry tourist visas are issued
on arrival at Wattay International Airport
in Vientiane, Luang Prabang International

Airport, Pakse International Airport, and
at the international border checkpoints
(see page 315). You will need one
passport photo and between US$30
and US$45 (visa fees vary depending on
what passport you are holding) for the
visa application. There is an "overtime"
charge of US$1 for entry after 4pm and
at weekends. Alternatively, 30-day tourist
visas and 30-day business visas can
be obtained in advance of your trip at a
Lao embassy or consulate, or at travel
agencies in any major city in Asia.

Extension of Stay

Visa extensions can be obtained from
the Lao Immigration Office at the
Ministry of the Interior in Vientiane,
opposite Talaat Sao (Morning Market),
tel: 021-212 529. The cost is US$2
per day up to a maximum of 30
days. Tour agencies, guesthouses
and some cafés can also arrange
visa extensions for a small fee.
Overstaying your visa will cost US$10
for each day.

W

Weights and Measures

Metric.

Women Travellers

Attitudes towards women in Laos
are somewhat contradictory. While
the socialist ethic espouses gender
parity, traditional Buddhist beliefs
give women a lower status than men.
Lao men have little of the conception
of foreign women as "easy" and the
woman traveller is unlikely to be
subjected to unwanted attention. On
the other hand, the Lao are very group-
oriented, and a woman travelling alone
would seem odd to the Lao.

LANGUAGE

UNDERSTANDING THE LANGUAGE

General

what? *nyang?*
who? *pai?*
when? *vila?*
where? *sai?*
why? *ben nyang?*
how? *nyow dai?*
What is this? *an nee men nyang?*
Do you speak English/French/Lao? *wow dai baw passa ungkit/falang/lao?*

Greetings

Hello *sabai dee*
Goodbye (person leaving) *la gon*
Goodbye (person staying) *sok dee*
Nice to meet you *nyin dee tee hu chak*
What is your name? *chao seu nyang?*
My name is... *koy seu...*
Where are you from? *chao ma tae sai?*
I come from the USA/England/Canada/France *koy ma tae amelikaa/ungkit/kanada/falang*
How are you? *sabai dee baw?*
I'm fine *sabai dee*
Excuse me *kho thoht*
Thank you *kop chai*
You're welcome *baw pen nyang*

Directions/Transport

Where is...? *you sai...?*
toilet *hong nam*
restaurant *han ahan*
hotel *hong haem*
bank *tanakan*
hospital *hong maw*
police station *satanee tamluat*
left *sai*
right *kua*
car *lot nyai*
bus *lot meh*

bus station *satanee lotmeh*
bicycle *lot teep*
aeroplane *nyon*
motorcycle *lot chak*
pedicab *sam law*
post office *bai sanee*
tourist office *hong kan tong teeow*
embassy *satantut*

Shopping

How much is...? *tow dai...?*
this one *toh nee*
that one *toh nan*
money *ngeun*
change *ngeun noi*
price *lakaa*
cheap *teuk*
expensive *peng*

Restaurants

eat *gin khao*
drink *deum*
drinking water *nam deum*
cold water *nam yen*
ice *nam kon*
tea *nam saa*
coffee *ka fei*
milk *nom*
sugar *nam tan*
rice *khao*
fish *bpa*
beef *sin ngua*
pork *moo*
chicken *gai*
plate *chan*
glass *jok*

Days and Time

Monday *wan chan*
Tuesday *wan angkan*
Wednesday *wan put*
Thursday *wan pahad*
Friday *wan souk*
Saturday *wan sao*

Language Schools

A number of language schools in Vientiane offer short-term Lao language classes:
Lao-American Language Center
152 Sisangvone Road
Tel: 021-414 321
www.lac.edu.la
Vientiane University College
That Luang Road
Tel: 021-414 873
Email: vtcollege@laopdr.com

Sunday *wan ateet*
today *meu nee*
this morning *sao nee*
this evening *meu leng*
tomorrow *meu eun*
yesterday *meu wan nee*
What time is it? *chak mong laeoh?*

Numbers

zero *soun*
one *neung*
two *song*
three *sam*
four *see*
five *ha*
six *hok*
seven *jet*
eight *baet*
nine *gao*
ten *sip*
eleven *sip-et*
twenty *sao*
twenty-one *sao-et*
twenty-two *sao-song*
thirty *sam-sip*
thirty-two *sam-sip-song*
hundred *loi*
two hundred *song loi*
thousand *pan*
million *lan*

FURTHER READING

Culture and Religion

Lao Textiles and Traditions by Mary Connors. The authoritative text on Lao textiles, this widely quoted volume offers a clear introduction to history, style and technique.
Traditional Recipes of Laos by Phia Sing. This book, written by the former chef and Social Director at the Royal Palace in Luang Prabang, contains recipes for traditional Lao dishes and Luang Prabang specialities.
Treasure from Laos. A beautifully produced cultural history of Laos featuring old black-and-white images.

History and Politics

Lao Peasants Under Socialism by Grant Evans. A harsh analysis of the Communist programme in Laos and the failure of socialism to better the lives of rural Lao citizens.
Politics of Ritual and Remembrance: Laos since 1975 by Grant Evans. An engaging work full of provocative observations about the period between the pre- and post-war regimes, the exploitation by the Party of religious symbols and traditions, and the challenges facing the current Communist regime.
Tragic Mountains: The Hmong, the Americans and the Secret Wars for Laos, 1942–92 by Jane Hamilton-Merritt. A former foreign correspondent in Laos, Hamilton-Merritt documents the Hmong struggle for freedom.
The Politics of Heroin in Southeast Asia by Alfred W. McCoy. The classic work on the politics and economics of opium production in the region.
The Ravens: Pilots of the Secret War of Laos by Christopher Robbins. This entertaining book relates the story of the American air war in Laos with an emphasis on tactical details.
In Search of Southeast Asia: A Modern History edited by David J. Steinberg. One of the most highly regarded introductions to the history of the region, this text includes limited material on Laos, but offers a discussion of the larger historical context from which the country has never been separate.
Buddhist Kingdom, Marxist State: The Making of Modern Laos by Martin Stuart-Fox. In this work on post-1975 Lao politics and history, the author provides one of the clearest discussions of the emergence, victory and rule of the Pathet Lao.
A History of Laos by Martin Stuart-Fox. The best English-language general history of Laos in print, this volume offers a clear and comprehensive narrative that focuses on the develop-ment of Lao nationalism in the years since World War II.
Shooting at the Moon: The Story of America's Clandestine War in Laos by Roger Warner. An enjoyable, though profoundly disturbing, history of the secret American war in Laos, using material gleaned from declassified US government material and extensive interviews.

Travel

A Dragon Apparent: Travels in Cambodia, Laos and Vietnam by Norman Lewis. A first-class travel narrative of the 1950s that gives you a sense of just how much – and how little – has changed in Indochina since the early post-war days.
The Lands of Charm and Cruelty: Travels in Southeast Asia by Stan Stesser. Originally published in *The New Yorker*, Stesser's section on Laos provides an entertaining and insightful look at Lao politics and society in the early 1990s.
Another Quiet American: Stories of Life in Laos by Brett Dakin. An amusing and informed account of life in contemporary Laos by a former American resident of Vientiane.

Contemporary Fiction

Mother's Beloved: Stories from Laos by Bounyavong Outhine. A collection of 14 short stories by a Vientiane-based novelist, these contemporary and near-contemporary tales reflect compassion and tradition, often in the face of adversity.
The Coroner's Lunch by Colin Cotterill. The first of a series of six books by English writer Colin Cotterill, all set in Laos and featuring an unlikely but endearing Lao detective, Dr Siri.

Natural History

A Photographic Guide to Birds of Vietnam, Cambodia and Laos by Peter Davidson. A handy guide to the colourful birdlife of Indochina.
The Birds of South-East Asia, a Field Guide by Craig Robson. The definitive comprehensive guide for birdwatchers.
A Field Guide to the Mammals of South-East Asia by Charles Francis. The first detailed guide to the wildlife of mainland Southeast Asia from Indochina south to Malaysia.

Send Us Your Thoughts

We do our best to ensure the information in our books is as accurate and up-to-date as possible. The books are updated on a regular basis using local contacts, who painstakingly add, amend and correct as required. However, some details (such as telephone numbers and opening times) are liable to change, and we are ultimately reliant on our readers to put us in the picture.

We welcome your feedback, especially your experience of using the book "on the road". Maybe we recommended a hotel that you liked (or another that you didn't), or you came across a great bar or new attraction we missed.

We will acknowledge all contributions, and we'll offer an Insight Guide to the best letters received.

Please write to us at:
**Insight Guides
PO Box 7910
London SE1 1WE**
Or email us at:
insight@apaguide.co.uk

TRANSPORT

GETTING THERE AND GETTING AROUND

GETTING THERE

By Air

Most international visitors to Cambodia arrive by air at either **Phnom Penh International Airport** or **Siem Reap-Angkor International Airport**. In response to the Cambodian government's open skies policy, an increasing number of airlines are flying into Cambodia via a number of regional airports in Asia, including Bangkok, Ho Chi Minh City, Hanoi, Kuala Lumpur, Singapore, Taipei, Kunming, Hong Kong, Seoul, Vientiane and Luang Prabang.

The airlines serving Cambodia include Bangkok Airways, China Southern Airlines, Dragon Air, Emirates Airlines, EVA Air, Lao Airlines, Malaysia Airlines, President Airlines, Progress Multitrade Air, Royal Phnom Penh Airways, Shanghai Airlines, Siem Reap Airways, Silk Air, Thai Airways and Vietnam Airlines. Budget carriers Jetstar Asia, operating from Singapore, and Air Asia operating from Kuala Lumpur, now offer flights to Phnom Penh and Siem Reap. Air Asia also flies from Bangkok to Phnom Penh.

A departure tax of US$25 is included in the price of all international flights. For a comprehensive list of airlines flying to and from Cambodia, as well as for flight details and schedules, call the airport information hotline (tel: 023-890 890), or visit www.cambodia-airports.com.

By Land

For foreign visitors, there are several points of entry into Cambodia by road.
From Thailand, the most popular

Airline Offices

Air Asia
179 Street Sisowath
Phnom Penh
www.airasia.com
Air France
Tel: 023-965 500
www.airfrance.com
Asiana Airlines
Tel: 023-890 441 2
http://ea.flyasiana.com
Bangkok Airways
61A Street 214, Phnom Penh
Tel: 023-426 624/707
www.bangkokair.com
Cambodia Angkor Air
206A Norodom Boulevard
Phnom Penh
Tel: 023-666 678 6
www.cambodiaangkorair.com
China Southern Airlines Co., Ltd.
c/o Shop F, G, H, I
Ground floor, Phnom Penh Hotel
53 Monivong Boulevard
Tel: 023-430 877
www.cs-air.com/en
Dragonair
Suite A4–A5, Regency Square,
168 Monireth Boulevard
Tel: 023-242 300
www.dragonair.com
EVA Air
Suite 8A, 298 Mao Tse Toung Blvd,
Phnom Penh
Tel: 023-219 911

www.evaair.com
Jetstar Airways
Tel: 023-220 909
www.jetstar.com
Korean Air
www.koreanair.com
Lao Airlines
58C Sihanouk Blvd,
Phnom Penh
Tel: 023-216 563
www.laoairlines.com
Malaysia Airlines
172–184 Monivong Blvd,
Phnom Penh
Tel: 023-426 688
www.malaysiaairlines.com
Myanmar Airways
www.maiair.com
Silk Air
MiCasa Hotel Apartment,
313 Sisowath Quay, Phnom Penh
Tel: 023-426 808
www.silkair.com
Singapore Airlines
www.singaporeair.com
Thai Airways International
294 Mao Tse Toung Blvd,
Phnom Penh
Tel: 023-214 359
www.thaiairways.com
Vietnam Airlines
41 Street 214, Phnom Penh
Tel: 023-363 396
www.vietnamairlines.com

points of entry are at Poipet/Banteay Meanchey, Cham Yeam/Koh Kong and O'Smach/Ordor Meanchey. In addition, there are now also entry points at Choam, Pruhm and Preah Vihear, but these crossings are located in the more remote areas of the country, and Preah Vihear is closed at present due to military tension.

When open, this crossing is used by visitors to the temple of the same name (known to the Thais as Khao Phra Viharn) who are travelling to the temple via the Si Saket province in Thailand – this is otherwise a good way to get there, as the Cambodian route is still a long drive and an unpleasant stint at the top of the hill.

TRANSPORT

ACCOMMODATION

EATING OUT

ACTIVITIES

A – Z

LANGUAGE

From Vietnam, you can enter at Bavet/Svay Rieng, Prek Chak/Xa Xia, Phnom Den/Tinh Bien, O Yadaw/Le Tanh, Trapaeng Thlong/Xa Mat, Trapaeng Sre/Loc Ninh, Banteay Chakrey/Khanh Binh and Kham Sam Nor/Kandal. From Laos, cross at Dom Kralor/Stung Treng, but the situation sometimes changes, so check with your consulate or travel agent before travelling.

Cambodian border guards are notorious for running scams and overcharging. Their efforts usually only amount to the loss of a few dollars, but it's a good idea to bring yourself up-to-date on the most recent border regulations before you cross, as a precaution.

By Sea

It is possible to travel between Kep or Sihanoukville and Phu Quoc, a large island resort controlled by Vietnam. Ferries and private charters run between the destinations but transportation must be confirmed in advance and likewise visas should be secured at embassies prior to departure.

GETTING AROUND

On Arrival

Phnom Penh International Airport

The airport is 10km (6 miles) from the centre of Phnom Penh, and the journey into town takes around 20 minutes. The average fare to Phnom Penh centre is about US$10 by taxi or US$5 by tuk-tuk.

Siem Reap-Angkor International Airport

The airport is located about 8km (5 miles) from town. The journey by taxi or moto will take 10–15 minutes. Most hotels, as well as some of the better guesthouses, provide airport transfers for guests who have confirmed reservations.

By Air

Siem Reap Airways, Royal Phnom Penh Airways and Progress Multitrade Air serve Siem Reap, Sihanoukville, and Koh Kong. Routes and timetables change frequently. Consult the airlines or your travel agent, or check flight schedules on www.cambodia-airports.com. A domestic airport tax of US$6 is levied and included in the ticket price.

By Bus

Several air-conditioned bus services offer comfortable and affordable trips between Phnom Penh and various destinations, including Siem Reap, Sihanoukville, Kampot/Kep, Battambang, Kompong Cham, Kratie and Poipet. The road to Sihanoukville is one of the best in the country. Shorter trips to places such as Udong or Kompong Chhnang can also easily be made by air-conditioned buses. Many bus services depart from the bus terminal near *Psar Thmay* (Central Market). You can also check with your guesthouse or a travel agent.

By Boat

Air-conditioned boats ply the route between Phnom Penh and Siem Reap, departing just beyond the Japanese Bridge at the northern end of Phnom Penh. Travelling up the Sap River, you will pass Cham fishing communities and, as the boat enters Tonlé Sap, large Vietnamese and Khmer boat communities can be seen. The journey takes around 6 hours and usually begins at 7am. Chances are that the boats are overcrowded and you will have to ride on the roof. With the improvement of the roads between the two cities, however, this mode of transport is fast losing its popularity to air-conditioned buses, which are cheaper, more comfortable and far quicker. Boat services to Kompong Cham or Kratie from Phnom Penh have been discontinued due to declining demand.

By Train

Passenger rail services are being renovated but their future schedules and development remains uncertain and precarious. Traditionally train travel in Cambodia was neither comfortable nor convenient though new projects may change this.

Taxis, Tuk-Tuks and Pedicabs

Motorcycle taxis, or "motos", as they are known, can be found all over the country. The drivers are usually recognisable by the fact that they wear hats of some sort (helmets are now required for the driver, but not the passenger). Because taxis are usually hard to find in Phnom Penh, the moto is the best way to get somewhere quickly. Many moto drivers speak some English. Expect to pay US$1 for a short journey, and US$2 for

longer ones. Always agree the fare beforehand. Motos normally wait at the airport, and this can be a viable way into town if you arrive alone. The fare is less than US$5.

In Phnom Penh and Angkor the "cyclo" or pedicab was once popular but has gradually fallen out of favour, as the tuk-tuk has risen to take its place. Tuk-tuks are large, four-wheel covered wagons that are pulled by motorbikes. Tuk-tuks can carry up to four passengers, though they are more comfortable for two. Among tourists, they are more popular than motos, though they can be up to double the price, and are not necessarily a safer mode of transport. Air-conditioned taxis are readily available at the airports. Within Phnom Penh city, they may be difficult to locate quickly. In Siem Reap, there are plenty of taxis ready and willing to take you around the temples at Angkor. At the time of writing they charge at least US$60 for a full day in and around Angkor and Siem Reap. You may have to pay up to US$100 to visit the temples further afield.

An option for long-distance travel is the share-taxi. These vehicles ply between Phnom Penh and all the major towns. The drivers may wait until they have filled the vehicle to overflowing, sometimes taking up to six or seven passengers, so this is not always a comfortable form of transport, although it is certainly a cheap way to get around.

Alternatively, freelance taxi drivers can be arranged via your hotel, guesthouse, or contact a taxi firm such as Vantha Ke (tel: 012-934 849) in Phnom Penh.

Bicycle and Vehicle Hire

In many parts of Cambodia, bicycles are offered to rent. These bicycles are often older-style road bicycles but are usually well maintained and the rental charges are small. Cycling around the smaller towns and cities of Cambodia can be a great way to see the sights. Never leave your passport as a guarantee for the bicycle you rent.

Tourists are not allowed to drive their own cars in Phnom Penh and Siem Reap, and must hire a driver. Motorcycle rental is allowed in most of Cambodia, but not in Siem Reap and Angkor. In Sihanoukville, car and motorcycle rentals are occasionally problematic due to the daily whims of local police. The car and motorcycle rental regulations change from time to time, so it is necessary to plan ahead of travel.

ACCOMMODATION

HOTELS, GUESTHOUSES, RESORTS AND BOUTIQUES

Choosing Accommodation

Luxury accommodation in Cambodia is limited to a few major centres: Phnom Penh, Siem Reap and Sihanoukville. Phnom Penh offers a fine choice of luxury accommodation at very reasonable prices, considering the amenities on offer. Mid-level accommodation can be found in abundance and is usually quite comfortable. At the lower end, guesthouses are common, and some of them are excellent. Compared with what was available a few years ago, the general situation in Cambodia has improved tremendously. Above the US$15 or $20 level all rooms will be air-conditioned and normally have satellite television and a refrigerator. Hot water is usually available in mid-level and luxury accommodation. Under US$15 usually gets you a cold shower and ceiling fan. You may or may not have windows and a TV with international cable stations.

Booking ahead is a good idea, particularly in Phnom Penh and Siem Reap, as well as Sihanoukville during high season (roughly October to March). It's best to book directly through the hotel or through an online service rather than a tour office. Tour offices will mark up the price considerably. Moto and tuk-tuk drivers can drive you around and help you find accommodation when you first arrive. However, be aware that they receive a commission from the hotel, which may be added to the price of the room. Beware of taxi drivers at the airport who try to tell you that your chosen hotel is already full, under renovation or full of prostitutes. This will rarely, if ever, be true. It's common for taxi drivers to pull a bait-and-switch, taking you to the wrong hotel (one where they collect a commission). If this happens, hold your ground (unless the other hotel looks like a better deal), and don't pay the difference in the fare to take you to the correct hotel.

Bed bugs can be a problem in Cambodia's budget hotels. Check for grey stains on sheets, tiny exoskeletons on the floor (particularly behind and under the bed), blood smears on walls, and tiny bugs (or black deposits of faeces in nests) in the folds of the mattress. Where signs are found, do not simply change rooms – it's best to find another hotel entirely.

Unlike in Vietnam or Laos, Cambodian hotels do not need to retain passports to present to police. Receptionists will copy basic information and then immediately return them to guests.

Useful hotel booking services include www.cambodia-hotels.com and www.agoda.com.

PHNOM PENH

Amanjaya Pancam
1 Street 154 and Sisowath Quay
Tel: 023-219 579
www.amanjaya-pancam-hotel.com
One of the best hotel locations in town as it sits across from Wat Ounalom and overlooks the river. Lots of dark-wood flooring and furnishings. The lobby opens onto the popular K-west restaurant and bar. **$$$$**

Boddhi Tree Aram
70 Street 244
Tel: 011-854 430
www.boddhitree.com

Located just south of the Royal Palace, this new member of the Boddhi family is a luxurious boutique hotel and requires advanced booking for one of the eight exclusive rooms. **$$$**

FCC Hotel Phnom Penh
363 Sisowath Quay
Tel: 023-210 142
www.fcccambodia.com
Located one floor below the renowned restaurant and bar, the FCC Hotel has spacious, well-appointed rooms with verandas overlooking the river. **$$$**

Goldiana Hotel
10–12 Street 280
Tel: 023-727 085
www.goldiana.com
An excellent mid-range hotel. Very popular with NGOs and consultants. **$$**

Holiday International
84 Monivong Boulevard
Tel: 023-427 402
Includes a 24-hour coffee shop, casino and the Manhattan disco. **$$**

Hotel Cambodiana
313 Sisowath Quay
Tel: 023-426 288
www.hotelcambodiana.com.kh

A splendid hotel overlooking the confluence of the Sap, Bassac and Mekong rivers. Contains all the amenities of a top modern hotel. **$$$$**

InterContinental
Regency Square, 296 Mao Tse Toung Boulevard

PRICE CATEGORIES

Price categories are for a double room in high season:
$ = under US$15
$$ = US$15–40
$$$ = US$40–200
$$$$ = more than US$200

ABOVE: luxury accommodation at Raffles Hotel Le Royal, Phnom Penh.

Tel: 023-424 888
www.ichotelsgroup.com
A five-star hotel with all the
facilities of this worldwide
chain. Good business facilities and one of the best
Cantonese restaurants in
the city. **$$$$**

The Juliana Hotel
16 Juliana, 152 Street,
Sangkat Veal Vong
Tel: 023-880 530
www.julianahotels.com
Away from the city centre,
with health club, sauna and
a good pool. Regards itself
as Phnom Penh's premier
business hotel. **$$$**

Mittapheap Hotel
262 Monivong Boulevard
Tel: 023-213 331
If you enjoy a game of
snooker this is the place to
come. **$**

Okay Guesthouse
38 Street 258
Tel: 023-986 534
Email: hello0325@hotmail.com
Right next to the Cambodia-
Vietnam Monument and
south of the Royal Palace,
Okay is in a quiet spot,
despite being the largest
and most popular back-
packer den in the city. Room
conditions vary, so take a
look before you book, but

overall it's a good bargain
and well managed. **$**

Paragon Hotel
219 Sisowath Quay
Tel: 023-222 607
This riverside hotel is a
great bargain. All 40 rooms
have air conditioning, satel-
lite TV, hot water and mini-
bars. **$$**

The Pavilion
227 Street 19
Tel: 023-222 280
www.thepavilion.asia
Located just below the
southwest corner of the
Royal Palace, The Pavilion is
a boutique hotel set in a
spacious French villa with
elements of fine Khmer and
Chinese decor. A beautiful
garden and pool area is hidden in the back. Unusually,
no children are permitted.
$–$$

Raffles Hotel Le Royal
92 Rukhak Vithei Daun Penh
(off Monivong Boulevard)
Tel: 023-981 888
www.phnompenh.raffles.com
A luxury hotel with a history,
it has seen a succession of
foreign guests including
journalists of the Vietnam
War, UN aid workers after
the defeat of the Khmer
Rouge and renowned

figures like Jacqueline
Kennedy. Restored to the
height of colonial splendour
by the Raffles group, it is
unrivalled in ambience (as
well as price). Set amidst
lush gardens with a choice
of fine restaurants and
swimming pools. Even if not
in residence, a drink at the
Elephant Bar is worth its
price. **$$$$**

Renakse Hotel
40 Sothearos Boulevard
Tel: 023-215 701
Email: renakse-htl@camnet.com.kh
Beautiful French colonial-
style hotel superbly located
opposite the Royal Palace
and close to the river front.
$$

Sharaton Cambodia Hotel
Street 47, near Wat Phnom
Tel: 023-360 395
Well located near the Wat
Phnom and the Sap river
front. **$$**

Sky Park Guesthouse
78 Street 111
Tel: 023-992 718
Located west of the
Independence Monument in
a part of town that is the out-
of-the-way budget tourist
venue district. The stylish
rooms have air conditioning,
hot water and satellite TV. **$$**

**Sofitel Phnom Penh
Prokeethra**
26 Old August Site, Sothearos
Boulevard
Tel: 023-999 200
www.sofitel.com
The Sofitel is the capital's
newest and grandest luxury
accommodation. Situated
on a southern stretch of the
Mekong across from
Diamond Island, the area is
destined to become a hot-
bed for the urban upper
class. Featuring multiple
swimming pools, a health
club, spa, and four separate
restaurants (Japanese,
Chinese, Italian and interna-
tional), Sofitel exceeds its
5-star class. Do Forni, their
Italian restaurant, is cer-
tainly the finest dining in the
city. **$$$$**

Sunday Guesthouse
97 Street 141
Tel: 023-211 623
This quiet favourite is
located just west of the sta-
dium. Sunday is run by a
friendly family who keep the
place clean and cosy.
Internet available. **$**

Sunway
1 Street 92, near Wat Phnom
Tel: 023-430 333
Situated in the heart of old

colonial Phnom Penh.
Facilities include jacuzzi,
swimming pool and sauna.
$$$
TAT
52 Street 125
Tel: 023-986 620
Quiet, comfortable and tidy,

this family-run guesthouse is
located near the stadium.
Shared and private bathrooms
are available. The rooftop res-
taurant serves Khmer, Chinese
and backpacker fare. **$**
Walkabout Hotel
109G Corner of Street 51 and

Street 174
Tel: 023-211 715
www.walkabouthotel.com
This popular place along
the well-known entertain-
ment strip includes a
24-hour restaurant and two
bars. **$**

SIEM REAP (ANGKOR) AND BATTAMBANG

Battambang

Angkor Hotel
Street No. 1
Tel: 053-952 310
Best location in town. Air-
conditioned, with TV and
refrigerator. Overlooks the
Sangker River. **$–$$**
Chhaya Hotel
Street 3
Tel: 053-952 170
This hotel has a good loca-
tion in the centre of town
and has rooms with air con-
ditioning, hot showers and
TV. **$**
Leng Heng
National Route 5
Tel: 053-370 088
Modern building set in
courtyard with nice garden.
Light and airy rooms. **$**

Royal Hotel
118 Street 3
Tel: 016-912 034
This backpacker favourite
across from the central market has 45 spacious rooms.
The windows in most of them
open on an enclosed atrium
rather than the outdoors. **$**
Spring Park Hotel
588 Romchek 4, Ratanak
Tel: 053-730 999
This new hotel is located on
the east river bank and is one
of the largest in town. There
are 90 spacious rooms and –
allegedly – the only function-
ing elevator in Battambang. **$$**

Siem Reap

Amansara
Road to Angkor

Tel: 063-760 333
www.amanresorts.com
A former villa of the present
king and host to Jacqueline
Kennedy, the exclusive
Amansara is now said to be
a favourite of the family of
Angelina Jolie and Brad Pitt.
With no signs out front and
a closed gate, not anybody
can just walk into the oasis
of serenity. Half the rooms
have sizeable private pools
in addition to several larger
swimming areas on site.
$$$$
Angkor Hotel
Street 6, Phum Sala Kanseng
Tel: 063-964 301
www.angkor-hotel-cambodia.com
Opened in 1999, this four-
star hotel has an excellent

restaurant and a large
swimming pool. **$$$**
Angkor Village
Wat Bo Road
Tel: 063-963 561
www.angkorvillage.com
Individual wooden bunga-
lows, swimming pool, nice
gardens and a French res-
taurant. Has its own ele-
phants available for rides. **$$**
City Angkor
Airport Road
Tel: 063-760 336
www.thecityangkorhotel.com
Still sometimes called by its
former name, Nokor Kok
Thlok, City Angkor is located
on the airport road and has
pleasant rooms with bath-
tubs. Swimming pool, res-
taurants and a lobby bar. **$$**

BELOW: Siem Reap has a range of comfortable places to stay.

TRANSPORT

ACCOMMODATION

EATING OUT

ACTIVITIES

A – Z

LANGUAGE

Freedom Hotel
Route 6, near Central Market
Tel: 063-963 473
www.freedomhotel.info
A very reasonable restaurant attached to the hotel, and a free pick-up service from the airport. **$**

Home Sweet Home
Wat Bo area
Tel: 012-693 393
Fairly new, friendly, very clean hotel. Upstairs rooms with hardwood floors. Good restaurant. Internet connection. Good value. **$**

La Noria
Achasvar Street
Tel: 063-984 242
Small but cool and quiet cottages with terraces set in a garden. The restaurant offers traditional Khmer puppet-theatre performances. **$**

La Résidence d'Angkor
River Road
Tel: 063-963 390
www.residencedangkor.com

The International Orient-Express hotel group specialises in unique properties in exotic locales such as Angkor Wat and Luang Prabang, Laos. All rooms are beautifully decorated in teak wood and Khmer cotton. The gardens surround a free-form swimming pool with a fountain. **$$$**

Le Méridien Angkor
Vithei Charles de Gaulle
Tel: 063-963 900
www.starwoodhotels.com/lemeridien
Sumptuous modern five-star with all the luxury facilities you would expect, including a large swimming pool, a spa, and several restaurants including a very good Italian. **$$$$**

Raffles Grand Hotel d'Angkor
1 Vithei Charles de Gaulle
Tel: 063-963 888
www.siemreap.raffles.com
This fabulous hotel sits in the centre of Siem Reap

opposite the Amansara and Victoria hotels. It has been refurbished by the Raffles group and can rightly claim to be one of Southeast Asia's grandest old hotels. Wide range of restaurants and bars, a large swimming pool, dinner theatre and spa, plus all the comforts of a luxury hotel. **$$$$**

Rithyrine Angkor Hotel
No.0509, Wat Bo Village,
Tel: 012-543 475
www.rithyrineangkorhotel.com
A pleasant mid-range hotel with large rooms and a courtyard swimming pool. Much of the hotel is exquisitely furnished in solid wood and carvings. Free breakfast and Wi-fi is included. **$$**

Shinta Mani
Om Khum Street and Street 14
Tel: 063-761 998
www.shintamani.com
Charming 18-room property, ideally located in the French

Quarter in the centre of Siem Reap. Facilities include a spa, swimming pool and a restaurant. The hotel also runs (and funds) a vocational hotel-training centre for the underprivileged. **$$$**

Skyway Guest House
Route 6, near Psar Samaki
Tel: 063-963 969
Rooms include TV, air conditioning, hot water, and benefit of the in-house restaurant. A small crocodile farm is located behind the hotel. **$**

Sofitel Royal Angkor Golf and Spa Resort
Angkor Wat Road
Tel: 063-964 600
www.sofitel.com
A modern low-rise with a cool, airy feel. A bit out of town. Beautiful garden and pools plus a variety of restaurants, a bar and an 18-hole golf course. Ideal for relaxing after temple-overload. **$$$$**

Ta Prohm Hotel
Near Old Market
Tel: 063-380 117
Email: taphrom@camintel.com.kh
Sometimes crowded with group tours, the Ta Prohm is very well situated next to the river, in the old French Quarter. The ground floor hosts a number of shops, including Monument Books and Toys. Conveniently located next to the old market and Pub Street. **$$**

Victoria Angkor Resort & Spa
Central Park
P.O. Box 93145
Tel: 063-760 428
www.victoriahotels.asia
A brand well known across Indochina, Victoria arguably has the loveliest property in Cambodia. Colonial-style architecture with dark wooden beams encircles floating courtyards where tall trees hang above fish pools, and even a pair of crocodiles! The expensive grandeur of the blue swimming pool is banked by the fine in-house restaurant, serving with all the quality but a fraction of the price of surrounding restaurants. **$$$$**

BELOW: friendly service.

CENTRAL CAMBODIA

Kompong Cham

Heng Heng Hotel
Preah Sumarit Road
Tel: 072-971 405
Go for the newer wing, which features spacious rooms with TV and hot showers. **$**

Mekong Hotel
Tel: 042-931 536
Overlooking the Mekong. The rooms on the river afford some good views. **$**

Mittapheap Hotel
Kosamak Ncary Roth Street, near the roundabout
Tel: 042-941 565
Smart rooms with TV and hot water. **$**

Oudom Sambath Hotel
439 Preah Sumarit Road
Tel: 072-971 502
Huge air-conditioned rooms overlooking the Mekong, but the service can be a bit lax. **$**

Rana Homestay
7km (4.5 miles) east of Kompong Cham off National Route 7
Tel: 012-682 240
www.rana-homestay.blogspot.com
Email: sreysiam@gmail.com
For a unique insight into Cambodian rural life, try this friendly homestay. Very popular, so it's essential to book ahead through the email address. **$$**

Santepheap Hotel
Preah Sumarit Road
Tel: 072-971 537
Email: santepheaphotel@yahoo.com
This is Kratie's best hotel, with very comfortable rooms that have air conditioning and hot showers. **$$**

You Hong
91 Street 8, north side of the market
Tel: 012-957 003
Email: youhong_kratie@yahoo.com
A great place to overlook Kratie's bustling market. Facilities include restaurant, bar and internet. **$**

Stung Treng

Sok Sambath Hotel
Street 2, near the river
Tel: 074-973 790
With its wide range of air-conditioned rooms, the Sok Sambath has long been Stung Treng's finest hotel. **$**

THE CAMBODIAN COAST

Kampot

Borey Bokor Hotel
Tel: 033-932 826
Located one block from the river, it has the most comfortable rooms in town, with air conditioning and TV. **$$**

Kampot Guesthouse
Off the River Road
Tel: 012-512 931
Basic but pleasant guesthouse away from the riverside on a backpacker hotel street. Rooms are tidy and efficient with hot water, fan or air conditioning and cable TV. Wi-fi is available in the very basic restaurant. **$**

Molieden Guesthouse
Makara Road
Tel: 033-932 798
A new guesthouse located a stone's throw from the river. Features spacious and very clean, single to family rooms with en-suite bathrooms. **$**

Sen Monorom Guesthouse
Opposite the Canadian Bank
Tel: 012-650 330
An attractive budget place with large, clean rooms and satellite TV. **$**

Koh Kong

Koh Kong Guesthouse
Tel: 099-800 200
The Koh Kong is a friendly, family-owned guesthouse. The upstairs restaurant serves Thai, Cambodian and backpacker fare. **$**

The Rainbow Lodge
Tatai Koh Kong (25km/16 miles from Koh Kong, on the way to Sre Amben)
Email: therainbowlodge@netkhmer.com
This charming eco-lodge offers river views from seven stilt-house bungalows. Prices include three meals a day. Booking is by email only. **$$$**

Sihanoukville (Kompong Som)

Chez Claude
Kam Pegn Hill (above Sokha Beach)
Tel: 012-824 870
The hilltop location is hard to beat with its commanding views of the Gulf of Thailand. There is a good in-house restaurant, and Claude also arranges group diving trips. **$$**

Chez Mari-Yan Bungalows
Sangkat 3, Khan Mittapheap
Tel: 034-933 709
Close to Independence Square, near Victory Beach, the Mari-Yan has a good open-air restaurant and the bungalows provide a great view of the ocean. **$**

Holiday Palace Hotel and Casino
Victory Beach
Tel: 034-933 808
Sihanoukville's casino hotel overlooks the ocean; 114 rooms and suites make it the biggest game in town. Not as glitzy as you might expect for a casino, which is a plus if you are just looking for a nice place to stay. **$$**

Mealy Chenda Guesthouse
Mondul 3, Sangkat 3, Khan Mittapheap
Tel: 034-933 472
The largest guesthouse in Sihanoukville. Some rooms have a balcony with sea view. The restaurant offers great views of the sunset. **$**

Orchidée Guesthouse
23 Tola Street, Ochheuteal Beach
Tel: 034-933 639
www.orchidee-guesthouse.com
An excellent villa-style guesthouse that features rooms with air conditioning, refrigerator and TV. There is an in-house restaurant and a swimming pool as well. **$**

Peak Hotel
Near the port
Tel: 034-320 301
This hotel has a unique location on top of the hill, overlooking the port. It offers refurbished rooms with en-suite bathrooms and cable TV, as well as tennis courts, a restaurant and mini-mart. **$$**

Sokha Beach Resort & Spa
Sokha Beach
Tel: 034-935 999
www.sokhahotels.com
Sihanoukville's first five-star hotel is set on a 15-hectare (37-acre) beachfront garden and a private beach. The comprehensive amenities include a good swimming pool, gym and tennis courts, two bars, three restaurants and a nightclub. **$$$**

Ratanakiri (Banlung)

Lakeside Chheng Lok Hotel
Tel: 012-957 422
www.lakeside-chhenglokhotel.com
While not an attractive building, the location on the lake on the edge of town is convenient and the staff are very friendly and speak enough English. **$**

Tree Top Ecolodge
Phum No.1, Laban Seak Commune
Tel 012-490 033
www.treetop-ecolodge.com
Easily the coolest budget accommodation in the country. In a town where run-down guesthouses are the norm, Tree Top's private villas with a tree-house feel provide the sort of atmosphere one might expect at a coastal boutique resort. The rustic, open-air restaurant and lounge have beautiful sunset views of the valley below. **$$**

PRICE CATEGORIES

Price categories are for a double room in high season:

$ = under US$15
$$ = US$15–40
$$$ = US$40–200
$$$$ = more than US$200

EATING OUT

RECOMMENDED RESTAURANTS, CAFES AND BARS

What to Eat

Cambodian food is similar in form to Thai and Vietnamese, though the flavour is milder, lacking a heavy reliance on chilli. The main national staple is, of course, rice, but French colonial influence has dictated that the Cambodians eat more bread than any other Southeast Asian country. Because of the country's incredible richness in waterways, freshwater fish and prawns are especially popular. Fresh seafood is also available from the Gulf of Thailand. Beef, pork, chicken, duck and other poultry are widely available. Soup is served as an accompaniment to nearly every meal.

Visitors upcountry will generally find themselves limited to Cambodian cuisine or to the ubiquitous baguette and pâté. In towns of any size Chinese food will also be available. In the west of the country Thai food is widespread, and in the east, Vietnamese influence is similarly common.

Cambodia overflows with fruit; among the most popular and widespread fruits are mango, coconut, rambutan, durian, mangosteen, starfruit, pineapple, watermelon and a wide variety of bananas.

Where to Eat

Eating "locally", as in Laos, is a little more challenging in Cambodia than Vietnam or Thailand. Cambodians are adventurous eaters, and dishes or snacks made with unusual creatures and internal organs are common on the street. Markets are the cheapest place to grab a hot meal or a take-away snack. They are busiest – and have the best variety – early in the morning and around dinner time. Cafés with foreign coffee and free Wi-fi are popular in the big cities. Many serve good food, but portions are generally small and on the pricey side. Truck stops are a great place to pick up pre-packaged snacks, ice cream and soft drinks. Most travellers will stick to the wide variety of tourist restaurants and bars, however.

Drinking Notes

Unlike Laos, Cambodia is not renowned for its beer. Draught is increasingly common in the form of Angkor or Tiger, but travellers are often limited to canned international beers such as Carlsberg, Heineken, Tiger, ABC, Victoria Bitter, Foster's, San Miguel and Singha; local brands include Angkor, Angkor Stout, Kingdom and Bayon. Imported wine – shades of the French colonial past – is readily available in major towns, while domestic rice wines promising strength and virility are widespread.

It is always best to drink bottled water in Cambodia. The traveller should also beware of ice of unknown origin, particularly upcountry or at street stalls. Soft drinks like cola and lemonade manufactured by internationally known companies are available everywhere. Caution should be exercised with fresh fruit juices and sugar-cane juice, but cartons and cans of fruit juice, milk and drinking yoghurt are available in supermarkets and convenience stores everywhere. Coffee – often very good – and tea are generally available throughout the country.

PHNOM PENH

Khmer

A good area for authentic Khmer food is across the Japanese Bridge over the Sap River. Here you will find 5km (3 miles) of restaurants on both sides of the road.
Frizz Restaurant
67 Street 240
Tel: 023-220 953
A renowned restaurant with renowned cooking classes.

The Cambodian cuisine here is spectacular. Set in a humble street-level building just west of the Royal Palace. Try the banana blossom salad and fish *amok*.
$$
Khmer Borane
389 Sisowath Quay
A large, popular Khmer restaurant with an emphasis on plenty of beer with your dinner, served by the ubiquitous "Tiger Girls". Balcony seating overlooks the riverfront in a prime location just north of the Royal Palace.
$$
Malis
136 Norodom Boulevard
Tel: 023-221 022
A highly regarded restaurant with artfully prepared traditional or contemporary Khmer dishes by celebrated Cambodian chef Luu Meng, and a full bar with an extensive wine list. Elegant dining environment, either indoors or outdoors in the terrace garden. **$$**
Manor House
6B Street 288
Tel: 023-992 566
This air-conditioned restaurant serves reasonably

priced Khmer food with a Western touch. **$$**

Romdeng Restaurant
21 Street 278
Tel: 092-219 565
Run by Mith Samlanh of Friends restaurant fame, Romdeng serves traditional Cambodian food. Like Friends, this is a non-profit restaurant whose aim is to arm former street youth with marketable skills. **$$**

Sugar Palm
19 Street 240
Tel: 023-220 956/012-818 143
Located along the atmospheric street of galleries, boutiques and small restaurants is this lovely two-storey restaurant-bar that serves good Khmer food. **$$**

Asian

Boddhi Tree
50 Street 113, opposite Tuol Sleng Genocide Museum
Tel: 016-865 445
A restaurant-café set in a Cambodian-style wooden house serving healthy Asian dishes, fresh juice and wine. Also a guesthouse. **$**

Little Noodle Shop
1 Street 172
Tel: 023-555 0511
A small eatery serving fresh, Chinese-style pulled noodles and dumplings. All noodle dishes available boiled or fried. Vegetarian options available. **$**

Mamak's
18 Street 114
A popular halal Malaysian restaurant since 1992. Food is akin to North Indian, with a large selection of curries, seafood, roti, and tarek (red milk tea). **$$**

Nouveau Pho de Paris
26 Monivong Boulevard
Tel: 023-723 076
Popular with both locals and expats, this is a good place for savoury Asian dishes. It focuses on Chinese cuisine, but also offers well-prepared Khmer and Vietnamese dishes. **$$**

Warung Bali
25 Street 178
Tel: 012-967 480
An Indonesian favourite in a rustic setting with a wide variety of spicy meat and vegetarian dishes. Go early in the evening as food may

run out in this popular spot. **$$**

French

La Croisette
241 Sisowath Quay
Tel: 012-876 032
This river-front restaurant serves a wide selection of French, Khmer and international dishes. Its charcoal-grilled beef skewers are popular. A good selection of ice cream, cocktails and wine, as well as breakfasts, is available. **$$**

Tamarind Bar
31 Street 240
Tel: 012-830 139
An old favourite serving French and Mediterranean dishes in a French colonial building. Choice of indoor, pavement or rooftop seating. **$$$**

Topaz
100 Sothearos Boulevard, near Hong Kong Centre
Tel: 023-211 054
Serves excellent French and Thai food in a refined environment. **$$$**

International/Western

The Blue Pumpkin
245 Sisowath Quay
Tel: 023-998 153
www.tbpumpkin.com
A cheerful white interior with tables and couches, overlooking the river. Blue Pumpkin has an extensive selection of the best baked goods in Cambodia. They also have a full menu of drinks, sandwiches and pasta. Branches also at Monument Books and at Phnom Penh airport. Free Wi-fi. **$**

Brown Coffee
Corner of Street 51 and Street 302
Tel: 069-737 567
One of the most popular cafés in Phnom Penh and all but impossible to get seats on Sundays. Similar to local Gloria Jean's Coffees in style and menu, though cheaper prices. Branches nearby at the corners of Street 57 and Street 294, as well as 17 Street 214 (off Norodom). Free Wi-fi. **$**

Foreign Correspondents' Club of Cambodia (FCCC)
363 Sisowath Quay

Tel: 023-724 014
www.fcccambodia.com
Easily the most atmospheric restaurant in Phnom Penh, with stunning views of the river and the National Museum. It has an excellent international menu. A travel agent and a souvenir section are located on the second floor. The FCC Hotel Phnom Penh is also located here. **$$$**

Friends
215 Street 13, near the National Museum
Tel: 023-426 748
www.streetfriends.org
This cosy non-profit tapas restaurant is run as part of a programme to teach former street youth useful skills. Very good snacks, salads and fruit shakes, as well as good service at reasonable prices. **$$**

Garden Centre Café
23 Street 57
Tel: 023-363 002
Set in a lovely garden courtyard, the "centre" serves a large array of affordable Khmer and Western dishes, including plenty of choices for vegetarians. **$$**

Lazy Gecko
1D Street 258
Tel: 023-500 1176
Relocated away from Boeung Kak Lake following the famous illegal government evictions, this backpacker favourite still serves all the "traveller classics" such as cheeseburgers, fries, pizza, banana pancakes and a few Khmer dishes to round things out. **$$**

Le Rendevous
127 Sisowath Quay
Tel: 023-986 466
Set on the river front, this popular restaurant has a large international menu which includes pizzas, salads, steaks and sandwiches in large portions. There is a well-sheltered pavement area for dining outside. Open until late. **$$**

Metro Café
Corner of Sisowath Quay and Street 148
Tel: 023-222 275
A smart design and trendy setting makes this one of the few chic offerings to be

found in Phnom Penh. Metro has a popular bar and serves fine French and Asian fusion cuisine. **$$**

The Rising Sun
20 Street 178, around the corner from the FCC
Tel: 012-970 719
A very popular British pub and restaurant serving affordably priced food and drinks. **$$**

Rory's Pub
33 Street 178
Tel: 012-425 702
A bar and restaurant serving a wide selection of Western, Irish and Khmer dishes. Beers and an impressive range of Irish spirits. **$$**

Tiger Feet
9 Street 118
Tel: 012-885 188
Other than Khmer food, this well-decorated restaurant-cum-bar serves a good variety of Western dishes such as meat pies and mash, lasagnes and burgers. A full bar offers cold beer and spirits. **$$**

USA Donut
Corner Street 51 and Street 302
Tel: 023-630 6040
Across from Brown Coffee, USA Donut arguably serves the best American-style donuts, burgers and hot dogs in all of Southeast Asia, at the front of a small convenience store. **$**

Italian

Happy Herb's Pizza
345 Sisowath Quay
Tel: 023-362 349
Famous place serving good pizzas. Depending on your mood, ask for "normal", "happy" or "very happy" versions. **$$**

Luna d'Autunno
6C Street 29
Tel: 023-220 895
Luna is a very popular, authentic Italian chain found in major cities throughout Indochina. Prices are a little higher

PRICE CATEGORIES

Price categories are per person for a meal without drinks:

$ = under US$5
$$ = US$5–20
$$$ = more than US$20

TRANSPORT
ACCOMMODATION
EATING OUT
ACTIVITIES
A – Z
LANGUAGE

than competitors, but you can taste the difference. Extensive wine list. Great brick-oven pizzas and seafood. **$$**

The Pizza Company
Sorya shopping centre near the Central market
This popular Thai-owned chain serves American-style pizza, with numerous toppings and crust styles – all a rarity in Indochina. It's one of the best Italian restaurants in the country, and very popular. Free, unlimited (soft) drink refills are available. **$$**

Pop Café
371 Sisowath Quay

Tel: 012-562 892
Pop Café serves up authentic Italian cuisine by an Italian owner and chef. All the basics are covered, including thin-crust pizza, spaghetti and pasta, gnocchi and lasagne. Located with the FCC. **$$**

Japanese

Ginga
295 Monivong Boulevard
Tel: 023-217 323
Sushi, sashimi and barbecued dishes are offered in this restaurant. Has another branch in Siem Reap. **$$**

Origami
88 Sothearos Boulevard
Tel: 012-968 095

This expat favourite offers set menus of artfully presented tempura, sushi and sashimi. Located just east of the Cambodia-Vietnam Monument. **$$**

Mexican

The Mex
115 Norodom Boulevard (next to Independence Monument)
Tel: 023-360 535/012-911 767
Serves good Mexican and American food in an air-conditioned environment. Open for breakfasts. **$$**

Thai

Baan Thai
2 Street 306 (off Norodom

Boulevard)
Tel: 023-362 991
A popular restaurant with a good selection of high-quality Thai and Khmer food in a Cambodian-style wooden house. Seating is Thai-style, on cushions around low tables. **$$**

Tonlé Bassac
177 Mao Tse Toung Boulevard
Tel: 023-210 019
This restaurant offers buffet-style dining. A wide range of Asian and Western food is served, including Japanese cuisine, grilled seafood and Mongolian barbecue.
$$

SIEM REAP AND BATTAMBANG

Battambang

Gecko Café
Street 3, one block south of Psa Nath Market
www.geckocafecambodia.com
This relatively new balcony restaurant sits upstairs in an old French-colonial shop. The menu includes authentic Western food and Khmer favourites. Offers the only free Wi-fi in town, massage and motorbike rentals, with information on how to visit all the local sights on your own. **$$**

Smokin' Pot
West of the Angkor Hotel
Tel: 012-821 400
This restaurant and café features Thai but serves great Khmer and Western food as well. Popular with expats. Cooking classes are also available. **$$**

Sunrise Coffee House
West of Royal Hotel
Tel: 053-953 426
This very quiet spot is located on the same street as the market. Sunrise serves authentic Western food and great coffee. The breakfast burritos and fresh cinnamon rolls are a real

winner. **$**

Vegetarian Foods Restaurant
North of Hôtel Asie
Tel: 012-501 408
This family restaurant serves Khmer, Vietnamese and Chinese vegetarian dishes. Menu items feature home-made tofu and soy milk. Located just south of NH5. **$**

Siem Reap

Abacus
Oum Khun Street
Tel: 012-644 286
Occupying a traditional two-storey Cambodian house, this restaurant and bar serves international cuisine with a good wine selection. Indoor, garden and balcony seating is available. **$$**

Angkor Café
In front of Angkor Wat
Tel: 063-380 300
Excellent Asian snacks, dishes and fruit juices. **$$$**

Bamboo Hut
Angkor Diamond Hotel, West bank of river
Tel: 063-380 038
Beer garden and restaurant serving Khmer, Asian and

international food and vegetarian dishes. **$**

The Blue Pumpkin
Old Market area
Tel: 063-963 574
Very popular place for its excellent pastas, salads, breads and freshly made ice cream. **$$**

Dead Fish Tower
Sivatha Boulevard
Tel: 012-630 377
Its architecture is as playful as its name suggests. This cool restaurant offers good Khmer and Thai food, and traditional Cambodian music and dance performances at lunch and dinner. **$$**

FCC Angkor
Pokambor Street
Tel: 063-760 283
The sister restaurant of Phnom Penh's famous FCC. Amid a refined atmosphere, choose from an extensive menu of international and local dishes, and a full bar. **$$**

Les Orientalistes
Wat Bo Street
Tel: 012-440 627
Fine French, Khmer and Mediterranean food is

served in an imaginatively designed setting. **$$$**

Little India
Near the Old Market, opposite Blue Pumpkin
Tel: 012-652 398
Siem Reap's oldest and best Indian restaurant. Try the delicious home-made breads. **$$**

The Red Piano
Near the Old Market
Tel: 063-964 750
One of the most popular places in town for Western and Asian food, as well as the extensive wine list. The Red Piano Guesthouse nearby has stylish rooms with small verandas. **$$**

Soup Dragon
Old Market area
Tel: 063-964 933
Enjoy Vietnamese and other cuisines in this airy, three-storey restaurant with a rooftop bar. **$$**

Viroth's
246 Wat Bo Street
Tel: 016-951 800
Well-prepared Cambodian cuisine with a contemporary twist and served in a modern setting. **$$**

CENTRAL CAMBODIA

Kompong Cham

Hao An Restaurant
Corner of Preah Monivong

Boulevard and Vithei Pasteur
Tel: 042-941 234
A large restaurant (for

Kompong Cham) serving good Khmer and Chinese food at reasonable prices. **$**

Lazy Mekong Daze
Preah Bat Sihanouk Road
A comfortable riverside bar

and restaurant catering to travellers with its tasty Khmer and international food. Open for breakfast, lunch and dinner. **$**

Mekong Crossing
Preah Bat Sihanouk Road
Tel: 042-941 773
A small restaurant and pub located by the Mekong River, with Khmer and Western dishes. **$**

Two Dragons
Ang Duong Road
Tel: 042-945 969

Some very good Chinese and Khmer dishes at this friendly family-run restaurant. **$**

Kratie

Heng Heng
Heng Heng Hotel,
Preah Sumarit Road
Tel: 072-971 405
One of the better restaurants in town, the Heng Heng serves very good Khmer fish dishes as well as some Chinese favourites. **$**

Red Sun Falling
Preah Sumarit Road, near Santepheap Hotel
A cosy restaurant and bar located in front of the river, with comfortable seats, good music and a second-hand bookshop. Very popular. **$**

Star Guesthouse
Next to the market
Tel: 072-971 663
Star Guesthouse offers a small restaurant with simple and tasty Western food, run

by young English-speaking locals. **$**

Stung Treng

Le Tonlé
Tonlé Tourism Training Centre, 500 metres/yds east of town
Tel: 074-973 638
A training centre for locals interested in joining the hotel and catering industry, the Tonlé doubles as both guesthouse and restaurant serving Khmer and international dishes. **$**

THE CAMBODIAN COAST

Kampot

Blissful Guesthouse
Tel: 012-513 024
Comfortable guesthouse restaurant and bar serving good local and Western dishes. Open until late. **$**

Little Garden Bar & Guesthouse
River Road
Tel: 012-256 901
This river-front, expat-managed restaurant and bar serves Khmer and Western food. Good cocktail and wine list. **$**

Rusty Keyhole
River Road
Tel: 012-679 607
Western-run restaurant and bar serving Asian and backpacker fare, ice cream and sweets. Best ribs in Cambodia. **$**

Ta Eou Restaurant
River Road
Tel: 033-932 422
Built on stilts over the river; enjoy a good Khmer or Chinese meal while watching the sun set. **$**

Kep

Located **opposite Kep Beach** is an area lined with sheltered picnic platforms, where vendors will present fresh seafood for you to browse and take your pick from. Other restaurants and bars are found in the lodges and guesthouses hereabouts.

Champey Inn
Kep Beach
Tel: 012-501 742
The restaurant at this bungalow resort overlooks the

ocean and serves French-style seafood. **$$$**

Le Bout du Monde
Tel: 012-198 9106
French and Khmer dishes are served at this restaurant-bar. **$**

Koh Kong

Riverfront Restaurant
Street 1
Tel: 011-943 497
Located on the waterfront between the Koh Kong City Hotel and the Phou Minh Koh Hotel. Specialises in tasty Khmer and Thai soups. **$**

Sauna Garden Bar
Street 3
Tel: 015-601 633
This expat favourite is set in a lovely garden and serves decent Thai, Khmer and backpacker fare. As the name suggests, there is also a sauna. **$$**

Sihanoukville (Kompong Som)

Angkor Arms
Ekareach Street
Tel: 034-933 847
Traditional English pub with draught beer, spirits, wines and cocktails, as well as Western and Asian dishes. Pool table and cable TV. **$$**

Caffe Venezia
Ekareach Street
Tel: 012-516 543
Good Italian cuisine in this guesthouse restaurant. **$$**

Chhner Molop Chrey Restaurant
Victory Beach
Tel: 034-933 708

A large seafood restaurant opposite the Holiday Palace Hotel. **$$**

Eden Bar
Serendipity Beach
Tel: 034-933 585
A popular beachfront bar and restaurant. Good music selection and late-night parties on Tuesday, Friday and Saturday nights. **$**

Holy Cow
Ekareach Street, near bus station
Tel: 012-478 510
Guesthouse restaurant and bar with good Western and vegetarian fare. **$**

Indian Curry Pot
Weather Station Hill
Tel: 034-934 040
The humble appearance of this place belies its really good halal Indian food. Arranges trips to Ream National Park and other nearby destinations. **$**

Mick & Craig's Sanctuary
Between the Golden Lions and Serendipity Beach
Tel: 012-727 740
A good selection of wood-fired barbecue and home-cooked meals. Sandwiches, salads and fresh fruit juices are served during the day. **$**

The Nap House
Serendipity Beach
Tel: 034-934 153
This modest restaurant and guesthouse is situated right on the beach, next to Eden Bar. There is a barbecue every night. **$**

Snake House
Victory Beach

Tel: 012-673 805
This unusual Russian-managed restaurant-bar and guesthouse has highly rated Russian, French and international food served within a herpetarium. **$$**

Treasure Island Seafood Restaurant
Koh Pos Beach, near Independence Hotel
Tel: 012-838 385
Treasure Island Seafood Restaurant specialises in fresh seafood and Hong Kong-style cuisine, with the added benefit of a very pleasant beach – albeit one with rough waters. **$$**

Ratanakiri (Banlung)

Tree Top Ecolodge
Phum No.1, Laban
Seak Commune
Tel 012-490 333
www.treetop-ecolodge.com
There are few places to eat in Ratanakiri apart from guesthouses serving local fare. Tree Top Ecolodge is a rare venue serving the sort of menu expected in Phnom Penh. The tree-house-style restaurant and lounge is atmospheric and has great views of the valley. Free Wi-fi. **$$**

PRICE CATEGORIES

Price categories are per person for a meal without drinks:

$ = under US$5
$$ = US$5–20
$$$ = more than US$20

ACTIVITIES

THE ARTS, NIGHTLIFE, FESTIVALS, SHOPPING AND SPORT

THE ARTS

Cultural Performances

Classical *apsara* dance performances truly bring life to the Angkor experience, as they directly portray the celestial maidens depicted in the bas-reliefs of the temples. They can be seen at the Chatomuk Theatre near the Royal Palace in central Phnom Penh, as well as at major (expensive) hotels in the capital and at Siem Reap.

Another interesting dance genre is called *tontay*, which portrays *Reamker*, a Cambodian version of the Indian epic, the *Ramayana*. Performances are held at various hotels and restaurants in both Phnom Penh and Siem Reap.

Phnom Penh

Sovanna Phum Art Association
111 Street 360
Tel: 023-987 564
www.shadow-puppets.org
Traditional dance and other cultural art performances, such as shadow puppetry and music, can be viewed at the Association every Friday and Saturday evening at 7.30pm.

Siem Reap

Raffles Grand Hotel d'Angkor
1 Vithei Charles de Gaulle
Tel: 063-963 888
www.siemreap.raffles.com
Have an Asian–international buffet dinner as you watch a cultural show at the hotel's outdoor restaurant, which is staged three evenings a week.
Chao Praya Restaurant
62 Angkor Wat Street
Tel: 063-965 052

The restaurant's buffet dinner (consisting of a range of Asian and European items) comes with a traditional dance performance.

Cinemas

Phnom Penh welcomed the country's first two American-style movie theatres in 2011, complete with reclining, stadium seating, air conditioning, surround sound and full 3D. Both offer American and occasionally Hong Kong or even Cambodian films. All but the Asian films are offered in original English dialogue with various subtitles.
Legend Cinema
City Mall (top floor)
Monireth Street
Tel: 093-300 400
www.legend-cinemas.com
Sabay Cineplex
Sorya Shopping Centre (top floor)
Street 53
Tel: 017-666 210
www.thecineplexs.com

NIGHTLIFE

The Cambodian nightlife scene is rather diverse. From the colonial elegance of the Elephant Bar at Le Royal Hotel to incredibly tawdry karaoke dens, there is certainly something for everybody. The substantial expat population has led to the establishment of quite a few Western-style bars. Most are couple-friendly, but clubs and bars down side streets leading away from the city river fronts tend to cater to the needs of the single male, with the services of paid dance partners and hostesses in abundance.

Phnom Penh and Sihanoukville are not always safe after dark, and more than a few of the patrons of the wilder nightclubs and discos are both armed and intoxicated. When travelling late at night anywhere in these cities, be sure to go with a friend or at least stay in the vicinity of your accommodation to avoid the attentions of muggers. The best (and safest) part of Phnom Penh for night revelry is along the Sap River at Sisowath Quay. There is a variety of low-key nightspots and the area is safer than most. Street 51 (Pasteur Street, otherwise known as "The Strip") between Streets 174 and 154 is also popular, though prone to more illegal (and dangerous) activity. The area just south of Independence Monument and west of Pasteur is another low-key but chic nightspot.

Phnom Penh

Bars
Elephant Bar
Hotel Le Royal, Street 92, off Monivong Boulevard
Tel: 023-981 888
A classy and cosy bar in a world-famous hotel.
Equinox Bar
3A Street 278
Tel: 021-586 139
Two floors with indoor and outdoor seating. Happy hour 5–8pm.
Foreign Correspondents' Club of Cambodia (FCCC)
363 Sisowath Quay
Tel: 023-724 014
www.fcccambodia.com
Expensive and touristy, but the iconic bar and restaurant is still one of the nicest spots in the city for evening drinks with views of the river front.
Green Vespa
95 Sisowath Quay

Tel: 012-887 228
A very popular Irish bar located by the ferry landing, with good food, snacks, and hot and cold drinks. Travel information available here.
Huxley's Brave New World
30 Street 136
Two floors with a restaurant upstairs. This posh British pub has a near-endless selection of drinks.
Talkin to a Stranger
21B Street 294
Tel: 012-798 530
A cosy bar in a garden setting with great bar food and even better drinks. Live music.

Nightclubs
Heart of Darkness
26 Street 51
Tel: 012-943 654
A hangout popular with expats and kids of wealthy locals (often armed and with bodyguards). Live music at weekends.
Martini Pub
45 Street 95, off Mao Tse Toung Boulevard
Tel: 011-874 416
Well-known pub and indoor disco bar, with live music on Friday and Saturday evenings. Outside is an open-air restaurant and bar with a 3-metre (120-inch) screen on which the latest movies are played every Friday.
Salt Lounge
217 Street 136
Tel: 012-289 905
Located 10 metres (30ft) from Sisowath Quay, this contemporary bar attracts a diverse clientele with good music, friendly staff and a variety of local food and cocktails.
Walkabout Bar
Corner of Streets 174 and 51
Tel: 023-211 715

A very popular and well-known place with two bars (the one upstairs is called Whale N Hoe) and a restaurant within a mid-range hotel. A full bar, full menu, cable TV and pool table. Open 24 hours.

Siem Reap

The Angkor What?
Pub Street (Old Market area)
Tel: 012-482 764
One of the oldest night hangouts here, this is an intimate late-night bar popular with both expats and travellers.
Aqua Sydney
Wat Damnak area
Tel: 012-181 4010
This could well be the coolest nightclub to be seen in – it even has a swimming pool.
Chilli Si-Dang
Stung Siem Reap Street
Tel: 012-723 488
Sip wine from the balcony overlooking the river or hide below and use the free Wi-fi. There is a happy hour 5–8pm.
FCC Angkor
Pokambor Street
Tel: 063-760 283
www.fcccambodia.com
The sister restaurant of Phnom Penh's famous FCC, this property has more of a chic pool-bar atmosphere.
Ivy Bar
Old Market area
Tel: 012-800 860
A popular place for food and drinks, with a relaxed and friendly environment and a well-stocked bar.
Temple Club
Bar Street
Two floors with Angkorian decor. The top floor hosts a popular restaurant

with live, traditional Khmer dance shows. There's free Wi-fi… if it's working. Happy hour 10am–10pm.

Sihanoukville

Fisherman's Den
Downtown
Tel: 34-933 997
A lively Westerner-managed rooftop bar, serving cold beer, spirits and whole-day breakfast. There is satellite TV for those who want to catch up on sporting events, and a pool table and darts for some indoor leisure. Fishing and snorkelling trips can be arranged here.
Revelation
Downtown, above Starfish Café
Tel: 012-185 6603
Vodka bar serving a huge selection of good, flavoured vodkas, as well as cold beer and other spirits. Party night on Thursdays.
Papayago
Weather Station Hill
Tel: 012-187 6110
A relaxed, cosy bar and lounge serving a delectable selection of tapas, a full bar of cocktails, beer and wines to chill-out and house music. A pool table and a big-screen TV entertain as well.

FESTIVALS

January

International New Year's Day (1 Jan)
A public holiday.
National Day (7 Jan)
Marks the overthrow of the Khmer Rouge regime by the Vietnamese with Cambodian rebel assistance.
Chinese Lunar New Year and Vietnamese New Year (Tet) (Movable)
Celebrated in late January or early February by Chinese and Vietnamese communities. Many shops close for three days. Witness this spectacle of exploding firecrackers in Vietnamese neighbourhoods.

February

Friendship Day (1 Feb)
Celebrates the signing of the Friendship Treaty between Vietnam and Cambodia in 1980.
Magha Bochea (Movable)
Celebrates the gathering of 1,200 disciples to witness the Buddha's last sermon. Candlelit processions take place at temples where devout Buddhists circle the main temple building in a clockwise direction three times. In some years it falls in February.

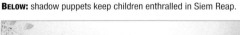
BELOW: shadow puppets keep children enthralled in Siem Reap.

March

International Women's Day (8 Mar)
Parades with floats are held in many towns around the country.

April

Chaul Chnam or Khmer New Year (13–16 Apr)
A three-day festival involving a lot of water-throwing similar to that in Laos, Thailand and Burma (Myanmar). Offerings are made at temples and houses are cleaned. This is a time of year for many overseas Khmers to return home. Children all over the country build miniature sand stupas in representation of Mount Meru.

ABOVE: the Elephant Bar at Raffles, Angkor.

May

International Workers' Day (1 May)
Genocide Day (9 May)
A solemn day commemorating the victims of the Khmer Rouge.
Birthday of HM King Norodom Sihamoni (13–15 May)
A public holiday.
Bon Choat Preah Nengkal or Ploughing of the Holy Furrow (Movable)
In mid- to late May; this marks the beginning of the rice-planting season. It is usually led by the royal family and was originally a Hindu rite. The sacred oxen are offered various foods to eat by the Brahmin priests, and from their choice of beans, maize, rice etc. the bountifulness of the coming harvest can be predicted.
Vesak Buchea (full moon) (Movable)
Commemorates the Buddha's birth, enlightenment and entry into Nirvana.

June

Birthday of HM Queen Mother (18 June)
A public holiday.
Armed Forces Day (19 June)
Commemorates the day the Revolutionary Armed Forces of Kampuchea were founded in 1951. Main parades and celebrations are held in Phnom Pehn.

July

Chol Vassa or Buddhist Lent (Movable)
Traditionally the most auspicious time for young Cambodian males to join the monkhood. Originally men spent the whole of the rainy season (three months) in the temples, but these days it is more usual to spend only two or three weeks.

September

Constitution Day (24 Sept)
This also marks the re-coronation day of the former King Sihanouk.
Bon Kathen or the end of Buddhist Lent (Movable)
Exact dates are decided by the lunar calendar and can sometimes fall in early October. Offerings are made to ancestors and devout Buddhists, and those wishing to accrue merit give monks new robes and other offerings. This major festival lasts for 29 days.
Bon Pchum Ben or "Spirit Commemoration Festival" (Movable)
In late September or early October; lasts for 15 days and culminates at full moon in Bonn Pchum Ben, which is the Cambodian equivalent of All Souls' Day. Ancestors are remembered, and respects are paid with offerings at temples throughout the country.

October

Bon Om Tuk (Water Festival)
In early November, this celebrates the beginning of the dry season. The current in the Sap River reverses at this time of year and begins to empty back into the Mekong. Boat races are held in Phnom Penh, and monks at many temples around the country will row ceremonial boats.
Coronation Day of King Norodom Sihamoni (29 Oct)
Commemorates the day King Sihamoni ascended the throne in 2004.
HM King Father King Sihanouk's Birthday (31 Oct)
There is a spectacular show of fireworks by the river-front at the Royal Palace when the sun has set.

November

Independence Day (9 Nov)
Marks independence from France in 1953 and Khmer National Day. There are grand parades in front of the Royal Palace, with spectacular floats, marching bands and banners highlighting Cambodia's national achievements.

December

National Reconstruction Day (2 Dec)
International Human Rights Day (10 Dec)

Sightseeing Tours

Compagnie Fluviale du Mekong
Office 20, 313 Sisowath Quay, Phnom Penh
Tel: 023-216 070
www.cfmekong.com
Cruises on the Mekong River in one of four boutique, colonial-style boats ranging from 10–24 cabins.
Hidden Cambodia

Adventure Tours
Siem Reap
Tel: 012-655 201
www.hiddencambodia.com
Organises adventure and activity-themed tours, including 4WD, dirt biking, trekking, motocross, as well as humanitarian, ecotourism and cultural-themed tours.

SHOPPING

Except in upscale hotels, tax is always included in the listed price. Unless a shop notes that prices are fixed, some bargaining is expected. Products made from wild animals should not be purchased. Likewise it is illegal to take antiquities out of the country.

Phnom Penh

The capital, along with Siem Reap, is the best place to shop. It has several large markets, shopping malls, art galleries and numerous boutiques offering all manner of souvenirs, including handwoven textiles, high-quality silks, handicrafts, clothing and furniture, art, paintings and artefacts, books and small gift items such as T-shirts or postcards. Of course, pirated CDs, DVDs and photocopied books are also widely available.

A popular souvenir item is the distinctively chequered scarf, *krama*, which Cambodians typically wear around their head and necks as protection against the sun (see page 222). Another good souvenir is the traditional handmade silver betel containers shaped like animals – small and easy to pack and carry.

For silk products, browse **Psar Tuol Tom Pong** (Russian Market) and boutiques such as Couleurs d'Asie (19 Street 360), Jasmine (73 Street 240) and Kambuja (165 Street 110).

Apart from the many traditional markets – the most notable of which are the **Central Market** (Psar Thmay) and **Psar Tuol Tom Pong** – of special interest to the visitor are **Street 178** and **Street 240** in the Royal Palace and National Museum area. Street 178, nicknamed "Art Street" by the locals, is home to various local art galleries, souvenir shops, boutiques and restaurants. The shorter stretch of Street 240 between Norodom Boulevard and Street 19 is lined with boutiques, bars, restaurants, travel agencies and bookshops.

In addition to commercial boutiques for art, paintings and prints, and clothing, there is also a scattering of non-profit shops selling good-quality handicrafts and textiles to benefit disadvantaged Cambodians. Among the latter are Rajana (Psar Tuol Tom Pong and 170 Street 450), Tabitha (Street 51), Cambodia Handicraft Association (CHA, Corner of Street 113 and Street 348), Reyum (47

Cycle Touring

There are a few practical steps you can take which will enhance your cycle touring experience in Cambodia, the major consideration being what to take. The most important thing to remember is that Cambodia, even in the rainy and cool seasons, is a hot place; packing light is crucial. Taking too much, both in terms of weight (either in panniers or in a trailer) and in terms of the number of panniers used, is to be avoided. Basically, take as little as possible, bearing in mind that cycling with backpacks or camel packs for water is not recommended either.

Accommodation is plentiful so there is no need to camp or take camping equipment. Likewise, most guesthouses will supply a towel and toiletries, even in the more remote areas of the country. Mines or unexploded ordnance can still be a real issue in the more remote parts of the country, therefore camping or straying away from the main roads should never be done.

Another major piece of advice is

Street 178; www.reyum.org) and Colours of Cambodia (373 Sisowath Quay).

Books (fiction and non-fiction), periodicals, maps and travel guides can be found in Monument Books (111 Norodom Boulevard), D's Books (two locations at 7 Street 178 and 79 Street 240) or Bohr's Books (5 Sothearos Boulevard).

Large, modern shopping centres include Sorya (near the Central Market) and City Mall (behind the Olympic Stadium).

A few interesting speciality shops include:
Artisans d'Angkor
12 Street 13 (opposite the Post Office)
Tel: 023-992 409
www.artisansdangkor.com
Phnom Penh showroom of the renowned Siem Reap silk workshop. The prices are relatively high compared to other shops but the quality is very good.
Citadel Knives and Swords
10 Street 110 Phnom Penh
Tel: 012-802 676
www.depdep.com
A world-renowned brand of hand-crafted knives made in Cambodia. The beautiful craftsmanship with natural wood, horn, bone and skin handles is readily apparent, even to the non-collector. The knives have been used as props in movies and TV. Check customs regulations in your

to take spares for your bike. Whilst most towns and villages will have a local bike mechanic, there are always places where none can be found. Take a spare inner tube, a puncture repair kit and a pump as a minimum. However, it is also prudent to take a spare spoke and a multi-tool to allow roadside repairs.

Maps and directional equipment are not essential, mainly due to the small number of roads and the reasonable signage in the country.

Finally, sunscreen, hats and sunglasses are all vital pieces of equipment. The average cyclist will spend 8–10 hours a day cycling in the sun. The choice of clothing needs to fit the conditions. Usually loose fitting tops and sportswear bottoms, with sandals or specific cycling shoes on the feet. Dust can be an issue in the drier seasons, therefore many cyclists opt to carry a mask. Comfort in the warm, humid environment is one of the most important factors when considering a cycle journey across Cambodia.

own country before purchasing, as regulations vary.
Sentosasilk
33 Sothearos (corner of Street 178)
Tel: 012-962 911
www.sentosasilk.com
A large selection of silk goods and souvenirs, including handbags, ornaments, fashion, pillow cases and whole silk fabrics sold by the metre.
Vichet Gem-Cutting Shop
52 Street 19
Tel: 023-631 4205
Phnom Penh's Central Market has a large selection of gem-sellers. However their authenticity and quality is often very questionable. Gem-cutting shops like Vichet appear to have more trustworthy stock.

Siem Reap

In Siem Reap, visitors head for the **Old Market** (Psar Chas), which has an excellent range of souvenirs. Most are similar to those found in the capital city, but some items are unique to the Siem Reap area. There are also numerous art galleries, boutiques and other shops selling pricier souvenirs in the Old Market area.

One item that is commonly sold is "temple rubbing", which is paper that has been moulded over a piece of bas-relief (most likely a reproduction) so that it bears the impression of the carving. Other

TRANSPORT
ACCOMMODATION
EATING OUT
ACTIVITIES
A – Z
LANGUAGE

popular souvenir purchases include silver work, handicrafts, and stone and woodcarvings.

For silk products, visit **Artisans d'Angkor** at the National Silk Centre (16km/10 miles west of town; tel: 063-963 330; www.artisansdangkor. com), where you can buy silk and, if you are interested, view the entire production process at the silk farm.

In general, be very careful when buying gems, as fake and low-quality stone scams are not uncommon. Also note that the purchase, and export from the country, of any authentic antiquities from Angkor is strictly forbidden.

SPORT

Cycling

Many companies offer cycling tours around Cambodia. In addition, many offer cross-border tours in Southeast Asia. These tours vary in duration and areas/ sights visited. The tours are mostly inclusive of hotel, guide and drinks/snacks. Many charge extra for bicycle rental and single participants. Tours can be tailored to individual needs. These tours can be excellent value for people with limited time or those who want to travel as part of a group. The companies generally will offer tours through the tourist highlights in Cambodia, including Phnom Penh, Angkor Wat/Siem Reap and Sihanoukville.

Spice Roads Cycle Tours
14/1-B Soi Promsi 2, Sukhumvit 39, Bangkok, Thailand
Tel: 662-712 5305
www.spiceroads.com
This Thai-based cycle tour company has been offering tours across the region for many years. The guides are all local and the tours are fully supported.

Cambodia Cycling
No. 03335, East River Road, Siem Reap, Cambodia
Tel: 063-963 440
www.cambodiacycling.com
This company is based in Cambodia and provides the most in-depth list of routes and itineraries.

Grasshopper Adventures
Tel: 662-280 0832
www.grasshopperadventures.com
Dedicated to Asian cycling adventure tourists, Grasshopper offers a number of Cambodian tours and cross-border tour options.

Bike Asia
42 Guihua Lu, Yangshuo, Guangxi, China
Tel: 867-73882 6521
www.bikeasia.com
Asian-wide company which offers good-value programmes and reasonable routes.

Diving

Chez Claude
Kam Pegn Hill, Sihanoukville (between Sokha Beach and Independence Beach)
Tel: 012-824 870
Claude specialises in group diving trips to the distant reefs and also organises boat tours.

EcoSea Dive
Ekareach Street, Sihanoukville (next to Angkor Arms)
Tel: 012-654 104
www.ecosea.com
Fred Tittle organises diving and snorkelling trips and also conducts dive courses.

Scuba Nation Diving Centre
20 Street 278, Phnom Penh
Tel: 034-933 700
Mohachai Guesthouse, Serendipity Beach Road, Sihanoukville
www.divecambodia.com
Gerard Leenen and Vicky Leah offer daily and live-aboard diving and snorkelling trips. They also conduct PADI dive courses.

Football

You will see people of all ages playing football (soccer) around the country, even in the compounds of the great temples of Angkor. The national team now competes in most international competitions, including the Southeast Asian Games and the larger Asian Games. Unfortunately it has not gained much success; but it does continue to improve.

Fitness Centres and Swimming

A number of the larger hotels in Phnom Penh and Siem Riep operate swimming pools and fitness centres that are open to public use for a fee, usually US$5–10 per day, sometimes a little more.

Phnom Penh

Royal Phnom Penh Hotel
Samdech Sotheáros Street
Tel: 023-982 673
Fitness centre and a large pool.
The Juliana Hotel
16 Juliana 152 Street,

Golf

Golf is still in its infancy in Cambodia, but as in other Southeast Asian nations it appears to be the de rigueur game for politicians, businessmen and top military officers.

Cambodia Golf and Country Club
35km (22 miles) south of Phnom Penh off Route 4, on the way to Sihanoukville
Tel: 023-363 666
Phukeetra Country Club
Tel: 063-964 600
Siem Reap's first international golf club, located along National Highway 6 in Pouk district, about 16km (10 miles) from town.
Sofitel Royal Angkor
Angkor Wat Road, Siem Reap
Tel: 063-964 600
www.sofitel.com
A newly opened international-standard golf course.

Shooting

CPSA (Cambodia Practical Shooting Association)
35 Street 240/55, Phnom Penh
Tel: 012-813 301

Snooker

Many clubs in Phnom Penh offer excellent snooker facilities with reasonable hourly rates.
Mittapheap Hotel
262 Monivong Blvd, Phnom Penh
Tel: 023-216 666
Sakura
30 Street 242, Phnom Penh
Tel: 023-810 383
Sampeov Meas
18 Street 48, Phnom Penh
Tel: 023-428 730
The Sharaton Hotel
Street 47, near Wat Phnom Penh, Phnom Penh
Tel: 023-360 395

Sangkat Veal Vong
Tel: 023-366 070
Health club, sauna and a good pool.
Inter-Continental
Regency Square, 296 Mao Tse Toung Boulevard (Issarak Street)
Tel: 023-424 888
Has a Clark Hatch fitness club.

Siem Reap

Angkor Hotel
Street 6, Phum Sala Kanseng
Tel: 063-964 301
Large swimming pool.

A – Z

A HANDY SUMMARY OF PRACTICAL INFORMATION, ARRANGED ALPHABETICALLY

A

Admission Charges

Admission charges vary widely. Sights off the beaten track generally have cheap admission charges, while places that receive lots of foreign tourists, notably Angkor Wat, can be relatively expensive. Many sights have free admission for Khmers or children.

B

Budgeting for Your Trip

Cambodia is the most expensive country in Indochina. The price difference between Cambodia and both Laos and Vietnam is partly due to Cambodia's reliance on the US dollar, and because so many products are imported. Also, the substantial numbers of foreign NGO workers living in Cambodia for the past two decades have contributed to inflation. Food and drink, transport, internet access, medications and supplies are more expensive here, but accommodation tends to be cheap.

C

Children

Phnom Penh and Angkor Wat have enough diversions and creature comforts to keep the young ones in a good mood, but more remote destinations are certain to be taxing.

Cambodians love children, but sometimes express this affection by a firm pinch, which can be a surprise for the child not used to this cultural trait. The beach at Sihanoukville and the temples of Angkor present spectacular "playgrounds" for children, while Phnom Penh can be a bit problematic. Beware of wild monkeys at Angkor and Wat Phnom in Phnom Penh. They are often attracted to children and do bite – and can carry dangerous diseases. Better hotels normally have swimming pools. Monument Toys in Phnom Penh and Siem Reap carry toys. A large Lego retailer is located beside the Cambodia–Vietnam Friendship Monument in Phnom Penh.

Climate

Cambodia's climate is dictated by the annual monsoon cycle. Between May and October the southwest monsoon brings heavy rainfall, usually for a few hours in the late afternoon on most days. The northwest monsoon, between November and early March, brings somewhat cooler temperatures and lower rainfall. The coolest months are between November and January, and this is generally the optimum time to visit, though even then minimum night-time temperatures seldom fall below 20°C (68°F). March and April see rising temperatures – the latter, which can be furnace-like, is best avoided. The driest months are January and February, when there is little or no rainfall, and the wettest months are usually September and October.

What to Wear

Cambodia is hot all year round, so it is unnecessary to bring a lot of heavy

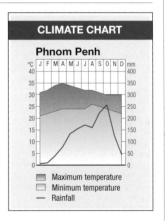

clothes. Even in the cooler months, the temperature does not usually drop below 20°C (68°F) so a light jacket or wind-breaker for chilly early mornings and evenings should suffice. If visiting higher elevations such as Bokor hill station (near Kampot town), however, warmer clothing is necessary, especially if you are staying overnight on the hill. During the monsoon season things get pretty wet, so do remember to bring along some lightweight protection against the rain.

A strong pair of shoes is essential if you are visiting the temples at Angkor. A hat is also recommended when visiting Angkor: much of the site is exposed, and it is amazing how quickly you can feel debilitated without something covering your head.

When visiting temples and mosques, men and women should dress appropriately: no skimpy clothing. Knee-length shorts are just about acceptable, but running shorts are not. To visit one of

Phnom Penh or Siem Reap's more exclusive restaurants you will require reasonably smart clothes. If you do forget anything you believe is essential you will almost certainly be able to pick it up in Phnom Penh at one of the many very good markets, malls or shops.

Crime and Safety

Cambodia has become a lot safer for travellers in recent years. However, parts of Phnom Penh and Sihanoukville are a little risky after dark, and at any time of day basic precautions should be taken to avoid falling victim to the many pickpockets found in markets and tourist areas. Always use a money belt, lock valuables in your hotel safe, and don't flaunt electronics and jewellery. Most travellers – especially men – will be confronted by tuk-tuk and moto drivers selling drugs and prostitutes. Hard drugs are readily available, including cocaine, heroin and opium – and all very much illegal.

Cambodia has long received attention as a source for human trafficking and haven for paedophiles. Recent laws both in Cambodia and abroad are serving to deter these heinous crimes.

Sihanoukville is one of the few places in Cambodia to have a growing reputation for serious crime. Armed robbery is reported often, and there have been some cases of rape, all on the beach. It is not safe to visit empty sections of the beach alone, nor go to the beach after dark without several people to accompany you.

The threat from bandits is diminished but still relevant in remote parts of the country such as the northeast and southwest. Another danger is unexploded ordnance (UXO): do not stray off paths in remote areas of the country,

Beware of strangers offering free drinks in bars. Druggings and robberies, as well as overdose, have been reported. Likewise beware of invitations from the Filipino mafia in tourist areas around Phnom

Electricity

The electric system runs on a 220V AC circuit, and most outlets use two-prong flat or round sockets. It is a good idea to bring along a torch with you, as temporary power outages are quite common.

Penh (particularly Sorya Shopping Centre and the river front). The mafia approach tourists and act out an elaborate scam in which they lure tourists to secluded locations and pressure them into rigged card games.

Customs

Travelling to and from the country is reasonably trouble-free. As elsewhere, weapons, explosives and narcotics are prohibited. Regulations otherwise are relaxed and simple formalities observed. Any amount of foreign currency can be brought into Cambodia, but the amount of Cambodian currency must not exceed 100,000 riel per person. It is illegal to take antiquities out of the country. The duty-free allowance for each visitor is one bottle of spirits, 200 cigarettes and a reasonable amount of perfume.

D

Disabled Travellers

Despite having so many disabled citizens, little is done in Cambodia to accommodate them. Fortunately most shops and restaurants have ground-floor entrances and seating. Some of the better hotels may have elevators and entry ramps, but budget accommodations rarely do.

E

Embassies and Consulates
Cambodian Embassies Overseas
Australia
5 Canterbury Crescent, Deakin ACT 2600, Canberra
Tel: 026-273 1259
www.embassyofcambodia.org.nz
China
9 Dongzhimenwai Dajie, Beijing 100600
Tel: 010-6532 1889
Hong Kong (Consulate)
Unit 616, 6/F, Star House,
3 Salisbury Road, TST, Kowloon
Tel: 852-2546 0718
Email: cacghk@netvigator.com
Indonesia
4th floor, Panin Bank Plaza, Jalan 52 Palmerah Utara, Jakarta 11480
Tel: 62 21-919 2895
Email: recjkt@indo.net.id
Laos
Thadeua Road, Km 2, Vientiane,
B.P. 34, Lao PDR

Emergencies

Police Tel: 117 or 023-924 484
Fire Tel: 118 or 023-786 693
Ambulance Tel: 119 or 023-724 891

Tel: 8562-131 4950/2
Email: recamlao@laotel.com
Thailand
185 Rajadamri Road, 10330 Bangkok
Tel: 66 2-254 6630
Email: recbkk@cscoms.com
United Kingdom
64 Brondesbury Park, London,
NW6 7AT
Tel: 44 20-8541 7850
www.cambodianembassy.org.uk
United States
4500 16th Street, NW
20011 Washington DC
Tel: 1 202-726 7742
Email: cambodia@embassy.org
Vietnam (Hanoi)
71A Tran Hung Dao Street, Hanoi
Tel: 844-3825 3788
Email: arch@fpt.vn
Vietnam (Ho Chi Minh City; Consulate)
No. 41 Phung Khac Khoan
Tel: 848-3829 2751
Email: cambocg@hcm.vnn.vn

Foreign Embassies in Phnom Penh
Australia: 11 Street 254
Tel: 023-213 470
www.cambodia.embassy.gov.au
Canada: 9 Street 254
Tel: 023-213 470
http://geo.international.gc.ca/asia/cambodia
China: 156 Mao Tse Toung Boulevard (Issarak Street)
Tel: 023-720 920
Indonesia: 90 Monivong Boulevard
Tel: 023-215 148
Laos: 15–17 Mao Tse Toung Boulevard (Issarak Street)
Tel: 023-982 632
Malaysia: 5 Street 242
Tel: 023-216 177
Malta: 10 Street 370
Tel/fax: 023-368 184
Philippines: 33 Street 294
Tel: 023-222 303
Singapore: 92 Norodom Boulevard
Tel: 023-221 875
Thailand: 196 Norodom Boulevard
Tel: 023-726 306-10
United Kingdom: 27–29 Street 75
Tel: 023-427 124
http://ukincambodia.fco.gov.uk
United States: 1 Street 96
Tel: 023-728 000
http://cambodia.usembassy.gov
Vietnam: 436 Monivong Boulevard
Tel: 023-362 531

Etiquette

The traditional Cambodian greeting is the sampiah, with hands brought together in front of the face, as if to pray. The higher one raises one's hands and the lower one makes an accompanying bow, the more respect is shown.

Always smile and never lose your temper, otherwise you will lose face and embarrass those around you.

G

Gay and Lesbian Travellers

Cambodians are not hostile towards homosexuals, but any display of public affection, regardless of sexual orientation, is frowned upon. There is no gay "scene" as found in Thailand.

H

Health and Medical Care

Unfortunately Cambodia's health infrastructure is still rather rudimentary, so it is advisable to take all the necessary precautions for a safe trip before you arrive. Immunisation is recommended for cholera, typhoid, tetanus, hepatitis A and B, polio and tuberculosis.

Mosquitoes carrying malaria and dengue fever are widespread in the countryside, but as long as you are staying close to the tourist areas there should be no real problems. Nevertheless, it is advisable to bring along some good mosquito repellent for use on exposed skin at night. After dark it is advisable to wear long-sleeved shirts and long trousers.

Avoid drinking water offered to you that has not come directly from a bottle. Bottled water is widely available. Ice is also best avoided. When travelling around the country, and especially walking, carry your own water bottle. Apart from being guaranteed clean, it will also help prevent dehydration. Heat exhaustion, salt deficiency and dehydration cause more problems than anything else, so don't forget sun block and keep drinking liquids.

It is recommended that visitors arrange a comprehensive overseas travel sickness insurance before leaving, including transport home if necessary. If you were to have a major health problem or an accident, it would be wise to consider evacuation to Bangkok or Singapore, where emergency health facilities are better.

Medical Services

Good hospitals in Cambodia are few and far between, although there are decent pharmacies in Phnom Penh and Siem Reap, such as UCare (www.u-carepharmacy.com). Minor ailments can be treated effectively, but for anything major it would be best to go to Bangkok or Singapore.

Calmette Hospital
3 Monivong Boulevard, Phnom Penh
Tel: 023-723 840
The Calmette is the largest hospital in Phnom Penh and has some French staff.

IMI Dental Clinic
193 Street 208
Tel: 023-212 909

International SOS Medical and Dental Clinic
161 Street 51
Tel: 023-216 911

Phnom Penh Healthcare Clinic
Wimawari Hotel
313 Sisowath Quay, Office No. 3, Ground Floor, Phnom Penh
Tel: 023-991 166

Sen Sok International University Hospital
91-96 Street 1986, Phnom Penh
Tel: 023-883 712

Tropical and Travellers Medical Clinic
88 Street 108, Phnom Penh
Tel: 023-366 802
www.travellersmedicalclinic.com
The best pharmacy in Phnom Penh is the **Pharmacie de la Gare**, tel: 023-430 205, near the railway station, recommended for all medicines.
U-Care, a pharmacy, is at the corner of Sotheeros Boulevard and Street 178, tel: 023-222 399. For optical needs, go to **I Care Optical Centre**, 166 Norodom Boulevard, tel: 023-215 778.

I

Internet

There are now several internet providers in Cambodia, including most mobile phone service providers, such as Metfone, MobiTel, Mfone, Beeline and Hello. Most restaurants, bars and cafés now offer free Wi-fi, but the speeds are much slower than in neighbouring Vietnam. Internet access at internet cafés is relatively slow and more expensive than in surrounding countries. While internet cafés still exist, they are becoming hard to find as most have been converted to dingy internet gaming rooms for students and the computer terminals have questionable security. Instead bring a Wi-fi-compatible device and surf the web at one of the many conventional, air-conditioned cafés with menus.

M

Media

Newspapers and Magazines

There is a variety of English- and French-language publications available in Cambodia. The *Phnom Penh Post* (www.phnompenhpost. com) is a tabloid newspaper, printed daily, which sticks fairly solidly with events within the country. The *Cambodia Daily* is available every day and will keep you up-to-date with world events, but in a rather limited format. The *Bangkok Post* and the *International Herald Tribune* are flown in daily from Thailand, and provide a far more comprehensive view of regional and world events.

There is a series of free monthly English-language magazines by *Canby Publications* (www.canbypublications. com) that contain thorough listings of most of the hotels, restaurants and all the local events that might interest a visitor. There are numerous expat magazines as well, of which *Asia Life: Phnom Penh* (www.asialifecambodia. com), like its Ho Chi Minh City version, is perhaps the best known.

The following shops sell English-language publications. Bohr's, D's and Boston sell second-hand books. D's also has as a lot of photocopies. Monument Books stores are the best (and perhaps only) source for new English-language books in Cambodia, Laos and Myanmar. As neighbouring Vietnam meticulously censors all publications, many expats come to Phnom Penh to buy books. Monument is also one of the only outlets for quality foreign toys.

Bohr's Books
5 Sotheeros Boulevard, Phnom Penh
Also Street 172, Phnom Penh
Tel: 012 929 148

Boston Books at Café
House 8, Street 240, Phnom Penh
Tel: 077-938 254
www.bostonatcafe.com

D's Books
79 Street 240, Phnom Penh
Also Street 178 Behind FCC, Phnom Penh

Monument Books
111 Norodom Boulevard, Phnom Penh
Also Taprohm Hotel, Siem Reap
Tel: 023-217 617
www.monument-books.com

ABOVE: the Cambodian currency – the riel.

Money

The Cambodian currency is called the riel, although the Cambodian economy is really based on the US dollar. Transactions of more than 4,000 riel usually involve American currency. Cambodian riel comes in denominations of 100,000, 50,000, 20,000, 10,000, 5,000, 2,000, 1,000, 500 and 100. The import and export of riel is prohibited.

At the time of writing, US$1 is approximately equivalent to 4,200 riel. For the sake of practicality, most locals are accustomed to rounding the rate down to 4,000 riel during transactions. It is a good idea to have plenty of small-denomination US dollars, as they are far easier to change than larger notes. It is also useful to carry some small riel notes (500 and 1,000) for minor purchases. One way of collecting small change in riel is to buy small items, such as mineral water and canned drinks, at the local shops – using small US dollar notes. All major currencies can be changed at the airports in Phnom Penh and Siem Reap, and also at upmarket hotels, although the latter usually reserve the service for their guests.

Gold shops also act as money-changers (for cash exchange only) and are found around the markets in town. Their rates are better than the banks' and hotels'. Note that while damaged riel notes are acceptable to the locals, even the slightest tear in a large US note renders it unusable in Cambodia.

Travellers' Cheques and Credit Cards

Travellers' cheques have become easier to cash in well-touristed areas such as Phnom Penh, Siem Reap and Sihanoukville, but they remain difficult to change upcountry. Again, it is preferable to have US dollar cheques.

Credit cards have also become more widely accepted. Most good hotels, restaurants and boutiques will accept Visa, JCB, MasterCard and sometimes Amex. Cash advances on cards are possible in some banks in Phnom Penh, Siem Reap, Battambang and Sihanoukville. Most businesses charge a 3 percent fee for credit card usage. ATMs are widely available in Phnom Penh, Siem Reap and large towns.

Tipping

Tipping is not a traditional part of Khmer culture, but it is becoming expected in tourist venues, and with wages being so low it is certainly appreciated. If you feel you have been well treated, a small token of your gratitude (suggested 10 percent) would not be out of place. Hotels and top restaurants will have already added a service charge to your bill.

Phnom Penh
Acleda Bank
28 Mao Tse Toung Boulevard
Tel: 023-214 634
ANZ Royal Bank
265 Sisowath Quay
Tel: 023-999 000
Cambodian Commercial Bank
26 Monivong Boulevard
Tel: 023-426 145
Canadia Bank Plc.
265 Street 110
Tel: 023-215 286
Emperor International Bank Ltd
230 Monivong Boulevard
Tel: 023-426 254
Ernst & Young
124 Norodom Boulevard
Tel: 023-211 431
Global Commercial Bank
337 Monivong Boulevard
Tel: 023-721 567
PricewaterhouseCoopers
41 Norodom Boulevard
Tel: 023-218 086
Singapore Banking Corporation Ltd
68 Street 214, PO Box 688
Tel: 023-211 211
Standard Chartered Bank
89 Norodom Boulevard
Tel: 023-216 685
Union Commercial Bank Ltd
UCB Building, 61 Street 130
Tel: 023-427 995

Kompong Som (Sihanoukville)
Canadia Bank Plc.
Independent Boulevard
Tel: 034-933 490
Union Commercial Bank Ltd
Ekareach Street
Tel: 034-933 833

TRANSPORT

O

Opening Hours

Banks are normally open Monday to Friday 8.30am–3.30pm and sometimes Saturday mornings. Government offices and official bodies open Monday to Saturday 7.30–11.30am and 2–5.30pm. Post offices open Monday to Saturday 7am–7pm. Banks, administrative offices and museums are closed on all public holidays and occasionally on religious festivals. Shops and supermarkets are usually open for longer hours. However, Cambodians tend to go home early. It's always safest to assume shops and offices (even very busy ones) will close 30 minutes to 1 hour earlier than posted.

P

Photography

Most shops provide digital camera-to-CD and print services. Memory cards or sticks are also widely available and very cheap. Print, slide and video film are increasingly difficult to find in Phnom Penh and Siem Reap.

Cambodians, on the whole, do not mind being photographed, although it is always advisable to ask first. Show restraint when photographing

Public Holidays

There are numerous official public Cambodian holidays, but keep in mind that many things will also close for major festivals and internationally celebrated holidays like Christmas.
1 January International New Year's Day
7 January Victory Over the Genocide
8 March International Women's Day
13–16 April Khmer New Year
1 May International Workers' Day
8 May International Children's Day
13–15 May The King's Birthday
18 June The Queen Mother's Birthday
24 September Constitution Day
29 October Coronation Day
31 October The King Father's Birthday
9 November Independence Day
10 December International Human Rights Day

people at prayer, and monks. Also, be careful when photographing soldiers or anything military. Government, police and military buildings generally should not be photographed.

Postal Services

The postal service, like many other services, has improved over the last few years, though it is still not entirely reliable. Mail is forwarded via Bangkok and therefore arrives much more quickly than ever before. Costs are very reasonable: a 10g airmail letter costs between 2000 and 6000 riel. Postcards are anything from 2000 to 4000 riel to anywhere in the world.
Ministry of Posts and Telecommunication
East of Wat Phnom on Street 13, Phnom Penh
Tel: 023-426 832

Courier Services
A number of international courier agencies offer their services in Phnom Penh:
DHL Express Cambodia
28 Monivong Boulevard
Tel: 023-427 726
TSP EXPRESS (Cambodia) Co. (FedEx)
701D Monivong Boulevard
Tel: 023-216 708
Mon–Sat 7.30am–5.30pm
TNT Cambodia
151F Street 154
Tel: 023-424 022

Public Toilets

Western sit-down toilets are a standard feature in hotels, restaurants and most other venues frequented by tourists. They will have toilet paper most of the time – if not, ask the staff.
What few public toilets exist are often dirty "squatty potties", and will always charge a small fee (usually 1,000 riel or less). Toilet paper will cost extra.

R

Religious Services
Christian
Cambodia Church of the Nazarene
3A Monireth Road
Tel: 023-366 109
International Christian Assembly
20 Street 71, World Vision Building
Tel: 023-720 597
Catholic Church – Residence of the Bishop
787 Monivong Boulevard

Sex Tourism

Cambodia has garnered an unfortunate reputation as a destination for sex tourists, particularly those who exploit young children. The Cambodian government and foreign NGOs like Child Safe Network (www.childsafe-international.org) have initiated a campaign to end these activities, and several foreign paedophiles are serving sentences in Cambodian prisons. Recently volunteerism which includes brief visits or stints "helping out" in local orphanages has come under fire for putting children at risk in the presence of strangers. Numerous fake orphanages have sprung up across the countries seeking to profit from well-meaning tourists and exploit street children in the process.

Tel: 023-212 462
Email: pphpar@online.com.kh

Buddhist
Buddhist Institute
Sisowath Quay
Tel: 023-212 046

T

Telephones

Telephone costs in Cambodia are high – international calls vary between US$1.60 and $3 per minute, domestic calls between 300 riel and 700 riel per minute. Telephone booths are installed around Phnom Penh and other major tourist destinations. Many of these booths take phone cards, and it is possible to telephone most countries directly. Cards for US$5, $20 and $50 can be purchased at post offices and many good hotels. To call abroad from Cambodia, dial the international access code 001 (or 007 from mobiles for a cheaper rate), followed by the country code, area code and telephone number. Mobile phone numbers begin with 01 or 09.

Mobile Phones
If you wish your mobile to function with the same number while you are in Cambodia, this is possible, although depending on your provider's system, you may be charged a very high rate to receive calls from callers who do not know you are abroad.
Alternatively, purchase a local

SIM card to install in the telephone. Metfone, MobiTel, Mfone, Beeline and Hello are four of the most popular mobile phone service providers based in Cambodia. Coverage is good in Phnom Penh, reasonable in Siem Reap, Battambang, Sihanoukville and Kampong Cham, but out in the countryside it is often nonexistent. Most offer 3G internet service plans as well. It is much cheaper and more convenient to pre-pay using phone cards, which are available at branded shops and kerbside vendors.

Another solution is to rent a mobile phone locally and use the local number assigned to the handset. Mobile telephones are offered for rent at the airport. Countless shops selling new and inexpensive used phones are in every town.

Telephone Area Codes by Province

Banteay Meanchey 54
Battambang 53
Kampot 33
Kandal 24
Kep 36
Koh Kong 35
Kompong Cham 42
Kompong Chhnang 26
Kompong Speu 25
Kompong Thom 62
Kratie 72
Mondolkiri 73
Oddar Meanchey 65
Phnom Penh 23
Preah Vihear 64
Prey Veng 43
Pursat 52
Rattanakiri 75
Siem Reap 63
Sihanoukville (Kompong Som) 34
Stung Treng 74
Svay Rieng 44
Takeo 32
Note: When dialling to a different area code within Cambodia or to a mobile telephone, dial 0 before the area code.

Tourist Information

Cambodia's tourist office is at 262 Monivong Boulevard in Phnom Penh. Tel: 855-23 216 66; info@ tourismcambodia.com; www. tourismcambodia.com

Websites

Tourism of Cambodia: www. tourismcambodia.com. The official website

Time Zone

Cambodia is 7 hours ahead of Greenwich Mean Time (GMT).

for information on visiting Cambodia.
General Information on Cambodia: With a comprehensive business directory. www.gocambodia.com
The Phnom Penh Post: The latest English-language news on events inside the country. www. phnompenhpost.com
Beauty and Darkness: Cambodia in Modern History: Documents, essays, oral histories and photos relating to the recent history of Cambodia, with an emphasis on the Khmer Rouge period. www.mekong.net/Cambodia
Extraordinary Chambers in the Courts of Cambodia: a UN-backed court website prosecuting five of the top Khmer Rouge leaders. www.eccc.gov.kh
Specialist books on Cambodia: White Lotus Press based in Bangkok carries new and out-of-print books about Cambodia. www.whitelotuspress.com
Cambodian Genocide Progamme: A regularly updated site on the political and criminal history of the Khmer Rouge in Democratic Kampuchea and afterwards. www.yale.edu/cgp
Andy Brouwer's Cambodia Tales: This site is by Andy Brouwer, a very keen Cambodia enthusiast. Personal experiences with interviews and the latest news. www.andybrouwer.co.uk
LTO Cambodia: The blog of a long-time expat living in Phnom Penh. ltocambodia.blogspot.com
Fish Egg Tree: an author's blog, highlighting adventures and current events in Vietnam and Cambodia. www.fisheggtree.com
Tales of Asia: Current information regarding local conditions in Cambodia, border crossings, security, etc. www.talesofasia.com
Canby Publications Cambodia Guides: The online edition of the city guides for Phnom Penh, Siem Reap, Sihanoukville and the rest of Cambodia. www.canbypublications.com
Bayon Pearnik: A free monthly tourist magazine. www.bayonpearnik.com
Maurice Glaize's Guide to Angkor: Glaize's definitive 1944 guide in English. www.theangkorguide.com
Apsara Authority: website of the authority responsible for the conservation of Angkor Wat and other heritage sites in Siem Reap. www. autoriteapsara.org
Travelfish: a comprehensive and up-to-date guide on travel in Cambodia and Southeast Asia. www.travelfish.org/country/cambodia
Khmer440: The expat guide to Cambodia with the inside scoop, and a notoriously edgy forum. www. khmer440.com
ThingsAsian: Publishers of the popular To Asia with Love series, the

site features submitted stories about Cambodia from both widely published authors and amateurs. http:// thingsasian.com/Cambodia
Bong Thom: an English-Khmer audio phrasebook with hundreds of free mp3 downloads. www.bongthom.com/akonline

Travel Agencies

Phnom Penh

5 Oceans
33 Street 178
Tel: 023-986 920
Email: info@5oceanscambodia.com
www.5oceanscambodia.com
Angkor Tourism Co. Ltd
178C Street 63,
Boeng Keng Kong 1
Tel: 023-427 676
Email: aktrep@online.com.kh
Apex
53 Street 63
Tel: 023-217 787/216 595
Apsara Tours
8 Street 254, R. V. Vinnavaut Oum
Tel: 023-216 562/212 019
Email: apsaratours@camnet.com.kh
Diethelm Travel
65 Street 240
Tel: 023-219 151
Email: pierre.j@kh.diethelmtravel.com
www.diethelmtravel.com
East-West Travel (Cambodia) Ltd
5A Street 288, Boeng Keng Kong 1
Tel: 023-216 065
Email: eastwest@online.com.kh
www.eastwest-travel.com
Eurasie Travel
176 Street 13
Tel: 023-427 114/426 456
Email: et.tvl@online.com.kh
www.eurasietravel.com
Hanuman Tourism
12 Street 310, PO Box 2321
Tel: 023-218 356, 218 396
Email: sales@hanumantourism.com
www.hanumantourism.com
KK International Travel & Tours Co.
No. 203E, Rue 13
Tel: 023-724 349/012-846 213
Email: kktravel@camnet.com.kh
www.kktravel.com.kh
K.U. Travel & Tours
38AB Street 240
Tel: 023-723 456/012-806 232
Email: info@kucambodia.com
www.kucambodia.com

Siem Reap

Asian Trails
587 Hup Guan Street, Mondol 1,
Khum Svay Dangkum
Tel: 063-964 595
Email: res@asiantrails.com.kh
www.asiantrails.info

Diethelem Travel
4 Road No. 6
Tel: 063-963 524

Eurasie Travel
National Road No. 6, Phum Krous
Tel: 063-963 449
Email: eurasierep@camintel.com

Hanuman Tourism Voyages
143 Mondol 3, Phoum Treang
Tel: 063-963 213/012-936 469
Email: sales@hanumantourism.com

PTM Travel and Tours
552, Group 6, Mondol 1,
Khum Svay Dangkum
Tel: 063-964 388
Email: siemreap@ptm-travel.com
www.ptm-travel.com

V

Visas and Passports

Your passport should be valid for at least 6 months. An entry visa is also required for citizens of all countries except Malaysia, the Philippines, Singapore, Vietnam and Laos. Single-entry Cambodian tourist visas, valid for 30 days, are issued on arrival at Phnom Penh International Airport and Siem Reap-Angkor International Airport. Cambodian visas are also issued at the Cambodia–Vietnam border checkpoints at Bavet and Kham Sam Nor, and at the Cambodia–Thailand border checkpoints at Cham Yeam/ Koh Kong, Poipet/Banteay Meanchey and O'Smach/Ordor Meanchey.

As visa requirements change from time to time, check the situation with your consulate or a reliable travel agent, or look up the Cambodian Immigration Department website (www.immigration.gov.kh) before you travel. You will need one passport-size photograph (10.2 x 15.2cm, or 4 x 6 inches) and US$20 in cash for the visa (US$5 extra if you enter by land and your bus driver processes it, sparing you the line through customs and immigration).

Visas can also be obtained through the Cambodian Embassy or Consulate in your own country. A list of embassies located outside of Cambodia can be found at www. embassyofcambodia.org/other_ embassies.html

To apply for an e-visa online, simply access the Ministry of Foreign Affairs and International Cooperation website at http:// evisa.mfaic.gov.kh. You will need to have your passport and credit card information ready, as well as a recent passport-size digital photograph. The e-visa will be sent to the email address you have provided. In addition to the usual visa fee, there is an extra processing charge of US$5. At present, e-visas are available for entry to Cambodia via Phnom Penh International Airport, Siem Reap International Airport and three border crossings with Thailand, and departure from the country via all points. Only tourist visas can be applied for online at the time of writing. For e-visa related questions, visit the website or email: cambodiaevisa@ mfaic.gov.kh.

Extension of Stay

Tourist visas can be extended only once at the Department for Foreigners (Mon–Fri 8–11am and 2–4pm; tel: 012-581 558; email: visa_info@online.com.kh). The office is located on Pochentong Road (Confédération de Russie) opposite Phnom Penh International Airport. A 30-day extension costs US$35 (28-day service) or US$40 (3-day service). Some guesthouses and travel agencies in Phnom Penh (try Lucky!Lucky! at 413Eo Monivong Boulevard) will also handle visa extensions for a nominal fee – a far more convenient option. Business visas (US$25 for the first month) can be extended indefinitely through guesthouses and travel agencies. Overstaying your visa will set you back by US$5 per day.

TRANSPORT
ACCOMMODATION
EATING OUT
ACTIVITIES
A – Z
LANGUAGE

Weights and Measures

Cambodia uses the metric system. Items in the market are sold by the kilogram. Petrol is sold by the litre. Hours are counted from 1–24.

W

Women Travellers

Women are unlikely to experience any unwelcome advances from Khmer men, but the usual common-sense caveats regarding conservative dress apply. Cambodian men are polite and respectful by nature, but excessive consumption of alcohol can obscure this, so pay attention in discos and the like. More serious is the danger of late-night muggings; women travelling alone are likely to be seen as an easy target, particularly in Sihanoukville and Phnom Penh. Only the foolhardy would resist an armed demand for money of this nature.

BELOW: a backstreet pharmacy in Phnom Penh.

LANGUAGE

UNDERSTANDING THE LANGUAGE

The Khmer Language

The Khmer language, also called Cambodian, is a Mon-Khmer language spoken by most of the people of Cambodia, as well as in parts of northeastern Thailand and southern Vietnam. Khmer belongs to the Austroasiatic group of languages, which is widely spread throughout mainland Southeast Asia. Other languages in this group, which is generally considered to have been one of the earliest in the region, include Mon, Vietnamese and Wa. Cambodian is a non-tonal language that has borrowed heavily from Sanskrit, Pali, Thai, Chinese and Vietnamese. It has been written since at least the 7th century AD, using a script derived from India. It is widely accepted that Thai script was derived from Khmer in the 12th century.

Because of the difficulty of learning Cambodian script, short-time visitors to the country are unlikely to achieve any great fluency in Khmer – though the lack of tones makes it easier for Westerners than, say, Vietnamese or Thai. It is relatively easy to acquire some basic vocabulary, however, and any such effort will be greatly appreciated by the Cambodians. English is rapidly becoming the second language, especially in Phnom Penh, Siem Reap and Kompong Som. Older people, particularly among the elite, may speak French. Some members of the Sino-Cambodian community speak Guoyu, or Mandarin Chinese. Thai is widely understood in Battambang and the west of the country; similarly Vietnamese is widely understood in the east of the country. Cham, the language of Cambodia's Muslims, is an Austronesian language related to Malay – but virtually all Cambodia's

ABOVE: heed the warning signs in Cambodia.

Chams are fluent in Khmer.

Language School

Offering Khmer language classes:
Khmer School of Language
Behind the Chinese Embassy, 13 Street 475 (off Street 183 Mao Tse Toung Boulevard), Phnom Penh
Tel: 23-360 938
Ask for either Miss Addheka or Miss Leaksmy.

General

what *ey*
who *niak nah*
when *bpehl*
where *eah nah*
why *haeht ey*
Does anyone speak English? *tii nih mian niak jeh piasah ohngkleh teh?*
I don't understand *k'nyom men yooul teh*

Greetings

Hello *jumreap sooa*
How are you? *tau neak sok sapbaiy jea the?*
I'm fine *k'nyom sok sapbaiy*

Good morning *arun suor sdei*
Good afternoon *tiveah suor sdei*
Good evening *sayoanh suor sdei*
Goodnight *reahtrey suor sdei*
My name is... *k'nyom tch muoh...*
What is your name? *lok tch muoh ey?*
Yes *baat*
No *dteh*
Please *sohm mehta*
Thank you *orgoon*
Excuse me *sohm dtoh*
Goodbye *leah suhn heuy*
Where are you from? *niak mao pi patet nah?*
I come from... *k'nyom mao pi...*

Directions/Transport

Where is...? *noev eah nah...?*
toilet *bawngkohn*
hotel *sohnthakia*
hospital *mon dtee bpeth*
police station *s'thaanii bpohlis*
turn left *bawt ch'weng*
turn right *bawt s'dum*
go straight on *teuv trawng*
car *laan*
bus *laan ch'noul*
bus station *kuhnlaing laan ch'noul*
boat *dtook*

train *roht plerng*
aeroplane *yohn hawh*
bicycle *kohng*
cyclo *see kloa*
post office *bprai sa nee*
embassy *s'thaantuut*

Days and Time

today *t'ngai nih*
tomorrow *t'ngai saaik*
yesterday *m'serl menh*
morning *bpreuk*
afternoon *r'sial*
evening *l'ngiat*
month *khaeh*
year *ch'nam*
last year *ch'nam moon*
new year *ch'nam thmey*
next year *ch'nam groy*
Sunday *t'ngai aadteut*
Monday *t'ngai jan*
Tuesday *t'ngai onggeea*
Wednesday *t'ngai bpoot*
Thursday *t'ngai bprahoaa*
Friday *t'ngai sok*
Saturday *t'ngai sao*
January *ma ga raa*
February *kompheak*
March *mee nah*
April *meh sah*
May *oo sa phea*
June *mi thok nah*
July *ka kada*

August *say haa*
September *kan'ya*
October *dto laa*
November *wech a gaa*
December *t'noo*

Numbers

one *moo ay*
two *bpee*
three *bey*
four *buon*
five *bpram*
six *bpram moo ay*
seven *bpram bpee*
eight *bpram bey*
nine *bpram buon*

Shopping and Restaurants

How much is...? *t'lay pohnmaan...?*
money *loey*
change *dow*
cheap *towk*
expensive *t'lay*
market *p'sah*
bank *tho neea kear*
restaurant *haang bai*
eat *bpisah*
I want a ... *k'nyom jang baan ...*
drinking water *dteuk soht*
ice *dteuk kok*

ten *dahp*
eleven *dahp moo ay*
twelve *dahp bpee*
sixteen *dahp bpram moo ay*
twenty *m'phey*
twenty-one *m'phey moo ay*
thirty *saam seup*
forty *seah seup*
fifty *haa seup*
sixty *hok seup*
seventy *jeht seup*
eighty *bpait seup*
ninety *gao seup*
hundred *mooay roy*
thousand *mooay bpoan*
ten thousand *mooay meun*
one million *mooay leeun*

tea *dtae*
coffee *kahfeh*
milk *dteuk daco*
sugar *sko*
rice *bai*
fish *dt'ray*
beef *saich koh*
pork *saich jruk*
chicken *moan*
plate *jahndtiap*
glass *kaehu*
beer *bia*

FURTHER READING

General Interest

The Land and People of Cambodia by David P. Chandler (1991). An excellent introduction to Cambodia by the foremost expert.
The Making of Southeast Asia by G. Coedes (London: 1966). A seminal account of the develop-ment of Indian cultural influence in Cambodia and elsewhere in Southeast Asia.
Swimming to Cambodia by Spalding Gray (1988). Strange, humorous and sometimes moving monologue by an actor and writer involved in the making of the film *The Killing Fields*.
Phnom Penh Then and Now by Michel Igout (1993). As the name implies, photographic record of the Cambodian capital before and after Democratic Kampuchea.

Eternal Phnom Penh by R. Werly and T. Renaut (Hong Kong: Editions d'Indochine, 1995). Well illustrated, with introduction by Jean Lacouture.

Pre-Angkor and Angkor History

The Ancient Khmer Empire by Lawrence Palmer Briggs (1999). Somewhat dated, but well illustrated.
Reporting Angkor: Chou Ta-Kuan in Cambodia 1296–97 by Robert Philpotts (1996). The account of the celebrated 13th-century Chinese ambassador seen through contemporary eyes.
The Customs of Cambodia by Chou Ta-kuan (Zhou Daguan) (Bangkok: The Siam Society, 1987). A must – beautifully illustrated

with photographs of contemporary scenes from the Bayon as well as 19th-century French engravings.
Society, Economics and Politics in Pre-Angkor Cambodia by Michael Vickery (Tokyo: Toyo Bunko, 1998). The definitive study of the period.

Post-Angkor History to the Colonial Period

Facing the Cambodian Past by David P. Chandler (Chiang Mai: Silkworm Books, 1996). Invaluable collection of essays and articles covering a period of Cambodian history which is usually ignored.
A History of Cambodia by David P. Chandler (Chiang Mai: Silkworm Books, 1998). The best introduction to Cambodian history available.

TRANSPORT

ACCOMMODATION

EATING OUT

ACTIVITIES

A – Z

LANGUAGE

Travels in Siam: Cambodia and Laos 1858–60 by Henri Mouhot (1986). Fascinating 19th-century account by the Frenchman who "discovered" Angkor before going on to die tragically at Luang Prabang in Laos.
Cambodia After Angkor: The Chronicular Evidence for the 14th to 16th Centuries by Michael Vickery (Michigan: 1977). Serious study for the specialist.

Independence and the Vietnam War

Politics and Power in Cambodia: The Sihanouk Years by Milton Osborne (1973). Perceptive account of the mercurial King Sihanouk's role in the making and breaking of independent Cambodia.
Sideshow: Kissinger, Nixon and the Destruction of Cambodia by William Shawcross (London: André Deutsch, 1979). Seminal – cannot really be beaten. This book deeply infuriated Kissinger.
River of Time by Jon Swain (London: William Heinemann, 1996). Magical account of this foreign correspondent's love affair with Vietnam and Cambodia. He was one of the journalists menaced by the victorious Khmer Rouge when they entered Phnom Penh – a chilling scene represented in the film *The Killing Fields* which, once seen, can never be forgotten.

The Khmer Rouge Years

When the War Was Over: The Voices of Cambodia's Revolution and Its People by Elizabeth Becker (New York: Simon and Schuster, 1986). Becker was one of only three Westerners in Phnom Penh as the Vietnamese invasion of Democratic Kampuchea began. Contains memorable accounts of her interview with Pol Pot and of the murder of Scottish academic Malcolm Caldwell by unknown assassins.
Brother Enemy: The War after the War, a History of Indochina since the Fall of Saigon by Nayan Chanda (New York: Collier Books, 1986). The best book written about the Third Indochina War by the experienced and knowledgeable editor of *Far Eastern Economic Review*.
Pol Pot Plans the Future: Confidential Leadership Documents from Democratic Kampuchea, 1976–1977 by David P. Chandler, Ben Kiernan and Chanthou Boua (New Haven: Yale University Southeast Asia Studies, 1988). An amazing book – check out the extraordinary Khmer Rouge "plans" to develop tourism

("must build hotels"), and the records of its illicit trade in endangered wildlife.
Brother Number One: A Political Biography of Pol Pot by David P. Chandler (Chiang Mai: Silkworm Books, 1992). Comprehensive biography of the Khmer Rouge leader.
The Rise and Demise of Democratic Kampuchea by Craig Etcheson (Boulder: Westview Press, 1984). Excellent, balanced account.
Genocide and Democracy in Cambodia: The Khmer Rouge, the UN and the International Community edited by Ben Kiernan (1993). Probably the best book on the DK regime.
Cambodia: Year Zero by F. Ponchaud (New York: Holt, Rinehart and Winston, 1978). By the French priest who first opened the world's eyes to the hideous excesses of the Khmer Rouge regime.

Personal Accounts

A Cambodian Prison Portrait: One Year in the Khmer Rouge's S-21 by Vann Nath (Bangkok: White Lotus, 1998). The author was one of the very few prisoners who survived incarceration in Tuol Sleng – saved because he was an artist who could paint and sculpt busts of Pol Pot.
Beyond the Horizon: Five Years with the Khmer Rouge by Laurence

Send Us Your Thoughts

We do our best to ensure the information in our books is as accurate and up-to-date as possible. The books are updated on a regular basis using local contacts, who painstakingly add, amend and correct as required. However, some details (such as telephone numbers and opening times) are liable to change, and we are ultimately reliant on our readers to put us in the picture.
We welcome your feedback, especially your experience of using the book "on the road". Maybe we recommended a hotel that you liked (or another that you didn't), or you came across a great bar or new attraction we missed.
We will acknowledge all contributions, and we'll offer an Insight Guide to the best letters received.

Please write to us at:
Insight Guides
PO Box 7910
London SE1 1WE
Or email us at:
insight@apaguide.co.uk

Picq (New York: St Martin's Press, 1989). This is a special book. Picq, a French Communist, was married to a mid-ranking Khmer Rouge cadre and voluntarily stayed on in Cambodia after the KR victory. She is the only Westerner to have remained in Phnom Penh throughout the Democratic Kampuchea years; as such her account is unique, though less informative than it might have been as she was never trusted by the top leadership.
Children of Cambodia's Killing Fields: Memoirs by Survivors by Dith Pran (1997).
The Death and Life of Dith Pran by Sydney Schanberg (1985). The basis for the film *The Killing Fields*.
Voices from S-21: Terror and History in Pol Pot's Secret Prison by David P. Chandler (2000). Accounts from the horrific prison of Tuol Sleng.

The Vietnamese Period and UNTAC

Kampuchea Diary 1983–1986: Selected Articles by Jacques Bekaert (1987). Perceptive record of Cambodia's reconstruction after the DK period. To be read in conjunction with the following book.
The China–Cambodia–Vietnam Triangle by Wilfred Burchett (1981). Political analysis by a veteran Australian Communist.
War of the Mines: Cambodia, Landmines and the Impoverishment of a Nation by Paul Davies and Nic Dunlop (1994). Excellent black-and-white photography.
Heroes by John Pilger (1986).
The Quality of Mercy: Cambodia, Holocaust and Modern Conscience by William Shawcross (André Deutsch, 1984). Critically examines collusion between the defeated Khmer Rouge, China and the West at the expense of Cambodia (and Vietnam).
War and Hope: The Case for Cambodia by Norodom Sihanouk (1980).

Contemporary Cambodia

The Tragedy of Cambodian History by David P. Chandler (Chiang Mai: Silkworm Books, 1994). A perceptive and highly readable history seen from the perspective of the late 20th century.
Off the Rails in Phnom Penh: Into the Dark Heart of Guns, Girls and Ganja by Amit Gilboa (Bangkok: Asia Books, 1998). The title says it all – but there is more to Phnom Penh than brothels and marijuana.
Sihanouk: Prince of Light, Prince of

Darkness by Milton Osborne (Chiang Mai: Silkworm Books, 1994). A dark portrait of the ruler.
Sympathy for the Devil by Nate Thayer (1999). Thayer is the *Far Eastern Economic Review* correspondent most closely associated with the Khmer Rouge leadership in its final days. He interviewed Pol Pot in the jungle at Anlong Veng before he died, and spoke at length with Ta Mok and other KR leaders.

Minorities and Religion

Islam in Kampuchea (Phnom Penh: NCUFK, 1987). Cambodia's Cham Muslim minority suffered horribly under the Democratic Kampuchean regime, as this book makes clear.

People and Society

The Warrior Heritage: A Psychological Perspective of Cambodian Trauma by Seanglim Bit (El Cerrito: Seanglim Bit, 1991). A fascinating interpretation of the various cultural and historical factors making up the Cambodian psyche from a Khmer scholar.
Cambodian Culture since 1975: Homeland and Exile edited by May Ebihara, Carol Mortland and Judy Ledgerwood (1994). Useful for its insights into overseas Cambodian communities.

Arts and Culture

Angkor: An Introduction by G. Coedes (1963). Essential reading – insightful, informed and readable.
Angkor Cities and Temples by Claude Jacques and Michael Freeman (1998). Large-format picture book of great beauty and detail.

The Royal Palace of Phnom Penh and Cambodian Royal Life by Julio A. Jeldres (1999). The author is a long-time friend and confidant of King Sihanouk, and so well placed to write this book.
Angkor: An Introduction to the Temples by Dawn Rooney (1997). The best-written and most informative guide to Angkor.

Khmer Culture Abroad

Khmer Heritage in Thailand by Etienne Aymonier (1999).
Northeast Thailand from Prehistoric to Modern Times by Peter Rogers (Bangkok: DK Books, 1996). Information on the Suai or ethnic Khmers of the Thai provinces of Surin, Buriram and Sisaket.

Travel

A Dragon Apparent: Travels in Cambodia, Laos and Vietnam by Norman Lewis (London: Eland, 1982). Classic travel writing.
A Pilgrimage to Angkor by Pierre Loti (Chiang Mai: Silkworm, 1996). Reprint of the 19th-century classic.
Silk Roads: The Asian Adventures of Clara and André Malraux by A. Madsen (London: 1990). Malraux planned and executed the theft of several important pieces of sculpture from Banteay Srei in 1923. He was caught and held under house arrest in Phnom Penh until the stolen pieces were returned.
Derailed in Uncle Ho's Victory Garden by Tim Page (1995). Return to Vietnam and Cambodia by the renowned British war photographer, now recording his impressions of Indochina at peace.

Linguistics

Introduction to Cambodian by Judith M. Jacob (Oxford University Press, 1990).
Seam and Blake's Phonetic English-Khmer Dictionary by Ung Tea Seam and Neil Blake (Bangkok: Asia Books, 1991).
Colloquial Cambodian: A Complete Language Course by David Smyth (London: Routledge, 1997).
The Cambodian System of Writing by Derek Tonkin (1996).

Filmography

Apocalypse Now (1979). Director: Francis Ford Coppola. Starring: Marlon Brando, Martin Sheen, Robert Duvall. Based on the novel *Heart of Darkness* by Joseph Conrad. During the Vietnam War, Captain Willard (Martin Sheen) is sent upriver into Cambodia with orders to find and kill Colonel Kurtz (Marlon Brando). Before reaching Kurtz, Willard embarks on an odyssey of epic and surreal proportions. There are many memorable scenes, not least the helicopter attack on a Vietnamese village to the accompaniment of Wagner's *Ride of the Valkyries*.
The Killing Fields (1984). Director: Roland Joffe. A *New York Times* journalist and his Cambodian assistant are caught up in the Khmer Rouge revolution of 1975. The film portrays the horrors of the Khmer Rouge period with Dith Pran, played by Haing Ngor, trying to escape the country.

Natural History

For books on the natural history of Cambodia and the region, see the Laos Further Reading section, page 342.

ART AND PHOTO CREDITS

INDEX

Main references are in bold type

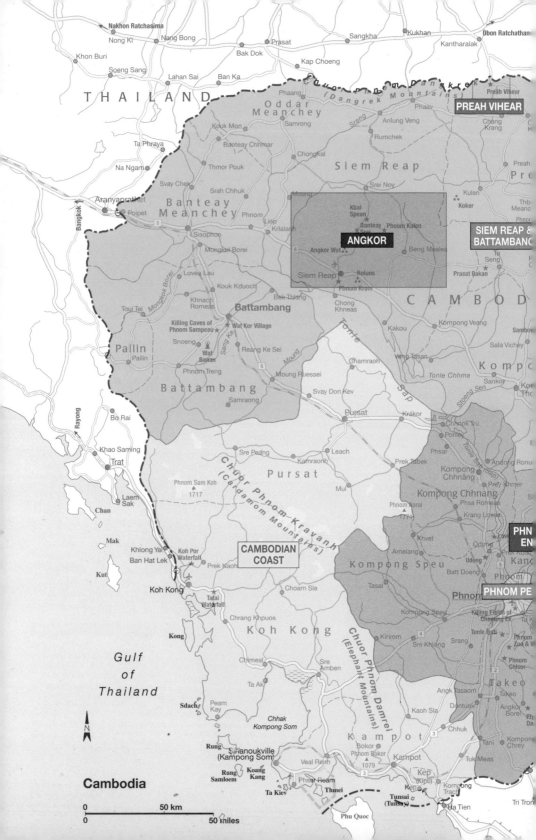